Y0-BVN-599

STATE AND WELFARE
USA/USSR

RESEARCH SERIES/NUMBER 71

State and Welfare USA/USSR

Contemporary Policy
and Practice

HN
59.2
.S72
1988
West

GAIL W. LAPIDUS &
GUY E. SWANSON, Editors

A15041 455700

INSTITUTE
OF INTERNATIONAL
STUDIES
University of California, Berkeley

Library of Congress Cataloging-in-Publication Data

State & welfare, USA/USSR : contemporary policy and
    practice / Gail W. Lapidus & Guy E. Swanson, editors.

        p. cm. — (Research series / Institute of International
Studies, University of California, Berkeley, ISSN 0068-6093 ;
no. 71)
    Includes index.
    ISBN 0-87725-171-1
    1. United States—Social policy. 2. Soviet Union—Social
policy. 3. Public welfare—United States. 4. Public welfare—
Soviet Union. I. Lapidus, Gail Warshofsky. II. Swanson,
Guy E. III. Title: State and welfare, USA/USSR. IV. Series:
Research series (University of California, Berkeley. Institute
of International Studies) ; no. 71.
HN59.2.S72 1988
361.6'1'0947—dc19   88-15444
                                                    CIP

©1988 by the Regents of the University of California

CONTENTS

STATE AND WELFARE:
SOVIET AND AMERICAN CHALLENGES

Gail W. Lapidus

It is one of the paradoxes of the mid-1980s that, in both the United States and the USSR, key features of the welfare state, and its consequences for economic productivity and social justice, are undergoing far-reaching reassessment. Notwithstanding fundamental differences in the organization of state-economy relations in their two systems, and in the underlying political and social values they embody, U.S. President Ronald Reagan and Soviet General-Secretary Mikhail Gorbachev appear to share the view that traditional social entitlements have undermined individual incentives and become an impediment to enhanced economic performance. In both countries new policy intiatives have been devised to cut back a number of social programs, and indeed to alter the terms of the implicit "social contract" between government and society.

That such a reexamination should be provoked by an important political realignment in the United States is not altogether unexpected. The enormous value historically attached to individual self-reliance, combined with long-standing distrust of governmental intervention, has traditionally made the United States relatively less hospitable than other industrial democracies to the welfare state; a vast literature documents the difficulties in legitimizing the New Deal in an environment dominated by anti-statist, individualist, and market-oriented values. In a number of respects the United States to this day remains a "welfare laggard" (Wilensky 1975; Skocpol 1987).

But sharp controversy over the economic impact and social purposes of the welfare state has hardly been confined to the United States during the past decade and a half; it has engulfed a broad range of Western industrial democracies. The assumption that economic development and social progress would go hand in hand with an expanding commitment to social rights, and a growth in the scope and scale of social benefits, has been called into question by the combined effects of demographic changes and fiscal crises. The rapidly growing burden of social entitlements on state budgets provoked far-reaching reassessments of the relationship between economic performance and social justice, and a renewed discussion of the proper scope and limits of individual entitlements and state responsibility. Although the pressures for retrenchment in public spending took different forms and produced varying outcomes, political realignments and changes in economic policy precipitated reconsideration of a range of social programs.

It is rather more surprising that this debate should have had its counterpart in the socialist world. The claim that socialism was by definition a "welfare society," and that public ownership of the means of production and centralized planning guaranteed both economic efficiency and social justice, appeared deeply entrenched in elite ideologies as well as in popular expectations.* In view of the considerable value attached to egalitarianism, collectivism, and social solidarity rather than competitive individualism, outside observers might reasonably have expected the socialist world to demonstrate a high degree of continuity and stability in social policies, but even there deteriorating economic performance prompted increasingly far-reaching reexaminations of economic organization and policy. From Eastern Europe to China and the USSR, economic reform moved to the center of the political agenda, and with it the problems of social welfare. The inescapable interdependence of state-economy linkages and social policy meant that debates over economic reform would inevitably engage issues of social justice. The need to strike a suitable balance between efficiency and equity—itself a condition of political legitimacy and continued political stability—required a reexamination of a broad range of social as well as economic policies.

The fact that similar questions have been raised in systems which have adopted such markedly different approaches to economic organization and social welfare is sufficiently intriguing to invite closer examination. Yet the burgeoning literature on the welfare state offers little as a point of departure. It has been devoted largely to studies of the evolution of welfare states and social policy regimes

---

*The positive attitude of former Soviet citizens toward the Soviet welfare state was first documented by the Harvard Project on the Soviet Social System in the 1950s. Studies of more recent emigrés have found a striking continuity of expectations and evaluations (see Gitelman 1977: 563–64).

in Western industrial democracies, and to comparisons among them, with virtually no effort at comparison across socioeconomic systems. Moreover, the emphasis on macrolevel analysis that uses aggregate data to test hypotheses about welfare effort tends to exclude analysis of the interplay of politics and markets in different types of systems. The task of comparison would in any case be exceedingly difficult, given the absence of any systematic, recent study of social welfare in the USSR.*

A number of studies have demonstrated that affluent industrial states demonstrate a high degree of convergence of welfare outcomes. Economic level and its demographic and bureaucratic correlates appear to outweigh the impact of differences in cultural and political traditions in accounting for social security effort; "holding affluence constant," Wilensky et al. have argued, many other factors lose the power to explain (1985: 10). This hypothesis is obviously addressed to a particular set of core programs and to a particular universe of outcomes. A rather different research strategy would be required if the focus of concern shifted to the internal features of social programs, or to their impact on individual welfare, or to efforts to explore the relationship between state-economy linkages and social policy regimes. How differences in the role and capacities of the state, and in its relationship to economic organization, affects social policy inputs and ultimately welfare outcomes deserves the serious attention of social scientists and policymakers alike.

Soviet and American approaches to social welfare differ significantly across a wide range of characteristics. They reflect important differences in the broader setting of social policy (levels of development, political and cultural belief systems and norms, the relationships of state and economy and of public and private realms, the ways in which the interests of social groups achieve political expression), in the content of policy (administrative arrangements, revenue and expenditure patterns, scope and forms of benefits and services provided), and in the overall quality of outcomes, including the distribution of benefits and the relationship of citizens to the welfare bureaucracy. Some of these variables can be readily manipulated by policymakers; others are less amenable to direct control.

The American "welfare state" is something less than the comprehensive, integrated, and universal system of social protection as it was conceived in Europe and virtually identified with the rights of

---

*The most comprehensive study remains Madison (1968). For a suggestive treatment of the East European experience, see Szelenyi and Manchin (1987).

citizenship. Indeed in the United States the very term still lacks legitimacy and even carries a certain pejorative connotation, reflecting the sharp distinction between those social programs such as Social Security, which are treated as "entitlements," paid by contributions over a lifetime of work, and those treated as "welfare," which are often viewed as a form of governmental handout to the undeserving as well as the needy.

The American approach is also characterized by several additional features. First, it involves extensive reliance on the market as a coordinating and allocative mechanism; the market is presumed to promote competition and efficiency while state intervention is viewed as a secondary and limited mechanism for regulation and redistribution to guarantee some degree of equity and social stability. Second, responsibility for financing and administering social programs is dispersed among different levels of government (federal, state, and local) as well as shared with private and voluntary organizations, and typically includes insurance as well as programs of direct grants. Finally, although levels of governmental effort in some areas are comparatively modest by comparison with a number of European industrial democracies, state investment in education in the United States is exceptionally high.

In the Soviet Union, by contrast, the functions of coordinating major economic and social processes are performed by a central state bureaucracy rather than by the market.* The bureaucratic function is also a redistributive one, intervening in the functioning of enterprises to reallocate revenues from profitable firms to others which would otherwise go bankrupt, and redistributing income in accordance with a variety of central objectives.† Productivity and welfare are joined in a single set of economic and social institutions: the enterprise serves as both employer and provider of social benefits. Job security has been a central feature of the Soviet approach to welfare, wherein the guarantee of the right to work carries with it the obligation to work. As a consequence, important welfare benefits are closely linked to production, with only limited social provision for those unable to work due to age, disability,

---

*This is not to say that a market is completely absent. Indeed the unofficial or "second" economy has played a rather substantial role in providing a corrective to the imperfections of the central planning system (see, e.g., Grossman 1977).

†This pattern is responsible for what Janos Kornai (1980) has called the "soft budget constraint," which in turn results in scarcities.

or family responsibilities. Pensioners, for example, are particularly disadvantaged by the absence of provisions adjusting pensions to increases in the cost of living. At the same time, the link of performance and reward in the Soviet system has been relatively weak; the combined effects of job security and increasing wage egalitarianism in recent years give workers a high degree of immunity from the discipline imposed by the marketplace in capitalist systems. Further distinguishing the Soviet from the American pattern is the centrality of the state as the ultimate provider. Private institutions or activities are deprived of any formal role and are virtually absent; indeed the term *charity* virtually disappeared from the Soviet lexicon for half a century.* Welfare functions are carried out through the administrative allocation of scarce goods and services, either in kind or at heavily subsidized prices, creating a relationship between provider and consumer that deprives the latter of significant influence.[†] The combined effects of overextension and underfunding, which contributed to an acute disequilibrium between the supply and demand for key goods and services, was an important catalyst in the growing pressures for reform in social as well as economic policy.

THE REAGAN "REVOLUTION"

By the early 1980s, key features of both these systems had come under attack by analysts and policymakers alike. In the United States, the Reagan administration inaugurated a major experiment in economic and social policy with potentially far-reaching consequences for the scope and purposes of the American welfare state. Faced with high rates of inflation, low rates of economic growth, and particularly low growth of productivity, rising federal expenditures, and a perceived inadequacy of military capabilities, President Reagan initiated a major reorientation of economic policy designed to scale back federal spending on domestic social programs and to transfer much of the fiscal and programmatic responsibility assumed by the federal government in past decades to state and local governments and to the private sector.

*The family, however, has remained a key institution in Soviet life and performs important welfare functions.

[†]Food, housing, and transport are heavily subsidized, and this practice has created in the Soviet population the expectation of an elastic supply at low prices.

This attempt at "rollback" in economic and social policy expressed a shift in social philosophy as well as a response to fiscal constraints. It was premised on the view that government had come to play an excessive and even harmful role in the American economy — that its responsibilities were too vast, its expenditures too high, and its impact problematic. Provision for social welfare, in this view, far exceeded the needs of a modest safety net. It had become, in the memorable phrase of David Stockman, who would later become President Reagan's budget director, the "great social pork barrel" (1975: 3-30; see also Palmer and Sawhill 1982). By reducing the force of market incentives, it was now serving to create and to foster dependence. In short, federal intervention was exacerbating economic and social problems rather than alleviating them, and the appropriate solution was to increase reliance on market mechanisms and on the private sector.

This approach reflected a narrower conception of the social safety net, an effort to reduce the scale of social benefits and to restrict eligibility for them, and a rejection of the view that greater egalitarianism was a legitimate or desirable objective of economic and social policy. Its central goal was to shift control over a greater share of income from the public to the private sector in the conviction this would promote more rapid economic growth and stimulate individual initiative. As the president's 1982 *Economic Report* put it: "Income redistribution is not a compelling justification in the 1980s for federal taxing and spending programs" (1982: 92).

In this, as in other areas of national life, the results of the Reagan experiment proved less sweeping than the original intention. Political expediency moderated social philosophy; while the initial attacks on welfare abuse gave expression to widespread popular resentment, the Administration eventually came under assault for threatening social programs which had the support of broad constituencies. Ironically it found itself defending its record by arguing it had increased social spending. By the end of the Reagan administration, a shift in public attitudes appears to be under way, with increased support for greater governmental intervention and for a shift in resources from military to social spending (*Washington Post*, 16-22 May 1988).

But the Reagan era had a potentially more lasting impact on American social welfare policy by changing the terms of debate: no longer is the dominant argument about which social programs government should finance next, but about whether even the existing range can be adequately sustained. In this respect the high budget deficits which are a central legacy of the Reagan administration will, intentionally or unintentionally, serve to constrain future administrations as they approach the problems of social welfare. Future investments are likely to be focused on improving the quality of the labor force rather than on expanding the scope of the social safety net.

THE GORBACHEV AGENDA

The economic reforms central to Gorbachev's effort to revitalize the Soviet system involve an effort to sharply reduce the scope of bureaucratic intervention in the operation of the Soviet economy and to expand the role of market forces. They would not only reduce the size and functions of the state bureaucracies, and compel enterprises to become self-supporting, but would also widen wage differentials in the state sector and encourage cooperative and private initiative, particularly in the spheres of agriculture and consumer goods and services (Hewett 1988; Hauslohner 1987).

These reforms would have a major impact not only on the Soviet economic system, but also on the entire system of social welfare. Over the long term they promise significant improvements in living standards for the population as a whole, but in the short run they threaten diminished security and welfare. By increasing the pressures as well as the rewards for high performance, by subjecting enterprises as well as individuals to the discipline of the marketplace, and by eliminating what is in effect the subsidization of failure, the reforms would create a novel separation between the functions of productivity and those of welfare. If the extensive subsidization of key consumer goods and services is indeed reduced, and prices allowed to rise to balance supply and demand, welfare will become more closely tied to productivity and to income. A more limited array of social entitlements will be combined with the opportunity for some segments of the Soviet population to use private resources to purchase higher quality goods and services outside the normal channels of state supply—from food and housing to medical care (already available at fee-for-service clinics) and possibly new forms of private or cooperative education for pre-schoolers. These opportunities will endow consumers with an unprecedented range of choices as well as unaccustomed power over providers.

These changes require major adjustments of values as well as of institutions. They challenge traditional conceptions of social solidarity, justice, and equity long equated with socialism itself. They seek to reverse the long-standing suspicion of private enterprise, while assigning unaccustomed virtue to competitive individualism and the marketplace. And they question an assumption that has gone unchallenged since the Stalin era: that an expanding role for the state is synonymous with social progress. These unaccustomed ideas and values have provoked widespread confusion and resistance from ordinary citizens as well as from party and state officials, compelling Soviet reformers to pay serious attention to public opinion in pursuing their larger objectives.

If the reforms proceed further, the Soviet system will require a new array of institutions to perform the new welfare functions that will become necessary: new tax policies to redistribute income if earnings become a function of profits generated, job training and placement services if redundant workers and officials are to be released, more extensive provision for the unemployed as well as the unemployable.

While reducing the scope of the social welfare system in some domains, the Soviet leadership also promises to come to grips with its severe underfunding. The system of medical care is acknowledged to be in acute need of improvement, and high-level attention is being devoted to improving its quality and resource base. To address widespread poverty among the elderly, a new pension law is under consideration which may bring some improvement in currently inadequate levels of support. The plight of female-headed households has been recognized by Gorbachev himself, and the system of family allowances is likely to be modified as well.

Moreover, new trends in Soviet public life, involving the emergence of a public arena, are likely to have an impact of their own on social policy. *Glasnost* has focused public attention on a broad range of previously invisible and unacknowledged social problems—from unemployment to homelessness, from drug addiction to the absence of day-care centers for the elderly—and has opened the door to public discussion of how to address them. The campaign for democratization promises to endow local soviets with enhanced powers and opportunities, which may permit new local initiatives in social policy. The emergence of a wide variety of unofficial organizations, with the tacit acquiescence of the leadership itself, has begun to create new organizational frameworks for private initiatives in the name of charity and compassion (Antic 1988). Even the Russian Orthodox church has begun to press for the right to engage in charitable volunteer activities such as nursing. In short, the reforms now under way in the USSR could well lead to a pattern of social welfare provision which joins public and private initiatives in novel ways.

The challenges and possibilities presented by current trends will give new importance to the role of social science in social policy-making. The mutilation of the social sciences during the Stalin era, and the ideological and political constraints under which it has continued to operate, deprived the Soviet Union of the self-knowledge essential to its further development. The current Soviet leadership is coming to recognize that it has been trying to govern an increasingly modern and complex society with instruments that are no longer appropriate (see Lapidus 1988). Fictions and stereotypes were taken for social reality, ideological dogmatism became a substitute for serious social research, and the myth of a solidary society prevented the acknowledgment and serious study of the diversity of needs and interests of different social and ethnic groups. It is therefore no accident that a number of social scientists — including a distinguished economist, Abel Aganbegian, and the once controversial economic sociologist Tatyana Zaslavskaya — have become leading advisors to General-Secretary Gorbachev, and that two new institutes for social research, including the first national center for the study of public opinion, have now been established to guide the formulation of new economic and social policies.

A RESEARCH AGENDA

As both the United States and the Soviet Union come to grips with new challenges which invite reassessment of attitudes and approaches toward social welfare, it is a particularly appropriate time to attempt to develop a baseline against which current controversies might be better understood and future new departures might be assessed. It may prove equally helpful to provide a framework which could stimulate more comparative research across socioeconomic systems. This volume seeks to serve both purposes by examining the central features and the characteristic shortcomings and dilemmas faced by the two systems in addressing universal problems of social welfare. It also makes use of two kinds of newly available materials on Soviet economic and social policy: published Soviet materials that reflect the greater openness of discussion of social problems in recent years, and the findings of Western research based on interviews with former Soviet citizens, made possible by the major new wave of emigration from the Soviet Union in the 1970s and early 1980s (Millar 1987).

Both the focus of this volume and the themes selected for treatment reflect these broader comparative concerns. While a comprehensive treatment of social welfare should embrace both public and private expenditures, particularly since many of the institutions of social protection in the Western industrial world are neither exclusively public nor private, the paramount role of the state in the Soviet case places it at one end of the broader comparative spectrum. The selection of topics reflects both their importance for the central theme and the availability of roughly comparable data; the relative paucity of both sources and research on the Soviet side precluded the inclusion of a number of other possible topics. Finally, the poorer quality of some of the Soviet data, and its more fragmentary character, resulted in certain asymmetries which it may prove possible to remedy in future research. If the development of Soviet social research produces a community of scholars able to join in the common enterprise, the experiments under way will yield new insights into the way in which state-economy relationships affect social policy regimes and their broader consequences for individual welfare.

REFERENCES

Antic, Oxana. 1988. "Discussion in the Soviet Press on Allowing the Church to Engage in Charitable Work." Radio Liberty Research, RL 179/88. April 27.

Economic Report of the President. 1982. Washington, D.C.: Government Printing Office.

Gitelman, Zvi. 1977. "Soviet Political Culture: Insights from Soviet Emigrés." *Soviet Studies,* October.

Grossman, Gregory, 1977. "The 'Second Economy' of the USSR." *Problems of Communism,* September–October: 25–40.

Hauslohner, Peter. 1987. "Gorbachev's Social Contract." *Soviet Economy,* no. 1: 54–89.

Hewett, Ed A. 1988. *Reforming the Soviet Economy: Equality versus Efficiency.* Washington, D.C.: Brookings Institution.

Kornai, Janos. 1980. *Economics of Shortage.* Amsterdam: North Holland.

Lapidus, Gail W. 1988. "State and Society: Toward the Emergence of Civil Society in the USSR." In *Politics, Society, and Nationality*, ed. Seweryn Bialer et al. Boulder, CO: Westview Press.

Madison, Bernice. 1968. *Social Welfare in the Soviet Union.* Stanford: Stanford University Press.

Millar, James, ed. 1987. *Politics, Work, and Daily Life in the USSR.* New York: Cambridge University Press.

Palmer, John L., and Sawhill, Isabel V., eds. 1982. *The Reagan Experiment.* Washington, D.C.: Urban Institute Press.

Rein, Martin; Esping-Andersen, Gøsta; and Rainwater, Lee, eds. 1987. *Stagnation and Renewal in Social Policy.* Armonk, NY: M.E. Sharpe.

Skocpol, Theda. 1987. "America's Incomplete Welfare State." In Rein, Esping-Andersen, and Rainwater, eds.

Stockman, David A. 1975. "The Social Pork Barrel." *The Public Interest*, Spring: 3-30.

Szelenyi, Ivan, and Manchin, Robert. 1987. "Social Policy under State Socialism: Market Redistribution and Social Inequalities in East European Socialist Societies." In Rein, Esping-Andersen, and Rainwater, eds.

Wilensky, Harold L. 1975. *The Welfare State and Equality: Structural and Ideological Roots of Public Expenditures.* Berkeley: University of California Press.

Wilensky, Harold L. et al. 1985. *Comparative Social Policy: Theories, Methods, Findings.* Berkeley: Institute of International Studies, University of California.

PREFACE

This book grew out of a conference on "Social Welfare and the Social Services: USA/USSR" held in Berkeley in November 1982 and jointly sponsored by the Center for Slavic and East European Studies and the Institute for Human Development. The conference focused on governmental assistance to individuals and families when they deal with certain major transitions or crises in their life-cycles: obtaining a higher education, coping with illness, insuring financial support when old or retired, and dealing with unemployment or underemployment. There were papers on American and on Soviet provisions in each of these areas and on the nature of relations between citizens and the welfare bureaucracies in the two countries. Two participants, Joseph Berliner and Alex Inkeles, agreed to review all of the papers and to set them in a broad comparative framework.

The conference benefitted from comments by the specialists who opened the discussions of the original papers and who contributed to their final updating and revision: Martha Derthick (University of Virginia), Mark Field (Boston University), and (from the University of California, Berkeley) Gregory Grossman, David Kirp, Ralph Kramer, and Harold Wilensky. George Breslauer and Harold Wilensky worked with us in designing the conference and this book. Dr. Elizabeth Shepard, Associate Research Specialist in the Center for Slavic and East European Studies, was an indispensable collaborator at all stages of our work. We owe a special debt of gratitude to Paul Gilchrist, Principal Editor of the Institute of International Studies, whose gifted editing has made an invaluable contribution to this symposium.

GAIL W. LAPIDUS

GUY E. SWANSON

NOTES ON CONTRIBUTORS

GAIL W. LAPIDUS is Professor of Political Science and Chairman of the Center for Slavic and East European Studies, University of California, Berkeley.

GUY E. SWANSON is Professor of Psychology and Director of the Institute of Human Development, University of California, Berkeley.

JOSEPH S. BERLINER is Professor of Economics at Brandeis University.

CHRISTOPHER M. DAVIS is Lecturer at the Centre for Russian and East European Studies, University of Birmingham.

RICHARD B. DOBSON is Resident Scholar, Kennan Institute for Advanced Russian Studies, Woodrow Wilson Center, Smithsonian Institution.

ZVI GITELMAN is Professor of Political Science at the University of Michigan (Ann Arbor).

YEHESKEL HASENFELD is Professor of Social Welfare at the University of California, Los Angeles.

ALEX INKELES is Professor of Sociology at Stanford University and Research Fellow, Hoover Institution on War, Revolution and Peace.

BERNICE MADISON is Senior Fellow, Kennan Institute for Advanced Russian Studies, Woodrow Wilson Center, Smithsonian Institution.

THEODORE R. MARMOR is Professor of Public Management and Political Science, Institution for Social and Policy Studies, Yale University.

GUR OFER is Professor of Economics at the Hebrew University of Jerusalem.

LEE RAINWATER is Professor of Sociology at Harvard University.

MARTIN REIN is Professor of Sociology, Department of Urban Studies and Planning, Massachusetts Institute of Technology.

MARTIN TROW is Professor of Public Policy and Director of the Center for Studies in Higher Education, University of California, Berkeley.

AARON VINOKUR is Professor of Sociology at the University of Haifa.

MAYER N. ZALD is Professor of Sociology and Social Work at the University of Michigan (Ann Arbor).

THE COMPARISON OF SOCIAL WELFARE SYSTEMS

Joseph S. Berliner

The wedding is nearly over. The family of the bride have consorted with the family of the groom, and each side is relieved to know that the other is at least of the same religious persuasion. They have found to their pleasure that they have much in common, but they have talked mostly to the members of their own family, with whom they are most at ease.

Some, however, traded gossip with the other family as readily as with their own, and seemed to move easily among both. Their world is that of the clan and not of the family. They are the comparativists.

There is always something slightly unsettling about the comparative exercise. Virtues that we have thought to be unique to our own family turn out to be shared by other families in the clan, and by other clans as well. One is never sure where the comparativist's loyalty lies. The anxiety provoked by the comparative exercise surfaced during this conference in the repeated, and sometimes irritated, requests for clarification of questions about why we are comparing, what we should be comparing, and what do we do when we compare.

My first encounter with the doubts generated by the comparative enterprise occurred when I was a newly minted graduate student. Standing on the outskirts of a circle surrounding a famous economic theorist, I heard him remark, cocktail glass in hand, "When you don't know what to do with your data, you compare it." That remark almost derailed what I hoped would be a brilliant career in comparative economics. Faith prevailed over reason, however, but I later came to believe that faith had its reason. The famous theorist had contributed to the development of macroeconomics, and had spent much of his life thinking about the relative merits of fiscal and monetary policy. That exercise may appear to be remote from comparative economics, but if one considers what is involved in the assessment of fiscal and monetary policy, it is apparent that it is fundamentally an exercise in comparative analysis. One compares two states of the world, each

1

consisting of a set of outcomes produced by different interventions into or constraints upon a system. From that somewhat imperialistic perspective, all systematic analysis can be regarded as comparative. One compares groups with different incomes and different fertility rates in order to study the systematic relationship between income and fertility. In the same way, one must compare different groups in order to study the relationship between social class and attitudes, or between income and consumption. All of us at this wedding have been guilty of some sort of social analysis, and are therefore comparativists, either overt or covert. Even Martha Derthick, who assured us that she had never knowingly committed comparativism, turns out to have been a closet comparativist all the time.

Since we all do it, it behooves us to clarify the scholarly function of comparative analysis—the sense in which it is an aid to understanding. It does entail the stretching of the mind, as Ted Marmor puts it, but it does more than that. It is a method of seeking to discover the systematic relationship among phenomena, or of testing a proposed theory of that relationship. Ideally we would like to compare objects that are similar in all respects but two—like families that are similar in all respects except income and number of children. With an appropriate sample of such families, we could proceed to study the relationship between income and fertility. One of the things that makes such a study interesting is that we can rarely find the ideal sample. The things we can observe are contaminated by all sorts of noise, and the task is finding ways of controlling for the noise in order to isolate the variables in which we are interested.

LEVELS OF RESEARCH

We can distinguish three levels of social research according to the degree of difficulty in isolating the variables to be compared. The first and simplest level deals with a single national society, such as the research that produced the conclusion that in higher-income countries the traditional relationship between life expectancy and per capita income has disappeared. One such study is a comparison of Utah and Nevada, which are similar in levels of income, medical care, and a great many other characteristics, but are vastly different in levels of health. What varies greatly are styles of life: there are Mormons in Utah and gamblers in Nevada. Most social research is of this kind, and it is not normally thought of as comparative at all.

The second level of social research is one in which the general features of the culture and the social system are similar, but there are large variations in their specific features. Many participants at this conference have operated on this level in some of their research. Hal Wilensky, for example, has compared the welfare state practices of the richest democracies, and Martin Trow has compared the American and European higher education systems. At this level there are so many sources of variation in the data that the relation among the specific variables of interest is difficult to establish because of the noise in the data. Experienced investigators can nevertheless produce plausible generalizations, and where quantitative data are available, statistical techniques can produce fairly robust results.

Most social analysts are at home with this kind of research, reasonably secure in the view that, in the matters with which their research is concerned, Great Britain is not that different from West Germany or Switzerland after all. Few hackles would rise to the point of prompting the impatient demand "What are we supposed to be comparing anyway, and why?" It is only when one throws the socialist countries into the sample that the hackles begin to rise and a certain tension develops among the wedding guests. Within the academy the distinction is often quite sharp. If the young scholar has written a dissertation on French politics or Swedish fiscal policy, his job candidacy will be treated like that of anybody else. But if he has written on Soviet party organization or Chinese agriculture, one has first to make sure that there is an appropriate slot.

It is this third level of comparative research with which we have been engaged at this conference. In comparing countries like the United States and the USSR, it would seem that almost nothing is held constant; in particular, even the most general properties of the social and economic systems are different. It may appear that such large socioeconomic differences are the major source of the complexity of comparative analysis at this level, but from another point of view it is precisely that difference that offers the greatest promise of productive research results. For the major purpose of this kind of comparative analysis is to understand the consequences of variations in socioeconomic systems—to understand, for example, how the distribution of income, or the economic status of women, or the delivery of social services differs according to whether a society employs some variant of a socialist society or some variant of a capitalist society. A typical question on the first two levels is "What is the relation between family income and children's education, given the socioeconomic system?" A typical question on the third level is "Is the relation between income and education in a socialist system similar to or different from that in a capitalist system?" The practical objective of the first two levels is to predict the outcomes of various policies in a given system. The practical objective of the third level is to predict the outcomes of the adoption of one system or another. The first two levels involve within-system comparisons. The third level involves between-system comparisons. Hereafter when I refer to comparative analysis, I shall have only the third level in mind, recognizing that serious research on the first two levels must also be fundamentally comparative—with a small *c*.

The basic methodological problem of comparative, between-system analysis is that one cannot observe systems. One can only observe the behavior of different people in different countries. The task then is to distinguish those differences in behavior that can be ascribed to the differences in the socioeconomic systems from those differences in behavior that should be ascribed to everything else. The question I shall try to answer is "How can one possibly draw inferences about the effects of the socioeconomic system relative to the effect of the vast number of other sources of variation?"

I take it as the objective of this conference to identify and explain the differences in outcomes in the United States and the USSR in four selected areas of activity: educational services, medical services, income support services, and bureaucratic encounters. The fourth area is somewhat different from the first three: it can be thought of as an aspect of the quality with which the three types of services are delivered. Alex Inkeles has urged that we not be content with merely identifying and explaining outcomes, but that we also seek to assess the implications of those outcomes for social well-being. That is a far more important (and far more difficult) goal than I propose to pursue. My more limited purpose is to summarize the conference by presenting what seem to me to be the common threads in the participants' efforts to explain the observed similarities and differences in outcomes. The threads of explanation fall into two groups: those that can be regarded as features of the social systems of the two societies, and those that are nonsystemic but nevertheless affect social outcomes.

NONSYSTEMIC FEATURES

Two nonsystemic features have figured most prominently in the proceedings of this conference. The first is culture, in the conventional sense of learned forms of behavior, historical traditions, beliefs, values, and so forth—all of which vary to some degree among ethnic groups and social classes within a society. Culture determines the content of the attitudes and preferences of the population regarding such matters as the value of education relative to other goods and the obligation of the group to assume responsibility for individual needs. Cultural differences have been cited by Inkeles and others as one of the main sources of the differences in outcomes between the United States and the USSR.

The second notable source of nonsystemic variation in outcomes is difference in levels of per capita income. There has been some controversy over the best way to measure income in such different societies. Moreover, the level of income may be determined in the long run by the nature of the social system, particularly its economic subsystem. However those issues are resolved, the proposition is still likely to stand that many of the differences we have found between outcomes are due to differences in income.

SYSTEMIC FEATURES

From the comparative perspective of the conference, the non-systemic features are the noise in the data. We need to identify them in order to get them out of the way, so to speak. Our real interest is in those other differences in outcomes that are due to the differences in social systems. Two systemic features appear to me to have figured most prominently in the efforts to account for the variations in outcomes: preference articulation and organizational arrangements.

The content and distribution of individual preferences are determined largely by the culture. Given the culture-based content of preferences, however, the method by which the mass of individual preferences is taken account of in the making of large social choices is a central feature of the social system—particularly of the economic and political subsystems. At one extreme of the range of possibilities is a decentralized system in which the outcomes are the result of a large number of individual decisions made by citizens on the basis of their individual preferences. At the other extreme is a centralized system in which a governing group like a political party makes all the decisions on behalf of the population. Most societies employ both of these methods in various proportions; the United States is closer to the decentralized extreme and the USSR closer to the centralized extreme. A number of the differences in outcomes identified at this conference appear to be consequences of this difference in the ways preferences are translated into action in the two countries.

The second systemic feature which exerts a strong influence on outcomes is the set of organizational arrangements. Differences in organization entail differences in outcomes in the following sense: if we know that in one society a certain service is delivered by a single supplier, while in another society it is delivered by multiple suppliers, we can make some reasonable guesses about the differences in the ways that service is delivered in the two societies. Among the many facets of organizational arrangements discussed at this conference, one that appears to have considerable explanatory power is the various ways in which the service providers earn their incomes and the service users exert their claims to service. If the service provider receives his income from a fixed, budgeted source, the outcome is likely to be different than it would be in an arrangement in which there is a direct link between the provider's income and the user's satisfaction with the service. If the service is provided without charge to the user, the outcome will be different from that resulting from an arrangement in which there is a charge. Organizational arrangements of these kinds are the subject matter of that portion of conventional economic analysis that deals with the pricing of goods and services and of the factors of production.

The four systemic and nonsystemic features I have listed by no means exhaust the explanation of variations in outcomes. One participant noted, for example, that the microbiological climatic environment may be the cause of certain differences in health outcomes. We might consider that as part of a third nonsystemic source of variation in outcomes—the natural resource endowment. That category might be extended to include human as well as natural resources—to encompass education for example, for the outcome of a given set of educational arrangements varies according to the kinds of persons to whom the educational services are provided. Human resources, however, may be viewed as just another way of talking about culture. I mention these points to emphasize that the four features I have identified are not presented as definitive, or as elements of a proposed general theory of social variation. They should be taken as a somewhat ad hoc set of categories presented for the purpose of summarizing the proceedings of the conference.

ASSESSMENT OF RELATIVE IMPORTANCE

The explanation of the variations in outcomes that have been reported here is of course multicausal, but of the four categories of causal influence, the one that appears to me to account for most of the variation is organizational arrangements. Second and third are preference articulation and income; they appear to be about equal in importance. Surprisingly the influence of cultural differences seems to be of least importance. After the other three influences are accounted for, there is very little left to be explained by the fact that Russians and Americans are running the two countries. The implication is that system plays a very powerful role relative to culture. In the balance of my remarks, I will provide some illustrations that will help explain this conclusion.

With respect to variations in the organizational form of social institutions, if we examine all the papers presented here, the most striking difference between the United States and the USSR is the role in Soviet institutions of illegal activity—bribery, the second economy, and so forth. This activity seems to have provoked more comment in the discussions than any other subject. Whatever can explain this vivid difference between the two societies has a claim to be regarded as of major importance. In my estimation the difference is due predominantly to organizational arrangements.

METHODOLOGICAL DIGRESSION

Before proceeding to defend this view, I would like to discuss a methodological issue that arose on a number of occasions. Some of the conference participants who are not Soviet specialists are understandably suspicious about the assertions regarding the extensiveness of illegal activity in the USSR. Concern has been expressed about the unreliability of emigré testimony, and about the possible distortions in perception due to the anti-Soviet sentiments, if not bias, of some of the Soviet specialists here. In addressing this concern I wish to point out that the primary source of material on Soviet social institutions at this conference is Soviet publications. The value of this material derives from a long-standing Soviet tradition called *samokritika*, or self-criticism. Lenin himself did much to establish that tradition as a vital instrument in defeating what he foresaw as a threatening tendency toward self-serving behavior in bureaucracies. Self-criticism is a solemn obligation of the Soviet citizen and particularly of party members. It obliges every journalist, official, and party member to expose the weaknesses and failures of his own and other organizations, and particularly to expose instances of violation of plan discipline and illegal activity. Soviet publications are therefore a rich source of detailed information on informal and illegal activity. Because of this officially sponsored whistle-blowing, we probably know more about the shadowy side of organizational behavior in the USSR than we do of corresponding behavior in organizations in the United States. The emigré testimony supplements the published sources by providing context, specifics, and a basis for estimating the extent of the practices.

Having worked with the published sources, I have never doubted that the practices are of more than marginal significance, but I have reserved judgment about whether they are as pervasive as they appear to be from emigré testimony. The more one probes, however, the more one is persuaded. I was impressed, for example, with a remark of an emigré scholar, who is now a good friend and colleague, when I asked what he regards as the major difference between ways of living in the two countries. He replied: " I am continually surprised by the fact that in the three years I have lived in the United States I have never once had the occasion to offer anyone a bribe. That would be impossible in the Soviet Union."

DISEQUILIBRIUM

Granted then that the kind of corruption described in the papers on the USSR is as pervasive as reported, how is it to be explained? I propose that it is largely a consequence of the organizational feature of Soviet society that Greg Grossman refers to as "disequilibrium." It applies to a social arrangement in which a good or service is usually supplied under such conditions that the demand for it exceeds the amount available for distribution, and some agent therefore has the power to decide which persons will receive the limited supply. The proposition is that any society that employs such arrangements will in the long run generate corruption in such forms as bribery of distributing agents and illicit production of the good or service. Since most goods and services are supplied under disequilibrium conditions in the USSR, including higher education and medical care, such practices are widespread. It should be noted that when the United States adopted a system of materials allocation under the pressures of the Second World War, many of the same practices emerged and became shockingly widespread. When the society returned to its traditional form of operation after the war, however, the practices ended. Hence the proposition says nothing about a difference between Russians and Americans: it purports to explain a major difference in the social outcomes of the two societies on the basis of a particular feature of social organization.

I have alluded only to bribery and illicit production as the probable consequences of disequilibrium. There are various others, among them one that has figured prominently in the papers on the delivery of social services. The power over the user that disequilibrium bestows on the distributing agent generally leads to a lower quality of service than would be provided under equilibrium conditions. Visitors from abroad are generally struck by what appears to be the lack of interest or even surliness of Soviet waiters and sales personnel. Again there is a close parallel with market economies under wartime restrictions. Hence the social outcome with respect to the quality of the delivery of welfare services in the USSR is no different from that of restaurant services, or housing, or television repair services, given the disequilibrium in the organizational arrangements.

ORGANIZATIONAL ARRANGEMENTS

Let me proceed to other organizational arrangements that affect social outcomes. Gur Ofer and Aaron Vinokur report that, in the distribution of poverty in the USSR, about half are retired persons and about one quarter are single-parent households. Give or take a few percentage points, those proportions are very similar to the historical experience of the United States, although in recent years the proportion of retirees has decreased and that of single-parent households has increased. That pattern of poverty can be largely explained by the way in which the societies organize the relationship between income and work. In this case both societies link the two: for most people the predominant source of income is participation in the labor force. Under such an organizational arrangement, the incidence of poverty will be greatest in those households with the least capacity to earn income from labor supply. Hence the two societies produce similar outcomes because of the similarity of their organizational arrangement. The outcomes could be changed, of course, by the introduction of a new organizational device that redistributed earned incomes according to a different set of rules.

Some surprising results emerged in the papers on bureaucratic encounters. Zvi Gitelman expressed what must have been the common expectation that here we would find large differences in outcomes between the two countries because cultural differences are likely to predominate. The two societies also differ in what Yeheskel Hasenfeld and Mayer Zald call the power-dependence relation between bureaucrat and client, as well as in the political power of client groups: there are no welfare-rights organizations or associations of retired persons in the USSR. Despite such differences between the societies, however, the research results point to surprising similarities in outcomes. The degree of satisfaction with bureaucratic encounters is unexpectedly high in the USSR as well as the United States. Moreover the ordering is similar: the highest degree of satisfaction occurs in the administration of retirement pensions, and the lowest degree in disability and income maintenance programs.

I am not sure that these results could have been predicted, but they are readily explained after the fact by organizational arrangements—at least in part. These are services in which political issues are not at the fore, and entitlements to them are governed by legal and administrative structures that are probably very similar in the two countries. Class structure is very likely more important than organization in explaining the higher satisfaction level for retirement pensions. In both societies pensions are an entitlement that is of great importance to the educated and middle classes, members of which are the administrators of the program. On the other hand, the beneficiaries of income maintenance programs, and to some degree disability programs, are generally of a different social stratum. In addition to the effect of social class, however, the low rating of the bureaucratic encounter in these programs also reflects an organizational element. Any society that establishes entitlements based on such categories as illness, inability to work, or income level is bound to create dissatisfaction among people required to prove a back ailment or to show they are destitute. Both the USSR and the United States have such categorical requirements for certification, which contributes to the similarity in outcomes of the encounters between bureaucrats and clients.

An interesting difference between the two countries relates to the supply of physicians. Christopher Davis reports a shortage in the USSR while Marmor reports an oversupply in the United States in recent years. The explanation in the Soviet case is primarily government preferences, but in the United States case Marmor offers a strong organizational explanation: the expansion of third-party payment methods encourages greater use of expensive procedures which induces an increase in the supply of those services. With respect to the sex composition of service providers, the comparative outcomes are more complex. The sex distribution in education is similar in the two countries, but in health services it is quite different: women predominate among Soviet physicians. The explanation again is to be found largely in organization—in this case, the way in which service providers earn their incomes. The relative wages of teachers are about the same in the two countries, but the relative wages of physicians are much lower in the USSR.

PREFERENCE ARTICULATION

The second systemic determinant of outcomes I have alluded to is preference articulation. The two countries differ substantially in this respect. A large range of social choices that are the result of individual decisions in the United States are made directly by the government in the USSR. One would expect that, because of this difference in the ways in which preferences are articulated, social outcomes would vary considerably between the two countries. One can see some such differences in education and health services. If those services could be purchased by individuals in the USSR in a manner similar to that in the United States, many of their characteristics would probably be more similar—for example, the incomes and sex composition of physicians would probably be more like that in the United States, and the number of students in higher education might well be higher. In both countries, however, income maintenance programs are provided by the government, and the outcomes prove to be similar. In the USSR the primary objective of such programs is to maintain a high labor force participation rate. In the United States, while the government is more responsive to individual preferences, it is interesting to note that, despite cultural differences, labor force participation has also been an important concern in its income maintenance programs. For example, a major objection to a negative income tax as the basis of an income maintenance program is the potential for a large-scale withdrawal of labor, and in government-financed experiments for evaluating such programs, the labor supply effect is always studied. To the extent that income maintenance programs in both countries are influenced by their labor supply implications, the similarity in their outcomes is due to the fact that both are based on government preferences.

Of the two nonsystemic factors, differences in per capita national income surely explain most of the differences in the quantities of resources allocated to pensions, education, and medical services, and therefore to the quantities of those services that are delivered, but they probably do not explain much more than that. That is to say, if the USSR and the United States had the same per capita income levels, the quantities of resources each allocated to the welfare services would probably be very similar, but the ways in which those services were delivered would differ because of systemic differences.

This leaves very little to be explained by cultural factors. Trow explains the difference between American and European higher education as the consequence of differences in the level of academic standards to which they are committed. That may be regarded as an instance of outcomes being influenced by cultural differences. Similarly, Gitelman notes that such phenomena as *protektsiia* are part of the Russian historical tradition, but in my view, if the USSR had operated under different organizational arrangements for the past half-century, the salience of that historical tradition would have been greatly diminished. Perhaps cultural differences play such a modest role because the place of the social services happens to be very similar in the cultures of American and Soviet societies. We saw this to some extent in the similarity of attitudes toward pension plans compared to income maintenance plans in the two countries. In a conference focused on political institutions rather than social services, we would surely find larger differences in cultural attitudes regarding political matters, and therefore more of the variation in outcomes would be explained by cultural factors. I must concede that if this inquiry were pushed to the point of asking "What accounts for the organizational differences that account for the outcomes?," culture would be likely to assume a more prominent role. In this conference, however, in which social organization is a "given," one of the unexpected results is that culture accounts for very little of what we have observed.

I conclude by proposing a game to test the propositions presented in this summary of what I think was learned at this conference.

Imagine a country somewhere on earth whose identity you do not know. You may ask twenty questions about the country, after which you will be expected to describe the size and character of its educational, health, and income support services. What questions would produce the most useful information? I contend that you should inquire first about the level of per capita national income, which would provide the basis for a good estimate of the quantities of resources devoted to those services. Second, you should ask a series of questions about the organizational arrangements for the delivery of these services: what rules govern the entitlement of people to the receipt of the services, how do the service providers derive their incomes, is there a single provider or do the recipients have a choice among several, and so forth. My view is that when you have completed this line of questioning, you will have most of the information you need to describe the service systems. A bit more of value might be learned by inquiring into the roles of individual preferences and government preferences in the decisions regarding the delivery of these services, but few if any questions should be devoted to the content of preferences or to cultural matters in general, because they would provide less useful information than the questions about organization you would have to give up in order to ask them. Others at this conference undoubtedly came away with different strategies for playing such a game of explanation-prediction, but we can all agree that we were better prepared to play after this conference than we would have been before.

ACCESS TO

HIGHER EDUCATION

HIGHER EDUCATION IN THE SOVIET UNION: PROBLEMS OF ACCESS, EQUITY, AND PUBLIC POLICY

Richard B. Dobson

> What, then, are the sought ends in the politics of education in modern Britain? The dominant slogans are combinations of efficiency and equality. Efficiency for modernity. Equality for efficiency and justice. But both the meaning of these combined ends and the means postulated as adequate to their attainment remain dubious and confused. Thus the combination of equality of educational opportunity with the goal of national efficiency has led to policies designed to create and maintain a meritocracy—a principle which by no means commands universal acceptance.
>
> —A.H. Halsey, *Educational Priority* (1972)

Higher education contributes to social welfare in diverse ways. Its most immediate influence is, of course, on its own "clientele"— the students enrolled. According to conventional wisdom, higher education endeavors to expand students' cognitive abilities, deepen their knowledge, and develop their capacity for analytical thinking. It may also mold their political worldview, refine their moral judgment, enhance their aesthetic sensibility, and encourage self-development in general. Beyond this, higher education often transmits marketable skills and, by means of grades and degrees, certifies its graduates for complex and specialized work. In short, higher education influences students' abilities, attitudes, and life-styles,

---

The preparation of this essay was supported in part by a National Fellowship from the Hoover Institution and a research grant from the Kennan Institute for Advanced Russian Studies of The Wilson Center, Washington, D.C. The author gratefully acknowledges this assistance. The views expressed herein are those of the author only—not of the U.S. government, the U.S. Information Agency, or any other organization.

and enables many to enjoy relatively high occupational status and enhanced earning power.

Higher education affects the welfare of the larger society as well. It may promote the advancement and diffusion of knowledge, help to preserve the society's cultural heritage, and stimulate economic growth and development by contributing to scientific-technological innovation and training skilled manpower. By expanding and equalizing avenues of access, it may also help to resolve social problems, reduce social disparities, and strengthen societal integration.

This essay, which complements Martin Trow's study of higher education in the United States, focuses on access to higher education in the Soviet Union. In the USSR, as in the United States, the differentiated educational system serves as a principal channel through which young people either rise or fall from their place of departure in the social-occupational hierarchy, or by which favored status is perpetuated from one generation to the next. The degree to which the Soviet system permits talented children to advance regardless of their origins affects the skills and qualities of persons occupying "elite" positions, shapes perceptions of the class structure, and influences the nation's overall scientific potential. It also casts light upon a central ideological claim—that the Soviet educational system is more democratic than those in capitalist countries and that remaining social-economic disparities are being reduced as Soviet society moves ever closer to a homogeneous (*odnorodnoe*), classless society.*

Soviet education's purpose, structure, and content continue to evoke controversy. The conflicts in British education described by A.H. Halsey above are no less evident in the USSR, where policymakers also struggle to reconcile efficiency with equality. The commitment to efficiency is seen most clearly in the attempt to integrate educational policy with manpower planning and general strategies of economic development, approved at the highest level by the Communist Party leadership and the USSR Council of Ministers. Equality, on the other hand, lies at the heart of the socialist promise—the creation of a society in which an abundance of goods

---

*For an overview of these issues, see Trow (1981) and Kerr et al. (1978). Among Western studies bearing specifically on access to higher education in the Soviet Union, see Matthews (1972), Dobson (1977), Yanowitch (1977), Connor (1979), Dobson (1980), Dobson and Swafford (1980), and Avis (1983a, b).

and services will be shared equally by all. Inasmuch as efficiency contributes to economic growth, it is viewed as a necessary condition for the movement toward a more affluent and egalitarian social order.

In the short term, however, the two values clash. Efficiency implies the strict accounting of scarce resources, the calculation of their costs and benefits. In higher education this means not only limiting the number of openings to the optimal number needed for economic development, but also entails selecting students whose abilities and prior training promise to bring the greatest economic returns. Such calculations fly in the face of equality by limiting access to higher education and fostering a meritocratic elite.

Within planned, socialist societies, as the Polish sociologist Wlodzimierz Wesolowski has pointed out, there is "ground for contradictions of interest between the social strata in regard to the criteria providing access to secondary and higher educational institutions":

> The culturally differentiated conditions of individual homes accounts for differences in the initial [academic] levels of children of different social strata. Hence [in Poland] workers and peasants accept the preferential system of access to schools, a system in which supplementary points are awarded to their children to compensate for their social milieu. This system acts against the chances of admission of the children of the intelligentsia. This is why the culturally privileged prefer a system of selection based exclusively on the result of examinations testing pure ability. The latter system tends naturally to reduce the chances of the children of workers and peasants (1969:142-43).

We shall explore such differences among social strata later in the essay, but first it is appropriate to compare general features of Soviet higher education with the American system.

COMPARING SOVIET AND AMERICAN HIGHER EDUCATION

The Soviet system, which in 1987 consisted of 897 higher educational institutions (*vysshie uchebnye zavedeniia*, abbreviated VUZy), differs from the American in several respects. One of the most significant relates to policymaking and administration. In contrast to the policymaking prerogatives enjoyed by individual institutions or local governmental bodies in the United States (for example, state legislatures or boards of trustees), Soviet educational policy is spelled out authoritatively at the national level by the USSR Ministry of Higher and Specialized Secondary Education and, on very important issues, by the Central Committee of the Communist Party. In conjunction with other ministries responsible for particular branches of the economy (public health, heavy industry, agriculture, etc.), the national and republic ministries of higher education devise and implement policies regarding admissions, the content of instruction, placement of schools, and so on. Whereas in the United States the number of openings for students in particular specialties is determined largely by student demand, admissions to Soviet institutions are determined by the central ministries on the basis of projected manpower requirements. (Since these, in turn, are derived from enterprises' estimates, employers have considerable influence in determining the number of openings in particular specialties.)

A second contrast between the systems is found in their academic orientations and institutional arrangements. Soviet higher education has a stronger technical emphasis, indicated by the predominance of students enrolled in applied specialties relating to industry, transportation, agriculture, and the like. In the United States, by comparison, there is a liberal arts tradition that stresses the value of the broadly cultured person over the narrow specialist (particularly in the more prestigious colleges and universities), and a large share of the students major in the humanities and social sciences. These different orientations have correspondingly different institutional forms. In the Soviet Union, technical institutes that offer a few narrowly defined specialties are the rule; in the United States, colleges and universities with broad and rather loosely structured curricula predominate.

A third difference between the systems lies in the values evidenced in student life and learning. American colleges generally allow much more choice and place a stronger emphasis on individual development, both in academic work and in extracurricular activities. Far more than Soviet institutions, American colleges are centers of free discussion and of diverse cultural, social, and political activities, ranging from Hari Krishna to Young Republicans and left-wing radicals. Such freedom and pluralism contrast sharply with the officially sponsored youth groups (notably the Komsomol), the more authoritarian character of academic life, and the uniform ideology and political line that Soviet students are obliged to follow—at least outwardly.

The list of differences could easily be extended. But it is important to recognize that the Soviet and American systems have certain traits in common, too. Both nations were "born of revolution" and have traditions that stress social equality among citizens, and the two countries' educational systems have been less closely linked with the culturally advantaged and propertied upper classes than they have been in most European countries. Like the United States, the Soviet Union ranks well above most European societies in terms of the percentage of young people who complete secondary education and are eligible to pursue higher education. And in part because higher education has not been so closely linked with social elites in these two countries, it has expanded more rapidly, been more responsive to changing economic needs, and trained a larger share of students in fields outside the traditional professions than European institutions of higher learning have (Ben-David 1966:469).

Furthermore, the Soviet and American systems of higher education are by far the largest in the world and reflect the diversity and the vast dimensions of their societies. In both nations, federal systems provide the framework within which their institutions of higher education are located. While the fifteen Soviet republics lack the political and legal independence the fifty American states enjoy, they are nonetheless important political and administrative units. In both cases, too, the ethnic variety of the populations has been a factor contributing to educational expansion. Mandatory primary and secondary education has been viewed as vital in both countries for socializing minorities into the dominant culture. The expansion of Soviet higher education has been prompted in part by the government's attempt to reduce regional and ethnic variations in level of social-economic development, while grass-roots ethnic politics and entrepreneurship have helped to spur growth in college enrollments in the United States (Collins 1978).

EDUCATIONAL EXPANSION IN THE USSR

In the past three decades, the overriding objective of Soviet educational policy has been "universal secondary education"—that is, to ensure that every youngster completes the equivalent of a ten-year secondary education. This policy, according to official spokesmen, is motivated by economic, political, and social imperatives. It is believed that a well-educated work force is essential for economic growth and innovation, that the requirements for civic competence are rising, and that as a matter of citizenship all should enjoy the right to secondary schooling. Accordingly, eight years of schooling were made mandatory in 1973, many small schools have been consolidated into larger units, teachers' qualifications have been raised, and more and more students have been enrolled in "complete secondary" schools (i.e., schools that combine grades one through ten in a single building). The increase in secondary school graduations has been dramatic. From 284,000 in 1950, the number of students who graduated from the tenth (or eleventh) grade of general-education schools rose to one million in 1960, 2.6 million in 1970, and nearly four million in 1980 (USSR 1977:26-27; USSR 1981: 458).

Beyond eight years of compulsory comprehensive schooling, Soviet secondary education is differentiated by type of school and curriculum. For every 100 young people who graduated from the eighth grade at the beginning of the 1980s, slightly more than 60 entered the ninth grade of the day general-education school. Approximately 20 entered secondary vocational-technical schools that give training in skilled blue-collar trades, 10 gained admission to specialized secondary educational institutions that train mainly semi-professional white-collar workers, and 8 continued their secondary education through evening or correspondence general-education classes while holding down a job or learning a trade (Usanov 1981: 28). Young people who complete a secondary education through any of these routes are eligible to compete for admission to higher education. In practice, however, the day general-education school still serves as the principal college track. Since the mid-1960s, nine out of ten full-time students in higher education had attended such schools. On the other hand, a sizable share of the students enrolled in part-time college programs graduated from evening general-education schools or from specialized secondary educational institutions (Medkov 1977:104; Rutkevich and Filippov 1978:129).

Soviet statistics testify to the Soviet population's increasing access to higher education. Among persons employed in the Soviet economy, individuals who had completed higher education comprised 1.3 percent in 1939, 3.3 percent in 1959, 6.5 percent in 1970, 10.0 percent in 1979, and 12.2 percent in 1986 (USSR 1986:27). In 1986 the proportion of the work force with a higher education was virtually identical for men and women (12.4 and 12.0 percent respectively), but was much higher in urban areas (15.2 percent) than in the countryside (5.7 percent) (28).

Let us turn now to some comparative data on college enroll- ments and graduations. In the United States there were 3,227,000 students enrolled in two- and four-year institutions in 1960—a number equal to 35 percent of all 18-21 year-olds (see Table 1). By 1978, enrollments had risen to 10,179,000, which equalled 60.1 percent of those between 18 and 21. In the USSR, enrollments in full-time and part-time higher educational programs grew from 2,396,000 to 5,110,000 during the same period. While the total number continued to mount each year, the proportion of the age group enrolled fluctuated because of pronounced shifts in the size of the college-age population. As a result of the "demographic echo" of World War II, when the birth-rate declined substantially, the size of the college-age cohort contracted sharply in the early 1960s, and the proportion of students shot up from 11.6 percent in 1960 to 31.2 in 1965. Then, as the college-age population increased, the proportion enrolled declined to 22.2 percent in 1970, reaching 20.4 percent in 1978.

Thus, relative to the total college-age population, the proportion of college students was three times greater in the United States than in the USSR in the late 1970s. Many American students were enrolled in two-year programs that do not always lead to the bachelor's degree, but the contrast is nonetheless striking—particularly in light of the fact that more than two out of five Soviet students were in part-time programs. The figures on college graduations show similar patterns, but there is less of a disparity between the two countries. In 1978 the number of undergraduate degrees conferred in the United States was equivalent to 25 percent of all American 22-year-olds; in the USSR the number conferred was equal to 16 percent of all Soviet 23-year-olds.

Table 2 compares the American and Soviet systems with regard to the transition from secondary school graduation to higher educa- tion and then to college graduation. In the United States, growth in college enrollments outstripped the increase in secondary school graduations in the 1960s and 1970s, with the ratio of college en- trants to high school graduates rising to over 60 percent. In the USSR, on the other hand, secondary school graduations increased much more rapidly than college enrollments, with the ratio of entrants to graduations declining from over 50 percent in the early 1960s to only 27 percent in 1980. However, comparison of the ratio

Table 1

UNDERGRADUATE ENROLLMENTS AND GRADUATIONS IN
UNITED STATES AND USSR, 1960-1978

Enrollments[a]	United States		USSR			
				Percent of Age Group[d]		
	Number (in 000s)	Percent of Age Group[c]	Number (in 000s)	Total	Full-Time	Part-Time
1960	3,227	35.0%	2,396	11.6%	5.6%	6.0%
1965	4,829	39.6	3,861	31.2	12.8	18.4
1970	6,889	48.7	4,581	22.2	10.9	11.3
1975	8,468	51.9	4,854	20.8	11.3	9.5
1978	10,179	60.1	5,110	20.4	11.4	9.0
Graduations[b]						
1960	395	17.6	343	7.8	5.2	2.6
1965	539	18.1	404	13.3	7.4	5.9
1970	833	23.9	631	19.3	10.2	9.1
1975	988	26.0	713	16.4	10.0	6.4
1978	998	24.9	772	16.2	10.1	6.1

Source: Ailes and Rushing 1982:66-67.

[a]U.S. enrollments include both four-year and two-year institutions; USSR figures include all higher educational programs—day, evening, and correspondence-extension (*zaochnye*).

[b]U.S.: bachelor degrees awarded; USSR: diplomas (*diplomy*) conferred for completion of higher education (day, evening, and correspondence-extension).

[c]U.S.: enrollments as percent of 18-21 year-olds because American higher education generally runs four years from entrance to graduation; graduations as percent of 22 year-olds.

[d]USSR: enrollments as percent of 18-22 year-olds because Soviet higher education typically extends five years from entrance to graduation; graduations as percent of 23 year-olds.

Table 2

SECONDARY SCHOOL GRADUATIONS, ENTRANCE INTO HIGHER EDUCATION,
AND COLLEGE GRADUATIONS IN UNITED STATES AND USSR, 1960-1980

United States

High School Graduates		First-Time College Students[a]		College Graduates		
Year	Number (in 000s)	Number (in 000s)	Percent of High-School Graduates	Year[b]	Number (in 000s)	Percent of Entrants
1960	1,864	923	49.5%	1964	502	54.4%
1965	2,665	1,442	54.1	1969	770	53.4
1970	2,896	1,780	61.5	1974	1,009	55.9
1975	3,140	1,910	60.8	1979	1,000	52.4
1978	3,147	2,422	77.0	1982	NA	NA
1980	3,063	NA	NA	1984	NA	NA

USSR

Graduates of Secondary School[c]		Admissions to Higher Education[d]		College Graduates		
Year	Number (in 000s)	Number (in 000s)	Percent of Secondary School Graduates	Year[e]	Number (in 000s)	Percent of Entrants
1960	1,055	593	56.2%	1965	404	68.1%
1965	1,340	854	63.7	1970	631	73.9
1970	2,581	912	35.3	1975	713	78.2
1975	3,564	994	27.9	1980	817	82.2
1978	4,162	1,026	24.7	1983	NA	NA
1980	3,966	1,052	26.5	1985	NA	NA

Sources: Ailes and Rushing 1982:51; United States 1981:165; United States 1982:18; USSR 1981:458, 468, 469.

[a] Two- and four-year institutions.

[b] Assuming four-year course of study for bachelor's degree.

[c] Graduates of tenth (or eleventh) grade of general-education schools — day, evening, and correspondence.

[d] Day, evening, and correspondence divisions.

[e] Assuming five-year course of study for *diplom*.

of degrees conferred in the two countries, relative to the number of college entrants, shows a reverse relationship. The number of bachelor's degrees awarded in the United States is equal to slightly more than half the number who entered college four years earlier, whereas the number of Soviet graduates is equal to some four-fifths of the class entering five years previously. In comparison to an American student, then, the Soviet secondary school graduate is less likely to enter an institution of higher education, but if admitted is more likely to go on to earn a degree.

ADMISSION PROCEDURES IN SOVIET HIGHER EDUCATION*

Applications to the day divisions that offer full-time study are accepted from graduates of general-education schools, specialized secondary educational institutions, and secondary vocational-technical schools. However, graduates of full-time specialized secondary and vocational-technical schools must first complete a three-year job assignment unless they rank at the top of their graduating class. Applicants to the day divisions must be under 35 years of age, but there are no age limits for those submitting applications to the part-time programs.

Soviet applicants must not only select a specific institution, but must also indicate the precise specialty they intend to pursue throughout their course of study (usually lasting five years in the day divisions, six or more in the part-time programs). Most applicants are required to take the entrance examinations given by the institution they have selected. The examinations, which may be written or oral, are essentially achievement tests geared to the secondary school curriculum. Before 1986, four examinations were required as a rule—one in Russian language and literature (or in the language of instruction at the institution selected) plus three others related to the chosen specialty; since 1986, the examinations have been reduced to three. They are graded according to a standard point system: 2 = unsatisfactory, 3 = fair, 4 = good, 5 = excellent.[†]

---

*The following discussion is based on a reading of the official admissions regulations published annually in *Biulleten' MVSSO SSSR* [Bulletin of the USSR Ministry of Higher and Specialized Secondary Education].

[†]Some types of applicants—notably graduates of preparatory divisions (discussed below)—are not required to take entrance examinations, and since

Some applicants are accepted "outside the competition" (*vne konkursa*)—that is, with only passing grades (3 on all exams). Those who qualify for such preferential treatment include reserve officers of the armed forces, the Committee for State Security (KGB), and the Ministry of Internal Affairs (MVD), as well as persons who made significant innovations in industry or were recognized for contributions to the "rationalization" of production, and graduates of technical schools who earned excellent grades and worked in their specialty before applying for full-time study in a related specialty.

Most applicants, of course, do not fall in any of these categories and so must undergo further competition (in Soviet parlance, enter *po konkursu*). Since 1965 they have been divided into two pools from which proportionate numbers are selected: (1) applicants with two or more years of work experience and (2) all others.* This division facilitates the admission of applicants who have been in the work force by taking them out of direct competition with recent secondary school graduates, who are generally much better prepared academically. Applicants in each pool are ranked according to the total points they earned on the entrance examinations. (Between 1972 and 1983 the average of their secondary school grades was also added to their examination scores.)

But here again preferences are applied. Priority in admissions is accorded to "advanced production workers" (*peredoviki proizvodstva*) who have been assigned for full-time study by enterprises or farms, permanent rural residents who have chosen to study agricultural or other specialties vital for rural development, and so on. In addition, among students with equal numerical scores, preference is given to those who have worked longest in a field related to their specialty or were awarded gold or silver medals in secondary school.

The regulations are complex, and only their main features are indicated here. Three points should be emphasized. First, although the rules are laid down authoritatively for all institutions, applicants to one or another school may differ greatly in their social characteristics, prior training, or academic competence. The standards applied in selection vary accordingly. Second, chances for admission depend

---

1980, entrance requirements have been relaxed for specialties in which there is an acute shortage of qualified personnel (*ostrodefitsitnye spetsial'nosti*). Applicants who earn high marks in secondary school are excused from some examinations under certain circumstances.

*In 1986, applicants were not divided in this fashion, but in 1987 the practice was resumed.

not only on examination scores, but also on the advantages (*l''goty*) the candidate may claim. Other things being equal, the applicant who has worked for two years or who was awarded a gold medal for academic excellence in secondary school will be favored. Third, there is ample room in the selection process for other criteria to be considered. The admissions committee may take into account an applicant's political reliability, nationality, social-class background, sex, vocational aptitude, and so on. Strong recommendations from party and Komsomol organizations and evidence of political reliability and activism are especially important for gaining admission to study philosophy, scientific communism, the other social sciences, and journalism.

HIGHER EDUCATION'S CLIENTELE

Sociological surveys and government statistics shed a good deal of light on higher education's clientele. In this section we will consider the evidence that ethnic background, place of residence, sex, and family social-economic status (SES) condition young people's chances for admission. In the sections following, we will focus on the causes and consequences of social disparities in access as well as policies designed to ameliorate inequities.

ETHNIC DISPARITIES

The Soviet population is composed of more than one hundred officially recognized ethnic groups, or "nationalities," which differ markedly in their histories, cultures, and levels of social-economic development. In light of comparative research on modernization and educational participation, it is not surprising that the various ethnic groups' rates of enrollment in higher education are related to their levels of social-economic development, political participation, age of marriage, fertility rates, and so on. As a rule, the more modernized ethnic groups (as measured by degree of urbanization or number of skilled mental workers per thousand) marry later, have smaller families, participate more in politics as party members, and have more of their children enrolled in higher education.*

* According to the 1970 census, for example, the percentages of different groups living in "urban-type" settlements was particularly high for Russian

In recent decades, however, there has clearly been a tendency for convergence among ethnic groups both in levels of development and in educational participation (see Jones and Grupp 1984; Ostapenko and Susokolov 1983, 1985; Arutiunian and Bromlei 1986; Arutiunian and Drobizheva 1987). Not only have ethnic differences in secondary school graduation decreased markedly with the transition to universal secondary education, but differentials in participation in higher education have also been reduced. This can be seen unmistakably in Table 3, which shows rates of graduation and enrollment for seventeen Soviet nationalities in relation to the USSR average in 1970. The first three columns indicate the relative rates of graduation by nationalities as recorded by the 1970 Soviet census for three successive cohorts—age groups 40-49, 30-39, and 20-29. The fourth column shows the relative rates of enrollment in 1970 within the broad 17-29 age group, and the fifth shows the percentages of females enrolled.

We see that among those aged 40-49 the Russians had a rate of graduation (106) lower than that of the Georgians (242) and Armenians (163), but well above that of the Ukrainians (81), Lithuanians (93), Belorussians (60), Kazakhs and Central Asians (50-79), Tatars (52), and Moldavians (24). The Russians maintained an above-average rate of participation in the next two cohorts (30-39 and 20-29), which has been especially significant since Russians have constituted roughly three-fifths of all Soviet students. Most nationalities, however, have converged toward the all-union average. Thus the Georgians' rate fell from 242 in the 40-49 cohort to 164 in both the 30-39 and 20-29 cohorts and to 148 among students enrolled in 1970, while most of the underrepresented groups moved upward toward the mean. For example, the Uzbeks' rate rose from 60 in the 40-49 cohort to 104 among students enrolled in 1970—that is, almost to parity with the Russians. The rise of the Kirgiz has been even more striking. From a point equal to that of the Uzbeks in the oldest cohort, their rate rose to the level of the Russians in the 20-29 age group and then surpassed it. Over several decades, in short, expansion of higher education was accompanied by an impressive levelling of inter-ethnic disparities in participation. As of 1970,

---

Jews (98%), Russians (68%), and Armenians (65%), while being far below the mean for others, such as the Kazakhs (27%), Tadzhiks (26%), Uzbeks (25%), Moldavians (20%), and Kirgiz (15%). For further details, see USSR (1973:20, 27-28).

Table 3

NATIONALITIES' RATE OF PARTICIPATION IN HIGHER EDUCATION,
RELATIVE TO USSR AVERAGE BY COHORTS AND SEX, 1970

Nationality	Degrees Earned per 1,000 in Age Group			Enrollments per 1,000 in 17-29 Age Group, 1970	Females as Percent of Enrollment, 1970
	40-49	30-39	20-29		
USSR Average	100	100	100	100	49%
Slavs					
Russians	106	109	108	108	52
Ukrainians	81	84	78	82	48
Belorussians	60	70	78	78	49
Balts					
Lithuanians	73	83	104	98	53
Latvians	97	100	88	87	53
Estonians	105	125	118	100	51
Caucasians					
Armenians	163	110	130	131	44
Georgians	242	164	164	148	45
Azeri	118	84	104	127	32
Kazakhs and Central Asians					
Uzbeks	60	74	96	104	33
Kazakhs	79	91	104	106	45
Tadzhiks	50	60	80	85	24
Turkmen	61	77	92	92	23
Kirgiz	60	82	108	123	43
Others					
Moldavians	24	43	56	60	48
Tatars	52[a]	56[a]	64[a]	80	49
Jews	NA	NA	NA	341	45

Sources: Degrees earned—USSR 1973:549-53, 559; Enrollment rates—Jones and Grupp 1982:119; Percent female—USSR 1971:196.

[a]Tatars resident in the Russian Republic (80 percent of all Tatars in the USSR in 1970).

however, some substantial differences were still evident. Jews had a rate of enrollment of 341 — over three times that of the Russians and over five times that of the Moldavians.*

Examining more recent trends, Jones and Grupp (1984:168-70) found no evidence of convergence among nationalities in access to higher education between 1970 and 1980. In fact, except for the Tatars, the Muslim nationalities lost ground during the 1970s. They suggest that this reversal of earlier gains resulted from the Soviet authorities' inability or unwillingness to commit the resources needed to keep up with the rapid population growth of the traditionally Islamic peoples. Recently there have been indications that the authorities are increasingly sensitive to charges of "reverse discrimination" against Russians (see, e.g., Bromlei 1987).

PLACE OF RESIDENCE AND SEX

Surveys of Soviet secondary school graduates show that young people who completed their secondary education in major cities are much more likely to enter higher education than those from provincial towns or villages. In many parts of the country, moreover, boys are more likely than girls to go to college after finishing secondary school. As Table 4 shows, in Novosibirsk Province, college plans and enrollment rates decrease steadily as one moves from the provincial capital to other towns and villages. While one in two boys from the capital secured admission to higher education, only one in eight village girls did.

To generalize these results to the entire country would be inappropriate, given the remarkable regional variations that exist in the Soviet Union. For purposes of illustration, it is sufficient to refer to Table 5, which gives secondary school to college transition rates for Lithuania, Tiumen Province in Siberia, and Tadzhikistan in Central Asia. In Lithuania, where an exceptionally high 36 percent of all graduates embarked on full-time college study in 1974, there are disparities in enrollment rates both between boys and girls (46 vs. 29 percent) and between urban and rural schools (39 vs. 26 percent). Obviously both sex and place of residence condition chances for

*The persistent charges of discrimination against Jews and some other groups raise a number of issues that cannot be adequately dealt with here. The discriminatory practices have limited the numbers of Jews admitted to certain institutions or departments (especially the more prestigious). (See, e.g., Zaslavsky and Brym 1983:105-10; DiFranceisco and Gitelman 1984:616-17; Karklins 1984.)

Table 4

COLLEGE PLANS AND ENROLLMENT RATES BY PLACE OF RESIDENCE
AND SEX: NOVOSIBIRSK PROVINCE IN THE EARLY 1970S
(In percent)

Place of Residence/ Sex	Percent of Tenth-Graders Planning to Pursue Full-Time College Study	Percent of Graduates Enrolled as Full-Time College Students
Provincial capital		
Males	78%	49%
Females	61	34
Other towns		
Males	51	27
Females	37	19
Villages		
Males	31	17
Females	30	12

Source: Konstantinovskii 1977:127,144.

Table 5

COLLEGE ENROLLMENT RATES BY PLACE OF RESIDENCE AND SEX:
LITHUANIA, TIUMEN PROVINCE, AND TADZHIKISTAN IN EARLY 1970S
(In percent)

Place of Residence	Percent of Tenth-Grade Graduates Entering Higher Educational Institutions (Day Programs)		
	Male	Female	Both Sexes
Lithuania (1974)			
Urban	49%	32%	39%
Rural	37	20	26
All	46	29	36
Tiumen Province (1972-74)			
Urban	40	41	41
Rural	18	19	19
All	29	31	30
Tadzhikistan (1972)			
Urban	34	35	34
Rural	20	7	13
All	27	21	24

Sources: Lithuania—Matulenis 1977:119; Tiumen Province—Konstantinovskii
1977:146; Tadzhikistan—calculated from Shoismatulloev 1976:126-28.

admission in a way similar to Novosibirsk Province. This is not the case in Tiumen Province, however, where urban graduates are twice as likely as those from rural schools to enter college (41 vs. 19 percent), but differences between male and female entry rates are negligible. Tadzhikistan presents a more complex picture. There the urban-rural disparity is very pronounced (34 vs. 13 percent), and boys are somewhat more likely than girls to enter college (27 vs. 21 percent), but both sexes have virtually identical enrollment rates in the towns, whereas boys' chances are roughly three times greater than girls' in the villages (20 vs. 7 percent).

To understand these differences, one must take account of the particular features of each region—the availability of educational institutions, the population's ethnic and social composition, regional traditions, and so on. In the case of Tadzhikistan, two cultural factors contribute to the conspicuous contrast between urban and rural women: (1) the village women are almost entirely of the indigenous nationality whereas a large portion of the urban women are of European descent, and (2) Muslim traditions set the pattern of life in the countryside to a far greater extent than in the towns. Most rural girls now attend secondary school (a dramatic change from their low rate of participation in secondary education several decades ago), but few choose to go further (Shoismatulloev 1976:93-132, app. table 10).

Why do fewer women than men proceed to college following secondary school in so many other parts of the country? In Lithuania, for example, where Islamic traditions obviously play no role, women are still only half as likely as men to enter college after graduating. In this case, however, the bare percentages fail to reflect the fact that there were 1.7 times as many girls as boys in the secondary school's graduating class; thus, despite their lower entry rates, females slightly outnumbered men among the entering college students (Matulenis 1977:120-21). The lower entry rates of non-Muslim women are a combined effect of their numerical predominance among secondary school graduates, their demands for specific types of education, and the limited number of openings in those disciplines. Because the fields to which women are most attracted—medicine, teaching, the social sciences, and humanities—have fewer openings and have been growing at a slower rate than other fields, the large numbers of women graduates have often found themselves competing against each other for scarce openings in the higher educational institutions (Dobson 1978:267-92). Nonetheless, women have increased their representation in higher education significantly in recent decades.

Their share of undergraduate enrollments rose from 43 percent in 1960 to 49 percent in 1970, 52 percent in 1980, and 55 percent in 1985 (USSR 1986:517).

FAMILY SOCIAL-ECONOMIC STATUS

Soviet children from families of high social-economic status (SES) are more likely to attend college than children from the lower social-economic strata. Consider the findings presented in Table 6 from the 1972 survey of secondary school graduates in Tadzhikistan. The proportion of graduates who entered college declines from 70 percent among children of the urban intelligentsia to 40 percent among children of urban white-collar workers, 31 percent of children of the rural intelligentsia, 22-26 percent of children of blue-collar workers in industry, construction, and communications, and 11-12 percent of children of farm workers. In short, the children of the urban intelligentsia who graduated were nearly seven times more likely to enter college than the collective farmers' children.

Table 6

INFLUENCE OF FATHER'S OCCUPATION ON SECONDARY GRADUATES' COLLEGE PLANS AND ENTRY RATES: TADZHIKISTAN, 1972
(In Percent)

Father's Occupational Status	Tenth-Graders Planning to Pursue Full-Time College Study	Graduates Enrolled as Full-Time College Students
Urban intelligentsia	78%	70%
Urban white-collar workers	63	40
Rural intelligentsia	55	31
Workers in industry and construction	48	22
Workers in transport and communications	44	26
Rural white-collar workers	39	18
Agricutural workers	28	12
Collective farmers	24	11

Source: Shoismatulloev 1976:108 (table 5), app. table 14.

One might expect that the differences between children of various occupational strata would be greater in Tadzhikistan than in the more developed areas of Russia or the Baltic region. Tadzhikistan, one of the least developed parts of the Soviet Union, has a large and rapidly growing rural population. (It is the only republic to record a relative increase in the size of its rural population between the 1970 and 1979 censuses.) Children from the small urban intelligentsia, composed largely of persons of European descent, might enjoy more of an advantage in securing access to advanced schooling than they would if they faced competition from children of a large skilled urban work force. Furthermore, the extremely low rate of participation in higher education of rural women might widen the gap between children of the skilled urban strata and those of the less-skilled rural occupational groups.

Comparing the Tadzhikistan survey with other studies, however, we find that Tadzhikistan is not as exceptional as might be expected. Investigations conducted in other rural and urban areas reveal similar disparities among social-economic strata. For example, in the rural areas of the Krasnodar region, where 12 percent of the secondary school graduates entered college in 1976, only 6 percent of the children of low-skill manual workers went to college compared with 34 percent of the children of highly trained white-collar workers (Komarov 1980:136-40). Although the college enrollment rate of children of the urban intelligentsia in Tadzhikistan is very high, studies conducted in such Russian cities as Leningrad (1968), Syzran (1968), and Sverdlovsk (1970) revealed that the urban intelligentsia's offspring were 2.5-3.5 times as likely as urban blue-collar workers' children to enter college after tenth-grade graduation.*

This general picture of social-economic disparities is confirmed by a much broader survey conducted in six regions of the Soviet Union in 1973-74. The data presented in Table 7 show the extent to which college students' social origins differ from those of eighth- and tenth-graders in the general-education school. Though taken from

---

*In Leningrad, more than six out of ten of the intelligentsia's offspring entered a college program compared with only one out of four graduates from working-class homes. (These figures refer to enrollments in all VUZ divisions, not just day programs; see Vasil'eva 1970:42-43). In Syzran and Sverdlovsk, about one in two graduates from the intelligentsia, compared to one in six from the working class, went on for full-time college study following the tenth grade (see Ksenfontova 1972 and Gendel' 1971 as reported in Dobson and Swafford 1980:257, 261).

separate cross-sectional surveys, rather than a study of a single cohort at different points in time, the samples are sufficiently representative to permit a rough estimate of the changing proportions. The "index of change" indicates the proportion of each student group in college compared to its proportion among eighth-graders (where eighth-grade = 100).

Table 7

SOCIAL-OCCUPATIONAL CHARACTERISTICS OF EIGHTH-GRADERS',
TENTH-GRADERS', AND COLLEGE STUDENTS' PARENTS:
SIX-REGION SURVEY, 1973

Parents' Occupational Status		Percent of Students			Index of Change[a]	Disparity Index[a]
Father	Mother	Eighth-Grade	Tenth-Grade	College		
Specialist	Specialist	13.1%	19.1%	36.3%	278	647
Specialist	Employee	5.4	6.4	9.6	178	414
Employee	Employee	2.7	3.5	3.4	126	293
Worker	Specialist	7.7	6.3	8.3	108	251
Worker	Employee	12.0	14.7	9.8	82	190
Worker	Worker	24.6	20.1	12.0	49	114
Farm worker	Farm worker	20.6	16.1	8.8	43	100
All others		13.9	13.8	11.8	—	—
Total		100.0	100.0	100.0		
Number surveyed		9,800	9,278	13,618		

Source: Rutkevich and Filippov 1978:115, 117, 235.

[a] For definition, see accompanying text.

We see that children from households in which both the mother and father are specialists (i.e., members of the intelligentsia) are nearly three times as numerous among college students as among eighth-graders; in contrast, children from families in which both parents are manual workers make up half as large a share of college students as of eighth-graders. The "disparity index" shows the degree to which the chances for becoming college students differ for children from various strata when the most underrepresented group—children of farm workers—is taken as the reference point (= 100). Thus in comparison to a child of farm workers, a child whose father is a blue-collar worker [worker] and whose mother is a nonspecialist white-collar worker [employee] is nearly twice as likely to become a college student, and a child from a home in which both parents are specialists is six-and-half times as likely. A more finely differentiated breakdown would magnify the differences, for the intelligentsia includes occupations as diverse as scientists with postgraduate degrees and elementary-school teachers, chief engineers and rank-and-file technicians, high-level party officials and minor administrators. Nonetheless, these data clearly reveal the overall pattern of relative advantage—a stratification of life chances that in its basic configuration is similar to that found in other industrialized countries (cf. Poignant 1973 and Husen 1975).

We should recognize also that significant variations exist from one institution to the next or from one field to another. Drawing again on the Six Region Survey, we find that children of specialists accounted for approximately three-fifths of the first-year students studying medicine and the natural sciences and about half of those majoring in engineering and in the humanities and social sciences at universities (see Table 8). Their share dropped to 39 percent in the

Table 8

FATHER'S OCCUPATION OF FIRST-YEAR COLLEGE STUDENTS
BY SPECIALTY: SIX REGION SURVEY, 1973
(In percent)

| Father's Occupation | Area of Specialization | | | | | |
| | Universities | | Institutes | | | |
	Natural Sciences	Humanities	Medicine	Engi-neering	Teaching	Agri-culture
Specialist	60.6%	52.6%	58.2%	49.8%	38.6%	27.9%
Employee	3.7	4.6	5.2	4.5	4.6	4.9
Nonfarm worker	28.8	32.4	28.6	40.0	42.3	24.6
Agricultural worker	7.2	10.3	7.9	7.9	14.5	42.6
Total	100.3	99.9	99.9	102.2	100.0	100.0

Source: Rutkevich and Filippov 1978:190.

less prestigious teacher-training institutes and to 28 percent in the agricultural schools. Blue-collar workers' offspring were especially numerous among students in engineering and teaching, where they made up some two-fifths of the enrollment, but they also accounted for nearly a third in the humanities, natural sciences, and medicine. Sons and daughters of agricultural workers comprised no more than 10 percent in all fields except teaching (15 percent) and the applied agricultural sciences (45 percent). Thus a young person's family background not only conditions his or her chances for advanced schooling, but also has a bearing on the type of education he or she is likely to obtain. In this connection we should note that the predominantly "applied" bias of most schools helps to account for the relatively high proportion of working-class children in Soviet higher education. The numerous institutes for industry, mining, transportation, construction, and agriculture are heavily populated by students born in the manual strata.

FACTORS AFFECTING ACCESS

Since admission to Soviet higher education is voluntary and for the most part competitive, entry depends in large measure on individuals' demands and the resources they can use to advantage. Resources are basically of two kinds: academic (credentials, scholastic records, quality and type of training) and social-economic (family income, connections, etc.), both of which are related to family social-economic status.

DEMAND FOR HIGHER EDUCATION AND FAMILY SES

The British sociologist Frank Parkin asserts that "parents' ambitions for their children are pitched much higher in socialist than in capitalist societies. A striking feature of the former is the extent to which commitment to higher education and the desire for professional careers have spread among members of the lower strata" (1971:156). Indeed some surveys report that most Soviet parents— even rank-and-file workers and collective farmers—would like their children to pursue higher education. It is important, however, to distinguish parents' idealized ambitions from their realistic expectations, or the advice they give their children at the age of 15-17. For example, when parents of 1,310 tenth-graders in Gorky were polled in 1968, clear-cut differences were evident among occupational strata: three out of four white-collar workers asserted that "it is essential that they enter college [VUZ] as full-time students"; only half as many blue-collar respondents named this as a necessary goal for their children.*

Such differences are consistently shown by surveys of Soviet secondary school students as well. Like their counterparts in the United States or other Western countries, the young people most likely to plan to attend college are those who live in major towns and whose parents have completed additional years of schooling, earn more money, or enjoy higher occupational status. To illustrate this point, Table 9 juxtaposes data from the Six Region Survey with findings from a 1974 survey of a nationally representative sample of American high school seniors conducted by the U.S. Bureau of the Census. In the Soviet case, we see that the proportion of tenth-graders who report college plans rises steeply from 23 percent of those from families with per capita incomes of no more than 30 rubles to 72 percent of those with incomes of more than 100 rubles. Similarly, in the United States, 26 percent of the high school seniors with family incomes of less than $5,000 plan to attend a two- or four-year college after graduation compared to 68 percent of those with incomes of $25,000 or more. Although there is less of a spread in the Soviet income distribution (partly because the figures refer to per capita income), the degree of differentiation in the students' plans is no less than in the American case. On the contrary, the difference in the percentage with college plans between the extreme high- and low-income categories (which approximate the top and bottom tenths of the distributions) is slightly greater in the Soviet sample (50 percent) than in the American (42 percent for two- and four-year colleges, 45 percent for four-year institutions only).

To understand the connection between SES and demand for higher education, it is useful to consider a simple model of rational decision-making (cf. Keller and Zavalloni 1964; Boudon 1974:29-31; LeGrand 1982:62-63). It is assumed that in making a decision about whether or not to demand an additional unit of schooling, individuals assess the perceived costs and benefits to them of that

*On the other hand, more of the working-class parents thought that "ten years of schooling is quite enough—let them go to work" (16 vs. 5 percent) or that "it is essential that they enter a technicum" (29 vs. 10 percent) (cited in Mar'ianovskaia 1976:174).

Table 9

RELATIONSHIP OF GRADUATING SENIORS' COLLEGE PLANS TO FAMILY INCOME:
USSR (1973) AND UNITED STATES (1974)

Soviet Tenth-Graders, 1973[a]			American Twelfth-Graders, 1974[b]			
					Percent Planning to Attend	
Family Per Capita Income in Rubles	Distribution in Percent	Percent with College Plans	Family Income	Distribution in Percent	Two- and Four-Year Colleges	Four-Year Colleges
Over 100	9.0%	72.2%	$25,000 or more	8.4%	67.6%	53.5%
71-100	26.2	61.2	$15-24,999	25.2	51.7	28.1
51-70	24.5	44.2	$10-14,999	26.9	41.3	21.7
31-50	26.2	32.9	$5-9,999	19.9	32.0	16.2
30 or less	11.2	22.7	Under $5,000	10.1	25.8	8.9
No information	2.4	—	No information	9.5	40.7	22.6
All	100.0	45.3	All	100.0	42.6	23.7

Source: USSR – Mar'ianovskaia 1976:178 and Rutkevich and Filippov 1978:79, 100; U.S. – United States 1975:12.

[a] Soviet tenth-graders from six regions of the USSR (N=9,915) who were surveyed in 1973 before graduation. Information on family income was provided by the students after consulting with their parents. "College plans" refers to the intention to pursue full-time study at an institution of higher education (VUZ) following graduation.

[b] A nationally representative sample of high school seniors (N=3,376,000) who were surveyed in October 1974. Information on family income was provided by the students. Students "with college plans" are those who expressed a definite intention to pursue higher education at a two- or four-year institution sometime following high school graduation; students who said that they *may* do so are not included.

unit. If the benefits outweigh the costs, they will demand it. The perceived benefits are of two kinds: consumption and investment. Consumption benefits are those which individuals receive while attending school (for example, satisfaction derived from learning, greater leisure, extracurricular opportunities for cultural activities, etc.); investment benefits are those which individuals receive after completing their education (higher income, enhanced prestige, a richer cultural life, etc.). The costs include satisfactions individuals must forego in pursuing their education, the direct costs they must bear (purchases of books, moving expenses, etc.), the estimated opportunity costs of income foregone by not working, and the social and psychological costs occasioned by moving to another locality, breaking ties with friends and family, having to study for examinations, and so on.

While the perceived benefits of education can be assumed to be invariant among social groups, it is reasonable to assume that the costs are not. Each unit of income foregone or spent for education represents a greater sacrifice for those from low-income families than for those from middle- and upper-income households. Conversely, the social and psychic costs for higher SES children *not* to demand additional schooling may be considerably greater than for those of lower SES origin. More upper-status children have been socialized to the norm of college attendance, as a rule many of their friends share that norm, and choosing not to obtain a higher education may expose them to the prospect of social demotion. In short, if the benefits of higher education are perceived in the same way by all, this model would predict that children of higher SES would be more likely to demand higher education because of differences in perceived costs.

This model is as applicable to the Soviet Union as to the United States. When contrasted with the tangible rewards afforded by employment, foregoing them for five additional years of study may appear too costly to many Soviet young people with limited means. Some Soviet economists maintain that this judgment is encouraged by a wage structure that does not offer working-class children a strong financial incentive for obtaining a college degree. The economist A. B. Dainovskii points out that "at the present time highly skilled workers have a higher wage than a significant portion of the specialists with secondary and even higher education. Thus the formation of hereditary workers' families is strengthened by purely financial considerations as well [as family traditions]" (1976:55-56).

Not only opportunity costs, but also direct costs must be reckoned with. Although in recent years seven out of ten full-time college students received state stipends, and more than half lived in state-subsidized dormitories, most families still have had to contribute to their children's support. According to Soviet economists and surveys of parents, the minimum amount needed to support a student was 50-60 rubles a month in the late 1960s. If a student received a stipend and lived either in a dormitory or at home, he or his family still had to provide some 15-25 rubles a month to make ends meet. Most families were able to do so, but the burden was considerable for poor families. And if the student did not get a scholarship or had to rent an apartment, the cost became excessive for many (Gendel' 1971:114-16; Sarkisian and Kuznetsova 1967:66; Aitov 1968:191; Rutkevich and Filippov 1978:130; Dobson and Swafford 1980:263-65).

Although education in the USSR is tuition-free, one should not minimize the importance of financial constraints in a society where a sizable share of the population has, by Western standards, quite a low standard of living. According to the 1973 Six Region Survey, half of the first-graders and two-fifths of the eighth-graders reported family per capita incomes of 50 rubles or less—a level deemed less than adequate for maintenance of a minimal standard of living (see Table 10).* Clearly, children who are in the upper grades come disproportionately from higher-income families. The share from families with per capita incomes over 70 rubles rises from less than one-fourth among the first-graders to more than half among seniors who plan to attend college.[†]

In September 1972, acknowledging the inadequacy of the stipends either as financial incentives or means of support, the Soviet

---

*In the mid-1960s, Soviet economists estimated that the amount needed to maintain a minimal but adequate standard of living was approximately 50 rubles per person a month for an urban family of four (Sarkisian and Kuznetsova 1967 and McAuley 1979:16-20). In the Six Region Survey, the first-graders' teachers collected information on income from the parents while the eighth- and tenth-graders were asked to report their families' income themselves. The data are subject to the biases that self-reporting of monetary income usually entails (especially underreporting).

[†]The sociologists who report these findings attribute this rise in part to "the fact that the older students' parents are, as a rule, persons with higher qualifications," but they also acknowledge that "the family's level of financial well-being is one of the factors that determines students' choice of a given form of education" (Rutkevich and Filippov 1978:79).

Table 10

FAMILY PER CAPITA INCOME OF STUDENTS AT VARIOUS GRADE-
LEVELS: USSR, SIX REGION SURVEY, 1973

(In percent)

Family Per Capita Monthly Income in Rubles	Student Grade-Level in the General-Education School			
	First Grade	Eighth Grade	Tenth Grade	College Applicants[a]
30 or less	17.3%	12.0%	11.2%	5.6%
31-50	34.3	27.8	26.2	19.0
51-70	23.9	22.5	24.5	23.6
71-90	12.4	12.9	17.2	22.7
Over 90	9.1	12.6	18.5	28.2
No information	3.0	12.2	2.4	1.4
Total	100.0	100.0	100.0	100.0
Number surveyed	*10,740*	*9,800*	*9,278*	*4,200*

Source: Rutkevich and Filippov 1978:79, 100.

[a]Tenth-graders who plan to pursue full-time higher education after graduating.

government increased the basic amount to 40 rubles a month.* Yet, the following year, when college students in the Six Region Survey were asked about their sources of livelihood, the majority said that they were counting on help from home to supplement their stipends (see Table 11). In fact, nine out of ten first- and fifth-year students mentioned money from relatives as a means of support.†

*The size of the stipend depends upon the student's year of study, specialty, grades, participation in public affairs, and, in some cases, financial need. The basic rate for students in the fifth or sixth year was raised to 45 rubles, but students in some specialties received substantially more. For instance, those at the prestigious Institute of International Relations in Moscow received 100 rubles. Special scholarships, such as the V.I. Lenin or Karl Marx stipends, also paid 100 rubles. Students who earned high grades and distinguished themselves by their civic activity received a 25 percent bonus (Rozanova 1972). In 1987 the size of the stipends was again increased, and additional incentives were given for high achievement.

†At the same time, most students lived modestly: 70 percent reported spending no more than 60 rubles a month on their personal needs, and one-third spent no more than 40 rubles (Rutkevich and Filippov 1978:131).

Table 11

PROJECTED AND ACTUAL SOURCES OF FINANCIAL SUPPORT
FOR FULL-TIME STUDENTS IN HIGHER EDUCATION:
SIX-REGION-SURVEY, 1973
(In percent)

Sources of Students' Income	First-Year Students (Projected)	Fifth-Year Students (Actual)
Stipend, help from relatives, and own earnings	18.2%	22.6%
Stipend and help from relatives	66.0	60.8
Stipend and own earnings	5.5	7.6
Help from relatives and own earnings	1.8	2.4
Only stipend	3.9	1.7
Only help from relatives	4.2	4.3
Only own earnings	0.4	0.4
No answer	0.0	0.2
All	100.0	100.0
Number surveyed	*6,208*	*7,372*

Source: Rutkevich and Filippov 1978:129.

"CULTURAL CAPITAL" AND ACADEMIC PERFORMANCE

Although access to Soviet higher education is conditioned by differences in family income and standard of living, educational advancement is also to a great extent meritocratic. Numerous studies demonstrate that secondary school graduates' academic records have a strong influence on both their college plans and chances for admission. Because of the selective nature of higher education and the emphasis on achievement, students' academic performance appears to be a stronger determinant of college entry in the USSR than in the United States.*

---

*In Syzran (1968), for instance, 85 percent of the "straight A" graduates entered higher education for full-time study as against 43 percent of the graduates with basically "good" grades and only 8 percent of those with "fair" grades. In Sverdlovsk (1970), four out of five students at the top of their class entered higher education immediately after graduating whereas only one in ten

Yet it is generally true that children from higher SES families tend to earn higher marks than their classmates from lower SES homes. Children of the intelligentsia are usually twice as likely as blue-collar workers' offspring to maintain a B+ (4.5 grade-points) average in secondary school. This surely reflects the fact that, like American upper-middle-class parents, the better educated parents create an environment conducive to early cognitive development, place strong emphasis on academic success, and often provide their children with educational resources—books, trips to museums or the theater, even private tutors—that help them prepare for college entrance examinations. The use of coaches is especially common among the urban intelligentsia. According to a 1974 survey of first-year students in Kharkov, for example, virtually no students from farm workers' homes had employed tutors to prepare for the entrance examinations, but 11 percent of the urban blue-collar workers' offspring, 20 percent of the white-collar workers' children, and fully 69 percent of the children of the intelligentsia had (Sheremet 1977:77).

A disproportionate share of the intelligentsia's offspring also gains advantages through study at "special-profile" schools (*spets-shkoly*)—general-education schools that give advanced training in academic subjects such as mathematics, physics, chemistry, and computer science, as well as in foreign languages. Essentially these are college-preparatory institutions whose teaching staffs are more qualified and whose standards are higher than those of the regular schools. Not only do almost all their students aspire to higher education, but most graduates perform well on the entrance examinations. As a rule some 65-99 percent of the graduates go directly from secondary school to college—a decided contrast to the one-in-five chances of the average graduate. Owing to their superior academic training and high prestige, the spets-shkoly are especially popular among the urban intelligentsia, who often take pains to ensure that their children are enrolled (Dunstan 1978; Dobson 1984).

---

of those with average grades did. Similarly, in Tadzhikistan (1972), academic marks were fairly strong predictors of admission: 61 percent of the graduates with grade-point averages of 5.00 became full-time students in the fall compared with 51 percent of those with GPAs of 4.50-4.99, 19 percent of those with GPAs of 3.50-3.99, and 10 percent of those with GPAs under 3.50 (see Gendel' 1971:230-31, 298; Ksenfontova 1972; Shoismatulloev 1976:table 29).

"PULL" AND BRIBERY

Despite Soviet education's strong meritocratic strain, the "competition of parents" that Premier Khrushchev publicly deplored in the late 1950s also figures prominently in the picture. Emigrés from the Soviet Union speak about the frequent use of connections *(blat)* or patrons *(proteksiia)*. One recounted: "My relative just called up somebody on the entrance commission and said: 'Will you take of my relative?' I know my answer on Russian grammar should have been absolutely unsatisfactory (2), but I received a 4 [good]" (cited in Swafford 1979:55-56).

Though the use of outright bribery might be thought rare, the Soviet press regularly carries articles on malfeasance in admissions, suggesting that the problem of corruption is both perennial and widespread. For instance, an account in the Georgian newspaper *Zaria vostoka* detailed the activities of P. Gelbakhiani, the former rector of the Tbilisi Medical Institute, and members of his staff, who were convicted in 1975 of accepting bribes in exchange for admitting children from well-to-do families to the institute. (In the course of the legal investigation, more than 500,000 rubles were confiscated from instructors who had been bribed for admitting twenty-nine young people!) Of the 200 applicants who entered the institute's therapeutic division in 1967, 170 were found to have done so illegally, and between 1966 and 1968, when Gelbakhiani reigned supreme, 90 to 95 percent of the students in the institute reportedly came from white-collar workers' families—especially from homes of highly placed officials (Inoveli 1976:3).

Young people with connections have found other ways to enter college as well. In 1959, enterprises and farms were given the right to send a certain number of their outstanding workers to raise their qualifications at institutions of higher learning, but there are repeated press reports that many "young workers" make use of fraudulent character references from influential patrons to gain entry. Writing in *Izvestiia*, M. Lvovsky denounced these "unscrupulous characters who have latched onto this good thing like barnacles":

They have found a back entrance to the higher school and are shamelessly descending on these schools in droves. While his less devious peers are studying their textbooks, solving problems, and sweating out entrance examinations, and while his peers' equally suffering fathers and mothers are unable to find openings for them in the higher schools, the smart operator arms himself with a patron, wrangles a recommendation, a character reference, and work record entries from that patron and marches off proudly to say to the admissions committee: "Accept me please!" He knows that they will accept him under the applicable statute even if his entrance exam results are below those of the average graduate from his school (1971:4; see also Lukash 1979:2).

The use of influence and bribery is probably much more common in the USSR than in the United States, where higher education is more responsive to market forces.* Not only has the American system expanded rapidly to meet demand, but many private and public institutions are available to middle-class children with undistinguished academic records. (Indeed some private colleges cater specifically to children from affluent families who are unable to gain admission to more selective institutions.) In the USSR, where the supply of vacancies is restricted and where private schools do not exist, ambitious parents are likely to use personal ties or bribes to accomplish what, in a freer market, they could do legally.

CONSEQUENCES OF INEQUALITY OF ACCESS

EDUCATIONAL ATTAINMENT AND SOCIAL MOBILITY

The evidence that we have reviewed shows pronounced variations in secondary school graduates' chances for attending college in the Soviet Union. To the extent that one can generalize from these diverse studies, it appears that a graduate from an upper-middle-class family in Leningrad was ten times as likely as a graduate from an unskilled farm worker's family in the Krasnodar region to enter the day division of a higher educational institution. A gap of comparable magnitude separates a graduate from an urban intelligentsia family in Tadzhikistan and a girl who finished school in one

---

*In a survey of former Soviet citizens, DiFranceisco and Gitelman found that most respondents would contemplate using bribery, connections, or semi-legal methods to get a mediocre student admitted to a prestigious university department. "Bribery," they note, "is (of necessity) the chosen method of the less educated, whereas *blat* [use of "pull" or connections] is the favored instrument of the intelligentsia" (1984:614).

of the republic's villages. These disparities do not reflect the full range of inequality between social-economic strata in access to higher education, however, for they take no account of the differences in secondary school graduation rates among various groups, nor do they indicate anything about the different types of higher education obtained.

The most obvious consequence of social differences in access is that children who start off with high social status are much more likely than their less-favored age-mates to gain the educational credentials that will enable them to perpetuate that status. Suitable credentials and appropriate training are probably even more important for attaining high status in the Soviet Union than in the United States, where the private sector allows alternative avenues for upward mobility. However, we must not overlook the important point that most Soviet college students have achieved upward mobility. According to the Six Region Survey, only one-third of the students in higher education came from homes in which the father had earned a college degree (Rutkevich and Filippov 1978:122). And as the data in Table 7 indicate, 30 percent have fathers who are blue-collar workers, and another 9 percent come from families in which both parents work the land. Thus though its clientele is biased toward the upper SES groups, Soviet higher education clearly allows many others to get ahead.

Yet because of the social differences in participation, public expenditures for Soviet higher education go disproportionately to children from well-to-do families and the intelligentsia. Hence the effect of subsidies for college students is regressive. In this respect the Soviet Union is certainly not unique. Evidence from Western societies suggests that while public expenditures on compulsory schooling favor to some degree the lower SES groups, expenditures on post-compulsory education favor the middle and upper SES groups to a considerable degree. In England and Wales, according to estimates by Julian LeGrand (1982:58-59), college students from the professional-managerial stratum receive 2.7 times the mean expenditures per person in the client population—and over five times the amount received by children of semi- and unskilled workers.*

---

*LeGrand's estimates do not include income maintenance awards, which (as he notes) would lead to a slight lessening of inequality. There has been a great deal of controversy over the degree to which subsidies have comparable regressive effects in the United States (see Hansen and Weisbrod 1969; Pechman 1970; Windham 1970). The original study by Hansen and Weisbrod was criticized

As others have noted, public subsidies not only make higher education more affordable for the less affluent, but also make it more attractive to the rich. Indirectly they may increase certain costs by attracting a larger pool of applicants who must invest greater time and effort in preparing for the entrance competition. The Soviet government's long-standing policy of awarding stipends primarily on the basis of academic performance rather than need contributes to the regressive effect of the public payments.

INEQUALITY AS A POLICY CONCERN

It cannot be said that the Soviet authorities have been oblivious to the social disparities revealed by the sociological studies, or to the implicit challenge they pose to the official ideology. Since its inception the Soviet regime has prided itself on providing wide opportunities for advancement through education, especially to children of manual workers. In the mid-1960s, as the Khrushchev reforms were abandoned and as results of the sociological studies became available, debate over the issue of equality of opportunity intensified.

In 1968, for example, A. Emel'ianov, executive-secretary of the admissions commission at Moscow State University, pointed out that selection committees frequently had to bend the rules to admit even a few rural applicants. "But why," he asked, "must the members of the admission commission who want to do something good, something necessary, violate the rules in order to do so?" He went on to observe that through special efforts to help young people from the villages, their share among students in the natural sciences had doubled in two years, but they still accounted for only 11 percent of the entering class. To rectify this situation, he urged that the admission plan allot vacancies for rural applicants in proportion to the number of applicants, just as planned admissions are distributed between so-called production workers (applicants with work experience) and recent secondary school graduates (1968:3).

Government spokesmen continually point to the steps that have been taken to broaden access to higher education. Aside from expanding secondary education at a rapid rate, the government has

by McGuire for omitting student financial aid. McGuire's estimates show that if student aid is included the effect is pro-poor (1976: see also Hansen and Weisbrod 1978).

made a concerted effort to upgrade rural schools. Huge investments have been made for the construction of modern facilities, small schools have been consolidated into larger ones, transportation has been improved, and greater attention has been given to the hardships that rural teachers face. Furthermore, some institutions have set up on their own initiative special programs to assist rural youth prepare for entrance examinations.

THE ROLE OF THE PREPARATORY DIVISIONS

The main policy innovation that addresses the problems facing disadvantaged youth is the 1969 decision to establish "preparatory divisions" *(podgotovitel'nye otdeleniia)* at higher educational institutions on a national scale (Abakumov et al. 1974:439-41; see also Avis 1983b). Organized as day or evening programs, the preparatory divisions provide a year's college preparatory study for secondary school graduates who have been employed for at least a year, have recently been discharged from the armed forces, or have grown up in rural areas. Individual institutions evidently have considerable discretion in selecting auditors and structuring programs within the rather broad guidelines laid down by the USSR Ministry of Higher and Specialized Secondary Education. "Auditors" *(slushateli)* are selected through competitive examinations from among those recommended by enterprise or farm managers, heads of military units, and party, Komsomol, and union organizations. Auditors accepted by the full-time (day) divisions begin study in the first half of October, receive stipends on the same basis as first-year college students, and take final examinations after ten months. Those in the evening programs, who are not eligible for stipends, pursue an eight-month course of study from December to July. If they pass the examination at the end of the year, they can enter regular day programs at the same institution without having to take the entrance examinations required of most applicants.

Following the 1969 resolution, the divisions rapidly increased in number and size. Between 1969-70 and 1972-73 the number of divisions increased from 191 to 540, and enrollments rose from 20,000 to 74,000. By 1978 preparatory divisions were operating at 638 institutions, with a total enrollment of 103,500. (If all auditors were admitted to day divisions, they would have accounted for 16.7 percent of the planned admissions that year.) Since the cost of instruction in the preparatory divisions is comparable to that of regular students, and since full-time auditors receive stipends, these programs demand a sizable investment of state resources (Lisovskii and Dimitriev 1974:47; Maksimova 1978:3).

These divisions have been in operation for nearly two decades, but there is no persuasive evidence that they have improved opportunities for substantial numbers of young people from disadvantaged backgrounds. For one thing, a high proportion of the preparatory divisions' graduates drop out of the full-time college programs.* The high attrition rate elicited calls for universities and institutes to improve both the selection and training of auditors. But the administrators pointed out that it is difficult to select well-qualified applicants when few apply, due in part to insufficient publicity and factory managers' reluctance to release able workers.†

Thus a large share of the auditors are not "advanced workers" who have distinguished themselves by several years' exemplary performance on the job, but rather young people who have been out of school for only a year or two. One out of three production workers enrolled in the preparatory divisions in 1974 had worked for no more than a year (Maksimova and Ovchinnikova 1975:12-13). Writing about the situation at the Belorussian State University in 1978, V. Slobozhanin and I. Novikov comment:

Isn't it strange that the majority of young people who call themselves workers or collective farmers are rushing into the humanities and shunning natural science and technical specialties? This

---

*In the Russian republic as a whole, just over a third of those who graduated from the preparatory divisions in 1970 reached the fifth year in the regular program by 1974. At some schools, only half of the graduates reached the second or third year (Maksimova and Ovchinnikova 1975:5).

†Throughout the Soviet Union, there were fewer than two applicants for each opening in the preparatory divisions in 1974. Though some schools or parts of the country experienced keen competition for admission, elsewhere there were scarcely enough applicants to fill the entering classes. In 1974, 31 persons submitted applications for every 10 vacancies at preparatory divisions in Moldavia, while only 12 applied in Tadzhikistan (*Pravda*, 25 May 1974, p. 3; Maksimova and Ovchinnikova 1975:12). A 1980 report in *Pravda* observed: "Not many executives of construction projects, plants, collective farms, and state farms willingly part with their best production workers—the best, and the most essential. But if they want to get rid of lazy or sloppy workers, it's quite handy to recommend them for the higher school. So that's where they are sent— and with glowing recommendations" (Slobozhanin and Novikov 1980:2).

happens, it would seem, because for these youngsters their year of work in production is only a bridge that provides the easiest access to higher education and, what's more, to a "fashionable" academic division (1980:2).

As one would expect, college dropouts are especially numerous among graduates of the programs that are undersubscribed. But more revealing from a sociological point of view, the attrition rate is positively correlated with the graduates' age. At Gorky State University, for example, the sociologist V. Iu. Kondrat'ev found that 7 percent of those who graduated from the preparatory divisions at the age of 18 dropped out in the first two years of study compared to 18 percent of those 19-20 years old, 28 percent of the 21-year-olds, and 36 percent of those 22 or older (1976:63-64).

Contrary to the stated purpose of these programs, a significant fraction of the auditors have never been employed. Two graduates from the town of Nikopol wrote to *Izvestiia* about one of their classmates who "entered the Kharkov Medical Institute and got a two [poor] in chemistry. The next year she left for the Zaporozhze Medical Institute, but she didn't pass the competitive exam. We felt sorry for her, not yet knowing that in December she had enrolled in the preparatory division of the Dnepropetrovsk Medical Institute. Just imagine—she enrolled as a collective farmer!" (Maksimova and Ovchinnikova 1975:12-18). This was by no means an isolated incident. Press accounts suggest that such problems have persisted:

> A random sample of the 1980 enrollment [in the preparatory division] at the Rostov Institute of the National Economy revealed that one student in five had been enrolled on insufficient grounds and one in 10 on the basis of fraudulent papers. At the Bashkir Medical Institute there were 21 cases of enrollment with such papers in one year. A check at the Ivano-Frankovsk Pedagogical Institute showed that enterprise managers think nothing of signing phony certificates. . . .
>
> Seven years ago our paper wrote about preparatory departments in Kiev. That was the time when the first worker-students were receiving their diplomas. There were cheaters then, too, but they were extraordinary cases. Today, when I asked at the republic Ministry of Higher Education where such things are happening. . ., I was told, "Everywhere, but most often where interest is intense" (Maksimova 1982:6).

Given their dubious record, why have the preparatory divisions continued to exist? The British scholar George Avis is no doubt correct in observing that the divisions are "essentially romantic or nostalgic in conception"—they represent "the urge to exercise again the sort of political and social control which produced results in the 1920s and 1930s," when the Communist party used the workers' faculties (*rabfaki*) to channel loyal proletarians into higher education (1983b:31).

CONCLUSION

Notwithstanding major differences between Soviet and American societies, there are some striking parallels with regard to access to higher education. In both countries, educational policymakers and administrators confront the dilemma of balancing commitments to equality with economic requirements. (In the United States, however, the economic issue is usually seen as a problem of finding jobs for graduates in a changing and competitive labor market, whereas in the USSR it is viewed as a question of dovetailing "output" with economic plans.) Both systems of higher education afford various avenues for entry, draw on a large pool of eligible clients who have gained secondary certification, implement programs designed to assist disadvantaged youngsters, and enroll large numbers of students from modest social backgrounds.

In both countries the question of access acquires political significance as a result of the conflict of interests among ethnic groups and social-economic strata regarding the norms governing admissions and the distribution of resources. In the American context, this often takes the form of calls for federally sponsored programs to improve inner-city schools, open admission at state institutions, and affirmative action (preferential treatment of groups that have suffered past discrimination). In the USSR, similar group interests and objectives lie behind programs designed to upgrade rural schools, decisions regarding the placement of higher educational institutions in various republics, and the establishment of preparatory divisions. The perceived need for such programs derives in both societies from the fact that under conditions of ostensibly free academic competition, children from socially advantaged backgrounds are more successful in gaining admission to higher education—especially to the more prestigious institutions and specialties—than children from lower-class backgrounds. In recent decades, however, educational expansion, along with programs addressing the special needs of the disadvantaged, has contributed to a narrowing of at least some of the disparities.

Postscript. As this volume goes to press, Soviet higher education is embarking upon a period of major change. In March 1987, the Central Committee of the Communist Party and the USSR Council of Ministers approved plans for a restructuring of the higher educational system. This reform, which follows a reform of general and vocational-technical education begun in 1984, seeks above all to improve the system's contribution to economic performance and to stimulate scientific-technological progress (see Dobson 1987). In line with the Gorbachev leadership's commitment to intensive economic development, the reform calls for improvements in undergraduate instruction, revised study programs, greater incentives for achievement on the part of both students and faculty, and greater use of computers.

The restructuring plan also seeks to establish a more flexible, decentralized system of manpower planning and training based on contracts between higher educational institutions and economic enterprises. Under such contracts, universities and institutes would train specialists for the enterprises, and the enterprises would partially reimburse them for the costs. The training would be directly targeted to manpower needs and would increase funds available to higher education institutions for capital investment and acquisition of equipment. Such restructuring is likely to reduce the demand for specialists—and hence the size of college enrollments, especially in the engineering specialties—by substantially raising the costs for employers.

REFERENCES

Abakumov, A.A., et al., comps. 1974. *Narodnoe obrazovanie v SSSR.* Moscow: Pedagogika. [Resolution of the CPSU Central Committee and the USSR Council of Ministers, "Ob organizatsii podgotovitel'nykh otdelenii pri vysshikh uchebnykh zavedeniiakh": 439-41]

Ailes, Catherine P., and Rushing, Francis W. 1982. *The Science Race: Training and Utilization of Scientists and Engineers, U.S. and USSR.* New York: Crane Russak.

Aitov, N.A. 1968. "Sotsial'nye aspekty polucheniia obrazovaniia v SSSR," *Sotsial'nye issledovaniia,* vyp. 2, 187-96. Moscow: Nauka.

Arutiunian, Iu.V., and Bromlei, Iu., eds. 1986. *Sotsial'no-kul'turnye oblik sovetskikh natsii (Po rezul'tatam etnosotsiologicheskogo issledovaniia)*. Moscow: Nauka.

Arutiunian, Iu.V., and Drobizheva, L.M. 1987. *Mnogoobrazie kul'turnoi zhizni narodov SSSR*. Moscow: Mysl'.

Avis, George. 1983a. "Access to Higher Education in the Soviet Union." In *Soviet Education in the 1980's*, ed. J.J. Tomiak, pp. 199-239. New York: St. Martin's Press.

_____. 1983b. "Preparatory Divisions in Soviet Higher Educational Establishments 1969-79: Ten Years of Radical Experiment." *Soviet Studies* 35, 1 (January): 14-35.

Ben-David, Joseph. 1966. "The Growth of the Professions and the Class System." In *Class, Status, and Power*, eds. Reinhard Bendix and Seymour Martin Lipset, 459-72. New York: Free Press.

Boudon, Raymond. 1974. *Education, Opportunity, and Social Inequality: Changing Prospects in Western Society*. New York: Wiley.

Bromlei, Iu. 1987. "Natsional'nye protsessy v SSSR: Dostizheniia i problemy." *Pravda*, 13 February.

Collins, Randall. 1978. *The Credential Society: An Historical Sociology of Education and Stratification*. New York: Academic Press.

Connor, Walter D. 1979. *Socialism, Politics, and Equality: Hierarchy and Change in Eastern Europe and the USSR*. New York: Columbia University Press.

Dainovskii, A.B. 1976. *Ekonomika vysshego obrazovaniia: Planirovanie, kadry, effektivnost'*. Moscow: Ekonomika.

DiFranceisco, Wayne, and Gitelman, Zvi. 1984. "Soviet Political Culture and 'Covert Participation' in Policy Implementation." *American Political Science Review* 78, 3 (September): 603-21.

Dobson, Richard B. 1977. "Mobility and Stratification in the Soviet Union." *Annual Review of Sociology* 3: 297-329.

_____. 1978. "Educational Policies and Attainment." In *Women in Russia*, eds. Dorothy Atkinson, Alexander Dallin, and Gail W. Lapidus, pp. 267-92. Stanford: Stanford University Press.

_____. 1980. "Equality and Opportunity." In *Contemporary Soviet Society: Sociological Perspectives*, eds. Jerry Pankhurst and Michael Paul Sacks, 115-37. New York: Praeger.

_____. 1984. "Soviet Education: Problems and Policies in the Urban Context." In *The Contemporary Soviet City*, eds. Henry W. Morton and Robert C. Stuart, 156-79. Armonk, N.Y.: M.E. Sharpe.

_____. 1987. "Objectives of the Current Restructuring of Soviet Higher and Specialized Secondary Education." *Soviet Education* 29, 9-10 (July-August): 5-25.

Dobson, Richard B., and Swafford, Michael. 1980. "The Educational Attainment Process in the Soviet Union: A Case Study." *Comparative Education Review* 24, 2 (June): 252-69.

Dunstan, John. 1978. *Paths to Excellence and the Soviet School.* Windsor, Engl.: NFER.

Emel'ianov, A. 1968. "Put' iz sela v VUZ: Pravilam priema v vysshuiu shkolu—nauchnuiu osnovu." *Pravda*, 11 November.

Gendel', V.G. 1971. "Sotsial'nye problemy podvizhnosti molodezhi pri sotsializme." Cand. Sci. dissertation, Leningrad State University.

Hansen, W., and Weisbrod, B. 1969. "The Distribution of the Costs and Direct Benefits of Public Higher Education: The Case of California." *Journal of Human Resources* 4, 2: 176-91.

_____, and _____. 1978. "The Distribution of Subsidies to Students in California Public Higher Education: Reply." *Journal of Human Resources* 13, 1: 137-39.

Husen, Torsten. 1975. *Social Influences on Educational Attainment: Research Perspectives on Educational Equality.* Paris: OECD.

Inoveli, I. 1976. "Corruption, Favoritism, Bribery." *Zaria vostoka*, 28 July. [Abstracted in *CDSP* 28, no. 38: 5]

Jones, Ellen, and Grupp, Fred W. 1982. "Measuring Nationality Trends in the Soviet Union: A Research Note." *Slavic Review* 41, 1 (Spring): 112-22.

_____, and _____. 1984. "Modernisation and Ethnic Equalisation in the USSR." *Soviet Studies* 36, 2 (April): 159-84.

Karklins, Rasma. 1984. "Ethnic Politics and Access to Higher Education." *Comparative Politics* 16 (April): 277-94.

Keller, Suzanne, and Zavalloni, Marisia. 1964. "Ambition and Social Class: A Respecification," *Social Forces* 43: 58-70.

Kerr, Clark; Millet, John; Clark, Burton; MacArthur, Brian; and Bowen, Howard. 1978. *12 Systems of Higher Education: 6 Decisive Issues.* New York: International Council for Educational Development and Interbook.

Komarov, V.B. 1980. "Realizatsiia zhiznennykh planov i sotsial'nye peremeshcheniia vypusknikov sel'skikh shkol." *Sotsiologicheskie issledovaniia* 3: 136-40.

Kondrat'ev. V.Iu. 1976. "Sotsial'naia effektivnost' deiatel'nosti podgotovitel'nykh otdelenii vuzov (Na materialakh Gor'kovskogo vuzovskogo tsentra)." In *Obrazovanie i sotsial'naia struktura*, eds. F.R. Filippov, Iu.N. Kozyrev, and D.I. Ziuzin, 60-68. Moscow: Institute of Sociological Research of the USSR Academy of Sciences.

Konstantinovskii, D.L. 1977. *Dinamika professional'nykh orientatsii molodezhi Sibiri.* Novosibirsk: Nauka.

Ksenfontova, V.V. 1972. "Zhiznennye plany shkol'noi molodezhi i ikh realizatsiia." Cand. Sci. dissertation, Urals State University.

LeGrand, Julian. 1982. *The Strategy of Equality: Redistribution and the Social Services.* London: George Allen & Unwin.

Lisovskii, V.T., and Dimitriev, A.V. 1974. *Lichnost' studenta.* Leningrad: Leningrad State University Press.

Lukash, A. 1979. "Roditel'skaia 'liubov.'" *Pravda*, 7 July.

Lvovsky, M. 1971. "Substitute Students." *Izvestiia*, 28 February. [Condensed in *CDSP* 23, no. 9: 26]

Maksimova, E. 1978. "Admissions to Higher Schools for 1978." *Izvestiia*, 4 March. [Condensed in *CDSP* 30, no. 9: 24]

_____. 1982. "Certified Fraud." *Izvestiia*, 8 January. [Condensed in *CDSP* 34, no. 1: 22]

Maksimova, E., and Ovchinnikova, I. 1975. "Whom Does the Workers' Faculty Need?" *Izvestiia*, 15 April. [Condensed in *CDSP* 27, no. 14: 12-13]

Mar'ianovskaia, I.S. 1976. "Orientatsiia vypusknikov srednikh shkol na vysshee obrazovanie." In *Obrazovanie i sotsial'naia struktura*, eds. F.R. Filippov, Iu.N. Kozyrev, and D.I. Ziuzin, 171-79. Moscow: Institute of Sociological Research of the USSR Academy of Sciences.

Matthews, Mervin. 1972. *Class and Society in Soviet Russia.* New York: Walker.

Matulenis, A. 1977. "Nekotorye tendentsii formirovaniia studencheskogo kontingenta v. Litovskoi SSR." In *Sotsial'no-professional'naia orientatsiia molodezhi i kommuniticheskoe vospitanie v vuze*, ed. P. Kenkmann, 115-28. Tartu: Tartu State University.

McAuley, Alastair. 1979. *Economic Welfare in the Soviet Union: Poverty, Living Standards, and Inequality.* Madison: University of Wisconsin Press.

McGuire, J. 1976. "The Distribution of Costs and Direct Benefits of Public Education: The Case of California." *Journal of Human Resources* 11, 3: 343-53.

Medkov, V.M. 1977. "Rol' vysshei shkoly v popolnenii sovetskoi intelligentsii." Cand. Sci. dissertation, Institute of Sociological Research of the USSR Academy of Sciences.

Ostapenko, L.V., and Susokolov, A.A. 1983. "Etnosotsial'nye osobennosti vosproizvodstva intelligensii." *Sotsiologicheskie issledovaniia* 1: 10-16.

_____, and _____ 1985. "Dinamika natsiolnal'nogo sostava studenchestva soiuznykh respublik v poslevoennye gody." *Sovetskaia etnografiia* 2: 46-54.

Parkin, Frank. 1971. *Class Inequality and Political Order: Social Stratification in Capitalist and Socialist Societies.* New York: Praeger.

Pechman, J. 1970. "The Distributional Effects of Public Higher Education in California." *Journal of Human Resources* 5, 3: 361-70.

Poignant, Raymond. 1973. *Education in the Industrialised Countries.* The Hague: Nijhoff.

Pravda. 1974. "To Higher Schools on a Worker's Pass—Preparatory Divisions Have Readied Another Class." 25 May. [Condensed in *CDSP* 26, no. 21: 29]

Rozanova, Ye. 1972. "The Student Stipend." *Izvestiia,* 30 September. [Condensed in *CDSP* 24, no. 39: 31]

Rutkevich, M.N., and Filippov, F.R., eds. 1978. *Vysshaia shkola kak faktor izmeneniia sotsial'noi struktury razvitogo sotsialisticheskogo obshchestva.* Moscow: Nauka.

Sarkisian, G.S., and Kuznetsova, N.P. 1967. *Potrebnosti i dokhod sem'i.* Moscow: Ekonomika.

Sheremet, I.I. 1977. "Sotsial'nyi sostav studenchestva." *Sotsiologicheskie issledovaniia* 2: 76-78.

Shoismatulloev, Sh. 1976. "Sotsial'nye faktory vybora professii (na materialakh issledovaniia vypusnikov srednikh shkol Tadzhikskoi SSR." Cand. Sci. dissertation, Institute of Sociological Research of the USSR Academy of Sciences, Moscow.

Slobozhanin, V., and Novikov, I. 1980. "Poteri v puti." *Pravda,* 18 December.

Swafford, Michael. 1979. "Political Attitudes and Behavior among Soviet University Students." Research Report R-17-79, Office of Research, U.S. International Communications Agency, Washington, D.C.

Trow, Martin. 1981. "Comparative Perspectives on Access." In *Access to Higher Education,* ed. Oliver Fulton, 89-121. Guildford: Society for Research into Higher Education.

Usanov, V. 1981. "Vstupaia v odinadtsatuiu piatiletku." *Narodnoe obrazovanie* 2: 27-30.

United States. 1975. Bureau of the Census. "College Plans of High School Seniors: October 1974." *Current Population Reports,* Series P-20, No. 284.

_____. 1981. Bureau of the Census. *Statistical Abstract of the United States, 1981.* Washington, D.C.: U.S. Government Printing Office.

_____. 1982. Department of Education, National Center for Educational Statistics. *Condition of Education.* Washington, D.C.: U.S. Government Printing Office.

USSR. 1971. Tsentral'noe Statisticheskoe Upravlenie. *Narodnoe obrazovanie, nauka i kul'tura v SSSR: Statisticheskii sbornik.* Moscow: Statistika.

_____. 1973. Ts.S.U. *Itogi vsesoiuznoi perepisi naseleniia 1970 goda,* vol. 4: *Natsional'nyi sostav naseleniia SSSR.* Moscow: Statistika.

_____. 1977. Ts.S.U. *Narodnoe obrazovanie, nauka i kul'tura v SSSR: Statisticheskii sbornik.* 2nd ed. Moscow: Statistika.

_____. 1981. *Narodnoe khoziaistvo SSSR v 1980 g.: Statisticheskii ezhegodnik.* Moscow: Statistika.

_____. 1986. Ts.S.U. *Narodnoe khoziaistvo SSSR v 1985 g.: Statisticheskii ezhegodnik.* Moscow: Finansy i statistika.

Vasil'eva, E.K. 1970. *Sotsial'no-professional'nyi uroven' gorodskoi molodezhi.* Leningrad: Nauka.

Wesolowski, W. 1969. "The Notions of Strata and Class in Socialist Society." In *Social Inequality*, ed. Andre Beteille, 122-45. Baltimore: Penguin Books.

Windham, D.M. 1970. *Education, Equality, and Income Distribution.* Lexington: Mass.: Heath.

Yanowitch, Murray. 1977. *Social and Economic Inequality in the Soviet Union: Six Studies.* White Plains, NY: Sharpe.

Zaslavsky, Victor, and Brym, Robert J. 1983. *Soviet-Jewish Emigration and Soviet Nationality Policy.* New York: St. Martin's Press.

AMERICAN HIGHER EDUCATION:
PAST, PRESENT, AND FUTURE

Martin Trow

American higher education differs from that in almost all other countries in offering access to some part of the system to almost everyone who wants to go to college or university without their having to show evidence of academic talent or qualification. Moreover, private attitudes and public policy—so consensual across the political spectrum that they occasion hardly any comment—affirm that the more people who can be persuaded to enroll in a college or university, the better. The budgets of most American colleges and universities are directly linked to their enrollments—private institutions through tuition payments, public institutions through a combination of tuition and funding formulas which tie state support to enrollment levels. This linkage is incentive for almost every institution to encourage applications and enrollments.

Since enrollment levels are so central to the financial health and social functions of American higher education, I will begin by reviewing current enrollment trends and forecasts. I will then explore the social and historical forces that gave rise to and sustain this unique system.

RECENT ENROLLMENT TRENDS

American higher education is the largest and most diverse system of postsecondary education in the world. In 1947, just after World War II, 2.3 million students were enrolled in some 1800 American colleges and universities—about half in public and half in private institutions (Andersen 1968: 8009). While both sectors have grown over the past forty years, the enormous growth of enrollments during the 1960s and 1970s was absorbed largely by public institutions, both four-year and two-year colleges. By 1986, enrollments in America's roughly 3300 colleges and universities were running at

---

My thanks to Janet Ruyle for her help with this paper.

over 12.4 million and holding fairly steady, with 77 percent enrolled in public institutions (see Table 1). No central law or authority governs or coordinates American higher education: the approximately 1800 private institutions are governed by lay boards of trustees; the 1500 public institutions (including some 900 public community colleges) are accountable to state or local authorities, but usually have a lay board of trustees as a buffer and preserve a variable measure of institutional autonomy.

Table 1

HIGHER EDUCATION ENROLLMENT IN THE UNITED STATES, 1947-1985

| | Total Enrollment (*in 000s*) | Type of Institution | | | |
| | | Public | | Private | |
Year		Percent of Total	Enrollment (*in 000s*)	Percent of Total	Enrollment (*in 000s*)
1947	2,338	49%	1,152	51%	1,186
1950	2,297	50		50	
1955	2,679	56		44	
1960	3,789	59		41	
1965	5,921	67		33	
1970	8,581	75		25	
1975	11,185	79		21	
1980	12,097	78		22	
1985	12,247	77	9,479	23	2,768
1986	12,398	77	9,600	23	2,797

Sources: 1947: Andersen (1968: 8009); 1950-1980: Ottinger (1984: 56, 59); 1985: *Chronicle of Higher Education* (1986b: 42); 1986: *Chronicle of Higher Education* (1987: A29).

Forecasts of future growth in higher education are almost always wrong, not only in the United States but also abroad. The efforts of the British to predict the growth of their system over the past three decades have been consistently wrong, within a few years and by large amounts (Williams 1983: 13). Clark Kerr (1980: 6-8) has noted that in the United States the Carnegie Commission's estimates of aggregate enrollments, numbers of new institutions, faculty salaries, and proportion of the gross national product spent on higher education were all too high. More recently, nearly every-one concerned with American higher education was predicting a marked decline in enrollments starting in 1979 — a decline that was "inevitable" given the decreasing size of the college-age cohorts starting in that year. Indeed the number of high school graduates declined from a peak of some 3 million in 1979 to about 2.6 million in 1984—about 13 percent. Demographic projections point to a further decline to about 2.3 million high school graduates from 1991 to 1994 (McConnell and Kaufman 1984: 29). But the fall in college and university enrollments that was anticipated has simply not occurred. On the contrary, aggregate enrollments in American higher education grew by about 6 percent between 1979 and 1984, and "colleges and universities had close to 1.5 million more students and $6 billion more revenues than predicted by the gloom and doomers" (Frances 1984: 3).

Although a further fall of about 10 percent in the number of high school graduates is projected by 1991, it is far from certain that enrollments in higher education will suffer an equivalent decline. Among the reasons for not anticipating a similar decline in enrollments over the next decade are these:

First, there has been a steady growth in enrollments of older students since the early 1970s. During the decade 1972-82, the greatest percentage increase in enrollments was among people 25 years old and older. Those 35 and older increased by 77 percent, and those between 25 and 34 increased by 70 percent, compared with a growth of 35 percent in total enrollments during that period.

Second, increasing numbers of students are enrolled part-time. During the decade 1972-82, part-time enrollments increased by two thirds while full-time enrollments grew by less than one fifth.

Third, in recent years there have been very large increases in the enrollments of women and minorities. The number of women in colleges and universities grew by 61 percent in the decade 1972-82, and minority enrollments increased by 85 percent as compared with 15 percent for men and 30 percent for white students (*Higher Education and National Affairs* 1984a: 3).

The growing enrollments of older students, working and part-time students, and women and minorities are all trends that are independent of the decreasing size of the college-age population. For example, while a relatively small proportion of Hispanics living in California currently go on to higher education, the number of Hispanics in California's population, and especially among its youth, is very large—and increasing. In 1981-82 about a quarter of all public school students in the state were Hispanic, and by the year 2000 they will begin to outnumber whites in the under-20 age group (PACE Project 1984: 11, ex. 4). Even a small change in the percentage of Hispanics who graduate from high school and go to college would have a major impact on enrollment levels in California colleges and universities. A long-term growth in the percentage of Hispanics going on to college seems likely simply on the basis of trends among other ethnic groups throughout American history. In addition, long-term changes in the occupational structure, such as the growth of the knowledge and information industries, are increasing the numbers of jobs that call for college-educated people. And many of our colleges and universities are eager to welcome older people who want to upgrade their skills and equip themselves for employment in the new industries as their old jobs are phased out.

Moreover, current efforts to improve secondary education, which are almost wholly directed toward strengthening the courses that prepare students for college, may well lead to increases both in high school graduation rates and in the proportions of graduates who go on to college (NCEE 1983; Boyer 1983; Goodlad 1983; Trow 1985b).

On the other hand, enrollment levels may yet fall over the next few years. Moreover, population movements, changes in the economy, and changes in the size of age cohorts will affect various states and regions differently. In addition, these factors will affect different kinds of institutions within the same region quite differently. There will be great differences in the effects of demographic and economic changes not only between institutions in, say, Ohio and Texas, but also between public community colleges, minor private four-year colleges, and elite four-year colleges and research universities within the same region. There almost certainly will be closures of some private colleges over the next decade, and perhaps some consolidation among public institutions, though recent figures show an unexpected increase in the number of private four-year colleges over the past four years (Tsukada 1986: 101). The birth and death of colleges in large numbers throughout American history has been a natural outcome of giving the market a great influence over a diverse and decentralized system of higher education. Such closures as occur are mostly of weaker institutions, and may well leave the system as a whole even stronger (Glenny 1983).

The effort to think about what American higher education will look like in ten or twenty years forces us to think more clearly about the forces that have shaped it and given it its unique qualities and character. Eric Ashby has pointed out that we cannot know "what the environments of tomorrow's world will be like," but "we already know what its heredity will be like" (1967). And, as Clark Kerr has observed, heredity in higher education is a particularly strong force. The universities of today can draw a direct line back to Bologna and Paris and Oxford and Cambridge. Compared to universities, even religious institutions—those custodians of the eternal verities—have changed more, and political and economic institutions incomparably more.

DEFINING CHARACTERISTICS

What are the defining characteristics of American higher education? Certain features leap out when one compares American higher education with the systems in other advanced industrial societies—features deeply rooted in our history and institutions which shape their capacity to respond to the events and developments of the next decades.

First is the very strong influence of the market and market-related forces on American higher education.

Second, and related to the first, is the enormous diversity among American colleges and universities—in their size, functions, curricula, sources of support, structures of authority, and academic standards. This diversity is mirrored in their student bodies—in their age distribution, purposes and motivations, social class, ethnic and racial origins, and much else.

Third is the internal differentiation of academic standards and educational mission of the comprehensive universities and many of the larger state colleges that gives those institutions great flexibility to respond to changes in the markets for undergraduates, faculty, graduate students, and research support. This differentiation *within* the largest institutions complements the differentiation *among* the colleges and universities that arises out of their diversity.

Fourth is a cluster of related characteristics of curricula, teaching styles, and patterns of assessment: the inclusion of general education as a component of nearly all undergraduate degree programs; the considerable freedom allowed students in the selection of courses based on the elective principle and "distribution requirements"; and the unit-credit—the academic currency that links 3300 different institutions together into an enrollment-driven, market-oriented system without central control or coordination.

Fifth is our unique mode of college and university governance: lay boards of trustees and strong presidents who command large administrative staffs located inside the institutions rather than in some central ministry or other governmental agency.

Let us consider some of these characteristics more fully.

The most distinctive feature of American higher education is surely its size and diversity. It is this diversity that has enabled our colleges and universities to appeal to so many and serve so many different functions in our national life, and it is through the preservation of diversity that our system will be best prepared to respond to changing demands and new challenges in the years ahead. To see why this is so, it may help to review briefly the historical roots of diversity in American higher education.

Actually, this diversity was present from the very beginning. The colonies had established nine colleges by the time of the American Revolution, when two—Oxford and Cambridge—were regarded as enough for the more populous and wealthier mother country. When the Civil War began, the United States had about 250 colleges, of which over 180 still survive. Even more striking is the record of failure: between the American Revolution and the Civil War perhaps as many as 700 colleges were started and failed (Rudolph 1962: 47). By 1880, while England was managing with four universities for a population of 23 million, the single state of Ohio, with a population of 3 million, already boasted 37 institutions of higher learning (47-48). By 1910 the United States had nearly 1,000 colleges and universities with a third of a million students—at a time when the sixteen universities of France enrolled altogether about 40,000 students, about the number of faculty in American higher education at the time.

The extraordinarily high creation and failure rates of American institutions of higher learning are still with us. In the six years between 1969 and 1975, some 800 new colleges (many of them community colleges) were created, while about 300 others were closed or consolidated, leaving a net gain of nearly 500. This is a phenomenon unique to the United States—one that resembles the pattern of success and failure of small businesses in modern capitalist economies. It is in sharp contrast to the slow, deliberately planned creation of institutions of higher learning in most other advanced industrial societies, and their even slower (and rarer) termination. And this points to the very strong link between higher education in the United States and the mechanisms of the market.

Two important features of markets are, first, that their outcomes are not the results of central planning and, second, when the sellers (producers) are relatively numerous, their competition for buyers is intense, which strengthens the influence of the buyers over the character and quality of the product and of the producer.

In higher education we can see this when the buyers are students and the producers are the colleges and universities competing for their enrollment. We can see it also when the sellers are graduates competing for job openings. The two processes together greatly influence the size of academic departments and programs because American colleges and universities have considerable autonomy to move resources between departments in response to changes in student enrollment and job demand. Similarly, when research groups compete for scarce funds, funding agencies gain influence over the character of the research they support. In the United States, apart from the unusual period of rapid growth of college enrollments between 1955 and 1975, buyers or potential buyers at both ends — students and employers of graduates — have had powerful influences on the behavior of the producers. This influence of buyer over seller is likely to be relatively constant in the decades ahead.

We think most readily of competition involving cash transfers — for example, for students who bring with them tuition fees or per capita subventions from public authorities, or both. But we can also think of academic markets as places for the competitive exchange of other values. For example, the spread of graduate departments in American universities between, say, 1870 and 1920 was largely a market-driven process involving competition by self-seeking actors — in this case, institutions — for status, prestige, and distinguished scholars.

We can see the emergence of strong market forces in the early history of American higher education, we can see them today in the very structure and workings of our institutions, and we can compare their strength here with the systems of other societies. Let us look at the market forces in each of these ways: historically, structurally, comparatively.

Among the multiplicity of forces and purposes behind the establishment of colleges and universities in American history, there have been a variety of religious motives, fears of relapse into barbarism on the frontier, needs for various kinds of professionals, state pride and local boosterism, philanthropy, idealism, educational reform, and speculation in land, among others, and in all combinations. But the number and diversity of institutions competing for students, resources, and teachers, bringing market mechanisms into the heart of an ancient cultural institution, has required the absence of any central authority that could restrain the proliferation of institutions of higher education. The states were not that restraining force: under the pressures of competition and emulation, they have tended throughout our history to create institutions and programs in the numbers and to the standards of their neighbors. Crucially important has been the absence of a federal ministry of education with the power to charter new institutions, or of a single preeminent university that could influence them in other ways.

The closest the United States has come to establishing such a central authority was the attempt—first by George Washington and then by the next five presidents—to found a national university at the seat of government in Washington, D.C. Washington, in fact, made provision for such a university in his will, and mentioned it in his first and last messages to Congress. His strongest plea for it came in his final message to Congress, where he argued that it would promote national unity, a matter of deep concern at a time when the primary loyalties of many Americans were to their sovereign states rather than to the infant nation.

In addition, Washington hoped it would be possible to create one really first-class university by concentrating money and other resources in it. As he noted in his last message to Congress:

> Our Country, much to its honor, contains many Seminaries of learning highly respectable and useful; but the funds upon which they rest, are too narrow, to command the ablest Professors, in the different departments of liberal knowledge, for the Institution contemplated, though they would be excellent auxiliaries (Hofstadter and Smith 1961: 158).

Here indeed Washington was right in his diagnosis. The many institutions that sprang up between the Revolution and the Civil War all competed for very scarce resources, and all suffered to some degree from malnutrition. Malnutrition at the margin is still a characteristic of a system of institutions influenced heavily by market forces.

Rejection of the proposed national university meant that American higher education would develop without a single capstone institution. Had we concentrated resources in one university of high standard early in our national life, it might have been the equal of the great old universities of Europe or the distinguished new universities then being established in Germany and elsewhere. As it was, whatever the United States called its institutions of higher learning, the nation simply did not have a single genuine university— an institution of first-class standing that could bring its students as far or as deep into the major branches of learning as could the institutions of the old world—until after the Civil War.

A national university would have profoundly affected American higher education. As the preeminent university, it would have had an enormous influence, direct and indirect, on every other college in the country, and through them on the secondary schools. Its standards of entry, its curricula, its educational philosophy, even its modes of instruction, would have set the patterns for every institution which hoped to send some of its graduates to the university in Washington. It would very likely have established national standards for the bachelor's degree, for the undergraduate curriculum, for qualifications for college teachers, even for entrance to college, and thus for curricula in the secondary schools. Eventually it would have governed, shaped, and surely constrained the growth of graduate education and research universities in the United States.

However attractive some of that may seem to us, the cost to American higher education would have been great. The national university, for all it could have contributed to our intellectual and cultural life in the nineteenth century, would almost certainly have prevented the emergence of the big, sprawling, unregulated system of higher education which developed in its absence—a system that, in the American context, proved to be far preferable to a neat, tidy system of smaller size and higher uniform standards.

A federal system of high standards would have inhibited the emergence of the hundreds of small, weak, half-starved state and denominational colleges that sprang up over the next 170 years. They could not have offered instruction to the standard that the national university would have set for the baccalaureate degree, and demanded of applicants to its postgraduate programs. The situation would have been familiar to Europeans, for whom the maintenance of high common academic standards throughout their systems of higher education has long been a valued principle. In the United States, since the rejection of the idea of a national university, no one has challenged the principle of high academic standards across the whole system because no one has proposed it; there have been no common academic standards, high or otherwise. If Europe's slogan for higher education has been "nothing if not the best," America's has been "something is better than nothing." In that spirit we have created a multitude of institutions of every sort, offering academic work of every description and at every level of seriousness and standard. By so doing we have offered Europeans nearly two centuries of innocent amusement at our expense.

The idea of a national university of the United States failed. We did not go that way, and the ironic result is that without any central model, or governmental agency able to create one or more national systems, all of America's 3300 institutions—public and private, modest and preeminent, religious and secular—are in some way part of a common system of higher education.

What holds the system together is common membership in a series of markets for students, support, prestige, faculty. Markets can function as arenas for both competition and integration, largely because there is no central power to suppress them, or to make decisions centrally and administratively that are made by the market and institutional responses to it.

Another major event in the early history of the Republic which had powerful effects on the shape and character of American higher education was the 1819 decision of the Supreme Court in the Dartmouth College case. It was a landmark decision in that it affirmed the sanctity of contracts between governments and private institutions. In so doing, it gave expression to the Federalist view that the government could not interfere with private property even to benefit the public welfare. John Marshall, then Chief Justice of the Supreme Court, had written earlier: "I consider the interference of the legislature in the management of our private affairs, whether these affairs are committed to a company or remain under individual direction as equally dangerous and unwise." He and his colleagues on the Court decided in the Dartmouth College case that a charter of a private college or university was a contract which a state could not retroactively abridge. The decision had important repercussions both for the growth of capitalist enterprises and for the future development of higher education in the United States.

The State of New Hampshire's rationale for proposing changes in the Dartmouth College charter was the plausible argument that, though the college was a private corporation, it had been established to benefit the people of New Hampshire, and that could best be accomplished by giving the public, through the legislature, a voice in its operation. The state wanted to improve the college by modernizing its administration, creating the framework for a university, and encouraging a freer, nonsectarian atmosphere conducive to republicanism.

These goals were very much in the Jeffersonian tradition of encouraging the growth of "republican" institutions to meet the needs of the new nation. In this spirit, in 1816 the New Hampshire legislature had passed a bill giving the state government broad powers to "reform" Dartmouth. Chief Justice Marshall, ruling in favor of the college trustees, declared that the charter originally granted to the college was a contract, and that state legislatures were forbidden by the Constitution to pass any law "impairing the obligation of contracts" (Hofstadter and Wilson 1961: 218). In seeking to change Dartmouth, the New Hampshire legislature was proposing to substitute the will of the state for the will of the founders, which would turn the college into "a machine entirely subservient to the will of government" (219). In many ways Marshall's opinion followed the traditional view of the role of educational institutions in English society.

The Dartmouth College decision preventing the State of New Hampshire from taking over the college sustained the older, more modest role of the state in educational affairs against those who looked to the government to take a greater role. Marshall's decision had the practical effect of safeguarding the founding and proliferation of privately controlled colleges. Thereafter, promoters of private colleges knew that once they had obtained a state charter they were secure in the future control of the institution. By this decision, state university development was slowed or weakened, though, paradoxically, it may be that by making it more difficult to create them, state universities were ultimately strengthened.

The failure to establish a national university and the success of Dartmouth College in its appeal to the Supreme Court were both victories for local initiative and private entrepreneurship. The first of these set limits on the role of the federal government in shaping the character of the whole of American higher education; the second set even sharper limits on the power of the state over private colleges. Together these two developments constituted a kind of charter for unrestrained private initiative in the creation of colleges of diverse sizes, shapes, and creeds. Almost any motive or combination of motives and interests could bring a college into being between the Revolution and the Civil War, and thereafter its survival depended largely on its being able to secure support from a church, or from wealthy benefactors, or from student fees, or even perhaps from the state. The colleges thus created were established relatively easily, but without guarantees of survival. As a result, a situation arose resembling the behavior of organisms in an ecological system — intensely competitive for resources, highly sensitive to the demands of their environment, and inclined over time, through the ruthless processes of natural selection, to be adaptive to those aspects of their environment that permitted their survival. That environment included other colleges and, later, universities. We see in this frog pond a set of mechanisms that we usually associate with the behavior of small entrepreneurs in a market: anxious concern for what the market wants, a readiness to adapt to its preferences, an effort to find a special place in the market through a marginal differentiation of the product, a willingness to enter into symbiotic or parasitic relationships with other producers for a portion of the market. Here we are employing a language that Europeans tend to find strange and often objectionable when used in connection with institutions of higher learning. But objectionable or not, American higher education is a network of institutions which in many respects behaves like the myriad of small capitalistic enterprises that were springing up everywhere at the same time and in the same places, and often in response to the same forces.

America is, and has been from the beginning, an acquisitive society, confronted by a continent whose ownership had not been settled by sword and custom since medieval times. As Louis Hartz (1955) has noted, in America the market preceded society, a crucial fact whose ramifications can be seen in all of our institutions and throughout our national life. We are, to put it crudely, not embarrassed by the market. We believe the market is a sensible mechanism for the ordering of most social affairs—not just economic affairs, but cultural and intellectual life as well. We did not inherit the corporatism of medieval life or the statism of absolute monarchy. We were from the beginning a liberal society, and our arguments have been the arguments of various branches of liberalism. But Europeans, even those who approve of the market in economic affairs, find its presence oddly embarrassing in the realm of culture, scholarship, religion, or statecraft.

Besides the market, societies organize and manage systems of higher education in three other ways:

1. Through political decisions—as the outcome of the play of power and interests in political arenas, in government, or in the academic institutions themselves;

2. Through bureaucratic regulation: essentially through management by a ministry and its civil service;

3. Through the power of organized professional guilds of academics, applying academic norms and values in the service of the university as defined by the professors (Clark 1983).

Every system of higher education organizes itself and makes decisions through some combination of these ways. But the relative weight of market mechanisms, professional norms, bureaucratic regulation, or political decisions varies greatly between national systems. I have been stressing the relatively large role of market mechanisms in higher education in the United States, and the historical origins of that role. By contrast, Europeans and their governments, now as in the past, dislike market mechanisms and processes in education, and do everything they can to reduce their influence. This difference arises out of our profoundly differing feelings about culture and cultural competence. Markets threaten the "integrity" of cultural institutions by increasing the power of consumers over producers—that is, over the people who are presumably most competent to supply some kind of cultural entity, whether it be an artistic performance or higher studies in philosophy or physics.

In colleges and universities, the consumers, ordinarily students or their parents, are by definition less competent than the teachers and academic administrators who provide instruction. Europeans try to reduce the influence of the incompetent mass on high cultural matters, and to preserve a realm of elite determination of cultural form and content. In the United States, surely the most populist society in the world, we accept a larger role for the influence of consumer preference on cultural forms—even on what and how subjects are taught in colleges and universities. Europeans try to reduce the influence of students on institutions of higher education by insulating their financing from student fees. By contrast, in the United States, the enrollment-driven budgets in all but a few institutions, both public and private, ensure that most of them are extremely sensitive to student preferences.

Another example of the comparative hospitality of American institutions to market forces in higher education can be seen in the ways Congress provides major public funding for colleges and universities. After sharp debate in the early 1970s, Congress chose to fund higher education chiefly by providing grants and loans to students rather than through direct support to institutions. The result was to substantially strengthen the relative power of consumers over producers without increasing the power of central government over the producers.

When one looks at broad patterns of organization and finance of higher education systems (for example, multiple versus single sources of support), one can see the differences between market systems and those dominated by other principles of organization and political decision-making. We can also see the influence of market mechanisms in the private life of higher education, in the processes of teaching and learning. One example is the peculiar American system of earned and transferable "credits"—a kind of academic currency taken for granted in American institutions. The unit credit system is not found in other countries, where degrees arre earned by passing examinations or writing dissertations. These credits can be accumulated, banked, and transferred and, within limits, are automatically accepted as legal academic tender toward an earned degree at any college or university in the country, making possible an extraordinary mobility of American students between fields of study and between institutions. They also enable students to drop out, or "stop out" for a few months or years, and return to college later on.

The strength of academic markets in the United States has also helped shape our conception of liberal education, a relatively unspecialized undergraduate curriculum not keyed to any specific occupation or profession, but emphasizing a broad familiarity with the major areas of learning. This is a strange concept to most Europeans, whose university work is highly specialized, and from medieval times has been closely keyed to specific careers and vocations. The American conception of a liberal education, especially with its emphasis on breadth of exposure and a high measure of free choice by the student (the elective principle), requires a system of transferable credits, which makes possible an undergraduate curriculum based on aggregate units of instruction rather than the cumulation of knowledge in a specialized area of study that can be examined at the end of three or four or five years, or produces a dissertation as evidence of competence achieved.

An inventory of the distinctive qualities of American higher education must include a reference to the multiplicity of subjects taught, reflecting the openness of its institutions to almost any subject that might have a claim to be useful, or to be rooted in a body of skill and knowledge that can be studied and taught. This range of offerings, often a source of derisive comment by Europeans, would not be possible if we had a central agency maintaining "high standards" and evaluating new subjects for their appropriateness as judged by traditional criteria of university subjects.

There are many other distinctive qualities of American higher education. We might include the various ways colleges and universities enter into the life of the larger society, in part through the continuing association of many former students with their colleges and universities, and the crucial political and material support this gives to the institutions, public and private. The multiplicity of sources of support for higher education in the United States breaks the monopoly of control by public agencies, both political and bureaucratic, and weakens the influence of the national professional guilds and the disciplines inside the institutions. There is little counterpart for this elsewhere. In this respect, we should also acknowledge the special role of American college sports as mass entertainment that provides a point of identification for the general population with universities and colleges. There is the striking phenomenon of "subway alumni," a classic example of which is the role of Notre Dame football for Irish-Americans who never went to Notre Dame — or to *any* college or university (Riesman 1954: 242-57).

We could also point to the intimate links between American colleges and universities and local industries, governments, and other institutions and private organizations of all kinds — relationships which are emulated in other countries but rarely matched in scope (Eurich 1985).

After one sketches an inventory of distinctive characteristics of American higher education, the question arises: How are these distinctive characteristics related to one another in their origins and current functioning? Let us look, for example, at a cluster of phenomena found in American higher education — lay board of trustees, strong presidency, weak professoriate, internal administration, no central ministry of higher education — and consider how they are all tied together. Let us start with two characteristics that arose out of the early weakness of the academic profession in America: the location of the institution's primary authority in a lay board of trustees and the related phenomenon of the strong college or university president. The precedent for the external non-academic board of trustees was set at Harvard. The founders of Harvard had intended to "carry on the English tradition of resident-faculty control" (Rudolph 1962: 166), but there was no faculty in residence. Harvard had to be founded, and not just developed. There was not a body of scholars to be brought together to teach and govern themselves, but a *president* could be found to take responsibility for the operation of the institution, and he could find some young men to help him with instruction as tutors. Harvard had been established for more than 85 years before it had its first professor; Yale, for more than 50. "For over a century and a half, American collegiate education relied chiefly on the college president and his young tutors" (*ibid.*). Until well into the nineteenth century,

> the only secure and sustained professional office in American collegiate education was that of the college president himself. He alone, among the working teachers of the early colleges, had, in the community and before the governing boards, the full stature of a man of learning. To this situation can be traced the singular role and importance of the American college or university president (Hofstadter and Metzger 1955: 124).

The lay boards that arose to govern America's first college and most of those which followed were created by groups of individuals, not by the state. These boards *had* to govern; there was no one else. They appointed a president, and as busy men themselves, they had to delegate to him the day-to-day running of the institution. He held his office wholly at the pleasure of this external board. For a very long time there was no body of learned men making academic life a career, and thus no challenge to the president's authority so long as he had the support of his board of trustees.

The near absolute authority of the college president was lost over time—especially with the rise of the great research universities and the emergence of a genuine academic profession. In this century, especially in the stronger institutions, a great deal of authority over academic affairs has been delegated to the faculty. But the American college or university president is still more powerful than his counterpart in European institutions, who faces a situation in which power is already held jealously by the professoriate, or the academic staff more broadly, or government ministries, or student organizations, or trade unions (Trow 1985a).

The relatively great authority of the American college or university president ensured that when institutions became very large, and needed a big bureaucratic staff to administer them, that staff would be an extension of the president's office rather than reponsible to a faculty body or to state authorities. By keeping the administrative staff within the university, the strong presidency has helped preserve the autonomy of the public university in the face of state authority.

For a long time the academic profession in America was non-existent. When professors did begin to appear, they did not have the enormous prestige and status accorded to the European professor. They were not part of a prestigious civil service, nor were they recruited from the highest social strata. Indeed, in a society which prized action and worldly success, they were rather looked down on as men who had stood aside from the real challenges of life. America, for the most part, has given its honors and respect chiefly to men of action rather than reflection, and for a very long time, the very choice of an academic career suggested that a man was incapable of managing such important matters as the affairs of a university (Hofstadter 1963: 24-51; Rudolph 1962: 160-61). This tended to strengthen the hand of the president, who *may* have been a scholar, but almost certainly was also a man of affairs.

The relatively low status and weakness of the professoriate also meant that, as the academic profession grew, it was not dominated by a handful of prestigious professors. The academic ranks were established during the growth of the research universities after the Civil War, with almost the whole teaching faculty holding the rank of some kind of "professor," and with a remarkably large degree of independence for even young assistant professors. This is due partly to the strong egalitarian elements in American cultural life, and partly to the historic weakness of the senior professor—his lack of power, prestige, even scholarly distinction. Academic ambition was directed not so much to personal rank—that could be assumed—as to the national reputation and distinction of the institution or department in which one gained an appointment.

Many of the most important qualities of American higher education have arisen not from the strength but from the weakness of its component institutions. For example, as I have suggested, the relatively egalitarian character of American academic life, and the independence and authority of its junior members, are products not of the historical strength of American higher education but of the weakness of the academic profession and the professoriate. America has thus avoided the bitter struggles between the professors and other ranks of the academic profession which have marked European systems since World War II. In America the rank of professor was no special honor and held no great rewards, but was the rank that almost every young instructor or assistant professor (and not just the few most talented ones) could expect to achieve in the fullness of time. That ease of access to the rank of professor has helped to keep its status relatively low both within the university and outside it, where the title "Professor" still often has slightly pejorative or comic overtones.

What is the connection between a weak academic profession, strong presidents, lay boards, and the power of the market in American higher education? Briefly put, the strength of market forces is determined by the weakness of other forces which constrain the self-interested actions of individuals and institutions in higher education. Most commonly those constraining forces in other countries are state authorities allied with the academic profession and its organizations or guilds. In the United States, central state power was weak in relation to higher education in part as a result of the failure to establish a national university, and the Dartmouth College case which guaranteed a private sector. The weakness of the professoriate limited *that* constraint on the market. On the other hand, strong presidents and their staffs could promote the interests of individual institutions, and lay boards could ensure that those institutions would be responsive to the larger society, and to its markets for students and graduates, rather than to the state or professional guilds. And that certainly will be a source of strength as these institutions face an uncertain future and a changing environment.

THE SUPPORT OF AMERICAN HIGHER EDUCATION

We have been looking backward in order to see ahead. Let us see if there are any recent or current trends and developments that might point toward major changes in the future.

In 1985-86 expenditures of all kinds on American colleges and universities were estimated to be over $102 billion—an increase in current dollars of 32 percent and in constant dollars of 17 percent over 1981-82. This is roughly 2.5 percent of the gross national product (*Higher Education & National Affairs* 1986: 3). A distinctive characteristic of American higher education is its diverse sources of support. This diversity of funding sources has large consequences for the autonomy of American colleges and universities, and for their tradition of service to other institutions, both public and private, as well as for their finances. Taken in the aggregate, American colleges and universities get support from federal, state, and local governments, from private sources such as churches, business firms, foundations, and individuals, from students in the form of tuition and fees, rental charges for halls of residence, food services, health services, etc., and from endowments and sales of their services to others.

Government at all levels together provides nearly half of all current revenues for American higher education, not including federal aid given directly to students, which shows up for the most part in tuition and fees (see Table 2). The federal government provides only about 13 percent of the total funds for higher education, including its support for research and development in the universities, but excluding the aid it provides directly to students. State and local governments (mostly state) provide one-third of the funds for higher education. Students provide another one-third of the funds for higher education, including federal aid they have received, and the institutions themselves about 15 percent from their endowments and other sources. If federal aid to students is counted as federal support, it increases the federal contribution to about 23 percent of the total, and reduces the student contribution to about the same percentage. About 6 percent is provided by individuals, foundations, and private business firms in the form of gifts, grants, and contracts.

These proportions differ between public and private colleges and universities, of course, though it must be stressed that all American colleges and universities are supported by a mixture of public and private funds. For example, while in 1981-82 public four-year colleges and universities got over 44 percent of their operating budgets from state governments, private institutions got less than 2 percent of theirs from state sources. (On the other hand, private colleges got a slightly larger proportion of their support from the federal government than did public four-year institutions.) Another big difference between public and private institutions lies in the much greater importance of student fees and payments for services in private schools: they account for less than one-fourth of the revenues of public institutions but about one-half of the support for private institutions. These proportions differ sharply among even finer categories of colleges and universities — for example, as between public research universities and public four-year colleges.

In 1985-86 student aid from all sources was running at over $21 billion a year — 23 percent higher than in 1980-81. In real terms, however, student support from all sources had fallen by 3 percent since 1980-81, and aid from federally supported programs fell by 10 percent when adjusted for inflation (College Board 1986: 2). In fiscal 1985 the federal government provided about $23.7 billion directly and indirectly to higher education, of which $10.2 billion was a complex combination of student grants and loans (*Chronicle of Higher Education* 1986: 12). Student aid has widespread support in the Congress as well as in society at large, and while the Reagan administration regularly proposed cuts in that aid, many of these proposals were defeated. In 1985, for example, Congress "blocked

Table 2

SOURCES OF CURRENT-FUND REVENUES FOR INSTITUTIONS OF HIGHER EDUCATION, BY CONTROL AND TYPE OF INSTITUTION: UNITED STATES, 1970-71 AND 1981-82

Year and Source	Total	Public Institutions		Private Institutions	
		4-Year	2-Year	4-Year	2-Year
		Millions of Dollars			
1970-71					
Total	$23,879	$13,260	$2,266	$8,115	$237
Government[1]	12,106	8,291	1,778	2,020	16
Federal[2]	4,601	2,616	153	1,819	13
State	6,595	5,528	924	140	3
Local	910	147	701	61	1
Private sources[3]	1,227	348	11	838	31
Students[3]	8,146	3,485	437	4,043	181
Tuition and fees	5,021	1,738	295	2,871	118
Auxiliary enterprises[4]	3,125	1,748	143	1,173	62
Institutional[5]	2,401	1,136	41	1,215	9
1981-82					
Total	72,191	38,715	8,556	24,181	739
Government[1]	33,378	22,302	6,225	4,802	49
Federal[2]	9,592	4,882	491	4,187	32
State	21,849	17,142	4,255	438	14
Local	1,938	279	1,478	177	4
Private sources[3]	3,564	1,236	41	2,230	57
Students[3]	23,896	9,583	1,935	11,792	586
Tuition and fees	15,774	5,014	1,381	8,896	483
Auxiliary enterprises[4]	8,122	4,569	554	2,896	103
Institutional[5]	11,353	5,594	355	5,358	46

Percentage Distribution

1970-71

Total	100.0%	100.0%	100.0%	100.0%	100.0%
Government[1]	50.7	62.5	78.5	24.9	6.8
Federal[2]	19.3	19.7	6.8	22.4	5.5
State	27.6	41.7	40.8	1.7	1.1
Local	3.8	1.1	30.9	.8	.3
Private sources	5.1	2.6	.5	10.3	12.9
Students[3]	34.1	26.3	19.3	49.8	76.3
Tuition and fees	21.0	13.1	13.0	35.4	49.9
Auxiliary enterprises[4]	13.1	13.2	6.3	14.4	26.4
Institutional[5]	10.1	8.6	1.8	15.0	3.9

1981-82

Total	100.0	100.0	100.0	100.0	100.0
Government[1]	46.2	57.6	72.8	19.9	6.7
Federal[2]	13.3	12.6	5.7	17.3	4.3
State	30.3	44.3	49.7	1.8	1.9
Local	2.7	.7	17.3	.7	.5
Private sources	4.9	3.2	.5	9.2	7.7
Students[3]	33.1	24.8	22.6	48.8	79.4
Tuition and fees	21.9	13.0	16.1	36.8	65.4
Auxiliary enterprises[4]	11.3	11.8	6.5	12.0	14.0
Institutional[5]	15.7	14.5	4.1	22.2	6.3

[1]Includes appropriations, restricted and unrestricted grants and contracts.

[2]Excludes Federal aid going directly to students, e.g., Pell grants. Includes appropriations, restricted and unrestricted grants and contracts, and independent operations such as Federally Funded Research and Development Centers (FFRDC).

[3]Includes Federal aid going to students, e.g., Pell grants.

[4]Includes revenues generated by operations that were essentially self-supporting within the institutions, such as residence halls, food services, student health services, and college unions. Nearly all such revenues are derived from students.

[5]Includes endowment income, sales and services of educational activities, sales and services of hospitals, and other sources.

Note: Details may not add to totals because of rounding.

Source: U.S. Department of Education, National Center for Education Statistics, *Financial Statistics of Institutions of Higher Education: Current Funds, Revenues and Expenditures, 1970-71, 1974;* Higher Education General Information Survey, Financial Statistics of Institutions of Higher Education for Fiscal Year 1982, unpublished tabulations (November 1983); Plisko and Stern (1985: 114, table 2.14).

virtually all the cuts in aid to college students that the Reagan administration proposed" and was "drafting legislation to keep grants, loans and work opportunities essentially intact for five years" (Friendly 1985: 15). While pressures on the federal budget arising from the current huge deficits will be reflected in further pressure on federal student aid programs, there is little likelihood of cuts so deep as to endanger the programs.

Increases in student aid at the state and institutional levels (which now comprise 22 percent of the total student aid reports from all sources) have helped to offset the drop in federal funds for student aid. At the federal level, the distribution of student aid has shifted substantially from grants to loans: in 1975-76, 75 percent of federal student aid was awarded in the form of grants, but by 1984-85 the share of grant aid had dropped to 29 percent while the share of loans had more than tripled—from 21 percent in 1975 to 66 percent (see Table 3).

Table 3

SHIFT OF FEDERAL STUDENT AID FROM
GRANTS TO LOANS, 1975-1985
(*in percent*)

Type of Aid	1975-76	1984-85
Grants	75%	29%
Loans	21	66
Work-Study	4	5

Source: Frances 1985: 5.

Many states cut their support for public colleges and universities during the recession of 1980-82, but the levels of state support tended to rise again about as fast as economic recovery and increasing revenues permitted. State tax funds for the operation of higher education (which does not include capital costs) were nearly $31 billion for 1984-85—up 19 percent over 1983-84. According to one report, "Over the last decade, [1974-84], [state] appropriations [for higher education] increased 140 percent nationwide. Adjusted for inflation, the increase was 19 percent" (Evangelauf 1985: 1ff.).

Between 1982 and 1985, federal support for research, also perceived by many as endangered by the Reagan administration, increased by 16 percent in real terms, reaching $6 billion in 1985.

Moreover, in that year nearly two-thirds of all federal academic R&D support was committed to basic research projects, compared to about one-half in 1975 (National Science Foundation 1985: 2; see also *Chronicle of Higher Education* 1986: 12).

All these figures provide encouraging evidence that higher education remains popular in the United States, and can count on continued public support in the future. A national survey done in 1984 showed that two-thirds of Americans considered the overall quality of higher education in the United States to be good or excellent, and on their list of priorities for U.S. government spending, aid to higher education was third, behind only aid for medical research and medical care for the aged (*Higher Education & National Affairs* 1984c: 12; Evangelauf 1984: 3). Another national survey in 1985 found that nearly two-thirds of the adults sampled believed it is "very important" to have a college education, up from only 36 percent in 1978 (Gallup 1985: 47). Nearly 90 percent of parents of public school children would like their oldest child to attend college, and two-thirds expected the child to do so (45).

Contributions to colleges and universities from individuals, alumni, and business and industry have been rising steadily in recent years. Total voluntary support to higher education in 1984-85 was estimated at $6.3 billion, a 13 percent increase in current dollars over 1983-84, and up from $2.2 billion in 1971-72 (*Higher Education & National Affairs* 1986: 3; 1984b: 3). These figures provide evidence that support for American higher education in the society at large is strong and growing.

INDIRECT EFFECTS OF MASS HIGHER EDUCATION

We should not place too much weight on these recent trends in enrollments and support. We know, especially from the sad example of British higher education, how rapidly these figures can change when they are built on shallow foundations. In Britain the university system has few friends anywhere—in industry, in the professions, in the trade unions, or in the political parties—and its friends in the civil service are unable to protect it against economic and political pressures from government.

But unlike in Britain, American higher education has many friends and supporters in the society and in government. And those friends and supporters are likely to be there in the future because they support an institution which serves and supports them. The absence of a strong central governing authority which controls the growth of American higher education, and the concomitant responsiveness of colleges and universities to market forces, has forced them to find ways to serve other institutions and groups in the society in their search for support. Americans have not been able to afford the luxury of high academic standards in all their degree-granting institutions. The result is a diversity of standards and functions in American colleges and universities that Europeans find very strange. So long as the governing assumption of a system of higher education is that only a minority of students can work at the required high standard, and can demonstrate that capacity in secondary school, that system is limited both in its size and in the functions it can perform for its students and for the larger society. Such a system may perform the functions of elite selection, preparation, and certification, as most European universities have done and still do, but it cannot penetrate as deeply into the life of society as American higher education has.

Some of the effects of mass higher education on American society are not widely recognized. In assessing the impact of higher education in America, we are overly influenced by the economists' conceptions of costs and benefits, which in higher education focus on rates of return to the individual graduate.

Economists refer to the large unplanned and unintended effects of higher education on society as "externalities"—that is, effects "external" to the particular causal relationships they are concerned with, or are able to develop quantitative measures for. Economists, who can be wise as well as clever, recognize that the effects of higher education which can be measured are only a small fraction of the total impact of higher education on society. But they often go on to say that it is better for them to measure carefully what can be measured, and leave to historians, sociologists, educators, and politicians the discussion of those larger effects which are often long delayed in their appearance, are more "outcomes" than intended effects, and whose sources are only partly in higher education and partly in society at large. (For an economist with views similar to these, see Bowen 1977: 359-87.)

What are some of those larger effects of mass higher education on American society?

1. Higher education has substantial effects on the attitudes of those exposed to it. A large body of research supports this assertion — and also that changes in attitudes occurring during the college years

persist throughout life (Hyman, Wright, and Reed 1975; Feldman and Newcomb 1969). Higher education broadens the perspectives of students by giving them an appreciation of other cultures and groups, making them more tolerant of cultural differences, and challenging the prejudices and stereotypes that are characteristic of uneducated people. Changed attitudes in a population in turn make possible real changes in social structures, if and when they are accompanied by changes in law and institutional behavior.

In the United States the years after World War II saw a steady decline in hostility toward black people among whites, and a growing readiness to give blacks equal treatment and fair access to education, housing, and jobs. These changes can be seen in studies of attitudes in the general population, and among students during the college years and after (Hyman and Wright 1979; Stember 1961; Stouffer 1955; Clark et al. 1972). I believe that the considerable progress in race relations in the United States since World War II has been made possible by the growth of mass higher education. If that is true, then it represents a very great contribution of higher education to the life of the society that is almost never acknowledged by economists as one of the "benefits" of American higher education.

Higher education has played a more visible role in the racial revolution by helping to expand and educate black, Hispanic, and Asian middle classes. In 1985 for the first time, the freshman class at the University of California, Berkeley, was made up of a majority (52 percent) of minority group members.

2. Other positive attitudes, values, and perceptions are engendered by the experience of higher education, quite apart from the specific intentions of college courses. For example, people who have been to college or university on the whole have longer time perspectives regarding public issues than do less well educated people. Nations and industries cannot plan or develop programs and projects without the help of people who have gained that longer time perspective, who can envisage outcomes that may lie years ahead. Helping people to acquire that perspective is very much a benefit of mass higher education.

In an increasingly complex world, the successful development and implementation of plans require that people with longer time horizons be found throughout society, and especially at the middle levels of management in both public and private enterprises. Long-range plans require continual adjustments and modifications at the levels where they are implemented; people at those levels must be able to understand the purposes of long-range programs and to implement and modify them within planning guidelines. The intelligence and initiative required for those programs to succeed are very much an outcome of mass higher education.

3. Another skill that is gained or enhanced by exposure to higher education is the capacity to learn how to learn. In a world marked by rapid social and technological change, where so much of what we learn in college or university is obsolescent in ten years and obsolete in twenty-five, it is impossible to exaggerate the importance of people who want to continue to learn after finishing formal schooling. Modern societies need all of those people that they can get, and that ability to keep learning is a product, if often a by-product, of higher education. Where facilities are provided for adult education, they are filled primarily by people who have a first degree or some postsecondary education, who already belong to the class of lifelong learners: "All the evidence shows that those who attend [adult] courses are atypical of the adult population as a whole. . . . The key determinant is the level of previous education: the higher that level, the more likely there will be participation" (OECD 1977: 27). I believe that mass higher education in the United States, and especially the generous provision of education for adults, engenders the habit of lifelong learning more widely than in most other countries.

The qualities of mind I have mentioned here—tolerance of cultural and ethnic differences, a longer time perspective, greater initiative among middle- and lower-level administrators, the desire to continue to learn—are all created or enhanced by postsecondary education. They are usually by-products of that education, but immensely important for the life and progress of any society.

4. In the political life of a nation, higher education has two distinct roles. The more familiar one is the university as a critic of the established political order, the nursery of radical and even revolutionary student movements. But less dramatically and less visibly, the democratization of access to higher education may work in the opposite direction. It may strengthen and legitimate the political and social order by demonstrating that it rewards talent and effort, and does not serve merely as the cultural apparatus of the ruling classes to ensure the preservation of power and privilege across generations.

In a time of rising expectations among all social strata, nations must provide opportunities for social mobility to able and talented people from modest origins, both for social and political reasons and for economic growth. In many countries the armed forces have provided an avenue of mobility, and have often gained the support of the poor even when other social institutions have lost it. But the military is not the best solution to the problems of maintaining political legitimacy and social order. Higher education may be a better instrument for a democracy. Where it has performed that vital function, as in the United States, it goes unrecorded on the accounting sheets of the cost/benefits analyst.

5. A potentially large benefit of American higher education is the possible effect of current efforts by American colleges and universities to come to the aid of secondary education in new ways. Many recent reports on public secondary education (e.g., NCEE 1983; Boyer 1983; Goodlad 1983) have led to the creation of hundreds of programs establishing new links between higher and secondary education. Some of these programs seek to strengthen the academic and college preparatory work of the high schools, not just provide remediation for ill-prepared students after they reach college (Trow 1985b). It may be that the task is too large, and that the structural weaknesses of American high schools will defeat all efforts to overcome their "bias against excellence" (Clark 1985: 391), but it will not be for want of trying. Some results can already be seen in individual schools, but the larger effects will be long delayed, and may be obscured by other inputs and forces.

CONCLUSIONS

In reflecting on the distinctive character of American higher education, I have looked to the past and to the present in an attempt to assess the shape of the future. It is futile to try to make specific predictions about the future of American higher education. All such predictions are proven false—usually in less than twenty years. But my review of the defining characteristics of American higher education leads me to believe that it is well-equipped to survive and to respond creatively to almost any new developments that may occur. The strength of the system lies precisely in its diversity, which allows it to respond to different needs and demands on different segments of the system. Over the past forty years enrollments have grown from about 2.3 million to over 12.4 million, and along with this enormous growth there has been further diversification and democratization of access. Since World War II the system has been able to grow by a factor of five without any fundamental change in its structure or functions, and to provide access to a broad spectrum of American society while still providing education of the highest standard for a small fraction of our youth and research at the highest standard in a broad range of scholarly and scientific disciplines.

What besides this massive growth have been the main changes in American higher education over the past forty years?

First, the federal government has become a major source of support for the system—both through its support of university-based research and through student aid—but it still supplies less than a quarter of all support. Moreover, the government's influence on the system has been muted because its support has been mediated through individual scientists and students rather than going directly to the institutions. While the federal government has become a major actor in shaping the agenda of American science, science still retains a large measure of autonomy to pursue problems and issues that arise from within rather than at the initiative of the government.

Second, the fifty states have steadily increased their support for public higher education. At the same time they have demanded greater accountability from the colleges and universities for the use of these state funds. Not long ago there was concern that these demands for accountability by public authorities were the fore-runners of a dangerous shift of authority and initiative away from the colleges and universities to the state legislatures and governors' offices (Trow 1975). Relations between public universities and state authorities vary too much for easy generalization, but my sense is that public authorities and university leaders in many states have been coming to more mutually acceptable relationships than were thought possible even ten years ago (Newman 1987). These relation-ships might well be threatened by budget cuts, however, and by the tendency to centralize in order to make the difficult decisions that cutbacks make necessary.

Third, higher education has expanded its relationships with industry in many ways. Universities have provided the ideas and pro-fessional staffs for new science-based industries, and are at the center of their physical clusterings from Boston to Silicon Valley. They also provide an organizational model and style of work for many other institutions, from consulting firms and industrial labs to legislative committees (Muir 1982). Moreover, community colleges enroll increasing numbers of students who already hold a bachelor's degree and are employed but want further training in another specialty — new patterns of continuing education and professional development.

Fourth, the democratization of access has meant a larger proportion of mature, part-time, and working students. These kinds of students have confounded earlier predictions of enrollment decline after 1979. There seems to be no limit to this development: a large segment of American higher education seems eager to provide some useful educational service to these nontraditional students. We have no reason to believe that this will be less true in the future as more and more of the labor force works in industries whose survival is predicated on rapid change, new skills, and new ways of thinking.

All of this leads me to believe that American higher education will be an even more important institution in the society in the decades to come — as a supplier of more advanced skills, a vehicle for greater social equality, a source of continuing social commentary and criticism, and the transmitter of an ever-broadening cultural heritage. Higher education is today, I believe, the key institution in American society, the source of many of its most important ideas, values, skills, and energies. I strongly suspect that will be increasingly true as far ahead as anyone can see.

REFERENCES

Andersen, Charles J., comp. 1968. *A Fact Book on Higher Education*, no. 1. Washington, D.C.: American Council on Education.

Ashby, Eric. 1967. "Ivory Towers in Tomorrow's World." *Journal of Higher Education*, November.

Bowen, Howard R. 1977. *Investment in Learning: The Individual and Social Value of American Higher Education*. San Francisco: Jossey-Bass.

Boyer, Ernest. 1983. *High School: A Report on Secondary Education in America*. New York: Harper & Row.

Chronicle of Higher Education. 1986a. "Higher Education Funds in President Reagan s Fiscal 1987 Budget." February 12.

_____. 1986b. "Fact-File Fall 1985 Enrollment." October 15.

Clark, Burton R. 1983. *The Higher Education System*. Los Angeles: University of California Press.

_____. 1985. "The High School and the University: What Went Wrong in America, Part I." *Phi Delta Kappan* 66, 6 (February): 391-97.

Clark, Burton R.; Heist, Paul; McConnell, T. R.; Trow, Martin, A.; and Yonge, George E. 1972. *Students and Colleges: Interaction and Change.* Berkeley: Center for Research and Development in Higher Education, University of California.

The College Board. 1986. *Trends in Student Aid: 1980 to 1986.* Washington, D.C.: Washington Office of the College Board.

Eurich, Nell P. 1985. *Corporate Classrooms: The Learning Business.* Princeton, N.J.: Carnegie Foundation for the Advancement of Teaching.

Evangelauf, Jean. 1984. "Poll Finds 63 Percent Want More Aid for Colleges." *Chronicle of Higher Education*, October 24.

_____. 1985. "States' Spending on Colleges Rises 19 Percent in 2 Years, Nears $31-Billion for '85-86." *Chronicle of Higher Education*, October 30.

Feldman, Kenneth A., and Newcomb, Theodore M. 1969. *The Impact of College on Students.* 2 vols. San Francisco: Jossey-Bass.

Frances, Carol. 1984. "1985: The Economic Outlook for Higher Education." *AAHE Bulletin*, December.

_____. 1985. "1986: Major Trends Shaping the Outlook for Higher Education." *AAHE Bulletin*, December.

Friendly, Jonathan. 1985. "Budget Ax Fails to Make Dent in Aid Programs for Students." *New York Times*, 24 September.

Gallup, Alec M. 1985. "The 17th Annual Gallup Poll of the Public's Attitudes Toward the Public Schools." *Phi Delta Kappan* 67, 1 (September): 35-47.

Glenny, Lyman A. 1983. "Higher Education for Students: Forecasts of a Golden Age." Paper delivered at a seminar sponsored by the Higher Education Steering Committee, University of California, Berkeley, July.

Goodlad, John I. 1983. *A Place Called School: Prospects for the Future.* New York: McGraw-Hill.

Hartz, Louis. 1955. *The Liberal Tradition in America: An Interpretation of American Political Thought Since the Revolution.* New York: Harcourt Brace.

Higher Education & National Affairs. 1984a. "Statistics You Can Use: "Growth in Nontraditional Students, 1972 to 1982." June 18.

_____. 1984b. "Statistics You Can Use: Voluntary Support to Higher Education." September 24.

_____. 1984c. "Americans Support More Federal Aid for Higher Education." November 5.

_____. 1986. "Higher Education Is a U.S. Industry." July 28.

Hofstadter, Richard. 1963. *Anti-Intellectualism in American Life.* New York: Alfred A. Knopf.

Hofstadter, Richard, and Metzger, Walter P. 1955. *The Development of Academic Freedom in the United States.* New York: Columbia University Press.

Hofstadter, Richard, and Smith, Wilson, eds. 1961. *American Higher Education: A Documentary History*, vol. 1. Chicago: University of Chicago Press.

Hyman, Herbert H., and Wright, Charles R. 1979. *Education's Lasting Influence on Values*. Chicago and London: University of Chicago Press.

Hyman, Herbert H.; Wright, Charles R.; and Reed, John Shelton. 1975. *The Enduring Effects of Education*. Chicago and London: University of Chicago Press.

Kerr, Clark. 1980. "The Carnegie Policy Series, 1967-1979: Consensus, Approaches, Reconsiderations, Results." In *The Carnegie Council on Policy Studies in Higher Education*. San Francisco: Jossey-Bass.

McConnell, William R., and Kaufman, Norman. 1984. *High School Graduates: Projections for the Fifty States (1982-2000)*. Boulder, CO: Western Interstate Commission for Higher Education. January.

Muir, William K. 1982. *Legislature: California's School for Politics*. Chicago: University of Chicago Press.

National Science Foundation. 1985. *Science Resources Studies Highlights*. May 9.

NCEE [National Commission on Excellence in Education]. 1983. *A Nation at Risk: The Imperative for Educational Reform*. Washington, D.C.: U.S. Department of Education.

Newman, Frank. 1987. *Choosing Quality: Reducing Conflict between the State and the University*. Denver: Education Commission of the States.

OECD. 1977. *Learning Opportunities for Adults*. Vol. 1: *General Report*. Paris: Organization for Economic Co-operation and Development.

Ottinger, Cecilia A., comp. 1984. *1984-85 Fact Book*. New York: American Council on Education and Macmillan Publishing Company.

PACE Project. 1984. *Conditions of Education in California, 1984*. No. 84-1. Berkeley: School of Education, University of California.

Plisko, Valena White, and Stern, Joyce D., eds. 1985. *The Condition of Education, 1985 Edition*. Washington, D.C.: National Center for Education Statistics.

Riesman, David. 1954. "Football in America: A Study in Cultural Diffusion." In *Individualism Reconsidered*. Glencoe, Ill.: The Free Press.

Rudolph, Frederick. 1962. *The American College and University*. New York: Alfred A. Knopf.

Stember, Charles H. 1961. *Education and Attitude Change*. New York: Institute of Human Relations Press.

Stouffer, Samuel A. 1955. *Communism, Conformity and Civil Liberties*. Garden City, N.Y.: Doubleday.

Trow, Martin A. 1975. "The Public and Private Lives of Higher Education." *Daedalus* 2 (Winter): 113-27.

_____. 1979. "Aspects of Diversity in American Higher Education." In *On The Making of Americans: Essays in Honor of David Riesman*, ed. Herbert Gans, pp. 271-90. Philadelphia: University of Pennsylvania Press.

_____. 1985a. "Comparative Reflections on Leadership in Higher Education." *European Journal of Education* 20, 2-3: 143-59.

_____. 1985b. "Underprepared Students and Public Research Universities." In *Challenge to American Schools*, ed. John H. Bunzel, pp. 191-215. New York and Oxford: Oxford University Press.

_____. 1986. "The State of Higher Education in the United States." In *Educational Policies in Crisis: Japanese and American Perspectives*, eds. William K. Cummings et al., pp. 171-94. New York: Praeger Publishers.

Tsukada, Mamoru. 1986. "A Factual Overview of Education in Japan and the United States." In *Educational Policies in Crisis: Japanese and American Perspectives*, eds. William K. Cummings et al., pp. 96-116. New York: Praeger Publishers.

Williams, Gareth. 1983. "Making Sense of Statistics." *Times Higher Education Supplement.* November 18.

THE DELIVERY OF

HEALTH CARE

THE ORGANIZATION AND PERFORMANCE OF THE CONTEMPORARY SOVIET HEALTH SERVICE

Christopher M. Davis

The medical system in the USSR merits careful study by Western scholars and policymakers for several reasons. First, it represents one of the major alternative models of organization: a national health service in a socialist society. Socialized medicine is thought by many to offer advantages over the mixed system of private and public medical care in the United States. Analysis of the oldest and largest socialist health system facilitates the evaluation of this premise and the determination of the relevance to the United States of Soviet experience in medical organization, finance, planning, and management.

The Soviet health service is also of interest because it is the social institution which serves people in their most vulnerable state — illness. Study of its organizational principles, resources, and distributional characteristics, especially with respect to infants, the disabled, and the elderly, can provide insights into the overall welfare orientation of Soviet society.

Another reason is that preventive and curative medical services have a significant influence on important indicators of social well-being such as morbidity, disability, and mortality rates. Statistics concerning the levels and trends of these indicators can be used to evaluate the success of Soviet social policy in both a domestic and international context.

Fourth, the Soviet health service is a major sector of the national economy in the USSR. In 1987 the health labor force comprised about 7 million persons, or 6 percent of the national total. In that

The author would like to thank the following organizations for their support of his research on the economics of the Soviet health sector in the period 1973–87: Clare College and the Faculty of Economics and Politics, Cambridge University; International Research and Exchange Board; Centre for Russian and East European Studies, University of Birmingham; Kennan Institute for Advanced Russian Studies; National Council for Soviet and East European Research; and Wharton Econometric Forecasting Associates.

year 5 percent of the state budget was spent on health, total health expenditure amounted to 4 percent of national income, and there were over 3 billion outpatient visits and 70 million patient hospitalizations. It is desirable to assess the performance of a social service which operates on so large a scale.

Although the focus of this chapter is on the Soviet medical system, it is recognized that developments in the health of a nation are influenced by numerous institutions as well as a variety of demographic, political, economic, medical and sociological factors. Thus in the next section a definition will be provided of the Soviet health sector, which is made up of all the institutions in the economy involved in preventing or curing illness.* A simple model of the Soviet health production process will then be presented to describe in a general manner how these institutions interact to generate health outcomes.

The empirical sections of the chapter will examine three of the health sector institutions as well as trends in health output indicators. First, an evaluation will be made of recent changes in health conditions, consumer behavior, and illness patterns to determine whether the tasks confronting the health service have become more complex over the past two decades. Second, the medical system itself will be described and analyzed. Although a comprehensive assessment of medical care provision cannot be carried out in this chapter an effort will be made to provide answers to a number of important questions:

Is there equality in the distribution of medical services across population groups defined by age, illness, socioeconomic status, and region of residence?

Are the supplies of labor, commodities, and finance to the medical system adequate to enable it to provide high-quality medical care to all patients?

Does the medical system make efficient use of allocated resources?

In the following section an assessment will be made of the effectiveness of the medical system in reducing morbidity, invalidity, and mortality. This will be done by identifying the likely objectives of the system and then evaluating trends in related health output indicators.

---

*The terms *health service, health system, medical system,* and *medical service* are used interchangeably to refer to the institution which directly provides preventive and curative medical services. "Health sector" is a broader concept and refers to the set of institutions that participate in health production.

The concluding section will examine the publicly expressed concerns and reform policies of the central health bureaucracy. It will show that its evolving health-promotion strategy includes a wide range of measures that affect all components of the health production process, reflecting a growing recognition that the state medical system plays only a limited role in determining developments in the health of the Soviet population.*

PRODUCTION OF HEALTH IN THE USSR

The health of the population in the USSR is determined by a complex interaction of demographic, environmental, social, political, medical and economic factors. To understand and analyze the process that generates changes in health outcomes, however, it is useful to employ models which both simplify reality and focus attention on key variables and relationships. In this chapter, the model presented is derived from an economic approach to the study of health production in the Soviet Union.

THE HEALTH SECTOR PRODUCTION PROCESS

The health sector in the Soviet economy can be defined by identifying its primary output, the population's health, and then assigning to the branch all the institutions closely involved in its production. On this basis the seven main institutions of the health sector are the consumers (households), medical system, pharmacy system, medical industry, biomedical research and development (R&D), medical foreign trade organizations, and the central health bureaucracy. The activities of these institutions include production of health by households, production of medical services and pharmaceuticals, distribution of medical commodities, and administration. Each of these institutions generates measurable outputs and uses

*While most of the ideas and material presented in this chapter are the products of the research efforts of the author, it should be noted that numerous Western scholars have made substantial contributions to the study of the contemporary Soviet health service. Among these are Mark Field (1967), Gordon Hyde (1974), Michael Kaser (1976), Michael Ryan (1978), Willian Knaus (1982), and Murray Feshbach (1983, 1986). Their works should be consulted to obtain information about the many aspects of the health system in the USSR not covered here. In addition there are informative Soviet books on the topic, such as Zhuk (1968), Vinogradov (1974), Popov (1976b), Golovteev, Korchagin, and Shilenko (1978), and Malov and Churakov (1983).

inputs of labor, capital, and intermediate goods. They function in a coordinated manner as components of the Soviet health sector production process, which is diagrammed in Figure 1.*

CONSUMERS

The institution with primary responsibility for the production of health is the consumer, or the household (Davis 1981). Consumers possess a "stock" of health which is determined primarily by demographic characteristics such as age and sex but also is affected by genetic factors and past experiences. In any given time household members consume goods and services, an activity which has both positive and negative effects on health. On the one hand, improvements in nutrition or educational standards and increased participation in physical exercise are beneficial. On the other hand, a poor diet which results in obesity or vitamin deficiency and excessive consumption of alcohol or tobacco undermine health. The health environment has a number of dimensions: residential, family, technological, natural, and microbiological. Its characteristics are strongly influenced by the policies of the state bureaucracy. As with consumption, changes in the environment can be either good or bad for health. Improvements in housing, family stability, or the work environment are beneficial, whereas increases in industrial pollution or the emergence of a new influenza virus can have adverse effects.

Preventive medical services can help to offset some of the negative influences of consumption and the environment. For example, health education can have a positive impact on consumption habits, as the anti-smoking campaign in the United States has shown. The same is true of public hygiene and anti-pollution and safety programs. Despite such preventive services, the population will suffer illness. The national illness pattern generates a need for curative medical services, but for a variety of reasons patients will demand medical treatment for only a fraction of the total number of cases of illness.

It is important to recognize that the production of health (or illness) by households is primarily the result of decisions by individual citizens and is only indirectly affected by actions of the government.

*More detailed analyses of the health production process are presented in Davis (1979, 1981, 1983a, 1986a, and 1987). Here attention is focused on the illness pattern, the medical system, and final health output. The Soviet pharmacy network, medical industry, biomedical R&D, and foreign trade organizations are analyzed in Davis (1984, 1985, 1986a, and 1987).

Figure 1. THE HEALTH PRODUCTION PROCESS IN THE USSR

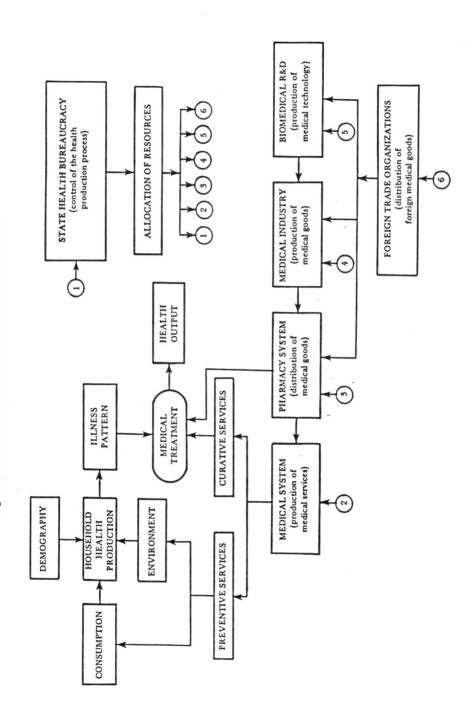

As a result, this is the component of the Soviet health production process least amenable to control by the state bureaucracy. Judging from recent U.S. experience, however, some of the greatest improvements in health output indicators are generated by more rational, health-maximizing behavior of individuals.

THE MEDICAL SYSTEM

The Soviet medical system plays a vital role in the health production process. Its primary responsibilities are to provide medical services to the population to prevent or cure illness and reduce mortality. The output of the system can be affected by changes in health policy, resource allocations, or production efficiency. In the USSR most preventive and curative medical facilities operate under the control of the Ministry of Health.

THE PHARMACY SYSTEM

In the Soviet Union medicines and medical equipment are distributed by the pharmacy system (Davis 1984, 1987; Gorenkov 1984). It purchases these commodities from the domestic medical industry and foreign trade organizations and sells them to medical facilities and consumers. In consequence, the performance of the pharmacy system exerts an important influence on both the provision of medical services and the import of goods from abroad.

The organization of pharmacies in the USSR is similar to that of the medical system. The national Ministry of Health controls most pharmacies, but several other ministries possess some pharmaceutical facilities. For example, the Ministry of Railroads manages over 1,000 pharmacies, 1,500 pharmaceutical points, and several pharmaceutical warehouses. Within the national Ministry of Health primary responsibility for planning and management of the pharmacy system is given to the Main Pharmaceutical Administration (Glavnoe Aptechnoe Upravlenie).

From 1970 to 1985 the number of pharmacies in the USSR increased from 22,900 to 29,150 and the number of pharmacists rose from 167,800 to 271,300 (Davis 1987). The total sales turnover within the pharmacy system increased from 1.9 billion rubles in 1970 to an estimated 4.4 billion rubles in 1985. Of this, wholesale transactions with the medical system accounted for 2.0 billion rubles (45 percent) and retail sales to the public 2.4 billion rubles (55 percent).

THE MEDICAL INDUSTRY

The Soviet medical industry is made up of the factories and farms that produce the medical goods which flow through the pharmacies to the medical system (Davis 1984, 1987; Shevchenko 1974). Many of the problems in medical service production in the USSR are caused by quantitative or qualitative inadequacies of inputs, which in turn are the result of deficiencies in the output of medical commodities. An analysis of the Soviet pharmaceutical and medical equipment industry is therefore vital to an understanding of the health production process.

Medical commodities are produced in several hundred factories and farms that are subordinate to over twenty different ministries (Davis 1987). For example, the Ministry of Health manages over 100 enterprises that make simple pharmaceuticals, bacterial and viral preparations, and eyeglasses. However, the dominant production organization for all medical commodities has been the Ministry of Medical and Microbiological Industry. In the early 1980s its 215 units produced over 6,500 different commodities per year, which accounted for 90 percent of the domestic output of medicines and 70 percent of medical equipment.

The Eleventh Five-Year Plan (1981–85) target for medical industry output growth was 44 percent, or 7.5 percent per annum. Production actually increased by 40 percent during the plan period, or by 7 percent annually. Although this was a relatively good performance, the plan in aggregate was underfulfilled. Reports make it clear that in the period up to 1987 the Soviet medical industry was unable to fully satisfy national demand for medical goods or to produce many of the sophisticated medicines available in the West.

BIOMEDICAL RESEARCH AND DEVELOPMENT

The technical sophistication and quality of the products of the Soviet medical industry are heavily dependent upon the effectiveness of the supporting work by the biomedical research and development sector. This is made up of a variety of medical, pharmaceutical, and engineering institutions which are involved in the four phases of the R&D cycle: fundamental research, applied research, development, and innovation. In the USSR these institutions and activities are managed by a number of different academic bodies and ministries (Davis 1985, 1986a, 1987). Three organizations are most important. The national

Academy of Sciences is the leading authority in fundamental research and has institutes working in the areas of biochemistry, biophysics, biology, and physiology. The national Ministry of Health has primary responsibility for biomedical research and controls a number of important research institutions. The third important organization is the Ministry of Medical and Microbiological Industry. In 1985 it controlled over forty scientific research and design bureaus which were responsible for applied biomedical and pharmacological research and prototype production.

During the Eleventh Five-Year Plan the biomedical R&D establishment fulfilled many of its targets, such as the number of investigations conducted and number of inventions. This work contributed to innovation in the medical industry, which introduced 170 new products during the plan period. On the other hand, numerous criticisms have been published during the past several years of the failings of the biomedical R&D system. In one recent authoritative article, high-ranking officials of the Ministry of Health attacked the inefficient and ineffective work of scientists and called for more discipline, greater productivity, and better results in the Twelfth Five-Year Plan period ("Rezervy nauki" 1985).

MEDICAL FOREIGN TRADE ORGANIZATIONS

The foreign trade sector is another important component of the health production process (Davis 1985, 1986a, 1987). Up to 1986 the foreign trade organizations (FTOs) of the Ministry of Foreign Trade imported commodities and sold them to the pharmacy system, medical industry, and biomedical R&D network (see below for a discussion of recent foreign trade reforms). The FTOs also purchased goods from Soviet producers and exported them. This trade was planned by the Health and Medical Industry Department of Gosplan (the State Planning Committee) in conjunction with the Ministry of Health and the Ministry of Medical and Microbiological Industry. The FTO with primary responsibility for implementing plans for imports and exports of pharmaceuticals was Medexport. Other bodies important to foreign trade in medical products were the State Committee for Science and Technology and the FTOs Litsenzintorg, Soyuzkhimexport, Tekhmashimport, and Teknopromimport.

From 1975 to 1980 Soviet pharmaceutical imports rose from 289.7 to 542.7 million rubles. They then increased by 36 percent in 1981, perhaps in response to growing concern by the leadership about the health situation. During the Eleventh Five-Year Plan period imports doubled to 1,160.9 million rubles (Davis 1987). As a result of this rapid growth, the share of pharmaceuticals in total Soviet imports went up from 1.1 percent in 1975 to 1.7 percent in 1985. This suggests that the priority attached to medical goods has risen in recent years. The Soviet Union sells only small amounts of pharmaceuticals abroad. In 1975 exports totaled 65.5 million rubles, or 23 percent of the import value in that year. Over the next decade exports grew slowly, reaching 104.8 million rubles in 1985, and their share of total exports fell to 0.1 percent.

CENTRAL HEALTH BUREAUCRACY

The central state health bureaucracy includes the various agencies above ministerial level that make resource allocation decisions, develop plans and budgets, and manage programs of the five state-controlled production and trade institutions of the health sector. As noted above, the bureaucracy has limited influence on household health production. It provides wages and benefits to households and determines consumption opportunities and environmental conditions, but it cannot force households to engage in health-maximizing behavior.

The top decisionmaking body of the central bureaucracy is the Politburo of the CPSU. It determines national objectives in all areas, decides on sectoral priorities, establishes performance targets for the state-controlled health institutions and ministries, allocates resources to major health programs, and promulgates general decrees on health matters. The Politburo's policymaking and resource-allocation decisions are assisted by inputs from party and state bodies. The CPSU Central Committee Secretariat is one source of information and advice. Its Non-productive Services Sector plays the leading role in the health field.

In the government under the Council of Ministers, numerous central bodies assist in health planning, budgeting, and management. Among those that have special health-related administrations or departments are Gosplan, the Ministry of Finance, the State Committee for Material and Technical Supply (Gossnab), the State Committee for Science and Technology, and the State Committee for Labor and Social Problems.

One other central organization with responsibilities in the health area is the Supreme Soviet. This national-level parliamentary body is divided into the Council of the Union and the Council of Nationalities. Both have Health and Social Security Commissions which review any health legislation.

HEALTH SECTOR OUTPUT

The primary objective of the Soviet health production process is to improve the various health-related output indicators. (Among the indicators which could be used are mortality, invalidity, recuperation time, and work-days lost from illness.) Figure 1 shows that these outputs are a function of both the illness pattern and medical service provision. It therefore is appropriate to evaluate health output after examining the performance of the various health sector institutions.

Measurement of health output is challenging even when one is dealing with individual cases. Even if a patient's progress is carefully monitored, it is difficult to determine causality. Not all credit or blame for individual outcomes should be automatically attributed to the medical treatment because there could be variability in the health stock of patients suffering from identical illnesses. It is even more difficult to measure the population's health status or effectiveness of a medical system at a national level. The necessary linked statistical records rarely exist. Even when data are available, they usually are not evaluated or published. As a result, the analysis must rely on simple indicators such as invalidity and mortality rates or life expectancy.

Below an empirical assessment is made of recent developments of Soviet mortality-related output indicators. This reveals a certain amount about the performance of the health production process in the USSR. However, given the uncertainties in measurements mentioned above, any conclusions about the role of the health service in determining outputs must be viewed as tentative.

HEALTH CONDITIONS, CONSUMER BEHAVIOR, AND
ILLNESS PATTERNS IN THE USSR

In order to evaluate the adequacy of medical care in the USSR, it first is necessary to assess the levels and trends in illness-determined needs and expressed demands for medical services. Figure 1 indicates that these are a function of household health production, which is carried out under the influence of demographic, consumption, and environmental factors. There are, in fact, many variables within each of these categories. The major ones are shown in Figure 2, which is a more detailed representation of the household component of the health production process. In this section an attempt will be made to review developments during 1965-85 in health conditions, consumer behavior, and the illness pattern in the Soviet Union.

HEALTH CONDITIONS AND CONSUMER BEHAVIOR

The demographic situation has changed significantly in the USSR in the period 1965-85 (*Narodnoe khozyaistvo SSSR v 1965 g. . . . 1985 g.*). The size of the Soviet population increased from 230 to 276 million, but its annual rate of growth fell from 1.3 percent to 0.9 percent. The age distribution altered markedly because of the decline in the birth rate. The share of young people fell and that of the elderly (over 60 years) rose from 9 to over 13 percent. It should be noted that many of the elderly in the USSR have lived through periods of considerable deprivation and stress. The sex distribution has shifted as well, with the share of males rising from 45 to 47 percent.

In recent years there have been positive consumption developments in the USSR. The index of real per capita income rose by 59 percent from 1970 to 1984, facilitating an 89 percent increase in retail sales over the same period (*ibid.*). The diet of the population also improved. The following advances were achieved from 1960 to 1984 in per capita food consumption (in kilograms): meat—from 39.5 to 60.4; vegetables—from 70 to 103; fruit—from 22 to 45. Educational standards went up considerably: the number per 10,000 population with higher and middle education increased from 483 to 686. This presumably facilitated more rational decisionmaking in the area of personal health.

On the other hand, there were several unfavorable trends in consumption. Adult per capita consumption of alcohol rose from 7.0 liters of absolute alcohol equivalent in 1965 to 12.3 liters in 1980 (Treml 1982b). Retail sales of tobacco products went up from 1,909 million rubles in 1965 to 6,547 million rubles in 1984. This suggests a continuing spread of the smoking habit. Despite the progress mentioned above, nutritional problems remain. The adult diet continues to have high shares of sugar, salt, fat, and carbohydrates. This has contributed to a substantial increase in the dietary cholesterol intake. According to one Western study, it rose by 26

Figure 2. DETERMINANTS OF POPULATION HEALTH STATUS

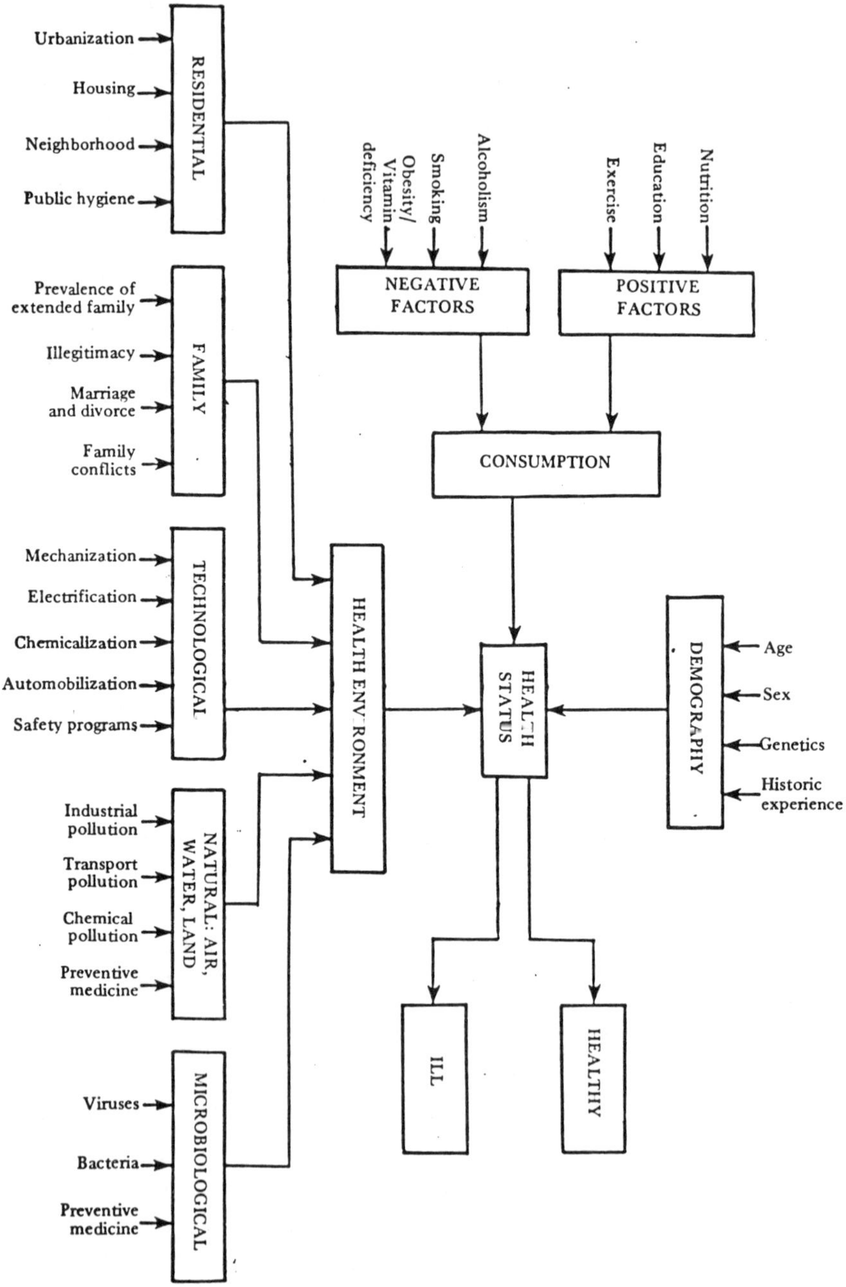

percent from the mid-1960s to mid-1970s (Cooper and Schatzkin 1982). Furthermore, there are inadequacies in the nutritional composition of available artificial milk and baby food.

Another shortcoming is in the supply of vitamins. A December 1985 *Izvestiya* article claims that the average citizen suffers from a 30-40 percent vitamin deficit ("Chto mozhet vitamin" 1985). Shortages are reported of vitamins A, B_1, niacin, C, and D. In population surveys it has been determined that levels of ascorbic acid are 2-3 times lower than norms and consumption deficits exist in the range of 50-75 percent for vitamin C and 20-70 percent for vitamin A. In response to this situation, the authorities have established, under the joint supervision of Gosplan and the State Committee for Science and Technology, a Scientific-Technical Program for the Creation of Production of Vitaminized Food Products.

The relationship between the environment and health in the USSR is an important but complex one. In the residential environment, there have been positive developments in housing. Although housing supply is still insufficient, the amount of urban residential space grew from 1,542 to 2,492 million cubic meters from 1970 to 1984. However, many of the new flats are in high-rise buildings located in underdeveloped districts on city outskirts, which are often deficient in supporting services such as schools, shops, public transportation, telephone exchanges, and creches. Furthermore, sanitation in public buildings is often substandard. Other negative environmental phenomena are the breakup of the extended family, excessively rapid mechanization and chemicalization of industry, increases in road traffic without adequate safety programs, and increased air and water pollution. For example, the April 1986 accident at the Chernobyl nuclear reactor released large amounts of radioactivity into the atmosphere which resulted in an increased threat to the health of a segment of the population.

Changes in the microbiological environment also have exerted an influence on health conditions. In recent years "antigenic shifts" in the influenza virus have contributed to the recurrence of epidemics of this disease (Davis and Feshbach 1980). The hepatitis virus appears to have become more virulent as well. There evidently has been some deterioration in the bacterial environment, largely due to hygienic problems. This has increased the risk of diseases such as typhoid fever, salmonellosis, and septicemia.

Preventive medical services can ameliorate the influences of negative consumption and environmental factors. The Soviet Union claims that its medical system has a preventive orientation, and the Ministry of Health contains a large sanitary-epidemiological organization which has programs in the areas of sanitation, epidemiology, disinfection, safety, pollution control, and health education. Despite these programs, serious problems exist in the prevention area. One reason is that preventive medicine has low prestige and receives inadequate funding. Another is that the sanitary-epidemiological service has little power relative to other economic and political institutions. The literature abounds with stories of factories which operate in unhealthy or unsafe conditions despite attempts of medical personnel to stop production in order to carry out remedial measures. A third reason is that vaccination programs are hampered by the initial poor quality of vaccines, inadequate transportation and storage facilities for serum, and chronic respiratory illnesses among children which make it difficult to administer hepatitis and other vaccines (Feshbach 1986). As a result of these deficiencies, the preventive medical services have been unable to fully offset demographic, consumption, and environmental developments which have adverse effects on the population's health status.

THE ILLNESS PATTERN

The study of the Soviet illness pattern is of considerable importance because it determines the underlying need for medical care. Research in this area is made difficult by the paucity of published data. The Soviet Union regularly publishes incidence and rate statistics for only a small set of selected infectious diseases. Nevertheless, there is sufficient material available about illness at regional and local levels for the analyst to obtain a good picture of the morbidity situation.

In order to evaluate trends in Soviet morbidity it is useful to divide illnesses into the following categories:

Degenerative disease—e.g., heart disease, cancer, and cirrhosis;

Accidents—e.g., fractures and poisonings;

Nutritional disease—e.g., rickets, scurvy, and obesity;

Infectious diseases—e.g., dysentery, typhoid, and influenza.

As a general rule, one would expect that as a nation becomes more urban and industrialized, living standards will improve and there will be a shift in its illness pattern. Usually this involves decreases in nutritional and infectious diseases and an increase in degenerative illness. In the Soviet case, however, available evidence suggests that due to its unbalanced development policy, especially its neglect of consumption, it has been unable to make the normal illness pattern transition and as a result has some of the features of both developed and underdeveloped countries.

One of the main categories of degenerative disease is cardiovascular. Published mortality information indicates that the death rate from all cardiovascular illness (per 100,000) rose from 247 in 1960 to 459 in 1975 to 535 in 1983 (Davis 1977; Feshbach 1986). Of the major types of cardiovascular disease, artherosclerotic cardiosclerosis exhibited the most dramatic rise. The 1975 rate was 2.5 times greater than that in 1960. Other data show that male heart disease mortality rates were about 30 percent higher than those for women and increased more rapidly. The evidence makes it clear that during the past twenty years the Soviet Union has experienced a coronary illness epidemic of growing severity (Cooper 1981).

Similar upward trends can be detected in cancer statistics. Death rates from malignant tumors rose from 115.5 per 100,000 in 1960 to 134.6 in 1973 (Davis 1977). Cancer of the digestive tract is the primary cause of death in this disease category, but its rate has fallen. On the other hand, mortality rates of cancers of the respiratory tract rose from 15.5 to 25.1 per 100,000 from 1960 to 1975, or by 62 percent. Male cancer mortality increasingly exceeds that of females. For example, in 1971–72 there were 51.7 deaths per 100,000 men from cancer of the respiratory tract versus only 6.9 for women. The trends and differentials probably are the result of variations between sexes in the consumption of tobacco.

From fragmentary evidence in the Soviet press, the accident and injury rate appears to be rising, primarily because of the interaction of high alcohol consumption and the growing complexity of the technological environment.

These trends in degenerative illness and accidents could be expected in a rapidly industrializing country. But other aspects of the disease pattern are more unusual. For example, Treml (1982a) has calculated that in the 1970s the number of deaths per year from alcohol-related poisonings was 60,000. The current anti-alcohol campaign undoubtedly is forcing many alcoholics into a desperate search for substitutes, which could lead to even more poisonings.

Another striking feature of the illness pattern is the prevalence of nutritional disease. The vitamin deficiencies discussed above undermine adults' work capacity, lower resistance to infections, and slow down illness recovery rates. Inadequate nutrition is reported to prevent many new mothers from breast-feeding properly. The effects of this are compounded by the insufficient nutritional content of artificial milk and baby food. In consequence, many infants in the USSR suffer from hypotrophy, rickets, and alimentary anemia (Davis and Feshbach 1980). One Soviet study in the 1970s found that 14 percent of all infant illness consisted of primary or secondary rickets, and a 1977 article reported that in a sample of 974 infants suffering from pneumonia, the rickets incidence rate was 474 per 1,000.

The Soviet population suffers from a very high incidence of respiratory illness (Davis and Feshbach 1980; Feshbach 1986). Influenza epidemics are routine occurrences and are virtually uncontrollable. The number of registered cases per year rose from 16 million in the 1970s to 30 million in the early 1980s. This illness is particularly dangerous for the very young and the elderly. If not treated promptly, influenza in infants leads to pneumonia. This, in turn, is the leading cause of infant death in the USSR. According to one survey, from 1968 to 1975 the influenza rate in the sample of infants up to three years of age was 636 per 1,000 and the pneumonia rate was 72 per 100 (Feshbach 1986). Respiratory illnesses not only directly cause death, but also interfere with vaccination programs and thereby raise the risk of other childhood diseases. According to Feshbach (1986), in 1984 primarily as a result of this factor 30–50 percent of children in the RSFSR did not receive diphtheria vaccinations.

Infectious diseases are unusually widespread in the USSR. Table 1 shows officially published rates for seven diseases. It indicates that by 1984 the rates of six were lower than in 1970, but that in five cases the rates were higher than previously attained minimum levels. Furthermore, Feshbach has shown that Soviet disease incidence levels are substantially above those in the United States, which is another large, multi-ethnic country:*

Typhoid and paratyphoid: The number of cases rose from 16,900 in 1980 to 18,900 in 1984. In contrast, the United States had 300 cases in 1984.

Diphtheria: Incidence went up from 200 in 1975 to 1,600 in 1984. The United States reported 5 cases in 1983 and 1 in 1984.

*Most of the information in this section is from Feshbach (1983, 1986). Statistics for U.S. disease incidence are from United States (1985).

Table 1

INFECTIOUS DISEASES IN THE USSR, 1970-84

Disease	Year						
	1970	1975	1980	1981	1982	1983	1984
Number of Cases (Thousands)							
Typhoid and paratyphoid	22.5	26.0	16.9	17.1	17.2	18.6	18.9
Scarlet fever	469.9	361.1	230.1	226.8	324.7	293.1	261.7
Diphtheria	1.1	0.2	0.4	0.6	0.9	1.4	1.6
Whooping cough	39.5	14.9	13.9	25.6	27.5	19.3	26.0
Tetanus	0.7	0.5	0.3	0.4	0.4	0.4	0.3
Poliomyelitis	0.3	0.1	0.2	0.3	0.3	0.2	0.1
Measles	471.5	363.8	355.7	342.8	466.2	233.8	252.5
Rates per 100,000							
Typhoid and paratyphoid	9	10	6	7	6	6	7
Scarlet fever	194	142	87	85	120	108	95
Diphtheria	0.5	0.1	0.1	0.2	0.3	0.5	0.6
Whooping cough	16	6	5	10	10	7	9
Tetanus	0.3	0.2	0.1	0.1	0.1	0.1	0.1
Poliomyelitis	0.11	0.05	0.06	0.11	0.10	0.07	0.04
Measles	194	143	134	128	173	86	92

Source: Narodnoe khozyaistvo SSSR v 1984g.

Whooping cough: Declined to a low of 13,900 cases in 1980 but climbed up to 26,000 in 1984. The U.S. incidence declined from 2,200 cases in 1977 to 1,200 in 1981 but rose to 1,900 in 1982.

Measles: The number of cases fell to 342,800 in 1981, then soared to 466,200 in 1982. In 1983 it dropped substantially but went up to 252,500 in 1984. The U.S. record shows a decline from 13,500 cases in 1980 to 1,400 in 1983.

Feshbach also has detected unfavorable trends in several infectious diseases not reported in the statistical yearbook of the USSR:

Mumps: Incidence rose from 621,400 in 1966 to an esimated 1,300,000 in 1982.

Hepatitis: Incidence went up from 339,100 in 1969 to 702,200 in 1975 to 1,400,000 in 1981-82. The United States reported 65,000 cases in 1984.

Sepsis of the newborn: According to one survey, this afflicted 0.9 percent of the newborn in the 1960s but 4.7 percent in the early 1970s.

Salmonellosis: Incidence increased twelve-fold from 1961 to 1977 due to growing problems in food hygiene. A similar, if less pronounced, trend could be observed in the United States, where the number of cases went up from 22,100 in 1970 to 40,900 in 1982.

The comparison of infectious disease incidence in the Soviet Union and the United States can be criticized on the grounds that the countries are at different stages of development. Some might say that it would be more appropriate to contrast the current Soviet record with that of the United States in an earlier period—e.g., the 1940s. On the other hand, the contemporary Soviet Union has a large medical system, medical science has advanced to the extent that infectious diseases are controllable, and vaccines or medicines are widely available in the world market. The poor Soviet record in infectious disease control therefore is more reflective of government policy than the level of development.

One final topic of relevance to the disease pattern is the scale of unreported illness in the USSR. In conjunction with the 1959, 1970, and 1979 censuses, the Soviet authorities have carried out large-scale surveys of the so-called "morbidity iceberg" (Davis 1979). The part of the iceberg above the "waterline" is reported illness, and the submerged component is unreported disease requiring treatment. The general finding is that in urban areas about two thirds of illness is reported and one third unreported. In rural areas, the ratios are reversed. This is shown in Table 2, which contrasts surveys of the city of Tselinograd and the rural region of Tambov. It shows that the share of unreported illness varies considerably by disease category. For example, inhabitants in Tambov failed to report only 12 percent of skin diseases but 88 percent of nervous illnesses.

In sum, it appears that during the past two decades there have been important developments in the Soviet disease pattern. The overall incidence of infectious diseases has remained high by international standards, but the rates of several diseases have been reduced. However, the rapid mechanization of Soviet society and growing consumption of alcohol have resulted in more accidents and poisonings. The most significant change has been the increase in degenerative diseases caused by the aging of the population, urbanization, stress, smoking, and pollution. These trends in illness have made the tasks confronting the Soviet health service more complicated and challenging.

Table 2

URBAN AND RURAL MORBIDITY ICEBERGS IN THE USSR: TSELINOGRAD AND TAMBOV REGION, 1969–71

(Cases of illness per 1,000 population)

WHO Classification of Illness (8th revision)	Tselinograd			Tambov Region		
	Reported Illness	Hidden Illness	Total Illness	Reported Illness	Hidden Illness	Total Illness
1. Infectious and parasitic illness	67.8	13.0	80.8	23.9	74.4	98.3
2. Tumors	9.9	9.7	19.6	4.5	16.6	21.1
3. Illness of endocrine system, nutritional disorder, and metabolic disturbance	12.0	9.0	20.9	5.1	28.6	33.7
4. Illness of blood and hematopoietic organs	3.3	3.0	6.3	2.1	8.0	10.1
5. Psychiatric disturbance	29.3	18.2	47.5	10.6	47.0	57.6
6. Illness of nervous system and sensory organs	134.3	78.9	213.2	37.2	264.5	301.7
7. Illness of circulatory system	84.3	41.4	125.8	33.9	179.1	213.0
8. Illness of respiratory organs	381.9	68.6	450.5	74.5	76.5	151.0
9. Illness of digestive organs	57.7	22.4	80.2	31.7	99.0	130.7
10. Illness of genitourinary organs	48.2	45.8	93.9	17.1	48.1	65.2
11. Pregnancy and birth complications	3.3	1.7	4.9	1.3	n.a.	1.3
12. Illness of skin and subcutaneous fat	54.6	14.1	68.8	26.2	3.6	29.8
13. Illness of osteomuscular system and connective tissue	65.3	17.5	82.8	25.1	47.6	72.7
14. Birth anomalies	5.7	4.9	10.6	0.6	6.7	7.3
15. Various reasons of perinatal illness and death	0.7	0.4	1.1	n.a.	n.a.	n.a.
16. Symptoms and unclearly diagnosed conditions	3.7	0.9	4.6	1.6	1.1	2.7
17. Accidents, poisonings, and trauma	78.0	6.5	84.5	25.5	28.6	54.1
Total	1040.0	356.1	1396.1	320.9	929.4	1250.3

Sources: For Tselinograd—Popov (1976a); for Tambov—Romazonovich and Golkova (1973).

ORGANIZATION AND PERFORMANCE OF THE
SOVIET HEALTH SERVICE

The ability of the medical system to provide preventive and curative services is influenced by numerous factors. Among them are: health principles and legislation; the organization of medical care; planning and budgeting; trends in the inputs, finance and outputs of the health service; the distribution of medical services; and problems of quality and efficiency. The objective of this section is to make an empirical assessment of the recent performance of the health service through an analysis of these factors.

HEALTH SERVICE PRINCIPLES AND LEGISLATION

Over the past seventy years there have been considerable modifications of Soviet health service principles, priorities, legislation, and organization in response to changing circumstances.* Although it is relatively easy to document changes in the last three categories, an assessment of Soviet principles is more challenging because in any given period there are alternative formulations, or at least varying interpretations of meaning. A further complication is in determining whether the principles represent only official propaganda claims or actually influence the behavior of decision-makers.

One authoritative formulation (Lisitsyn 1972) puts forward the following six principles of health organization and strategy in the USSR: the state, socialist character of the health service; provision of free-of-charge, widely available, and qualified medical care; the unified and planned character of the health service; the preventive orientation of the medical system; the unity of medical science and practice; and popular participation in health service activities.

Whatever the actual principles are, the health service operates in a complex legislative and administrative environment determined by the constitution, laws, Communist Party decrees and resolutions, and ministerial orders. Until recently the Soviet Union functioned, at least in theory, in accordance with the Constitution of 1936. In October 1977 the Supreme Soviet adopted a new constitution.

---

*Numerous Western and Soviet authors have discussed health principles and legislation so no attempt is made to reproduce basic information. See Field (1967), Hyde (1974), Vinogradov (1974), Kaser (1976), Safonov and Loginova (1976), Serenko et al. (1976), Ryan (1978), and Knaus (1982).

Article 42 states that "Citizens of the USSR have the right to health protection" and that provision of necessary services will be in accordance with principles similar to those outlined above. A more detailed legal description of citizens' rights to medical care can be found in the law on the Principles of Legislation of the USSR and Union Republics on the Health Service, which was passed by the Supreme Soviet in December 1969 (Ryan 1978). As Kaser (1976) has correctly observed, it was not until the enactment of this law that the Soviet health system became truly comprehensive.

The health service receives general guidance from the party and government. The program of the CPSU, most recently revised in 1985, expresses the party's long-term development strategy ("Programma" 1985). At the party congresses which take place every five years, the health situation is briefly discussed and exhortations are made to further improve medical care. The Twenty-Seventh Party Congress in 1986 conformed to this pattern ("Central Committee's Political Report" 1986). When problems in any sector become serious and significant changes are required, joint party and government decrees are issued. Three such decreees have been concerned with health since the mid-1960s: "On measures for the further improvement of the health service and development of medical science in the nation" (1968); "On measures for the further improvement of the national health service" (1977); and "On additional measures for the improvement of the population's health protection" (1982) (*Zabota partii* 1980) (Tsentral'nyy Komitet 1982).

On the basis of these general directives, the national Ministry of Health develops detailed plans, orders, and instructions for its subordinate units. Five-year and annual plans are constructed taking into account the current health service strategy, targets, and norms/standards. Approved plans become legally binding for the ministry and its subordinate units. Numerous ministerial orders (*prikazy*) govern activities throughout the health system. In 1985, 4,720 orders were issued ("Utverzhdat delom" 1986). In addition, the Ministry of Health, like any bureaucracy, generates vast quantities of detailed instructions, manuals, methodological letters, and regulations.

THE ORGANIZATION OF MEDICAL CARE

The Soviet medical system is made up of thousands of personnel and institutions which fulfill four different but complementary functions (Davis 1979). The two most obvious are to provide preventive and curative medical services. A third function is education of medical personnel. Fourth, the medical system acts as a sickness validation agency for social security and other organizations.

In theory, the Soviet Union has a unified medical system planned and managed by the Ministry of Health. In reality, several subsystems provide medical care of differing quality to a variety of population groups (Davis 1979). The structure of the health service is shown in Figure 3. There are six types of legal subsystems of medical care, five of which are administratively subordinate to the Ministry of Health: elite, capital city, industrial, provincial city, and rural. The departmental subsystem is controlled by other ministries or organizations.

Soviet medical facilities in the departmental system serve people affiliated with the controlling organization and are closed to the public. Among those which have polyclinics for their members are the Ministries of Foreign Trade, Finance, Higher and Intermediate Education, Foreign Affairs, the Aviation Industry, and the Academy of Sciences. The Ministry of Defense maintains its own complete system of medical care, which is administered by the Central Military Medical Directorate. The Committee of State Security (KGB) and the police (MVD) have their own medical systems as well. The Ministry of Railroads has an extensive network of at least sixteen hospitals which is run by its Main Medical-Sanitary Administration. The Ministry of Merchant Marine has a special system of clinics and hospitals for its sailors, as do the Ministries of Inland Waterways, Transport, and Civil Aviation. The level of medical care in the departmental subsystem is on average higher than that in the public sector because the economic and political importance of the controlling organizations ensures better access to available resources.

The majority of medical establishments are administered by the national Ministry of Health and the fifteen republican ministries.* Although this public system is unified in the sense that it is subordinate to one ministry, a number of distinct subsystems coexist which serve different population groups with varying standards of medical care.

The Ministry of Health is managed by a minister and a collegium made up of about twenty senior officials. The detailed planning and management of the medical system is left to the subordinate

*The organization of the Ministry of Health medical system is described in detail in Field (1967), Hyde (1974), Lisitsyn (1972), Ryan (1978), Safonov and Loginova (1976), Serenko et al. (1976), and Vinogradov (1974).

Figure 3. THE ORGANIZATION OF THE SOVIET MEDICAL SYSTEM

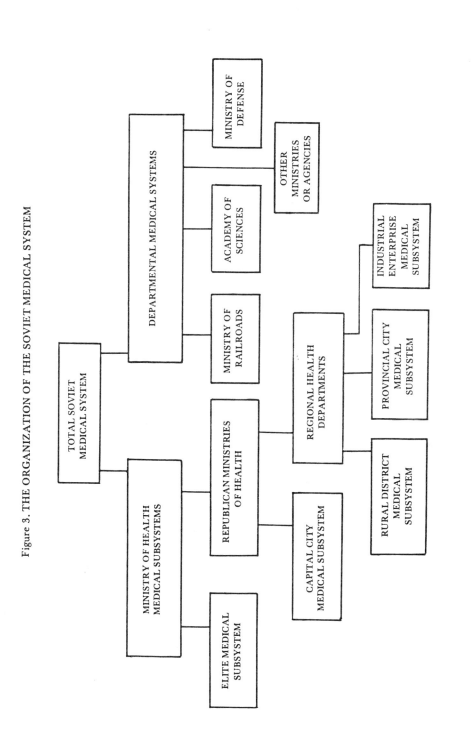

republican ministries, while the national ministry concentrates on: policy formulation; foreign liaison; plan and budget methodology; monitoring of medical, research, and educational services; and the procurement of pharmaceutical products and medical equipment.

The Ministry of Health also directly controls and finances a number of outside institutions. One of the most important is the Academy of Medical Sciences, which has a scientific staff of five thousand. The academy is divided into three departments: clinical medicine; hygiene, microbiology, and epidemiology; and medical and biological sciences. These departments are responsible for coordinating and monitoring research in the academy's twenty-nine research institutes and ten laboratories and in other medical institutions throughout the USSR. Other institutes under the Ministry of Health include the All-Union Semashko Institute of Social Hygiene and the Organization of Health Services. Finally, the ministry finances several advisory bodies, among which the most important is the Scientific Medical Council, a consultative body which reviews and assesses advances in medical research.

As noted, there are five systems of curative-preventive medical care subordinate to the national Ministry of Health. The easiest of these to define is the one which serves the Soviet party/government elite and their families. This nationwide subsystem is administered by a branch of the Ministry of Health called the Fourth Main Administration. Each of the republican ministries administers elite medical facilities located in its territory. From published Soviet sources, twelve hospitals, eight polyclinics, one laboratory, one research institute, and fifteen sanitoria of the Fourth Main Administration can be identified (Davis 1979). Available evidence suggests that the elite medical facilities are well supplied with modern Soviet and foreign medicine and equipment and staffed by the best medical personnel in the USSR. As a result of the generous allocation of resources to these facilities, the quality of its medical care is reported to be relatively high.

Most Soviet citizens receive their medical care in one of the other four subsystems. The best of these, the capital city system, is directly subordinate to the republican ministries, whereas the others are administered by regional health departments.

Capital city health systems are found in large urban areas such as Moscow, Leningrad, Tallin, and Kiev. They are managed by the main administration of public health in the city soviet. Although the capital city system has problems, it provides the best public

medical care in the USSR: services are free, institutions are specialized, the quality of the staff is relatively high, modern equipment
and medicines are available, and the urban transportation network
facilitates home care and emergency aid.

The industrial subsystem is comprised of paramedic (*feldsher*)
posts, doctor posts, and medical sanitary centers that are attached
to particular economic enterprises and provide medical care to
workers and their families. Industrial medical facilities are constructed and equipped by the individual enterprise profit funds,
but current costs are covered by the Ministry of Health. Medical
care in these establishments is better than that in provincial city or
rural subsystems because of more generous staffing and support,
access to additional factory resources, and the closed nature of the
service.

The provincial city subsystem is in medium-sized cities which
are subordinate to regional authorities but are not regional capitals.
It is likely to have adequate numbers of hospital beds, doctors, and
other basic medical inputs. However, a number of weaknesses exist.
First, medical facilities and personnel are not as specialized as those
in capital cities. Second, the quality of personnel is lower because
of the tendency of professionals to move toward political centers
as they ascend the medical hierarchy. Third, resource constraints
are tighter and supplies of all kinds are more erratic.

The majority of the Soviet population are served by the rural
health subsystem in rural districts containing subordinate villages,
small cities, and worker settlements. Rural inhabitants who live in
collective or state farms outside cities are treated first in small clinics or
hospitals (containing 3–4 beds) on the farm. Rural district city inhabitants obtain medical care at the district polyclinic/hospital. Patients
in the countryside are referred to the district hospital for more
specialized services (weather permitting).

Rural Soviet medical care is still years behind that in the cities.
One problem is the shortage of medical personnel in rural districts.
A second is that the low priority given to the countryside in the past has
meant that roads, public sanitation, and the supply system are poorly
developed. Shortages of all commodities are endemic. Furthermore, there are few sources of supplemental funding due to the
absence of industrial enterprises. Although farms make contributions
to support village medical facilities, these are modest in scale due to
the unprofitable nature of most agricultural activities. The rural
district has few effective channels of appeal because of its low

status in the power hierarchy and geographical isolation. As a consequence, the rural population in the USSR receives medical care which on the whole would be considered inadequate by prevailing Western standards.

HEALTH SERVICE PLANNING AND BUDGETING

Because the Soviet medical system operates within the centrally planned economic system, its activities and performance are determined by state plans and budgets rather than by market forces. This does not mean that the system as a whole, or an individual medical facility, operates in a mechanical and perfectly anticipated manner. In reality, results are often different from objectives because of unexpected developments in health conditions or illness patterns, planners' errors, substandard performance of medical institutions, or shortages of inputs (Ellman 1973).

The national Ministry of Health has the primary responsibility for preparation and implementation of plans for the medical system. The Planning-Finance Main Administration of the ministry provides subordinate units with methodological assistance and information about plan objectives. This work is coordinated with the Health and Medical Industry Department of Gosplan. Each of the fifteen republican ministries of health also has a planning-finance administration which has responsibility for health planning in the republic. Under the ministry are regional, city, and rural district health department planning sections.

As a rule, Soviet health planning is more concerned with the quantitative development of inputs, such as doctors and hospital beds, than with health outputs, the quality of medical services, or the efficiency of production.* In theory, planning begins at the local level with demographic projections and estimation of requirements for hospital bed-days or outpatient visits by medical specialty. These requirements are compared with existing facilities and personnel and the likely availability of resources. This leads to the selection of key plan targets. Norms and standards are then used to calculate requirements for other physical and labor inputs. The plans of local facilities are aggregated by district, region, and republic to determine the national health plan. Typically the plans call for modest, steady growth of inputs and medical service outputs.

*Among the good Soviet books on health planning and finance are Zhuk (1968), Popov (1974, 1976b), Babanovskii (1976), Golovteev and Shilenko (1977), Kant and Golovteev (1979), and Malov and Churakov (1983).

Health budgets are financial reflections of the physical targets, and their main function is to finance planned programs and activities. The budgets are prepared by planning-finance departments of Ministry of Health institutions under the supervision of the Ministry of Finance. The budget is broken down into fourteen expenditure "'articles" such as wages, administrative expenses, food, medicines, and capital investment. Budget estimates are made for each category using financial norms to convert physical plan indicators into monetary terms (Kant and Golovteev 1979). For example, polyclinics estimate their annual budget for medicines by multiplying the planned number of outpatient visits by an expenditure norm (until recently, it was four kopeks per visit). Hospitals use a financial norm linked to planned patient bed-days.

INPUTS TO THE MEDICAL SYSTEM

Medical services in the USSR are provided using combinations of capital, labor, and intermediate goods such as pharmaceuticals. The traditional Soviet strategy has been to employ cheap labor, simple facilities, and modest material inputs to generate large quantities of inexpensive services. In this section an assessment is made of recent trends in the inputs of facilities, equipment, medicines, and personnel.

Table 3 shows that the number of hospitals fell from 26,200 to 23,300 from 1970 to 1985, largely as a result of a decision to close down small, outmoded facilities and introduce larger, modern ones. Reflecting this policy, the average size of a Soviet hospital rose from 101 beds in 1970 to 155 in 1985. The number of outpatient clinics dropped from a peak of 38,900 in 1968 to a low of 35,600 in 1978 but rose to 39,100 in 1985. Furthermore, the share of modern facilities increased over time.

The most obvious piece of medical equipment in the health service is the hospital bed, an indicator used by the Soviets in planning the hospital system and assessing its performance. Table 3 shows that the number of beds increased from 2,663,000 in 1970 to 3,607,700 in 1985, or by 35 percent. The number of beds per 10,000 population went up from 109.4 to 129.6 over the same period. Caution should be observed in interpreting this trend, however. Hospital bed provision is a valid proxy indicator of the equipment input if a constant relationship between beds and other machines and instruments exists. In the unstable Soviet supply environment, this condition probably does not hold. Another point to keep in

Table 3

SOVIET MEDICAL SYSTEM RESOURCES AND OUTPUTS, 1970–85

Indicator	Year				1985 as Percent of 1970
	1970	1975	1980	1985	
Facilities and Personnel					
Hospitals (thousands)	26.2	24.3	23.1	23.3	89%
Outpatient clinics (thousands)	37.4	35.6	36.1	39.1	105
Hospital beds (thousands)	2,663.3	3,009.2	3,324.2	3,607.7	135
Hospital beds (per 10,000 population)	109.4	117.9	124.9	129.6	118
Doctors (thousands)	668.4	834.1	997.1	1,170.4	175
Doctors (per 10,000 population)	27.4	32.6	37.5	42.0	153
Middle-level medical personnel (thousands)	2,123.0	2,515.1	2,814.3	3,158.9	149
Expenditures					
State health budget (billion rubles)	9.2	11.4	14.7	17.5	190
Health share of total state budget (percent)	6.0	5.3	5.0	4.6	77
Non-budget sources (billion rubles)	2.5	3.1	4.1	4.9	196
Total expenditures (billion rubles)	11.7	14.5	18.8	22.4	191
Health expenditure per capita (rubles)	48	57	71	81	169
Health expenditure share of national income (percent)	4.1	4.0	4.1	3.9	95
Outputs					
Outpatient visits plus doctor home visits (millions)	1,938.4	2,296.9	2,750.5	3,168.4	163
Outpatient visits per capita	8.0	9.0	10.4	11.4	143
Preventive screenings (millions)	101.3	106.9	112.5	123.2	122
Hospital bed-days (millions)	828.3	962.9	1,063.7	1,162.1	140
Hospital bed-days (per capita)	3.4	3.8	4.0	4.2	124
Hospitalizations (millions)	52.2	57.3	62.7	69.6	133
Hospitalizations (per 100 population)	21.5	22.7	23.7	25.1	117

Sources: Narodnoe khozyiastvo SSSR v 1980 g. . . . 1985 g.

mind is that the pace of expansion in the bed stock has slackened as a result of both lower plan targets and construction bottlenecks. From 1975 to 1980, 315,000 hospital beds were added, at a growth rate of 2.1 percent per year. In contrast, the increment to the stock between 1980 and 1985 was 283,500, which represents an addition of 1.7 percent per year.

The bulk of the domestic supply of medical equipment comes from thirty-five enterprises of the medical industry which produce over 4,000 different pieces of equipment (Davis 1984, 1987). It is estimated that the value of their medical equipment output rose from 220 million rubles in 1970 to 645 million rubles in 1985. Other branches of Soviet industry produced an additional 263 million rubles worth of medical equipment in 1985. The Soviet Union also imports equipment and instruments (Davis 1984, 1985). About 20 percent of republican health budget capital spending is for the procurement or repair of equipment. Republican-level spending on noncapital equipment and instruments, which absorbs roughly 3 percent of the budget, rose from 193 million rubles in 1970 to 587 million rubles in 1985 (Davis 1985; Ministerstvo Finansov SSSR 1987).

Medicine and other medical supplies (bandages, vitamins, sutures) are purchased from the pharmacy system using state budget funds. From 1970 to 1985 republican-level budget expenditures on medicines rose from 733 to 1,508 million rubles. Pharmacy sales of all products to the health service increased from 892 million rubles in 1970 to 1,973 in 1985. The pharmacies in turn purchased these goods from either domestic industries and farms or foreign trade organizations. The value of Sovict imports of pharmaceuticals went up from 166 to 1,161 million foreign trade rubles from 1970 to 1985 (Davis 1985, 1987).

The health service requires numerous inputs of a non-medical nature — e.g. fuel for buildings, water, budget and planning forms, food for patients, automobiles, telephones, and academic journals. Total republican-level health budget expenditure on these commodities increased from 1,627 million rubles in 1970 to 3,207 in 1985.

As noted, the Soviet medical system in 1985 employed about 7 million people, or about 6 percent of the total labor force. The most important category of employee is doctors. Their number rose from 668,400 in 1970 to 1,170,400 in 1985 — a 75 percent increment. The indicator of doctors per 10,000 population climbed by 53 percent, from 27.4 in 1970 to 42.0 in 1985, one of the highest ratios in the world. However, Soviet doctors are less well trained than their Western counterparts and are poorly paid (Knaus 1982). The number of middle-level medical personnel (e.g., nurses) went up from 2,123,000 in 1970 to 3,158,900 in 1985. Their growth rate was lower than that of doctors, a disparity that has been evident for some time. As a result, the ratio of middle-level medical personnel per doctor fell from 3.2 in 1970 to 2.7 in 1985.

In sum, it appears that most inputs to the Soviet medical system increased substantially between 1970 and 1985. However, these basic statistics do not describe trends in the quality of inputs or the efficiency of their use. Also, the different categories of inputs have grown at varying rates. It is unclear whether this has been intentional or a by-product of poor planning and erratic supplies.

EXPENDITURES ON THE HEALTH SERVICE

There are five major sources of finance for the Soviet medical system: the state budget, economic ministries, individual industrial enterprises, social organizations, and the population. Of these, the Ministry of Health budget is most important: it accounts for 75–80 percent of the national total. There are additional budget expenditures from program areas such as "administration" and "science" or from budget-financed organizations such as the Ministry of Defense. Various economic ministries, such as the Ministry of Railroads, pay for their departmental medical systems out of their profits. At a lower level of the economic hierarchy, individual factories and collective farms contribute funds for capital investment and operational support of medical facilities which serve their workers and families. Social organizations such as trade unions pay for various preventive and curative medical services for their members. Finally, the Soviet population pays directly for a small number of medical services, such as abortions.

Table 3 presents official statistics about health spending in the USSR. State health budget expenditures rose from 9.2 billion rubles in 1970 to 17.5 in 1985. Although this represents a substantial increase, growth has been slowing. In 1975–80 health spending went up by 29 percent, or about 6 percent per annum. The equivalent annual increment in 1980–85 was under 4 percent. The table suggests that the relative importance of health in the state budget has declined, since its share of the total dropped from 6.5 percent in 1965 to 4.6 percent in 1985. Since 1970 the contributions from other sources have risen by 96 percent, from 2.5 to 4.9 billion rubles. As a result, total health spending went up from 11.7 billion rubles in 1970 to 22.4 billion rubles in 1985.*

The scale of and trends in Soviet health spending can be put into context by comparing them with appropriate indicators in the United States. At the official Soviet exchange rate of 1 ruble = $1.23, Soviet expenditure in 1983 was $25.7 billion. Total U.S. health spending in that year was $355.4 billion (United States 1985). Even if we take into account input price differentials and exchange rate problems, this disparity is large. From 1965 to 1983 Soviet spending rose 2.8 times in current rubles. Over the same period U.S. total health spending in current dollars went up from $41.9 billion to $355.4 billion, or by a factor of 8.5. There was, however, a more significant element of inflation in the U.S. figures than in the Soviet ones: the U.S. medical price index rose from 100 in 1967 to 357 in 1983. Thus U.S. health spending in constant 1967 dollars rose from $41.9 to $99.6 billion, or by a factor of only 2.4.

In the USSR medical expenditures per capita increased from 34 rubles ($43) in 1965 to 77 rubles ($93) in 1983. Over the same period, the American indicator went up from $207 to $1,459 in current dollars—or to $425 in constant dollars. In the USSR medical expenditure as a share of net material product (NMP) utilized fell from 4.1 to 3.9 percent from 1965 to 1983. An authoritative Western reconstruction of Soviet national income in GNP terms shows this share declining from 2.7 percent in 1965 to 2.4 percent in 1980 (U.S. Congress 1982). In contrast, the health share of GNP in the United States rose markedly from 6.1 percent in 1965 to 10.8 percent in 1983.

The analysis of Soviet health finance statistics reveals that in either a domestic or international context the medical system in the USSR has low priority and is subject to tight resource constraints (Davis 1987, forthcoming). This is evident in the low wages of medical staff and stingy financial norms governing capital investment and purchase of intermediate goods such as medicines. These constraints contribute to widespread shortages in the medical system and to the inferior quality of services provided.

*The total health expenditure shown in Table 3 probably understates the actual sum spent by about 5 percent because contributions from the population and various nonhealth state budgets are not included.

OUTPUT OF MEDICAL SERVICES

The Soviet medical system has responded to the demands of the growing population and of the evolving illness pattern by producing an increasing quantity of outpatient and hospital services. Trends in several aggregate indicators are shown in Table 3. From 1970 to 1985 the number of outpatient visits to doctors and doctors' home visits increased by 68 percent, from 1.9 to 3.2 billion. On a per capita basis this represents a rise from 8.0 to 11.4 visits per year. During the same period the number of patients receiving screenings for diseases went up from 101 to 123 million, or by 22 percent.

The hospital output indicators improved at a relatively more modest rate. The number of hospital bed-days provided increased from 828 million in 1970 to 1,162 million in 1985, or from 3.4 to 4.2 days per capita. Over the same period, the number of patient admissions to hospitals rose from 52.2 to 69.6 million and the number of hospitalizations per 100 population increased from 21.5 to 25.1.

Although trends in these output indicators are uniformly favorable, it is important when evaluating them to appreciate several problems with the output statistics. First, the indicators in Table 3 do not provide information about the quantities of specific services provided during a visit to a doctor or a hospital bed-day. Second, available indicators do not measure all the outputs of the health system, which has multiple functions. As noted, it provides not only preventive and curative services, but also engages in social insurance validation, scientific research, medical education, and administration. Third, little evidence is available about variations in the quality of medical services over time, regions, or subsystems. This information is important because a tightening of resource constraints can provoke the standard Soviet response of lowering quality of output in order to achieve quantity targets.

DISTRIBUTION OF MEDICAL SERVICES

In this section an attempt is made to assess the important and complex issue of the degree of inequality in the distribution of medical care in the Soviet Union.* It is important in doing so to distinguish

*In considering the issue of inequality in the USSR, it should be noted that since the early 1930s the Soviet regime has supported in theory and practice a differentiated approach to the distribution of wages, income, and social services (Davis

between the distribution of medical service outputs, such as poly-clinic visits and hospitalizations, and inputs, such as doctors and hospital beds. Furthermore, the standard measurements of distribu-tional inequality by geographic zone (republic, region, urban-rural) or population age group should be supplemented by an evaluation of the distribution of the population by the subsystems of medical care noted above. Accordingly, trends in the distribution of basic medical inputs across republics will be examined first. Then an estimate will be made of the numbers receiving medical care in the six subsystems. Finally, the effects of second economy activity on medical care distribution will be discussed.

Table 4 summarizes developments in the distribution of three basic medical input indicators across the fifteen republics from 1970 to 1985. The average number of doctors per 10,000 population in the USSR as a whole rose from 27.4 to 42.0. The indicator for Tadzhikistan was consistently the lowest, increasing from 15.9 to

Table 4

REPUBLICAN DIFFERENTIALS IN THE DISTRIBUTION OF
MEDICAL INPUTS: 1970, 1975, 1980, AND 1985

Input Indicator	Year	All USSR	Republican Minimum		Republican Maximum		Maximum as Percent of Minimum
			Number	Republic	Number	Republic	
Doctors	1970	27.4	15.9	Tadzhikistan	36.4	Georgia	229
per 10,000	1975	32.6	20.6	Tadzhikistan	41.4	Georgia	201
population	1980	37.5	23.5	Tadzhikistan	48.1	Georgia	200
	1985	42.0	26.6	Tadzhikistan	54.2	Georgia	204
Middle-level	1970	87.2	51.4	Tadzhikistan	93.8	Estonia	182
medical	1975	98.4	60.8	Tadzhikistan	105.2	RSFSR	173
personnel	1980	105.7	65.0	Tadzhikistan	115.9	Latvia	178
per 10,000	1985	113.5	71.7	Tadzhikistan	126.2	Latvia	176
population							
Hospital	1970	109.4	85.6	Armenia	118.9	Latvia	139
beds per	1975	117.7	85.4	Armenia	127.6	Latvia	149
10,000	1980	124.9	83.4	Armenia	136.8	Latvia	164
population	1985	129.6	83.5	Armenia	140.0	Latvia	168

Sources: Narodnoe khozyaistvo SSSR v 1980 g.: 496–99 and *v 1985 g.*: 540–44.

1983b). It is believed that under socialism inequalities are necessary in order to provide material incentives to workers. Distribution according to need will be appropriate only in the future, under full communism. See McAuley (1979).

26.6, and for Georgia it was consistently the highest, going up from 36.4 to 54.2. The maximum provision as a percentage of the minimum declined significantly from 1970 to 1980, but then went up slightly. The number of middle-level medical personnel per 10,000 in the USSR increased from 87.2 in 1970 to 113.5 in 1985. Tadzhikistan again had the lowest provisions. The ratio of maximum to minimum dropped from 1970 to 1975 but then increased; by 1985 the indicator in Latvia was 176 percent of that in Tadzhikistan. The indicator for hospital beds per 10,000 population in the USSR rose uninterruptedly from 109.4 in 1970 to 129.6 in 1985. However, the indicator for Armenia declined from 85.6 in 1970 to 83.5 in 1985. Latvia was the consistent republican leader. The ratio of the Latvian to the Armenian indicator grew from 139 in 1970 to 168 in 1985.

In sum, Table 4 indicates that significant inequalities existed between republics in basic medical inputs. Further research would be needed, however, to determine whether these differences were justifiable in light of variations in age distributions, health conditions, and illness patterns. In any event, it appears that there was a general improvement in provision levels during 1970–85, but that progress in reducing republican inequalities ceased after 1975.

One cannot evaluate inequality in the USSR by measuring only republican or regional discrepancies because not everyone within these territories has equal access to medical care. Furthermore, straight urban-rural comparisons understate differences because small cities and workers' settlements are in fact integrated into rural district subsystems of medical care. It is therefore necessary to calculate the distribution of the population across the six medical subsystems.

An estimate has been made of this distribution for 1975 (Davis 1979). The 1 January 1975 population of 253.3 million was divided into urban and rural. In 1975, 100.2 million people lived in 3,097 rural districts, and 153.1 million lived in 2,013 cities and 3,739 worker settlements. However, 1,138 cities and virtually all worker settlements are subordinate to rural district authorities. On the assumption that district-subordinate cities are the smallest ones, the population in the 1,138 cities was estimated at 15.8 million. There were 21.3 million inhabitants in the worker settlements. This indicates that 137.3 million people lived in rural districts and 116.0 million in cities subordinate to regional or republican authorities.

Capital cities are defined as those with a population of over 250,000. This category includes all republican capitals and most capitals of regions. In 1975, 63.9 million people lived in these cities. The remainder of the urban population, 52.1 million, lived in provincial cities (with populations of 27,000-250,000).

It is estimated that departmental medical subsystems serve 5 percent of the population (12.7 million) and the industrial subsystem another 8 percent (20.2 million). One can assume that these facilities are distributed proportionately to urban populations: rural districts — 24 percent; provincial cities — 34 percent; and capital cities — 42 percent. Thus appropriate deductions should be made from the three territorial subsystems. Finally, it is assumed that the elite medical subsystem serves the upper level of the *nomenklatura* and their families — about one million people. Virtually all of them live in capital cities, so another deduction should be made.

Table 5 shows the results of these rough calculations. It indicates that in 1975 about 25 percent of the Soviet population had access to medical care of a relatively high standard in elite, departmental, and capital-city facilities. Another 24 percent obtained decent services in industrial or provincial city subsystems. However, it appears that 51 percent were served by the relatively low-quality rural medical subsystem.

The influence of the second economy should also be considered when assessing the distribution of medical services in the USSR

Table 5

DISTRIBUTION OF SOVIET POPULATION AMONG SIX SUBSYSTEMS OF MEDICAL CARE IN 1975

Medical Subsystem	Number of Population (*Millions*)	Percent of Total
Elite	1.0	0.4%
Departmental	12.7	5.0
Capital city	49.1	19.4
Industrial	20.2	8.0
Provincial city	40.9	16.1
Rural district	129.4	51.1
Total	253.3	100.0

Sources: Population statistics from *Narodnoe khozyaistvo SSSR v 1975 g.* Assumptions and methodology are described in text and Davis (1979).

(Knaus 1982; Feshbach 1983). In the Soviet Union private medical practice is legal, although subject to severe constraints, and some fee-for-service outpatient clinics exist in the largest cities. However, most private activity in the medical sector is illegal in nature. Doctors, nurses, and other staff supplement their low wages by accepting side payments which are made to secure rapid admission for patients to better public hospitals, treatment by top specialists, improved dental work, medicines in short supply, discreet treatment of socially embarrassing medical conditions, and more considerate care in hospital wards.

The second economy undoubtedly affects the distribution of medical care. For example, it is widely recognized that highly remunerative private practice flourishes in Georgia. Table 4 shows that Georgia also happens to be the republic with the highest level of doctor provision. One could conclude that the high real wages of the medical profession there are partially responsible for the greater than average doctor supply indicators. Nonetheless, intensity of private practice probably varies considerably among regions and urban-rural areas. Furthermore, the second economy is more influential in distributing scarce services within a subsystem than in redistributing the population among subsystems. It is unlikely that even a substantial side payment would enable a member of the public to obtain medical care in a closed subsystem (elite, departmental, industrial) in the absence of official entitlement to access. On the other hand, it might be possible to arrange a move from a medium city to a capital city public medical facility. Given these restrictions, the second economy probably has only a small influence on the distribution shown in Table 5.

QUALITY AND EFFICIENCY PROBLEMS IN THE HEALTH SERVICE

To fully evaluate the Soviet health service one should examine not only the quantities of outputs and inputs, but also financial constraints, shortages of inputs, efficiency in resource utilization, and the quality of medical care. These issues are assessed in this section for the period 1965-85.

Tight financial constraints on the health system were evident in three areas (Davis 1983a). First, prices of many inputs were set at such low levels that they adversely affected decisions about production or supply. For example, in 1965 the medical system average wage was only 82 percent of that for the whole national economy.

Over the next twenty years, growth of medical wages did not keep up with the general trend. By 1984 they were only 71 percent of the national average.* These low wages affected the quality of entrants to medical and nursing schools and, in a situation of growing labor shortages, made it difficult to retain middle-level medical personnel. Furthermore, wage increases were not linked to performance, so there were few incentives for higher productivity and innovation.

Second, the financial norms which governed capital construction and repair were unrealistically low, making it difficult for the Ministry of Health to complete buildings on time and to maintain them subsequently. Third, there were miserly budget norms governing the purchase of pharmaceutical goods and medical equipment. Although they hampered the production of high-quality medical services, these constraints were necessary in order to maintain a balance between health system demand and the limited supplies available from pharmacies.

The financial constraints, in combination with the general supply problems of the Soviet Union's shortage economy, led to pervasive deficits of all types of health inputs. There is ample evidence that shortages existed of labor (total, by specialty, and by region), building space, machinery, equipment, instruments, medicine, and even basic commodities such as bed linens (Davis 1983a, 1987). One result of these shortages was bottlenecks in the production of medical services. For example, the limited availability of modern diagnostic machinery generated higher rates of patient referrals to hospitals by polyclinics. Once in hospitals, patients waited several days before the overburdened diagnostic departments could see them.

The quality of Soviet medical care was adversely affected by the financial constraints, shortages, and bottlenecks. One problem area was the doctor-patient relationship. Most sources suggest that because of large caseloads, lack of incentives, and authoritarian Soviet traditions, doctors did not provide their patients with adequate information or psychological support. Another problem area was equipment-related inadequacies in diagnosis. Deficient supplies of medicines and equipment constrained the effectiveness of treatment of disease. The risk of infection while undergoing treatment probably

---

*In 1965 the average monthly wage in the whole economy was 96.5 rubles, and in the health, physical culture, and social security sector it was 79 rubles. By 1984 the respective figures had risen to 184.8 and 131.4 rubles (*Narodnoe khozyaistvo SSSR v 1984 g.*: 417–18).

was higher in the USSR than in the West because of low hygiene standards in medical facilities and the absence of "throw-away" medical technology such as disposable syringes, paper bedding, and plastic products (Knaus 1982).

TRENDS IN SOVIET HEALTH OUTPUT INDICATORS

The primary objective of the Soviet health production process is to improve the various indicators of final output, such as recovery, invalidity, and mortality rates. Figure 1 shows that this output is a function of both the illness pattern and medical service provision. Since trends in these areas have been analyzed, it now is appropriate to evaluate developments in measures of health output. In this section, attention will be focused on mortality rates.

It can be assumed that Soviet political leaders and planners have the following implicit or explicit output targets for the four major mortality indicators:

(1) *Age-specific death rates* should decline or remain stable.
(2) The *infant mortality rate* should be reduced to the level of the advanced capitalist nations.
(3) The *crude death rate* should decline or remain stable, despite the aging of the population.
(4) *Life expectancy at birth* should be raised to levels achieved by advanced capitalist nations.

These objectives can be fulfilled by either reducing illness rates through programs designed to improve consumption and environmental health conditions or upgrading the effectiveness of curative medical services.

Between 1945 and 1964, mortality and life expectancy indicators showed improvement in the USSR. All age-specific death rates declined, and the crude death rate fell to 7.1 deaths per 1,000 by 1964–65. Life expectancy at birth rose from 47 years in 1938–39 to 70 years in 1965–66. For men life expectancy was 66 years in 1965–66 and for women it was 74 years. These improvements were taken by many in the Soviet Union to be proof of the effectiveness of the socialist health service. Although it was acknowledged that other social programs implemented by the government in the fields of housing, diet, and income distribution assisted in the attainment of targets for mortality reduction, the medical system was given most of the credit for the evident progress.

During the next decade, however, there was a striking reversal in mortality trends.* The USSR crude death rate, which was at a post-World War II minimum of 7.1 deaths per 1,000 population in 1964-65, rose to 9.4 per 1,000 in 1975-76. Infant mortality fell from 27.2 to 22.9 between 1965 and 1971, but then increased by 36 percent to an estimated 1976 value of 31.1 deaths per 1,000 live births (Davis and Feshbach 1980). As one might expect, a similar pattern is observed for the 0-4 age group. In the next three quintiles, covering ages 5-19, minimum postwar rates were maintained up to 1975-76, but all older age groups exhibited increases from the minimum which were in the range of 5-41 percent. Death rates of those in the prime productive years, 30-59, rose substantially, by an average of 27 percent.

The Soviet government clearly became embarrassed by these adverse mortality developments and stopped publication of age-specific death rates after 1976. However, censorship did not help the problem. From 1965 to 1984 the crude mortality rate rose dramatically, from 7.1 to 10.8 deaths per 1,000, or by 52 percent. Since the U.S. rate declined from 9.4 to 8.6 deaths per 1,000 over the same period, the Soviet experience does not represent an immutable process caused by the aging of the population. Instead, the unrelenting upward trend implies that there were further increases in age-specific death rates after 1976.

In October 1986 the USSR resumed publication of infant mortality statistics, providing data for 1980 and 1983-85 ("Naselenie SSSR" 1986; Davis 1986b). The new information confirms that infant mortality rose during the early 1970s and shows that it went up again in the 1980s.† The pattern now appears to be that the infant

---

*There is a growing Western literature on mortality trends in the contemporary USSR. Relevant contributions include Davis (1977), Dutton (1979), Davis and Feshbach (1980), Cooper (1981), and Cooper and Schatzkin (1982). The Soviet Union is not the only socialist society to have experienced rising mortality. Davis (1982) notes that most adult age-specific death rates in Poland increased by over 10 percent from 1970 to 1980.

†The Soviet infant mortality increase during the 1970s is analyzed in Davis and Feshbach (1980). Jones and Grupp (1983) criticize the Davis–Feshbach report, making the argument that much of the infant mortality rise was due to improved statistical reporting. This author believes that Jones and Grupp do not fully support their hypothesis and exaggerate both the scale of improvements in statistical recording and the effects on the national infant mortality rate. The infant mortality statistics published in "Naselenie SSSR" (1986) confirm that there was an increase during the 1970s and again in 1983-85.

mortality rate dropped to its historic low in 1971 but then rose to a peak in 1976 or later. It fell to 27.3 in 1980 and then to 25.3 in 1983, but went up again in 1984 and 1985, reaching 26.0 deaths per 1,000 live births in 1985. This upward trend is in striking contrast with the experience of most industrialized countries. In the United States, infant mortality has decreased uninterruptedly, from 20 deaths per 1,000 live births in 1970 to 10.6 in 1984.

The Soviets also have revealed that the total number of infant deaths per year climbed from 103,000 in 1970 to 140,000 in 1985. One explanation for this is that the birth rate rose as well, from 17.4 births per 1,000 population in 1970 to a peak of 19.8 in 1983. Thus there were more babies at risk. However, a rising birth rate is no excuse for increased deaths since modern medicine can cope with challenges of this sort. In the United States, for instance, the birth rate rose from 14.6 in 1975 to 15.9 in 1982, yet the number of infant deaths fell from 51,000 to 42,000 (United States 1985). Over the 1970-84 period the United States reduced infant deaths from 75,000 to 39,000.

During the 1980s the trends in age-specific death rates in the USSR became more varied. Of the fifteen age groups for which official statistics are available, nine had declining rates from 1980/81 to 1984/85, one remained stable, and five rose. Those that exhibited increases were the groups 40-44, 50-54, 55-59, 65-69 and over 70 years. The final column of Table 6 shows that in 1984/85 the death rates for age groups 0-4 and all above 30 years were higher than previously attained minimum rates.

Life expectancy estimates are derived from mortality statistics. It is therefore to be expected that in the USSR they should reflect the country's mortality experience. From the mid-1960s through 1971, Soviet life expectancy at birth remained stable. After that, though, rising mortality rates drove it down. Feshbach (1983) estimates that by 1982 life expectancy at birth was 62 years for males and 73 years for females. Even in later years there is some evidence of a decline in this key indicator. For example, in an April 1986 speech, Moscow party leader Boris Yeltsin revealed that life expectancy in the capital of the USSR declined from 70 years in 1983 to 68 years in 1985 ("Can Moscow Believe in Yeltsin?" 1986). In contrast, the United States registered uninterrupted increases in life expectancy from 70.8 years in 1970 to 74.7 years in 1983.

It is evident from the statistics presented that during the past two decades none of the targets for mortality-related indicators

Table 6

AGE-SPECIFIC DEATH RATES IN THE USSR, 1970/71–1984/85

(Deaths per 1,000 in the age group)

Age Group	Years								1984/85 as Percent of Minimum Since 1964/65
	1970/71	1971/72	1972/73	1973/74	1974/75	1975/76	1980/81	1984/85	
All ages[a]	8.2	8.4	8.6	8.7	9.0	9.4	10.3	10.7	152%
0 to 1[b]	22.9	24.7	26.4	27.9	29.4	31.1	26.9	26.0	114
0 to 4	6.7	6.8	7.2	7.7	8.2	8.7	8.1	7.7	115
5 to 9	0.7	0.7	0.7	0.7	0.7	0.7	0.7	0.6	86
10 to 14	0.5	0.5	0.5	0.5	0.5	0.5	0.5	0.5	100
15 to 19	1.0	1.0	1.0	1.0	1.0	1.0	1.0	0.9	90
20 to 24	1.6	1.6	1.6	1.6	1.7	1.7	1.8	1.5	100
25 to 29	2.2	2.1	2.1	2.0	2.1	2.1	2.3	2.0	100
30 to 34	2.8	2.8	2.8	2.8	3.0	3.0	3.0	2.8	112
35 to 39	3.8	3.7	3.6	3.6	3.7	3.8	4.4	3.6	116
40 to 44	4.7	4.8	4.8	4.9	5.2	5.3	5.6	5.7	150
45 to 49	6.0	6.1	6.2	6.4	6.7	6.9	8.0	7.3	146
50 to 54	8.7	8.8	8.6	8.8	9.0	9.3	10.8	11.3	145
55 to 59	11.8	11.9	12.5	12.3	13.0	13.4	13.9	15.1	140
60 to 64	17.9	18.1	18.0	18.2	18.3	18.9	20.6	20.4	119
65 to 69	26.9	26.8	27.2	27.0	27.4	28.0	29.5	31.1	127
Over 70	74.9	74.8	75.5	73.5	73.3	75.0	77.2	78.7	123

Sources: 1970/71–1975/76—Davis and Feshbach (1980: 2); 1980/81–1984/85—Statisticheske (1986: 71).

[a]Crude death rate.

[b]Infant mortality rate—deaths during first year of life per 1,000 live births. Rates are for the latest year shown in column heading.

were achieved in the USSR. This raises serious questions about the effectiveness of the medical system with respect to final output. Although the production of medical services and inputs to the health system increased, it appears that the improvements were insufficient to cope with the new tasks confronting the system. It is possible that between 1965 and 1985 the standard of medical care in the USSR improved in absolute terms but that simultaneously the effectiveness of the health service declined relative to the challenges of the evolving, more complex contemporary illness pattern.

SOVIET GOVERNMENT EFFORTS IN THE 1980S TO IMPROVE HEALTH SERVICE PERFORMANCE

During the 1980s Soviet party and state authorities have made repeated criticisms of the institutions in the health sector and have introduced numerous measures to improve their performance. For example, the 26 August 1982 decree of the Central Committee CPSU and the Council of Ministers USSR, entitled "Supplemental measures to improve the population's health protection" (Tsentral'nyy Komitet 1982), criticized many of the deficiencies described above, ordered a remedial program, and established an interdepartmental council under the Ministry of Health to supervise fulfillment.

In the period since Mikhail Gorbachev assumed the position of CPSU General Secretary (March 1985), he and other leaders have drawn attention to deficiencies in the health system and have called for urgent remedial action ("Central Committee's Political Report" 1986; "Ryzhkov's Report" 1986). The media have published detailed criticisms of the medical system, pharmacies, and medical industry with great frequency. In response to this concern, the Soviet government has initiated a radical reform program in the health area that involves changes in strategy, personnel, labor policy, organization, economic mechanisms, and planning.

PERESTROIKA IN THE HEALTH SECTOR

In developing its health strategy the Gorbachev regime appears to have recognized the complexity of the health production process and the need to carry out a restructuring (*perestroika*) of the health sector. This was evident in Gorbachev's speech at the Twenty-seventh Party Congress in which he stated that

For every person, and indeed society, there is nothing more valuable than health. The maintenance and strengthening of the people's health is a matter of utmost importance. We must view problems of health from broad social standpoints. It is primarily defined by conditions of work and life and the level of well-being, and of course public health care has enormous significance. We must satisfy as soon as possible the population's requirements for high-quality curative, preventive and medicinal help everywhere. And all this poses in a new way the matter of the material and technical base of the health service and how to tackle many urgent scientific, organizational and cadre problems. Considerable funds will, of course, be required, and we shall have to find them (Central Committee 1986).

The new health strategy appears to be one of raising the effectiveness of public health programs and shifting the medical system onto an intensive development path.

The policies announced or implemented by the Gorbachev regime have been influenced by this health strategy as well as by general reformist ideas and programs (Burenkov 1986). Many measures have been devoted to improving public health and preventive medicine. The national anti-alcohol campaign has an important health component because a reduction in alcohol consumption should reduce the incidence of accidents, some degenerative diseases, and birth defects. An energetic effort is being made to progress toward comprehensive screening of the entire population for diseases. Greater attention also is being given to improving public sanitation and reducing environmental pollution. With respect to curative medicine, policies have been introduced to upgrade the quality of medical care, to promote efficiency, and to improve the performance of supporting health sector institutions. These include: wide-scale replacement of ineffectual health sector leaders, substantial pay increases for medical staff and increased differentiation of wages, expansion of the network of fee-for-service polyclinics, crackdown on second economy activity, intensification of pressure on construction organizations to fulfill contracts for the building and repair of medical facilities, improvement of the distribution of medicaments and medical equipment, acceleration of technical progress in medical industry and biomedical R&D establishments, and reform of medical foreign trade structure and mechanisms.

CHANGES IN PERSONNEL AND LABOR POLICY

During the two years since Gorbachev came to power there have been substantial changes among top administrators in the health service, pharmacy system, and medical industry. Furthermore, there have been strict reprimands administered to most republican ministers of health, several deputy ministers of health, the deputy president of the Academy of Medical Sciences, and many heads of main administrations in the Ministry of Health. In sum, by 1987 many of the most important leaders of health sector institutions had been fired or reprimanded for poor performance by the Gorbachev regime.

There also have been substantial changes in policies affecting the work conditions and wages of lower-level personnel in the health sector. In recognition of the lack of material incentives for medical staff, the government has introduced wage reforms that over the next several years will substantially increase average medical wages and differentiate them in accordance with performance and job difficulties. Sticks have been used as well as carrots, however, to improve management and labor productivity. In the two years since Gorbachev came to power, 165 heads of medical establishments have been fired for substandard work, and criticism has been directed against many others by the media and party organizations. A tough anti-corruption campaign has been launched against the medical and pharmacy staff who engage in second economy activities. In the biomedical R&D system, procedures are being used to weed out incompetent scientific and technical staff. Efforts have been made throughout the health sector to tighten labor discipline of workers and employees, with the objectives of raising on-the-job productivity and reducing absenteeism.

CHANGES IN ORGANIZATION AND THE ECONOMIC MECHANISM

The Gorbachev regime believes that many of the deficiencies in the economy during the 1970s were caused by ministries' conservatism, departmentalism, and bureaucratic meddling in the affairs of subordinate units. As a result, steps have been taken to decrease the powers and rationalize the organization of ministries, and give subordinate enterprises more independence. A number of changes of this type have been introduced in the health sector (Davis 1987).

The medical industry has been especially affected by these reforms. In 1985 a new Ministry of the Medical and Microbiological Industry was created by amalgamating the old Ministry of the Medical

Industry and the Main Administration of the Microbiological Industry. In 1987 all of the industrial enterprises of the new ministry changed their operating procedures in accordance with the national economic reform. This entailed a moderate decentralization of decisionmaking power from the ministry to the enterprises, which now have more rights to decide on the composition, quantity, and prices of medical commodities produced and to retain profits for self-determined investments and bonuses. New pricing and bonus formulas reward firms that produce high-quality, innovative products and penalize those churning out inferior, obsolete goods.

The new ministry has been awarded expanded rights to conduct export-import operations with foreign partners. Since the primary objective of this reform is to promote exports, the ministry is being allowed to keep a substantial portion of the hard currency its enterprises earn as an incentive. It can use these funds to finance imports of technology and intermediate products needed in pharmaceutical manufacturing. The ministry also has enhanced rights to engage in scientific-technological cooperation and to establish joint ventures in medical commodity production with Western companies.

Under Gorbachev the Soviet government is trying to encourage an expansion of production of non-food goods and services for consumers (Kompleksnaya programma 1985). One health-related objective is to expand the number of fee-for-service outpatient clinics and raise the quality of their facilities and services. Although these establishments have existed for many years, they have been deliberately limited in number and starved of resources.

In conclusion, it is evident that the Gorbachev regime is aware of the recent adverse trends in health output indicators and of the many deficiencies in the health sector. The government appears to recognize the complexity of the health production process and the need to implement a program of wide-ranging remedial measures. However, effective reform will be difficult to accomplish. Much of the population's illness is caused by low living standards and health-damaging consumer behavior. Many health service performance problems are the results of years of neglect of medical institutions and their low priority status in a shortage economy. As a result, it undoubtedly will take years of sustained effort to improve health conditions and medical system performance and to bring Soviet health output indicators up to Western standards. The new policy measures of the Gorbachev government therefore should be viewed as promising first steps rather than as final solutions of existing difficulties.

REFERENCES

Babanovskii, I. V. 1976. *Voprosy finansirovaniya zdravookhraneniya v SSSR.* Moscow: Meditsina.

Burenkov, S. P. 1986. "Zadachi Sovetskogo zdravookhraneniya i meditsinskoi nauki v svete reshennii XXVII S'ezda KPSS." *Sovetskoe zdravookhranenie*, 7.

"Can Moscow Believe in Yeltsin?" 1986. *Detente*, no. 7: 2–5.

"Central Committee's Political Report Presented by Gorbachev." 1986. *Summary of World Broadcasts*, 26 Feburary; SU/8193/C/2–14, SU/8194/C/1–53.

Chernyak, A. 1986. "Zdorovye dorozhe bogatstva." *Pravda*, 15 October.

"Chto mozhet vitamin." 1985. *Izvestiya*, 13 December.

Cooper, R. 1981. "Rising Death Rates in the Soviet Union: The Impact of Coronary Heart Disease." *New England Journal of Medicine* 304: 1259–65.

Cooper, R., and Schatzkin, A. 1982. "Recent Trends in Coronary Risk Factors in the USSR." *American Journal of Public Health* 72: 431–40.

Davis, Christopher. 1977. "An Analysis of Mortality and Life Expectancy Trends in the USSR: 1959–1975." Cambridge, England; discussion paper.

_____. 1979. "The Economics of the Soviet Health System: An Analytical and Historical Study, 1921–1978." Dissertation for Ph.D. degree, Cambridge University.

_____. 1981. "The Health Care System." In J. Berliner, B. Schwalberg, and C. Davis, *The Economics of Soviet Social Institutions*. Washington, D.C.: Final Report to the National Council for Soviet and East European Research.

_____. 1982. "The Polish Health Crisis." *Current Analysis* 2, 3. Washington, D.C. Wharton Centrally Planned Economies Services.

_____. 1983a. "The Economics of the Soviet Health System." In U.S. Congress, Joint Economic Committee, *Soviet Economy in the 1980s: Problems and Prospects*. Washington, D.C.: Government Printing Office.

_____. 1983b. "Economic Problems of the Soviet Health Service: 1917–1980." *Soviet Studies* 35: 343–61.

_____. 1984. *The Health and Pharmaceutical Sectors in the Soviet Economy*. Washington, D.C.: Wharton Econometric Forecasting Associates, Special Report.

_____. 1985. *Opportunities in the Soviet Pharmaceutical Market in the 1980s*. London: Scrip Country Report.

_____. 1986a. *Developments in the Soviet Health Sector and Pharmaceutical Foreign Trade*. Birmingham: Special Consulting Report. May.

_____. 1986b. "Reviewing Soviet Health Care Problems." *Wall Street Journal* (European edition), 31 October.

_____. 1987. "Developments in the Health Sector of the Soviet Economy: 1970–90." In U.S. Congress, Joint Economic Committee, *Gorbachev's Economic Plans*. Washington, D.C.: Government Printing Office.

_____. Forthcoming. "Priority and the Shortage Model: The Medical System in the Socialist Economy." In *Models of Disequilibrium and Shortage in Centrally Planned Economies*, eds. Christopher Davis and Wojciech Charemza. London: Chapman and Hall.

Davis, Christopher, and Feshbach, Murray. 1980. *Rising Infant Mortality in the USSR in the 1970's.* Washington, D.C.: Bureau of the Census Report, Series P-95, no. 74.

Dutton, J. 1979. "Changes in Soviet Mortality Patterns, 1959-77." *Population and Development Review* 95: 267-91.

Ellman, Michael. 1973. *Planning Problems in the USSR.* Cambridge; Cambridge University Press.

Feshbach, Murray. 1983. "Issues in Health Problems." In U.S. Congress, Joint Economic Committee, *Soviet Economy in the 1980s: Problems and Prospects.* Washington, D.C.: Government Printing Office.

_____. 1986. "Recent Research on Soviet Health Conditions." Cambridge; paper presented at NASEES Annual Conference, March.

Field, Mark. 1967. *Soviet Socialized Medicine: An Introduction.* New York: Free Press.

Golovteev, V. V., and Shilenko, Yu. V. 1977. *Finansirovanie zdravookhraneniya.* Moscow.

Golovteev, V. V.; Korchagin, V. P.; and Shilenko, Yu. V. 1978. *Zdravookhranenie i narodnoe khozyaistvo.* Moscow.

Gorenkov, V. F. 1984. *Organizatsiya i ekonomika sovetskoi farmatsiya.* Minsk: Vysheishaya Shkola.

Hyde, Gordon. 1974. *The Soviet Health Service: An Historical and Comparative Study.* London: Lawrence and Wishart.

"Industriya zdorovye." 1980. *Pravda*, 9 February.

Jones, E., and Grupp, F. W. 1983. "Infant Mortality Trends in the Soviet Union." *Population and Development Review* 9: 213-46.

Kant, V. I., and Golovteev, V. V. 1979. *Spravochnik organizatora zdravookhraneniya: planirovanie, finansirovanie.* Kishinev: Kartya Moldovenyaske.

Kaser, Michael. 1976. *Health Care in the Soviet Union and Eastern Europe.* London: Croom Helm.

Knaus, William. 1982. *Inside Russian Medicine.* New York: Everest House.

"Kompleksnaya programma razvitiya proizvodstva tovarov narodnogo potrebleniya i sfery uslug na 1986-2000 gody." 1985. *Ekonomicheskaya gazeta*, no. 41.

Lisitsyn, Yu. 1972. *Health Protection in the USSR.* Moscow: Progress Publishers.

Malov, N. I., and Churakov, V. I. 1983. *Sovremennye osnovy i metodi planirovaniya razvitiya zdravookhraneniya.* Moscow: Ekonomika.

McAuley, A. 1979. *Economic Welfare in the Soviet Union: Poverty, Living Standards and Inequality.* London: Macmillan.

Ministerstvo Finansov SSSR. 1987. *Gosudarstvennyy byudzhet SSSR 1981–1985: Statisticheskii Sbornik.* Moscow: Finansy i Statistika.

Narodnoe khozyaistvo SSSR v 1965 g . . . v 1984 g. Moscow: Finansy i Statistika.

"Naselenie SSSR." 1986. *Ekonomicheskaya gazeta,* no. 43.

Popov, G. A. 1974. *Problemy vrachebnykh kadrov.* Moscow: Meditsina.

_____. 1976a. *Ekonomicheskie problemy v upravlenii lechebno-profilakticheskimi uchrezhdeniyani.* Moscow: Meditsina.

_____. 1976b. *Ekonomika i planirovani zdravookhraneniya.* Moscow: Moscow University Press.

"Programma kommunisticheskoi Partii Sovetskogo Soyuza (Novaya redaktsiya)." 1985. *Pravda,* 16 October.

"Rezervy nauki." 1985. *Meditsinskaya gazeta,* 25 December.

Romazonovich, G. V., and Golkova, M. L. 1973. *Kompleksnoe izuchenie sostoyanie zdorovya naseleniya tambovskoi oblasti v svyazi e vsecoyuznoi perepisyn naseleniya 1970 g.* Tambov.

Ryan, Michael. 1978. *The Organisation of Soviet Medical Care.* London: Martin Robertson.

"Ryzhkov's Report on the Basic Guidelines at the 27th Party Congress." 1986. *Summary of World Broadcasts,* SU/8200/C/1–30.

Safonov, A. G., and Loginova, E. A., eds. 1976. *Osnovy organizatsii statsionarnoy pomoshchi v SSSR.* Moscow: Meditsina.

Serenko, F.; Ermakov, V. V.; and Petrakov, B. D. 1976. *Osnovy organizatsii poliklinicheskoy pomoshchi naseleniya.* Moscow: Meditsina.

Shevchenko, A. P. 1974. *Voprosy ekonomiki khimiko-farmatsevticheskoi promyshlennosti.* Moscow: Meditsina.

SSSR v tsifrakh v 1985 godu. 1986. Moscow: Finansy i Statistika.

Treml, Vladimir. 1982a. "Death from Alcohol Poisoning in the USSR." *Soviet Studies,* no. 4.

_____. 1982b. *Alcohol in the USSR: A Statistical Study.* Durham, N.C.: Duke University Press.

Tsentral'nyy Komitet KPSS i Sovet Ministrov SSSR. 1982. "O dopolnitel'nykh merakh po ulucheniyu okhrany zdorov'ye naseleniya." *Pravda,* 26 August.

United States. 1985. *Statistical Abstract of the United States.* Washington, D.C.: U.S. Bureau of the Census.

U.S. Congress, 1982. Joint Economic Committee. *USSR: Measures of Economic Growth and Development, 1950–80.* Washington, D.C.: Government Printing Office.

"Utverzhdat delom." 1986. *Meditsinskaya gazeta,* 15 October.

"Vashe mnenie, Tovarishch Ministr?" 1986. *Meditsinskaya gazeta,* 5 February.

Vinogradov, N. A., ed. 1974. *Rukovodstvo po sotsial'noi gigiene i organizatsii zdravookhraneniya.* Moscow: Meditsina.

"V Politburo TsK KPSS." 1986. *Meditsinskaya gazeta,* 17 September.

Zabota partii i pravitel'stva o blage naroda. 1980. Moscow: Meditsina.

Zhuk, A. P. 1968. *Planirovanie zdravookhraneniya v SSSR.* Moscow: Meditsina.

DELIVERY OF HEALTH CARE IN THE UNITED STATES AND SOME COMPARISONS WITH THE USSR

Theodore R. Marmor

A broad sketch of American medical care, as it compares with that in the Soviet Union, can in some measure make the obvious juxtapositions: indicators of health status, relative expenditures, numbers of facilities and doctors, and medical advances. These, while significant, say little about fundamental differences in the organization of services and their provision; they do not illuminate the particular dynamic that characterizes the health sector in each country. It is this dynamic which is the best predictor of future developments.

Medical care in the Soviet Union is in theory constrained by a commitment to distribute access to medical care equally, to make care available to everybody. The reality falls considerably short of the model, of course, because of the rigid Soviet managerial structure, the sector's relatively low priority in the national budget, and metropolitan chauvinism. By comparison, the United States has neither the ideological commitment to equal access nor national programs to produce approximations of such a result. Instead it has national health programs for particular groups, with other groups literally shut out. American medical care is expensive and operates in an environment where expenditures, free of overall budgetary constraint, rise rapidly; profit-making is a barely concealed driving force; and innovation, both organizational and scientific, abounds in the face of considerable doubts about the marginal efficacy of medical care. Medical care in the United States, when compared with most other developed nations (the USSR included), occupies a unique position. American medical care is not primarily a public service. But

The preparation of this chapter was supported in part by a grant from the Kaiser Family Foundation to the Institution for Social and Policy Studies, Yale University. The assistance of Richard Smithey, Elizabeth Auld, and Karyn Gill is gratefully acknowledged.

widespread insurance for medical care means that it is no longer a private good in the ordinary sense either.

A U.S./USSR comparison represents perhaps the most radical of comparisons among developed nations. The Soviet Union presents the extreme of a centralized monopolistic version of medical care in which the state is the prime payer and provider. The United States presents the other extreme, where the government, although the major payer for health care, has a much more pluralistic form of financing. The result is a system in which there are considerably greater discrepancies in access to care than in countries like Britain, Sweden, France, Germany, and Canada.

America's pluralist structure of public support for health care, with its selective programs for discrete groups and little central control, leaves open significant opportunities for change in many directions. One can envision such possibilities as further erosion or—less likely—expansion of the government's role; further rapid growth or—less likely—drastic retrenchment in scope of services; organizational innovation; and even the redefinition of health care.

America's pluralist system of health care distribution has evolved over the decades since the end of World War II. We will describe briefly the changes in American medical care since 1945 and then turn to an analysis of current trends and an examination of possible futures for this disparate system. We will conclude with reasons for making cross-national comparisons of social policy so as to highlight the U.S./USSR contrast.

AMERICAN MEDICAL CARE SINCE 1945

POLICY INITIATIVES

The postwar period of American medical care has been marked by an extraordinary form of government intervention in financing and distribution. It is unusual in that national health programs expanded slowly by aggregation toward a much expanded role of the government. Since World War II there has been steady and substantial growth in general health expenditures (see Table 1). Public policy has at the same time shifted several times, with profound changes for medical care institutions and personnel. We began the postwar period with a substantial veterans' program for medical care. (Veterans' programs in the United States have always been an

Table 1

HEALTH EXPENDITURES IN THE UNITED STATES
SINCE WORLD WAR II

Year	Amount (*Billions of dollars*)	Percent of GNP
1950	$ 12.7	4.4%
1955	17.7	4.4
1960	26.9	5.3
1965	41.9	5.9
1970	75.0	7.4
1975	132.7	8.3
1980	248.0	9.1
1985	425.0	10.7

Sources: U.S. Department of Health and Human Services (1984: 137); Waldo, Levit, and Lazenby (1986: 13).

acceptable form of "socialized" medical finance.) The Hospital Survey and Construction Act of 1946 (usually referred to as Hill-Burton, after the act's sponsors) led to an increased supply of hospitals. The substantial endowment of the National Institutes of Health in the late 1940s greatly increased and improved biomedical research facilities. The result has been a highly technological form of health services centered in medical schools and their affiliated institutions. Under the impact of federal aid and the growth of private health insurance, American hospitals have grown progressively more elaborate, sophisticated, and expensive.

In the 1960s the emphasis of federal policy shifted from expansion of facilities to redistribution of services. With the enactment of Medicare and Medicaid in 1965 and the Great Society War on Poverty in the mid-1960s, health policy more explicitly addressed class and racial inequalities. Federal policy shifted from its earlier preoccupation with hospitals, research, and manpower to a broader interest in access to care. Programs were adopted to increase the number of physicians, set up community mental health centers and other neighborhood clinics, and bring about other changes in the pattern of services. One result of this shift in emphasis was that although the government's share of health spending increased, public ownership of medical facilities actually diminished. Medicare and Medicaid, in particular, made it possible for patients formerly dependent on public institutions to receive care in nongovernment hospitals and from private physicians.*

The new programs of the 1960s did not at first replace those of the 1940s; policymakers did not yet see a need for a choice of priorities or for regulation of growth. In the late 1960s and early 1970s congeries of programs arose—uncoordinated, often competing for funds, and pursuing contradictory objectives. The National Health Service Corps, for instance, was created to attract new physicians toward service in primary health care and in underserved communities. Although this measure added significant numbers of doctors to areas in need, some questioned whether short-term, young physicians were an adequate substitute for a stable body of local doctors. In a second response to the limited supply of needed general practitioners, Congress required medical schools receiving federal funds to channel students into primary care. Without centralized control of advanced training programs, however, the United States lacked the means to make such restrictions operationally adequate.

Parallel with these programs to stimulate demand and supply were regulatory schemes which experimented with various ways to

*The United States shares with the Soviet Union the problem of "undersupplied" regions. Particularly in rural areas, both societies find it difficult to match the numbers, mix, and quality of medical practitioners in urban areas. In the United States, for example, the ratio of physicians per 100,000 population in 1980 varied from a low of 107 in rural states like Idaho and Mississippi to a high of 272 in Massachusetts, 268 in Maryland, 267 in New York, and 230 in California—all states with large urban populations (*Selected Data* 1983: 108). There are three somewhat different aspects of this problem. The first is the unavailability of physicians in some rural areas, the familiar lament of the United States that a small town cannot find a replacement for its older physicians who retired, moved away, or died. This issue arises in the medical press of America under the rubric of "counties without physicians," a problem which the Soviet system can address more directly by assigning doctors and nurses to undersupplied areas. The extent to which rural areas have comparable availability is the second "face" of this issue. Neither the Soviet Union nor the United States has solved that problem—a case of convergence, so to speak, that parallels the experience of all of the OECD nations with undersupplied regions. The third aspect is the inevitable difference in speed of access of rural areas to the most specialized care. Modern technology can bring helicopters to aid in this area, but all modern societies face the difficulty of physician reluctance to practice in settings distant culturally, socially, and technically from the urban settings of their advanced training. On the other hand, there is ample evidence that programs like Hill-Burton increased sharply the technical sophistication and expertise of medical care practice in American rural and small town hospitals. Within the convergence, in short, there remain sharp differences in the technical capacities of American and Soviet medical care.

control the medical inflation encouraged in part by federal largesse. Among the schemes of the 1970s was the Professional Standards Review Organization (PSRO), a program that subjected doctors' judgments on hospitalization and other aspects of treatment of patients receiving federal funds to an audit by a board of colleagues. The PSRO law established agencies that allowed some doctors to set and enforce standards governing the practice of their colleagues. The agencies generally contracted out their functions to hospitals; the results, from the viewpoint of cost control, were disappointing. Nor were the state- and area-wide quasi-regulatory planning bodies (health systems agencies, or HSAs) much more successful at cost restraint. The HSAs were given a mixture of planning and regulatory responsibilities, but narrow authority. Although they had the legal authority to review institutional proposals for capital expenditures over $150,000, HSAs in fact only acted in an advisory capacity for state governments, which granted the required "certificates of need" (Morone and Marmor 1981; Morone and Dunham 1985: 274-75).

Medical care inflation proved invulnerable to these and other surprisingly imaginative measures, all promulgated in the naive belief that national health insurance was on its way. Ultimately, in its absence, these flawed programs became, by the early 1980s, impressive testimony to the failure of the liberal vision of the 1960s (Wing 1986; Marmor 1986). By the end of the 1970s the debate over federal health insurance had largely shifted away from national health insurance, and away from general regulation, to the specific issue of cost containment. In 1977 congressional stalemate frustrated the reform efforts of the Carter administration. In 1978 the hospital industry and the American Medical Association (AMA) promised a "voluntary effort" to control health-care costs, with no visible effect.

The health policy of the early 1980s, under President Reagan, has been marked by four elements: reduced public medical budgets, reduced benefits for and more cost-sharing by recipients of publicly supported care, cutbacks in payments to Medicare providers, and an adherence to the belief that excessive insurance drives medical inflation, at the expense of all other issues (Marmor and Dunham 1985).

FINANCING

What remains distinctive about American medical care is the pluralistic financing of personal medical care services. Public financing extended first to the poor elderly in the late 1950s and the early 1960s, and then in 1965 to the elderly under the Medicare program and to the poor under the Medicaid program. Care for the old, the poor, and veterans, along with some other special clientele groups (such as members of the armed services, dialysis patients, and the Indian Health Service), added up to spending by governments at all levels of close to 41 percent of the total $425 billion in national health expenditures in 1985 (Waldo, Levit, and Lazenby 1986). Although a significant share of these expenditures comes from public sources, the public outlays themselves are dispersed (see Table 2).

Table 2

U.S. PUBLIC EXPENDITURES FOR HEALTH SERVICES
AND SUPPLIES BY PROGRAM, 1985

Program	Amount (*Billions of dollars*)	
	Federal	State and Local
Medicare	$72.3	--
Medicaid	23.2	$18.6
Other public assistance programs	--	1.9
Veterans' Administration	8.7	--
Defense Department	8.4	
Workers' compensation	0.3	7.9
State and local hospitals	--	7.3
Other public programs for personal health care	2.9	1.8
Government public health activities	1.4	10.5
Total	117.2	48.0

Source: Waldo, Levit, and Lazenby (1986: 19).

Pluralism stands out even more starkly when one examines the 59 percent not financed by government programs. Medical care in the United States, although widely insured, is not insured comprehensively by the same kinds of programs. About 90 percent of hospital expenditures, for instance, are paid by third parties of all sorts. These include diverse government programs as well as different kinds of insurance institutions—Blue Cross, Blue Shield, commercial carriers, and self-insured firms (see Table 3).

Table 3

EXPENDITURES FOR HOSPITAL CARE BY SOURCE OF FUNDS, 1985

Source of Funds	Amount (*Billions of dollars*)	Percentage of Total
Direct patient payments	$ 15.5	9.3%
Third parties	151.2	90.7
Private		
Health insurance	59.3	35.6
Other funds	2.1	1.3
Government		
Medicare	48.5	29.1
Medicaid	14.8	8.9
Other federal	15.1	9.0
Other state and local	11.4	6.8
Total	166.7	100.0

Source: Waldo, Levit, and Lazenby (1986: 16).

Through the dizzying succession of reforms, subsidies, and regulatory initiatives, the basic format of health-care financing has remained unscathed, structured by the old Blue Cross "cost plus" reimbursement formula. Successive federal attempts to contain medical inflation have only prompted perverse gaming practices by hospitals in a culture that thrives on federal business while making obligatory ritualistic noises about regulation. This has had the effect of waving a red flag in front of the federal bull, which proceeds unaware that it is supplying the very adrenalin that stimulates the commercial trends in medical care. Partial reforms of a pluralistic system of payment simply have not produced anything like equitable distribution of either access or finance.

HEALTH STATUS

During the decades following World War II, Americans' health status improved significantly in a number of areas. Between 1960 and 1975 the infant mortality rate was cut by 38 percent (Rogers and Blendon 1977). Between 1970 and 1976 the age-adjusted mortality rate dropped 16 percent for coronary artery disease and 22 percent for strokes (United States, Executive Office 1979). In the late 1960s public concern about environmental and safety issues increased, and by the early 1970s a host of new laws had been enacted in these areas. Accidental deaths in the workplace fell by half in the wake of new occupational health and safety legislation (Kelman 1978).

The exact causes of these gains are not well understood; it is unclear whether better prevention, better access to better care, or other changes are responsible. The debate over preventive measures versus increased levels of expenditure on medical care has been intensified by increasing doubts about the efficacy of medical services, or at least about the efficacy of marginal improvements in those services. On the other hand, the investment in prevention, and especially environmental protection, has come under attack in a new atmosphere of increased international competition and higher energy costs. Furthermore, environmental measures have encountered stiff opposition from powerful interests, such as the tobacco and packaged food industries and the industrial sector at large.

Neither of these debates, however, has had any significant impact on the continuing increase in the relative cost of medical care services. Attention has shifted from an emphasis on government regulation to a growing tendency to trumpet the benefits of letting the market or—better—competition determine the nature of services, placing substantial administrative latitude in private hands. These "pro-competitive" reforms are typified by one survivor of the early 1970s federal reform initiatives—health maintenance organizations (HMOs). (For more information see Brown 1984; Marmor 1983: ch. 12.) Originally a cost-control organizational innovation, HMOs became increasingly an attractive investment opportunity for for-profit corporations.

CURRENT TRENDS IN U.S. MEDICAL CARE

The increasing cost of American medical care constitutes perhaps the most evident trend in progress. The cost has inflated enormously since the 1960s, rising from some $42 billion in 1965 to more than $400 billion in 1985, without commensurate improvements in quality or utilization. Moreover, there is widespread concern that rising insurance costs and pressure for further cost reductions in government programs threaten not only access to care, but also the quality of care available to Americans when they get it. This became an even greater concern in the face of the anti-inflation measures of the Reagan administration which were aimed at overall program cuts to reduce federal deficits, not medical inflation itself.

A related trend, which has increased the severity of the impact of the cutbacks in public programs, is the growing number of Americans who lack any, or sufficient, health insurance. In 1982 at least 33 million Americans under age 65—16 percent of the population—were without any insurance coverage, private or public (Davis 1985). In 1977, 25 percent of those under 65 who had some medical insurance had no protection against unusually expensive hospital stays (Farley 1985). And fully one third of elderly Medicare beneficiaries have no hospital coverage beyond Medicare's 150-day limit (Farley 1985).

The causes of this medical inflation are worth noting. Clearly one part of the increased costs, common to many nations, is the extent to which the financial barriers to medical care are being removed by some form of government or nongovernment protection. The United States has in effect moved to almost 100 percent third-party payments for hospital care without 100 percent public financing, regulation, or provision of such care. Insurance itself has increased the demand for and use of medical care services. Yet, as noted above, the existence of widespread third-party payment for hospitals has not meant universal coverage.

Second, we need to take into account the impact of the increased supply of personnel on costs. In the 1960s the Western democracies were concerned with increasing the supply of medical care practitioners. Twenty years later, we may have been too successful. The number of medical school graduates in the United States has doubled since 1960, and by the end of the century projections indicate that the country will have 260 physicians per 100,000 population—up from 156 in 1970 (see Tables 4 and 5). Many health economists

Table 4

ACTIVE PHYSICIANS IN THE UNITED STATES, 1960–2000

Year	Number (MDs and DOs)	Per 100,000 Population
1960	259,600	140
1970	326,500	156
1975	384,500	174
1980	457,500	197
1985[a]	527,900	221
1990[b]	594,600	238
2000[b]	706,500	264

Source: U.S. Department of Health and Human Services (1984: 137).

[a]Estimated.

[b]Projected.

Table 5

GRADUATES OF U.S. MEDICAL SCHOOLS, 1960–2000

Year	Number
1960	7,081
1970	8,367
1975	12,714
1980	15,135
1990[a]	16,240
2000[a]	16,080

Source: U.S. Department of Health and Human Services (1984: 125).

[a]Projected.

believe that increasing the supply of medical care personnel increases the costs of medical care—i.e., supply creates much of its own demand (Evans 1984).

Another trend in evidence is change in organizational structure. The service sector has become the frontier of corporate business. Medical care, long the province of independent practitioners and independent, nonprofit hospitals, is now witnessing the growth of for-profit hospital chains as well as nonprofit multihospital systems and diversified health care companies of all kinds (Gray 1985; Marmor et al. 1986)—see Table 6. HMOs, which were nearly all

Table 6

MARKET SHARE OF FOR-PROFIT, PRIVATE NONPROFIT, AND
PUBLIC HEALTH-CARE PROVIDERS IN THE UNITED STATES,
EARLY 1980s

Institutions Offering Services	Measurement Used	Percent of Services Provided by		
		For-Profit Institutions	Nonprofit Institutions	Public Institutions
Acute hospitals	Beds	8.5%	69.6%	21.9%
Psychiatric hospitals	Beds	6.0	4.7	89.3
Nursing homes	Beds	67.6	21.3	11.0
Homes for mentally handicapped	Residents	46.2	37.7	16.5
Blood banks	Facilities	63.3	5.8	30.9
Dialysis centers	Facilities	38.5	44.3	17.2
Health maintenance organizations	Enrollees	15.8	84.2	n.a.
Health insurance	Enrollees	45.2	42.7	12.0
Home health agencies	Patients	25.5	64.1	10.4

Source: Schlesinger (1984).

nonprofit and locally controlled in 1970, are increasingly operated by large national corporations, some of them insurance firms. Added to this structural change is the increased tendency of doctors to form group practices; more than a quarter of the profession now practices in groups (Freshnock and Jensen 1981).

A fourth trend has been decreased faith in the efficacy of medical care—a growing skepticism as to whether this is an area of desirable welfare-state expansion. Faith in the progress of medicine is everywhere being eroded, with an interesting implication. Without national health insurance or a national health service, the United States, aware of the relatively limited role that medical care is likely to play in future improvements in health status, has increasingly emphasized the role of environment and personal health habits, using these conceptions of the causes of illness as part of the argument against increased public investment in medical care.* Paradoxically, however, while relaxing the impetus toward national health insurance and new public programs, these arguments have in no way impeded the almost frenetic growth of private investment in medical care.

A fifth trend, stemming in part from the loss of faith in medical care, is a preoccupation with how to constrict the supply of both personnel and facilities—a perhaps vain preoccupation in light of the powerful counterforces currently at work in the hospital and health-services sector. This preoccupation is all the more ironic in view of the rather extraordinary growth since 1970, stimulated in large part by the favorable incentives offered and the new "markets" opened by government programs such as Medicare. This politically controversial issue is likely to be with us for a long time. In this respect, the Soviet system has anticipated the politics of constraint.

THE FUTURE OF AMERICAN MEDICINE

What is the likely future of a system that has been through a decade of preoccupation with its limits, worry about its costs, and a sense of incompleteness in the postwar reforms? Four possible futures might provide us points of contrast (Starr and Marmor 1984).

---

*In most other OECD countries the preoccupation with the nonmedical care determinants of improved health status followed the removal of financial barriers to care. In the United States the preoccupation with environmental and personal habits has preceded the universalization of financial access to health care and is partly an argument against going down that road.

The first of these futures is in fact already evident, a result of economic austerity and an administration dedicated to a belief in the private sector's superior efficiency. The Reagan administration's desire to reduce the federal role in health care is leading to the accelerated reprivatization of medical care—a preoccupation with how to reduce public expenditure and expand the role of the patient as consumer and payer. This trend is already evident in an extraordinary reevaluation of the principles under which Medicare and Medicaid have been operated.

This future has rather frightening possibilities—permanent, unrestrained cost increases and the decline of the vaunted autonomy of the physician in the face of a growing corporate presence. Who will benefit, and who will be accountable to whom, will change. The small entrepreneurs—particularly physicians—seem to be losing power to the larger organized corporate institutions, exemplified by Humana, Hospital Corporation of America, and (in part) the new nonprofit systems which are forming large chains with for-profit subsidiaries.

Some of the changes now occurring, particularly the vertical and horizontal integration of medical care facilities—chains are buying HMOs, investing in home health-care agencies, and attempting to control large hospital supply companies—are historically unprecedented in medicine. Yet this is a quite familiar stage in the development of Western capitalism, the displacement of smaller units by larger ones in the name of rationalization. In this milieu, however, the argument is not simply about the legal form of organization, but rather about control over patients, profits, and professional privilege. It is about the incremental decline of a service ethos—more naked in one sector, more camouflaged in the other.

A very different kind of future might come about if economic austerity continues and a political change brings to power an administration somewhat more to the political left. Under such conditions, the United States might well rediscover a quasi-British form of medical care finance—with centralized budgeting and a smaller portion of GNP spent on medical care than is now the case, but under politial control to ensure equity of access. The big contrast between the first and second futures is that in the first, policies to reintroduce cost-sharing and reduce public expenditure may make personal wealth and personal income the key determinants of access to medical care.

The other two possible futures reject the presumption of austerity and imagine a world of increasing economic growth and varying political auspices. Under the auspices of parties to the right in the United States we could expect something like the German system of medical care insurance. This would mean widespread third-party insurance and relatively ineffective centralized cost control, with expanding portions of national resources going to medical care, yielding diminishing marginal returns. Under the auspices of a party to the left we are likely to have something much more similar to Canada's federally funded but provincially administered national health insurance program. In that scheme the ministries of health in the ten provinces restrict the annual outlays for medical care to roughly the same proportion of GNP as the previous year plus an adjustment for GNP growth. The budgeting is marked by extraordinarily conflictive bargaining arrangements between the personnel of medical care and the monopolistic buyers of medical care in the state (Evans 1984; Marmor 1983: ch. 9).

CROSS-COUNTRY COMPARISONS IN MEDICAL CARE

In broad terms, there are two quite different reasons for comparing social policies across nations, each of which would seem to require a rather different research strategy. First is *policy learning* (Klein 1983; Marmor 1983)—that is, we look at the social policies of other countries in order to derive lessons or models which can be applied at home. To judge from the literature, this study would require a single-issue approach in a small number of "most similar" countries—i.e., a comparison of countries that are judged to be roughly similar in terms of economic development, social organization, and political ideology—for if the concern is the transplantability of ideas or models, it is clearly essential that the two environments should not be too different. This obviously does not apply in a comparison between the United States and the Soviet Union, even when examining a discrete policy area such as medical care.

The second reason is *policy understanding*. Here the emphasis is not so much on learning as on explanation. The associated research strategy would seem to be a systems approach in "most different" countries, using large numbers. The focus of interest is on the factors that help explain either the evolution or the behavior of a system as a whole. The nature of the analysis positively requires differences in economic development, social organization, or political ideology of the countries being examined, for it is obviously impossible to test the significance of a specific factor if it is common to the cases being examined.

A variant of the "different systems" approach addresses an admittedly very different sociopolitical community, contrasts its practices with another country, and highlights the cultural and other factors which set the two societies apart. Profound cultural differences are brought out more clearly by asking similar questions of the two cultures. Anthropologists do this for a living, but the practice has its own tradition of caution in drawing any policy lessons at all. The legitimate purpose of this variant is analytical illumination without policy transplantation (Klein 1983; Marmor 1983).

One might describe the analytical perspective here as yet another variant, one that combines the single-issue approach associated with policy learning with the different systems approach of policy understanding. Compared to a "most similar" system like Canada, the Soviet Union is clearly closer to a "most different" system. In comparing the United States with very different systems, one frames questions of access, expenditure, and patterns of illness quite differently. If similarities show up across widely differing countries, one has some powerful uniformities, especially if they dominate all the other ways in which the two systems differ. Two important U.S./USSR contrasts merit specific comment.

The first is the sharp divergence in the postwar experience regarding expenditures for medical care. The United States, like the Soviet Union, has a very large medical care industry that has grown rapidly in the postwar period. In the United States, however, expenditures rose from roughly 4 percent of GNP in 1950 to almost 10 percent of GNP in 1980, while the health share of the total Soviet budget fell. The U.S. increase in outlays has been particularly marked in the last decade. It can be highlighted by a comparison with Canada, where comprehensive national health insurance was introduced in 1971. The United States and Canada both began the 1970s spending roughly 7 percent of GNP for medical care. The United States ended the decade spending 10 percent, while Canada was still spending roughly 7 percent (see Figure 1). The problem in this country remains one of overall expenditures, not simply government outlays.

Unlike medical care in most of the Western industrial world, Soviet medical care has been restrained in its command of national resources. Across almost all Western industrial countries, medical care is both a standard and core feature of the welfare state and

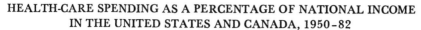

Figure 1

HEALTH-CARE SPENDING AS A PERCENTAGE OF NATIONAL INCOME
IN THE UNITED STATES AND CANADA, 1950-82

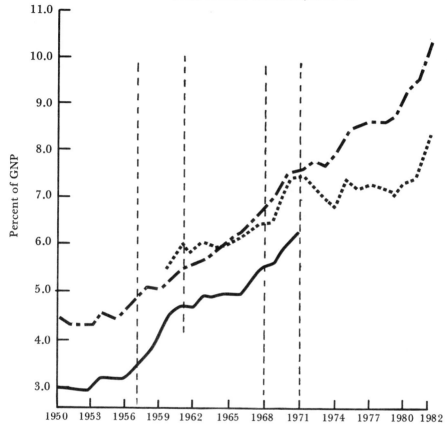

Source: Evans (1984: 10).

everywhere regarded in trouble. That trouble is almost always
described as an increasing expenditure of national resources and
a decreasing faith that this expense is worthwhile in terms of health
or other benefits.

Second, although unified in theory, the Soviet Union is in
practice quite pluralistic in its arrangements for the delivery and
financing of and access to medical care, but in comparison the
United States can only be described as extraordinarily pluralistic.
American medical care is pluralistic in the sources and character
of its financing, in the levels of care Americans receive at similar ages
by geographic region, and in the likelihood of equal response to
equal medical circumstances across class and region.

It is one thing to say that there is not uniformity. It is another to ask what characterizes the direction of change. On the one hand, if we try to place the United States' present circumstances and likely futures in an international context, attention is called not to a common pattern, but to the possibilities of quite different patterns of development depending on the political and economic circumstances in the 1980s and beyond. On the other hand, if we look only at where we have come from, the United States in the postwar period appears to resemble a large number of other regimes in the expansion of insurance and the growth and preoccupation with medical care costs. Unlike the Soviet Union, we do not have control over this welfare-state component, which in the United States has driven out the margins of adjustment for lots of other programs. Increases in U.S. expenditures for medical care and social security pensions alone represent the largest constraint on all other social welfare activities in this country.

Thus what is striking about a U.S./USSR comparison is divergence rather than convergence. Some elements of contrast are illuminating, calling attention to the very special circumstances of the United States, which has paralleled the rest of the world in every other area of the welfare state except medical care. The United States remains very much a maverick in the role of public authority over the distribution of access to medical care.

REFERENCES

Brown, Lawrence D. 1984. *Politics and Health Care Organization: HMOs as Federal Policy.* Washington, D.C.: The Brookings Institution.

Davis, Karen. 1985. "Access to Health Care: A Matter of Fairness." In *Health Care: How to Improve It and Pay for It.* Washington, D.C.: Center for National Policy.

Evans, Robert G. 1984. *Strained Mercy: The Economics of Canadian Health Care.* Toronto: Butterworths.

Farley, Pamela J. 1985. "Who Are the Underinsured?" *Millbank Memorial Fund Quarterly* 63, 3 (Summer): 476-503.

Freshnock, Larry J., and Jensen, Lynn E. 1981. "The Changing Structure of Medical Group Practice in the U.S., 1969-1980." Chicago: AMA, Center for Health Policy Research.

Gray, Bradford H. 1985. "Overview: Origins and Trends." *Bulletin of the New York Academy of Medicine* 61, 1 (January-February): 7-22.

Kelman, Steven. 1978. "Regulation That Works." *New Republic*, 25 November, pp. 17-18.

Klein, R. 1983. "Strategies for Comparative Social Policy Research." In *Health and Welfare States of Britain*, ed. A. Williamson and G. Room. Portsmouth, N.H.: Heineman Educational Books.

Marmor, Theodore R. 1983. *Political Analysis and American Medical Care.* New York: Cambridge University Press.

_____. 1986. "Commentary on American Health Policy in the 1980's." *Case Western Reserve Law Review* 36, 4: 686-92.

Marmor, Theodore R., and Dunham, Andrew. 1985. "The Politics of Health Policy Reform: Origins, Alternatives, and a Possible Prescription." In *Health Care: How to Improve It and Pay for It.* Washington, D.C.: Center for National Policy.

Marmor, Theodore R.; Schlesinger, Mark; and Smithey, Richard W. 1986. "A New Look at Nonprofits: Health Care Policy in a Competitive Age." *Yale Journal on Regulation* 3, 3 (Spring): 313-49.

Morone, James A., and Dunham, Andrew B. 1985. "Slouching Towards National Health Insurance: The New Health Care Politics." *Yale Journal on Regulation* 2: 263-91.

Morone, James A., and Marmor, Theodore R. 1981. "Representing Consumer Interests: The Case of American Health Planning." *Ethics* 91: 431-50.

Rogers, David E., and Blendon, Robert J. 1977. "The Changing American Health Scene: Sometimes Things Get Better." *Journal of the American Medical Association* 237 (18 April): 1710-14.

Schlesinger, M. 1984. "Public, For-Profit and Private Nonprofit Enterprises: A Study of Mixed Industries" Ph.D. dissertation, University of Wisconsin-Madison.

Selected Data on Health and Nutrition. 1983. Reprinted from the *U.S. Statistical Abstract*, with additional analyses by Jules M. Sugarman for the National Health Constitutional Convention, 24 October.

Starr, Paul, and Marmor, Theodore R. 1984. "The United States: A Social Forecast." In *The End of an Illusion*, ed. Jean de Kervasdoué, John R. Kimberly, and Victor G. Rodwin. Berkeley: University of California Press.

United States, Department of Health and Human Services. 1984. *Health, United States, 1984.* Washington, D.C.: Government Printing Office.

_____, Executive Office of the President. 1979. *Outlook Report*, 15 February. Washington, D.C.

Waldo, Daniel R., Levit, Katharine R., and Lazenby, Helen. 1986. "National Health Expenditures, 1985." *Health Care Financing Review* 8, 1 (Fall).

Wing, Kenneth R. 1986. "American Health Policy in the 1980's." *Case Western Reserve Law Review* 36, 4: 608-85.

PENSIONS AND SOCIAL SECURITY

FOR THE AGED

THE SOVIET PENSION SYSTEM AND
SOCIAL SECURITY FOR THE AGED

Bernice Madison

Programs and activities falling within the expanding realm of social security are being instituted all over the world by newly developing countries and enlarged by those who have reached a higher degree of industrial and technological development. Sums spent on these programs and activities have mounted steadily, especially in the second half of the twentieth century. In this chapter I shall discuss the evolution of the Soviet pension system from the 1917 Revolution to the present, focusing attention on current pension provisions for the aged—the largest program in the Soviet social security firmament (as it is in many industrialized countries, including the United States). In addition to published Soviet and Western sources, my evaluation of this program, as it affects the lives of its clientele and government policy, will include the views of a sample of Soviet emigrés who had been pensioners in the Soviet Union and a sample of personnel employed in social security whom we interviewed in Israel.

The most important social insurance law inherited by the new regime from the tsarist government was the Health and Accident Act of 1912—the result of lengthy discussions energized by the 1905 Revolution. Because it applied to only 19 percent of the labor force and granted low benefits, this law was extremely unpopular among workers (Astrakhan 1961: 20).* Its primary merit was that it included representatives from both employers and workers in its local administrative organs, thereby recognizing the right of workers to participate in organizing and managing programs concerned with their welfare.

While the 1912 law was still being debated, Lenin made a counterproposal to it at the Sixth Conference of the Russian Democratic Party in Prague (1912). He advocated a state system of social insurance

---

*In 1912 about 40 million rubles was spent for sickness benefits and medical care for factory workers. This represented 36 kopeks per person in the population—one tenth of the German expenditure (Danskii and Komarovskii, eds. 1913: 29-36).

built on four principles: (1) coverage of all risks that bring about loss of ability to work; (2) benefits equal to total earnings, financed entirely by employers and government; (3) coverage of everyone working for hire and members of the worker's family; (4) administration by unified organs of a territorial type in which the insured exercise complete control (Lenin 1948: 427; Aralov and Levshin 1959: 8-9). These principles, as used by Lenin and his followers, became an effective means for raising class consciousness among the proletariat. Their propaganda for their own social insurance program developed into a full-blown campaign which acquired a vividly political character and which went on in spite of arrests, searches of party offices, and other repressive measures. "Social insurance strikes became a common occurrence (Solov'ev 1913: 2-3; Ankudinov 1962: 7; "Strakhovanie rabochikh" 1913: 4).*

Developments following the assumption of power by the Soviets fall into three well-defined periods:

(1) 1917-21: War Communism. Decrees of December 1917 were designed to carry out the government's promise for "full social insurance" based on workers' "slogans." But they were short-lived. By the middle of 1918 the state became virtually the sole employer of all employables and thus obligated to guarantee a minimum income for all, either in the form of wages and salaries or in monetary assistance. In October 1918 a program of social security (*sotsial'noe obespechenie*), rather than social insurance (*sotsial'noe strakhovanie*), was enacted. Approved by Lenin, it extended coverage to all persons supporting themselves by their labor and to members of their families; related benefits to average "norms for minimum subsistence"; covered all risks, including old age if it was accompanied by disability; and transferred administration to the state. Financing, primarily by employing establishments, was to be supplemented by the national budget (Astrakhan 1971: 30). In effect, the 1918 legislation replaced social insurance with assistance—"to each according to his need"—a move toward egalitarianism. Given the cataclysmic destruction of economic resources of that era, the new program could not be implemented to any significant extent.

---

*In 1914 a bill incorporating Lenin's principles, drafted by worker representatives to the social insurance council established by the 1912 law, was submitted to the Social Democratic faction of the Duma, but no action was taken. Lenin's followers later emphasized what in their view was the abysmal inadequacy of actions by the Provisional Government.

(2) 1921-28: The New Economic Policy (NEP). With NEP came a drastic reorganization of social security, guided from then on by the socialist maxim "To each according to his work." Hence benefits were related to former earnings and a distinction was made between wage and independent workers, the latter deemed unsuitable for coverage because they were not hired and there was no giver of work. They were to get help from mutual aid. An old-age pension system freed from the disability requirement was introduced in 1927 for textile workers, extended to all manual workers in 1928 (and to all workers by 1937). It required a twenty-five-year work record, the beneficiary's labor contribution to society. Administration was shifted to Commissariats of Labor.

(3) 1928 to date: The Five-Year Plans. As the forced industrialization drive enormously increased the number of workers, social security became an ever more important instrument for achieving the economic objectives of the regime.* The Commissariats of Labor were severely criticized for allowing only those incapable of productive work to receive pensions. In 1929 the party demanded a "break from the past": social security was to concentrate on increasing labor productivity, strengthening work incentive, and encouraging socialist competition. In 1930 unemployment benefits were abolished. In 1931 Stalin denounced as a heresy egalitarianism (*uravnilovka*) that treated all insured workers alike. What was needed, he said, was differentiation, which would apply less stringent eligibility requirements and a more advantageous benefit formula to shock workers, union members, those in "leading" industries and unhealthy occupations, and those with long or uninterrupted work records. Funds for pensions were cut sharply, resulting in exceedingly low benefits throughout the 1930s.† In 1933 the Commissariats of Labor were abolished; administration was transferred to the All-Union Central Committee of Trade Unions (AUCCTU) operating as an arm of the state apparatus. The extension of benefits in Stalin's program was enshrined in the 1936 Constitution, Article 120 of which declared that "Citizens of the USSR have the right to material security in old age as well as in the event of sickness and loss of capacity to work."

---

*In 1928 the nonagricultural labor force numbered 15.5 million, while 70.6 million were engaged in agricultural occupations; by 1959 the former went up to 56.2 million while the agricultural work force went down to 52.6 million (Eason 1963: 77).

†In relation to wages, the average monthly pension dropped from 36 percent in 1927 to 29 percent in 1937 to 23 percent in 1955 (Minkoff 1959: 25).

The pensioners' situation deteriorated further after World War II, when huge differences were permitted between pensions for "privileged" and ordinary recipients, the former sometimes receiving fourteen times as much as the latter.* The level of ordinary old-age pensions was decisively influenced by the maximum on earnings (30 rubles a month), on the basis of which pensions were fixed. This limit was in effect from 1932 to 1956, although the average earnings of workers during this period went up almost ten times (Novitskii and Mil' 1981: 27-28)—a situation which often forced the aged to live in harrowing conditions. The "independent" contingent was still left to mutual aid, even though its meagerness, often accompanied by "cleanings [of] parasites" and *kulaks*, led to unrelieved hardship for many disabled, old, and helpless people. Despite all this, public assistance for the needy was ruled out.

The death of Stalin (1953) heralded a more humanitarian approach. At the Twentieth Party Congress (1956), Khrushchev called for a better pension program. Following wide public discussion, a new all-union law went into effect in October 1956—a date hailed by Soviet planners as inaugurating a brighter era. Its most beneficial features were substantial increases in amounts, extension in coverage, elimination of gross inequalities, supplements for unable-to-work dependent family members, introduction of a benefit formula weighted in favor of the low wage earner, and partial pensions. Public assistance finally appeared.† It was, however, to be implemented at the discretion of each republic. All of this was achieved while maintaining the major purposes of social security as in preceding years. Overall the 1956 law brought about a degree of harmony between the welfare needs of the people and the economic objectives of the regime but still left the weakest and neediest at the bottom.

The next breakthrough, in 1964, introduced a "guaranteed" pension system for collective farm workers (*kolkhozniki*), albeit on less generous terms than for nonagricultural workers and employees. ("Employees" are for the most part office workers, in either industry

---

*"Privileged" workers are in specific categories of difficult work and in leading industries; see below under "Coverage."

†The minimum old-age pension was set at almost 50 percent above the maximum sum generally allowed previously, while the minimum disability pension was raised to six times its former amount. On the average, old-age pensions rose 100 percent, disability pensions 50 percent, and pensions for survivors 64 percent. The greatest increases were for low-paid workers, for whom pensions increased almost threefold. For public assistance, see Zakharov (1974: 407-13).

or farms, or other types of administrative personnel.) The preamble to the 1964 Collective Farm Members' Pensions and Allowances Act stated that "sizes of pensions . . . will be gradually raised to the level of state pensions for workers and employees [in tandem] with the growth of national income, particularly collective farm [*kolkhoz*] income." This policy has been slowly implemented by a variety of devices which have diminished but not eliminated the inequalities in pension size. Furthermore, collective farmers are still ineligible for supplements and partial pensions. The current situation is seen as "transitional," caused primarily by low productivity, which does not generate sufficient farm income to provide pensions for collective farmers at the same level as for state farm workers (*sovkhozniki*), workers, and employees, or to make available to them grants and other forms of social security in line with norms fixed for workers and employees (Gushchin 1975: 22). It is generally agreed that "perfecting" pensions to do away with distinctions between separate groups can be achieved only if economic prerequisites exist.

After 1933 the AUCCTU was gradually divested of many of its administrative duties. In 1937 old-age and disability pensions were transferred to the republic Ministries of Social Security. Union power was also curtailed by the USSR Council of Ministers' Union-Republic State Committee on Labor and Social Questions. This body, created in 1955, serves in an advisory role to the Council of Ministers and exercises a key interpretive function designed to strengthen uniformity in the implementation of welfare policy throughout the nation. While AUCCTU has the right of legislative initiatives "in the supreme bodies of state power," the Committee on Labor and Social Questions has the right to review them and make recommendations which undoubtedly weigh heavily in final decisions.

THE PENSION SYSTEM

We turn now to the present system, shaped by seventy years of development and reenshrined in the 1977 Constitution, Article 43 of which guarantees material security for the aged, the totally and partially disabled, and survivors. As noted, we will present the views of a sample of Soviet emigrés who had been old-age pensioners in the Soviet Union.*

*The sample, gathered in 1980, includes 232 workers and employees. (Two collective farm workers were excluded from the sample.) Most (88 percent) left

COVERAGE

Entitled to old-age pensions are persons of retirement age who have the requisite work record; to disability pensions, adults disabled by general and work-connected causes, the former with the requisite work record, the latter without reference to the work record, and

their country between 1977 and 1980, the rest somewhat earlier. We located most of them in the United States, in 14 cities in nine states, and a few in Toronto, Canada, usually through resettlement welfare agencies and occasionally through contacts in emigré communities. Although not all emigrés who were approached wished to participate, most did, and their number was sufficient for our purposes. Our sample was not random, but our respondents were competent and earnest, and we believe that they provided reliable data. A careful analysis of the pattern of distribution of their answers shows unambiguously that they gave serious thought to our questions before answering them and that they were not responding in an undifferentiated manner. They ranged in age from 55 to 85. In the Soviet Union they had worked in 63 different occupations, in establishments whose work forces ranged from one to 15,000 workers.

In some respects our respondents constitute a distinctive sample. Only 131, or less than 57 percent, were women—a lower percentage than in the USSR generally—and only two women had received partial pensions—a much lower percentage than is true of the Soviet female old-age pensioner group.

In several important respects, however, our respondents appear to be representative of urban old-age pensioners in the Soviet Union generally, especially those in the largest and large cities, which contain relatively the greatest numbers of old-age pensioners in their populations. They came from 29 cities in 10 republics: 88 from 11 cities in the Ukraine; 84 from 4 cities in the RSFSR; 35 from 7 cities in Belorussia, Armenia, and Latvia; and the remaining 25 from 7 cities in Azerbaizhan, Georgia, Uzbekistan, Moldavia, and Lithuania. The cities included (among others) Moscow, Leningrad, Kiev, Rostov-on-Don, Odessa, Kharkov, Tashkent, L'vov, Minsk, Baku, Tbilisi, Riga, and Erevan. (It is predicted that in twenty or thirty years, inhabitants of pension age will make up 30-40 percent of Moscow's population. Pertinent is the finding that in 1970 the proportion of persons of pre-pension age [women, 50-54, men, 55-59] was higher in the RSFSR, Ukraine, Latvia, and Estonia than in the country generally. Since mobility among elderly people is not marked, most remain in the same republics, and in the same cities, after reaching pension age. Three of these republics were represented in our sample. See Dmitriev 1980: 97 and 31.) If we compare certain key characteristics of our respondents with those of urban pensioners in the categories of largest and large cities studied by Soviet investigators, a number of similarities emerge in terms of family composition, educational level, age and occupational distribution, percentages of women and men who continue to work after claiming their pensions, association between amount of pension and continuance of work, differences among men and women in rates of poor health, and views concerning qualifying pension age. Especially striking are the similarities in percentages of those who continue to work in the same since 1968, totally disabled children;* to survivor pensions, unable-to-work dependents whose breadwinners had the requisite work record;† to long-service pensions, some in scientific and creative professions; and to personal pensions, individuals for special services to the state. Partial pensions are paid to some with work records too short for full pensions.

Not all in these categories are in covered occupations, and not all in covered occupations meet other eligibility conditions:

(1) Occupational exclusions. Ineligible are those who either work without a labor contract or under civil law agreements or as nonstaff workers in trade and procurement; self-employed craftsmen and "free professionals"; institutionalized disabled and mentally ill employed on subsidiary farms and in neuropsychiatric facilities; "protectors" *(patroniruiushchie)* of the mentally ill; and meat-cutters in kolkhoz markets paid by private citizens (!) (Simonenko 1980: 57-58).**

(2) Work history requirements for old-age pensions are based on sex, working conditions, and physical condition of the worker. For

---

places and in the same jobs and in reasons for continuing; most important, for our respondents, on average, pensions replaced 51 percent of pre-pension earnings, while nationwide the replacement rate was 52 percent in 1976 (Ministerstvo 1982: 23; see also Shapiro 1980 and Dmitriev 1980). The 52 percent replacement rate is a sharp decline since 1959, when the average old-age pension equaled 71 percent of average earnings of workers who became pensioners in that year; in 1966, 66 percent; in 1972, 62 percent; in 1975, 52 percent.

*From 1968 to 1980 only children who had attained 16 years of age; since 1980, congenitally disabled children from birth.

†All legal children of breadwinners and illegitimate children whose paternity has been established in court, under age 16, or 18 if in school; brothers, sisters, and grandchildren, if they have no parents able to work; parents and spouse, if they have reached retirement age or are disabled; parent or spouse, regardless of ability to work, if he/she is raising any of the children in the above categories who are under age 8; and grandparents, if there is no one required by law to maintain them.

**Some idea of the size of the uncovered contingent may be gained from Simonenko's (1980) listing of just one segment: those who work for private citizens without labor contracts—laundresses, cleaning women, cooks, tailors, seamstresses, middle and junior medical personnel attending sick persons in the home, stenographers, typists, maintenance workers, servants, home teachers, teachers of music and drawing, coaches, and watch and clock repairmen. Simonenko includes no less than twenty-four excluded groups of occupations. Temporary workers are those whose work for a given employer does not last more than five consecutive days, or not longer than ten days a month.

male workers and employees in ordinary work, the minimum is twenty-five years; for females, twenty years. For both sexes these minimums are reduced if for at least half of the working period their work was "privileged": for work underground, in harmful conditions, or in hot shops pensionable age is lowered by ten years (to age 50 for men, 45 for women), and the work record minimum is reduced by five years (twenty years for men, fifteen for women). For those who worked under other onerous but less difficult conditions, pensionable age is lowered by five years (to 55 for men, 50 for women), but there is no reduction in the requisite work record. Mothers of five or more children raised to age 8 need five years less; blind and dwarfs of both sexes, ten and five years less respectively.

Following a series of liberalizing decrees, in 1980 former kolkhozniki were finally permitted to combine their farm work with work in state establishments and organizations, giving them the necessary "composite" (smeshannyi) work record for pension purposes.

To be eligible for a partial pension, an individual must possess a work record of at least five years; attain pensionable age while at work; complete not less than three years of work immediately preceding application (during these three years, interruptions in work that did not exceed a total of six months are permitted); and apply during the month following cessation of work. "Privileged" status is denied. The overwhelming majority of partial pension receivers, who on average lack 2.5 years of work for full pensions, are women. As a result, women tend to receive lower pensions than men (Ministerstvo 1982: 54). In November 1981 mothers of large families and of disabled children who reach age 8 or die between the ages of 8 and 16 were exempted from all requirements except the five-year work record, but they cannot retire before age 55 (Shedrova 1982: 54-56). Since most mothers of such young children are not likely to be this old, the new law "stimulates" them to work in the interim. For workers and employees disabled by general causes the work requirement rises with age from two to twenty years for men and one to fifteen years for women; in "privileged" jobs, from one to fourteen years for both sexes. For kolkhozniki and breadwinners of survivors requirements are the same, except that for the former there are no "privileged" jobs other than in the Far North.

(3) Age requirements. Since 1928, for male workers and employees in ordinary work, the retirement age has been 60, for females,

55. For both sexes these ages are reduced by ten years for arduous conditions of work for which the work record is reduced by five years (criteria enumerated above) (Zakharov 1983: 14). Retirement age is reduced by five years for those employed in difficult conditions of work (list (2) above), but the work record for eligibility remains twenty-five years for men and twenty years for women (*ibid.*). Mothers of large families, women with twenty years in "intensive" textile occupations (since 1968), and those whose twenty years of work include a fifteen-year stint as machine operators (since 1975) are entitled to a five-year reduction. Since 1968 men and women who worked fifteen years in the Far North, or those who were employed for twenty years in regions equivalent to the Far North, or have a twenty-year combined work record in the Far North and equivalent regions can also retire five years earlier. Male blind and dwarfs can retire ten and fifteen years earlier, respectively; female, fifteen years earlier. The minimum retirement ages for kolkhozniki (65 for men and 60 for women in 1964) were equated to those for workers and employees in 1968. They can receive reductions only for work in the Far North or the Far North and equivalent regions, a stipulation introduced in 1970.*

Between 1960 and 1981 the total number of pensioners rose by more than 143 percent, most of the rise caused by a more than 650 percent increase in old-age pensioners (see Table 1). Among the latter, workers and employees are a steadily growing majority, while kolkhozniki are a steadily declining minority. Survivors and disabled, extremely numerous between 1940 and 1950, in recent years have stabilized at about one third of all pensioners.

Despite the huge rise in old-age pensioners, it is likely that at least 13-15 percent of persons of pensionable age do not receive pensions (Madison 1978: 77, fn. 42, with later corrections).† They are ineligible owing to the occupational exclusions described above. To these must be added women who have not worked outside the home or worked for periods too short to entitle them to any kind of pension. Some women worked for the required number of years

---

*Those among my respondents who became eligible for pension earlier than at usual ages represented almost all "privileged" work categories: workers in hazardous occupations, workers in the Far North, those who achieved requisite work records before minimum retirement age, and those who worked under "special" circumstances.

†Most of the work on this estimate was done by Murray Feshbach, to whom I am most grateful. Also see Porket (1982: 261).

Table 1

PENSIONERS IN THE USSR, 1940-83

(In thousands)

Year	Total Number of Pensioners[a]	Old-Age Pensioners					Survivors and Disabled[b]	
		Workers and Employees		Kolkhoz Members				
		Number	Percent of All Old-Age Pensioners	Number	Percent of All Old-Age Pensioners	Percent of Total	Number	Percent of Total
1940	3,638	225	100.0%	--	--	6.1%	3,413	93.8%
1941	4,000	200	100.0	--	--	5.0	3,800	95.0
1950	19,829	846	100.0	--	--	4.3	18,983	95.7
1960	20,606	4,531	100.0	--	--	21.9	16,075	78.1
1961	21,900	5,400	100.0	--	--	24.6	16,500	75.3
1966	32,000	8,100	50.6	7,900	49.4	50.0	16,000	50.0
1970	40,100	13,200	55.7	10,500	44.3	59.1	16,400	40.9
1975	44,400	18,200	63.2	10,600	36.8	65.0	15,600	35.0
1976	45,200	19,000	64.6	10,400	35.4	65.0	15,800	35.0
1977	45,900	19,800	66.0	10,200	34.0	65.3	15,900	34.7
1978	46,700	20,800	67.5	10,000	32.5	66.0	15,900	34.0
1979	47,600	22,000	69.0	9,900	31.0	67.0	15,700	33.0
1980	48,700	23,100	69.8	10,000	30.2	68.0	15,600	32.0
1981	50,200	24,200	71.0	9,800	29.0	67.7	16,200	32.3
1982	51,400	25,500	73.0	9,500	27.0	68.1	16,400	31.9
1983	52,400	26,700	74.1	9,300	25.9	68.7	16,400	31.3

Sources: Vestnik statistiki, no. 7 (1976: 85), and no. 2 (1979: 79); *Narodnoe khoziaistvo SSSR* (1980: 411, and 1982: 417).

[a]Includes certain ranks of war veterans and their survivors.
[b]Includes survivors of war veterans.

but failed to fulfill other eligibility conditions, especially in regard to partial pensions. In the 1930s and 1940s worker families had to provide for nine out of ten elderly relatives, for five to six in the late 1950s, and for one to two in the early 1970s. Since 1980 the easing of work requirements for kolkhozniki and for mothers of large families or disabled children—if these mothers applied for partial pensions—has reduced the uncovered group to some extent, but the failure to cover all who work for hire remains a problem.

Most pensioners approve of the sex differential in the work requirement. Acceptance of ages fixed for ordinary work is quite widespread—much more so for men than for women—but a majority consider them too long for both sexes for "privileged" work, especially if it is dangerous. Workers in such jobs, particularly women, are said to find them exhausting, and many are concerned for their health.

FINANCING PROVISIONS

For workers and employees financing provisions date to 1956, when contribution rates were established for enterprises. The rates, between 4.4 and 9 percent of payroll, were in force until 1979, despite recommendations by many Soviet scholars and administrators that for the short run they be raised. They now range from 4.4 to 14 percent of payroll, depending in part on the degree of hazard of employment.* The intent was and still is to tie pensions squarely to output; when output rises, it is reasoned, so does the payroll, and so do contributions into the state social insurance fund. Subsidies from the national budget would be minimal. This last assumption has not been met: subsidies to cover deficits have increased steadily and by 1980 amounted to more than half of the total spent.

Financial arrangements for kolkhozniki date to 1965 and 1970. Their pensions are financed by the Central All-Union Social Security Fund for Collective Farmers. Its resources are formed by a 5 percent tax on the gross income of all self-contained kolkhozy (since 1978,

---

*Although all enterprises in a particular industry pay the same percentage, each branch of the economy has a different tariff. For a detailed breakdown of contribution rates from 1956 to 1979, see Krulikovskaia, Kiseleva, and Gorbunov (1959: 17) and Lantsev (1976: 42). In 1975 the average rate was 6.75 percent. It should be noted that the rates are not differentiated actuarially—i.e., not in direct relationship to the degree of hazard. For 1979 rates, see decree of the Soviet of Ministers, no. 18 (1979: 118).

6 percent of those that show more than a 15 percent return on investment); 3 percent of gross income when members work in inter-kolkhoz enterprises that show a return on investment in excess of 40 percent; plus a 5 percent payroll tax. In 1965 the national budget covered 38 percent of kolkhoz pensions; in 1970, 60 percent (Lantsev 1973: 250). Pensions of workers and employees in collective farms are paid from the state social insurance fund.

The national budget also absorbs total costs of institutions for the aged and disabled, of pensions for former military personnel and their survivors, and for personnel in state agencies equated to the military. An exception is the working partially disabled, whose pensions are paid out of designated funds in the systems for workers and employees and kolkhozniki respectively.

Since 1960 pensions have been the most expensive item in the social security/social insurance budget, using more than 70 percent of it (see Table 2). Increases in expenditures during 1960-69 were primarily on extended coverage and permitted only modest raises in benefit levels; during 1970-79 increases were primarily to raise benefit levels, while also covering the growing number of pensioners. (For a discussion of benefit levels for the 1970s, see Madison 1973: esp. 117.) These increases were reflected in expenditures on pensions as a rising percentage of the social consumption budget (Table 3) and GNP (Table 4).

Table 2

PENSIONERS AND EXPENDITURES ON PENSIONS, 1960-82

Year	Total Number of Pensioners (*In millions*)	Total Social Security/Social Insurance Expenditures (*Billions of rubles*)	Expenditures on Pensions (*Billions of rubles*)	Pension Expenditures as Percent of Total Expenditures
1960	21.0	10.0	7.2	72.0%
1969	39.0	20.7	15.0	72.4
1970	40.1	22.8	16.2	71.0
1979	47.6	42.3	30.6	72.3
1980	48.7	45.6	33.3	73.1
1981	50.2	48.3	35.4	73.3
1982	51.4	51.3	37.8	73.7

Sources: *Narodnoe khoziaistvo SSSR* (1922-72: 381; 1922-82: 419; 1977: 744; 1980: 381; 1982: 417); *Vestnik statistiki*, no. 5 (1983: 77), and no. 1 (1984: 75).

Table 3

PROPORTION OF SOCIAL CONSUMPTION BUDGET
EXPENDED ON PENSIONS, 1960-81

Year	Social Consumption Budget (*Billions of rubles*)	Percent Spent on Pensions from All Sources[a]
1960	27.3	26.0%
1965	41.9	25.2
1970	63.9	25.4
1975	90.1	27.0
1979	110.2	27.8
1980	116.5	28.3
1981	122.2	29.0

Sources: Narodnoe khoziaistvo SSSR (1981: 381); *Vestnik statistiki* 5 (1983: 77).

[a]The major source of funds for financing pensions is the social consumption fund. This fund is formed from allocations by the state budget and by social insurance contributions from employing establishments, social organizations, and collective farms. Currently revenues for social security accumulate in four systems: allocations from the state budget, state social insurance fund, Central All-Union Social Security Fund for Collective Farmers (since 1965), and Central All-Union Fund of Social Insurance for Collective Farmers (since 1970).

Table 4

PROPORTION OF GNP EXPENDED ON PENSIONS, 1976-83

Year	Gross National Product (*Billions of rubles*)[a]	Expenditures on Pensions from All Sources (*Billions of rubles*)	Percent of GNP Spent on Pensions
1976	530.8	25.7	4.8%
1977	558.1	27.1	4.9
1978	586.6	28.9	4.9
1979	606.2	30.6	5.0
1980	635.8	33.3	5.2
1981	669.7	35.4	5.3
1982	720.2[b]	37.8	5.2
1983	754.2[b]	40.0	5.3

Sources: GNP in 1976 and 1980: United States, CIA (1983); GNP in 1977, 1978, 1979, 1981, 1982, and 1983: extrapolated approximately by Gregory Grossman from official data on national income (produced) using multiplier of 1.376 (ratio of CIA GNP estimates to official national income figures for 1976 and 1980). The official Soviet national income (produced) figures are as follows (in billions of rubles): 1976: 385.7; 1977: 405.6; 1978: 426.3; 1979: 440.6; 1980: 462.2; 1981: 486.7; 1982: 523.4[b]; 1983: 548.1.[b] Expenditures on pensions, 1976-80: *Narodnoe khoziaistvo SSSR* (1980: 381); expenditures on pensions, 1981-83: *Narodnoe khoziaistvo SSSR* (1984: 427).

[a]In established prices.   [b]Preliminary.

Soviet theorists maintain that although pensions are wage-related, they are not a contract based on an exchange of benefits for premium payments. The failure of enterprise contributions to fully cover expenditures does not jeopardize the right to benefits. Hence while benefits are a fundamental right of eligible individuals, they are also a gift from the state—a reward for carrying out the duty to work, but not a payment for work done (Rimlinger 1971: 252-57). Despite continuing Soviet "gift" propaganda, fewer than 2 percent of pensioners see their benefits as gifts: 91 percent are convinced that they paid for them in full, and the rest, that they paid for them in part. Copious comments stress not only that they paid much more than in full by many years of hard work for which they received a pittance, but also that they paid indirectly through "limitless" taxes.*

BENEFIT ARRANGEMENTS

Soviet scholars do not describe economic resources other than pensions that may be available in old age. Rather they stress repeatedly that "for people who have crossed over into the non-able-bodied age, a pension is the chief and frequently the only source of their means of subsistence" (Pavlova, Rabkina, and Rimashevskaya 1979: 26). The amount of pension is therefore of overriding concern to the elderly. This amount is related to average past earnings, decreased by 15 percent for workers and employees who reside in rural communities and are "connected" with agriculture (Vul'f 1981: 49). Below we summarize the major arrangements.

(1) Old-age pensions. A worker or employee can choose earnings during the "five best out of the last ten years" or the year preceding

*Pensioners' rejection of the "free" pension concept is borne out by a prominent Soviet economist, who gave the following "perspective": "By the time a person reaches majority, society's expenditures on his upbringing amount to 15,000 rubles; during his working life (40-45 years), a worker creates 125-137,000 rubles of new value; of this he receives 60-65,000 rubles in wages, contributing 65-72,000 rubles to capital accumulation. From the latter he pays off his debt of 15,000 to society; 'makes an advance' of 13,000 rubles toward his old-age pension, *covering its cost for an average of 15 years*; and places the remaining 37-44,000 rubles at the disposal of society for further development of productive force. [Thus] if one approaches the evaluation of 'free' distribution through social funds from this perspective, it turns out that it is not at all free" (Namal'tsev 1976: 85; emphasis mine). Namal'tsev draws some of his material from *Planovoe khoziaistvo*, no. 12 (1972: 107); *Kommunist*, no. 8 (1972: 41); and *Pravda*, 27 July 1973.

application, whichever is more favorable. He is entitled to a 10 percent increase of the basic pension if his work record was ten years longer than the general qualifying period or if he had an uninterrupted work record of fifteen years.* A decree that became operative on 1 January 1983 raised the supplement to 20 percent if (a) men, and women who had never had children, had uninterrupted work records in the *same* enterprise of not less than twenty-five years (for women who had children, not less than twenty years); (b) the applicants' general work records were longer by ten years than the record generally required for old-age pensions; and (c) they were employed on 1 January 1983 as workers and employees. Since 1983 this supplement is not governed by the maximum pension limitation: it can be added to the maximum, as well as to the higher pension earned for working beyond retirement age, but cannot be greater than 10 percent of pension. Nonworking pensioners with unable-to-work or below-working-age dependents are eligible for a 10 percent supplement for one dependent and 15 percent for two or more. However, with the exception of the long or uninterrupted work supplement, a maximum pension receiver among nonworking pensioners is not entitled to additional increases or supplements.

Partial pensions are based on what the full pension would have been in proportion to the number of years worked, but never less than one fourth of the full pension. A kolkhoznik is limited to choosing any five successive years of earnings from the ten years preceding application and is not eligible for increases or supplements.

(2) Pensions for the disabled. The system adheres to the principle of compensating for loss of wages rather than for physical or mental harm sustained. Cause and degree of disability and type of work are decisive. All disabled are divided into three groups: Groups I and II, the totally and permanently disabled—the former needing constant care, the latter partially able to look after themselves; Group III, permanently partially disabled who are expected to work. For kolkhozniki, coverage to Group III was extended in 1968, but only if the disability is work-connected and occurs at the work place itself, not merely on land belonging to the farm. The benefit formula legislated in 1956 resulted in dire deprivation for many disabled. It was finally changed in 1974, but only for Groups I

---

*In 1972, 92 percent chose to base their pensions on earnings during the year preceding application because these earnings included increases in minimum pay. In the same year 42.8 percent of pensioners qualified for uninterrupted status and 9.4 percent for "long" status (Acharkan 1971: 124).

and II, for whom pensions are now calculated as a percentage of old-age pensions that ranges from 90 to 110 percent, depending on group and cause of disability. Supplements for dependents were changed from percentages to flat amounts, in some cases raising them by 300 percent (Komarova 1974: 3-8).* For Group I a 15 percent nursing supplement is granted. But all supplements combined cannot exceed 30 percent of the basic pension; the total pension cannot exceed the maximum pension or (except for Group I) average monthly earnings.

(3) Adult survivors' pensions. Eligibility is severely restricted. The spouse or parent of a deceased breadwinner is eligible only if he or she is caring for a child under age 8, or reaches retirement age, or becomes disabled within five years after the death of the breadwinner. Again the obvious intent is to "stimulate" young and middle-aged widows to work. Children (including illegitimate children if their paternity has been established, adopted children, and stepchildren) and dependent siblings and grandchildren receive pensions until age 16, or 18 if in school, or indefinitely if they become disabled before those ages. Pension amounts are computed in the same way as for the disabled.

(4) Benefit formula weighted in favor of low wage earners. For workers and employees in ordinary work and for kolkhozniki (since 1971) in all except Far North work, this formula grants pensions ranging from 100 percent to 50 percent, applied to earnings from 35 rubles a month or less to 100 rubles or more; for "privileged" work, the range is from 100 to 55 percent.† This means that proportionately low earners receive larger subsidies than high earners. However, in absolute terms, the reverse is the case.

(5) Restrictions regarding maximum and minimum amounts. In old-age pensions for workers and employees the 1956 maximum still applies—120 rubles a month; in old-age and disability pensions for kolkhozniki the 1965 maximum still applies—102 rubles a month. Maximums were raised in 1975 for disabled workers and employees— to 120 rubles for Groups I and II and 70 rubles for Group III.

---

*This change was largely motivated by the finding that the proportion of disabled with dependents was three times higher than among the aged, and that 86 percent of these dependents were children.

†Prior to 1971 a kolkhoznik's pension was equal to 50 percent of the first 50 rubles of average monthly earnings, plus 25 percent of earnings above 50 rubles—a formula considerably less advantageous than the one for workers and employees.

Minimums are based on an unable-to-work-person's minimum budget, researched since the 1950s and carefully defined in 1967.* The method used to develop it produced an austere standard for 1965-70: 51.1 rubles per person per month for a family member and 56 rubles for a person living alone; for 1970-75 the former figure rose to 66.4 rubles. Neither has been raised to date, despite Soviet scholars stressing that budgets must be adjusted to each higher stage in the country's economic development, and Western scholars' findings that prices have been subject to inflation (Chapman 1979).

Table 5 summarizes developments in minimum pensions since 1956. In 1981 the minimum pension for workers and employers exceeded the minimum wage for workers and employees (70 rubles a month) only for Group I disabled and for survivor families with three or more unable-to-work dependents by only five rubles a month. All others fell short of the minimum budget for 1965-70. Despite significant progress, kolkhozniki were still behind workers and employees. While some farmers can increase their incomes by selling produce grown on their private plots, such an option is not available to the totally helpless Groups I and II nor undoubtedly to many aged whose younger family members have moved to the cities. The most likely to fall below the austere historical poverty line are survivors (mostly women and children) and Group III disabled. The adults in these categories are "stimulated" to work (as noted), although their earning capacity is often severely curtailed by two-thirds disability or old age or both.

Minimums are supposed to assure modest adequacy; maximums (and the weighted formula) are supposed to partially level off differences in wage scales on the basis of which pensions are calculated. But these goals require that minimums and maximums keep up with rising earnings or prices; if they fall behind and stay behind for long periods, deprivation can become acute. Between 1956 and 1978 minimum wages for workers and employees went up four times, increasing by 160 percent; between 1956 and 1981 minimum old-age pensions went up twice, increasing by 67 percent. Hence the widening gap between the level of living of pensioners and the working population. Kolkhozniki did better: their minimums increased by 133 percent in fifteen years, but they started

*Sarkisian and Kuznetsova (1967), pp. 423 and 108 for time spans included in the "current period" and "coming period," and pp. 166 and 133 for the "rational budget"; also Karpukhin and Kuznetsova (1968) and Madison (1978: 47-49) on how the minimum budget is constructed.

Table 5

MONTHLY MINIMUM AND MAXIMUM PENSIONS, 1956-85

(In rubles)

Type of Pension	Minimum							Maximum			
	1956	1965	1968	1971	1974	1980	1981	1956	1965	1974	1980
Workers and employees											
Old age	30			45			50	120	120	120	120
Disability: Group I-A[a]	36	50			70		75	120	120	120	120
Disability: Group I-B	30	50			70		75	90	90	120	120
Disability: Group II-A	28.5	35			45		50	90	90	120	120
Disability: Group II-B	23	30			45		50	60	60	120	120
Disability: Group III-A	21	21			25		30	45	45	60	60
Disability: Group III-B	16	16			21		26	40	40	60	60
One survivor–A	16	21			23		28	45	45	60	60
One survivor–B	16	21			23		28	40	40	60	60
Two survivors–A	23	30			45		50	90	90	120	120
Two survivors–B	23	30			45		50	60	60	120	120
Three or more survivors–A	30	50			70		75	120	120	120	120
Three or more survivors–B	30	50			70		75 b	90	90	120	120 b
Pneumoconiosis											

Collective farmers	1956	1965	1968	1971	1974	1980	1985	1956	1965	1974	1980
Old age		12		20		28	40		102	120 (102)[c]	120 (102)
Disability: Group I-A		18	30	35		45			102	120 (102)	120 (102)
Disability: Group I-B		15	25	30		45			76.5	90 (76.5)	120 (102)
Disability: Group II-A		14.4	20	25		28			76.5	90 (76.5)	120 (102)
Disability: Group II-B		12	16	20		28			51	60 (51)	120 (102)
Disability: Group III-A		12		16		16			38.25	45 (38.25)	60 (51)
Disability: Group III-B											
One survivor–A		10.8		16		20			38.25	45 (38.25)	60 (51)
One survivor–B		9		16		20			34	40 (34)	60 (51)
Two survivors–A		14.4		20		28			76.5	90 (76.5)	120 (102)
Two survivors–B		12		20		28			51	60 (51)	120 (102)
Three or more survivors–A		18		30		45			102	120 (102)	120 (102)
Three or more survivors–B		15		30		45			76.5	90 (76.5)	120 (102)

Sources: (among others): Zakharov (1975: 29, and 1983: 25, 55, 71); Vul'f (1981: 49); Stiller (1983: 139, 160).; For kolkhozniki, see in addition *Current Digest of the Soviet Press* 19, 39: 5; *Pravda,* 27 September 1967, p. 2, and 21 May 1985, p. 1. It was stated in the latter issue of *Pravda* that pensions for kolkhozniki who are disabled or survivors will be increased proportionally—when, not stated.

a "A"—work-connected disability; "B"—nonwork-connected disability.

b Minimums for Groups I, II, and III are 75, 50, and 30 rubles respectively; maximums are 120, 120, and 70 rubles respectively.

c Amounts in parentheses are after deduction for agricultural connection (15 percent) if the farmer has a private plot that is larger than permitted by kolkhoz regulations, and for workers and employees if they reside in rural areas and have a connection with agriculture.

at an extremely low level. Pavlova, Rabkina, and Rimashevskaya summed up as follows:

> The satisfaction of the basic, including new, needs of pensioners presupposes maintaining a constant ratio between pensions and wages for every person during the entire period the pension is received (1979: 27).

Instead the Eleventh Five-Year Plan provided a five-ruble raise, even though "practice has confirmed that an increase in minimum pensions alone does not solve the problem of material support for pensioners as a whole" (Pavlova, Rabkina, and Rimashevskaya 1979: 26). In 1981 perhaps as many as 30 percent of all pensioners among workers and employees and 40-50 percent of old-age pensioners among kolkhozniki received minimum pensions (V TsK KPSS 1981: 7; Lopata 1980: 13). So far, no dynamic relationship between minimum pensions and average wages has been established—a crucial flaw.

(6) Average pensions. Table 6 shows average monthly pensions paid under different schemes during the years 1970-80. When these are compared to the official poverty lines for the periods 1970-75 and 1965-70, it is evident that as yet no average pension has reached the 1970-75 poverty line (66.4 rubles). Average pensions from all sources did not cross the 1965-70 poverty line (51.1 rubles) until 1978, pensions from state insurance until 1975; by 1980 they outpaced the line by only 4 and 9 rubles respectively. All average pensions from other sources are still below the 1965-70 standard.

(7) Absence of indexing and supplementation. The Soviet system does not provide for indexing, an anti-inflation device, and there is no supplementation of below-poverty-line pensions. Newly awarded pensions tend to rise with the wage level because most are based on average earnings during the last twelve months, but the longer a pensioner lives, the greater the disparity between his pension and current wages. The Eleventh Plan proposes to increase pensions of those who retired more than ten years ago on less than 60 rubles a month "to bring them closer to the level of pensions now granted to workers with analogous qualifications."

(8) Public assistance, introduced for aged workers and employees in 1956, was in 1981 available for the aged in only nine republics, and in all fifteen republics for Groups I and II disabled. It requires applicants to be ineligible for pensions, without "any

Table 6

AVERAGE MONTHLY PENSIONS PAID UNDER
DIFFERENT SCHEMES, 1970-80
(In rubles)

Year	Average Pension, All Sources	Average Pension from State Insurance[a]	Average Pension from Other Sources[b]
1970	33.6	41.1	23.0
1971	36.3	42.8	26.5
1972	39.2	44.6	30.6
1973	40.5	45.9	31.4
1974	42.3	47.7	32.9
1975	45.9	51.7	35.3
1976	47.4	53.3	36.4
1977	49.2	55.2	37.3
1978	51.5	57.1	40.1
1979	53.0	58.9	41.7
1980	55.6	60.1[c]	45.4

Source: McAuley (1982: table 6.4).

[a] For workers and employees.

[b] For collective farm members and war pensioners.

[c] Using "unpublished statistics from Gosplan," Sternheimer (1982: 86) gives the average pension for 1980 for "urban blue-collar workers and employees" as 70 rubles. Writing in 1981, the director of the Belorussian affiliate of the Institute for Scientific Research of Labor (Nauchno-Issledovatel'skii Institut Truda) and candidate of economic sciences calculated the average pension that year to be 77 rubles a month. He arrived at this figure by taking 50 percent of the average monthly wage of 154 rubles, the 50 percent being the rate applicable to this amount of earnings for pension purposes. For Belorussia his average pension came to 69 rubles (Slobozhanin 1981: 50-51). In a different context from that used for this table, McAuley prognosticated that by 1980 pensions for retired workers would reach 66-73 rubles (in Porket 1983: 306-7 and footnotes 27-29).

means for existence" and without relative legally responsible for support.* For residents of urban communities, until 1981 assistance averaged 10 rubles a month; in rural areas, 9 rubles. Since 1981 the average was raised to 20 rubles a month (to 28 rubles for "nationalities")—but only in the RSFSR. In 1970 only one third of kolkhoznik farms had "mutual material-assistance funds," which on average granted less than 65 rubles a year to the needy (Madison 1978: 55). By no stretch of the imagination can it be said that these

*Under the family code promulgated in 1968, responsible relatives include children, stepchildren, and grandchildren. Support payments can be exacted by civil suit if necessary and are set at levels proportional to the supporter's income.

grants provided an income of "modest adequacy." This was truly a blot on "socialist humanism" and explains why the more forward looking and concerned scholars and administrators were calling for more adequate support of this underclass. But it was not until 1985 that public assistance grants were raised to 30 rubles a month— obviously a great improvement but still below a harsh poverty line, still not a truly humane program for the "nonproductive."

(9) Institutional care. In 1979, the USSR's 1,500 institutions accommodated 360,000 aged and disabled, meeting roughly half of the need.* In many localities there are no institutions. Furthermore, a majority of them (878 in 1977) have always been located in the RSFSR, leaving but a small number for the remaining fourteen republics.

Given the benefit arrangements described above, it is not surprising that

> half of all pensioners live with working relatives. The size of their pensions is generally less than those of people who live by themselves and who depend on the pension as the chief source of income. And in many cases inadequacy of means of subsistence and not desire . . . compels pensioners to live in the families of their children, whose dependents they in some sense become (Pavlova 1976: 1196-1200).†

Our findings show that on average pensions replace 51 percent of earnings, ranging from 46 percent for high earners to 61 percent for low earners. Benefits are indeed weighted in favor of the latter, but in 1981 this helped only 11 percent of under-minimum earners to raise their pensions above the 1965-70 poverty line; very low earners (70-100 rubles) were more successful, yet 46 percent of them

---

*The extent of unmet need is indicated by a Soviet study carried out in 1971. It divided the country into five zones and found that institutional care was required by 1.4-4.0 persons (depending on the zone) for every 1,000 persons in the population. According to reliable estimates, the Soviet population was 264.5 million in 1979. If the average need for institutional care is arbitrarily set at 2.5 persons for every 1,000, the total needed places would come to 661,000 (cited in Kravchenko 1979: 42). Kravchenko believes that the time has come to build apartment complexes and furnish them in line with the special needs of the aged and disabled, including various facilities and services such as stores.

†Pavlova points out that "this causes a fairly large proportion of highly paid workers to end up, as far as per capita income is concerned, in the ranks of the relatively not-so-well-off, this having an adverse effect on their work."

also remained below the poverty line (see Table 7). In short, in absolute terms low earners remain at the bottom of the system.

A large majority of our respondents report that the economic gap between pensioners and the general population is wide (see Table 8). They are almost unanimous (96 percent) in declaring that minimums should provide a level of living comparable to that of the general population. All reject the 50 ruble minimum, arguing that such a sum cannot prevent deprivation; three quarters say that at

Table 7

INFLUENCE OF PRIOR EARNINGS ON PENSIONS
FOR OUR RESPONDENTS
(Percent)

	Prior Monthly Earnings					
Monthly Pension	Less than 70 Rubles	70-100 Rubles	101-150 Rubles	151-200 Rubles	More than 200 Rubles	Percent of Total
Less than 46 rubles	78%	28%	--	2%	--	18% (N=29)
46-51 rubles	11	18	3%	--	--	
Poverty Line						
52-70 rubles	11	54	45	--	1	21 (N=49)
71-119 rubles	--	--	50	84	12	34 (N=79)
120 rubles	--	--	2	14	87	32 (N=74)
Total	4 (N=9)	17 (N=39)	24 (N=56)	22 (N=50)	33 (N=77)	100 (N=231)

Table 8

PENSIONERS COMPARED WITH THE GENERAL POPULATION
IN FOUR AREAS (BY OUR RESPONDENTS)
(Percent)

	Area of Comparison			
Compared to general population, pensioners are:	Economic Well-Being	Medical Care	Housing	Leisure-Time Activities
Better off	1%	--	--	1%
Same	14	73%	87%	54
Worse off	85	27	13	6
Total (N=232)	100	100	100	61[a]

[a]Thirty-nine percent (90 respondents) had never heard of these activities.

least 101-150 rubles is necessary; the rest, that one could scrape through on 71-100 rubles. All believe that current supplements for dependents are too meager; most (94 percent) advocate 31-50 percent of basic pension for one dependent. Most (93 percent) want the current maximum raised or eliminated.

Three quarters of the respondents urge that supplementation be made available by the pension system for all persons with below-poverty-line pensions. Some would make drunkards and those able to work ineligible, and only 2 percent would make individuals with relatives ineligible because "relatives themselves have little." They stress that help from unions is not only rare and irregular, but also is not given for living expenses, and that help from kolkhozy— "erratic handouts"—has no practical significance. Perceptions of institutional care are negative in the extreme: only aged persons in desperate circumstances are said to be willing to enter institutions.*

WORKING PENSIONERS

An unprecedented and increasing amount of attention is being devoted by Soviet investigators to the problem of "stimulating" pensioners to work during "pension life." Calculations show that each working pensioner, even if his productivity is 10-12 percent below average, creates 3,500-3,600 rubles of national income annually. This is enough to "significantly" cover both his earnings and the cost of his pension, thus enabling the government to absorb the expense of pensioner care out of current rather than prior income produced by pensioners (Novitskii and Mil' 1981: 242). Since average life expectancy after reaching retirement age is now said to be between fifteen and seventeen years for men and about twenty-five years for women, work during pension life can also be significantly prolonged (Povarov 1980: 10). To this end, differentiation in "broad" stimulating policies, initiated in 1964, has become steadily more unmitigated and promises to exert even greater pressure in the future when policies are "deepened" (Zakharov and Povarov 1979: 45-46).

*Fifty-eight percent of the respondents are university and college graduates, and 49 percent worked as high- and middle-level professionals. Two thirds received pensions higher than the minimum wage, and nearly a third received the maximum pension. Nevertheless, for more than 20 percent pensions ranged between the 1965-70 poverty line and the minimum wage, and for 13 percent they fell below this line—both levels judged by all the respondents as too low to prevent deprivation.

The current situation is defined by a 1979 decree which in effect divides working pensioners into privileged and ordinary. Among workers and employees the most privileged engage in either arduous and hazardous occupations or jobs designated as essential for the economy; they are entitled to full pensions and full earnings. The somewhat less privileged work in the Urals, Siberia, and the Far East; they receive 75 percent of pension plus full earnings. The still less privileged are in moderately important jobs, among them managerial and supervisory; their pension-plus-earnings must not exceed 300 rubles a month. The least privileged are in only fairly important occupations; they get 50 percent of pension, which combined with earnings must not exceed 300 rubles. Some privileged are exempt from the 15 percent rural deduction. All must work full time and have the requisite work record for full pensions. The status of ordinary workers and employees is unaffected by "character or place of work"; they are permitted to retain pension and earnings, but only up to a combined ceiling of 150 rubles a month. This group takes in both full-time and part-time workers, and none is now subject to the two-months-a-year limitation on employment. They too must have requisite minimum work records. Kolkhozniki and sovkhozniki, in line with a 1964 decree, receive full pensions and full earnings if they continue to work in agriculture (Novitskii and Mil' 1981: 29).

For workers and employees the 1979 decree established an increment of 10 rubles a month for each year worked beyond retirement age up to a maximum of 40 rubles; however, pension plus increment is limited to 150 rubles. This is now called the "new maximum," although it is rather a device for lengthening the requisite work record and raising retirement age. The extra pay becomes available following cessation of work. The pensioner can receive either both pension and earnings without the right to increment, or receive only earnings while accumulating the increment.*

Table 9 presents data on labor force participation of old-age pensioners among workers and employees. Among the disabled, 40 percent were working in 1979—a relatively high proportion because more than 77 percent of Group III (the most numerous) are employed. Among kolkhozniki the proportion working dropped from 60 percent in 1959 to less than 34 percent in 1970. To an important extent, this decrease—in contrast to the post-1962 increase

*If work beyond retirement age took place before January 1980, the increment is not payable (Tsederbaum 1980a: 48-54, and 1980b: 48-50).

Table 9

LABOR FORCE PARTICIPATION OF OLD-AGE PENSIONERS
AMONG WORKERS AND EMPLOYEES, 1956-82

Year (as of 1 January)	Number of Old-Age Pensioners (*In thousands*)			Workers as Proportion of All Old-Age Pensioners (*Percent*)
	Total	Workers	Nonworkers	
1956	1,877	1,107	770	59.0%
1957	2,711	775	1,936	28.6
1958	3,493	670	2,823	19.2
1959	4,007	605	3,402	15.1
1960	4,531	532	3,999	11.7
1961	5,379	545	4,834	10.1
1962	6,040	554	5,486	9.2
1963	6,729	631	6,098	9.4
1964	7,436	748	6,688	10.1
1965	8,180	1,025	7,155	12.5
1966	9,020	1,268	7,752	14.1
1967	10,015	1,528	8,487	15.3
1968	10,987	1,748	9,239	15.9
1969	12,019	2,272	9,747	18.9
1970	13,185	2,500	10,685	19.0
1971	14,299	2,942	11,357	20.6
1972	15,290	3,252	12,038	21.3
1973	16,186	3,616	12,570	22.3
1974	17,197	4,019	13,178	23.4
1975	18,242	4,424	13,818	24.2
1976	19,056	4,649	14,407	24.4
1977	19,893	5,068	14,825	25.5
1978	20,827	5,503	15,324	26.4
1979	21,962	6,115	15,847	27.8
1980	23,100	7,022.4	16,077.6	30.4
1981	24,200	7,671.4	16,528.6	31.7
1982	25,500	8,160	17,340	32.0

Sources: For 1956-79—Novitskii and Mil' (1981: 37); for 1980 and 1981—Shchennikova (1984: 72); for 1982—Kolesnikov (1983: 3).

NOTE: Novitskii and Mil' (1981: 28-29) interpret the data in this table as a clearcut demonstration that the major influence on the decision of old-age pensioners to continue to work or not is the level of pension. After 1956, as a result of a substantial increase in average pensions and limits on payments to working pensioners, labor force participation declined precipitously, from 59 percent in 1956 to 9.2 percent in 1962. In 1955 every other old-age pensioner was working; in 1962, every tenth.

among workers and employees—is due to a growing number of kolkhozniki (especially women) being busy on their private plots rather than in the national economy—not only a more lucrative source of income, but also one that is now encouraged by the government. A higher proportion of men than of women work—in 1970, 15.9 and 9.6 percent respectively. However, in absolute numbers women constitute a majority of working pensioners because nearly three fourths of old-age pensioners are women. Participation of urban women is twice as high as that of kolkhoz women. On average men continue to work 5.4 years; women, 4.2 years. Not surprisingly, the highest labor participation is among privileged pensioners. Branches of the economy with the highest proportion of old-age pensioners in their work forces are health, physical culture and social security (6.5 percent), local public services (4.5 percent), and commerce and public catering (4.3 percent). Lowest is transport, with only 2.3 percent (Krukhmalev 1979: 46; Novitskii and Mil' 1981: 32, 70-72, 138-39, 206).

Pensioners are employed in three settings: in regular enterprises and organizations which guarantee maximum utilization of their experience; in 900 specialized enterprises for the disabled or those with limited work capacity; and in home work. A large majority of old-age pensioners continue to work in the same place where they worked prior to retirement; even if they change, two thirds remain in the same professions and occupations. The specialized enterprises employ only 150,000 old-age and disabled pensioners. The number of home workers increased more than 2.5 times in the 1970s; in 1978 it was said to be 250,000. Thirty percent, or 75,000, were pensioners, mostly disabled. Home work was still regulated by a decree of November 1928.*

In 1978 almost all working old-age pensioners (98 percent) worked full time (forty-one hours per week) which, it was claimed,

---

*Despite far-reaching changes in the employment situation since 1928—from unemployment to a shortage of labor—no changes in regulations for home work were made until 29 September 1981. Currently labor contracts for home work give priority to women with children under age 15; the disabled and pensioners; those who have reached retirement age but are not receiving a pension; persons with a lower than normal work ability for whom home work is recommended; persons who are nursing severely disabled family members or members suffering from lengthy illnesses; and persons whose seasonal work leaves free periods. Old-age pensioners employed in home work receive full pensions if, combined with earnings, their income does not exceed 300 rubles a month (Pankin 1982: 51-54).

"[was] not in the interest of the country or the health of the pensioners themselves" (Novitskii and Mil' 1981: 177). Most of the 140,000 who worked part time were home workers. Seventy percent who worked part time in regular enterprises received pensions below 60 rubles a month; only 7.4-8.2 percent among them worked part time because of "material security" (Novitskii and Mil' 1981: 133, 157-58, 173-76).

The single most important reason for working continues to be the pensioners' need for additional income. In this context, an influential factor has been the growth of average earnings in comparison with the growth in average pensions; during 1960-80 the difference between the two increased more than threefold and came to 70 rubles. Novitskii and Mil' conclude as follows: "Although this is a negative characteristic, it encourages higher labor participation among pensioners" (1981: 35). Generally, material "incentives" were the determining factors for 40 percent of pensioners in 1976-77, and for 49 percent of kolkhozniki. Other reasons, grouped under "social motivation," include a psychological need to work, desire to be in a congenial group, to do work useful for society, to keep up physical fitness, to help children financially, to improve one's standard of living, and to become eligible for a higher pension.* The higher the educational level, the higher the proportion who wish to continue to work (Novitskii and Mil' 1981: 75). Labor force participation rises among recipients of minimum pensions, drops somewhat when pensions are slightly higher, and rises again when pensions are fairly high or near maximum (Ministerstvo 1982: 11).

Most pensioners are critical of official judgments about the relative importance of occupations and jobs. As one of our respondents noted, these judgments result in "pensioners whose income from pension plus earnings is 300-500 rubles, while others do not receive even a half of either pension or earnings."† Our respondents

---

*Some of the reasons listed under social motivation are undoubtedly economic in nature and are characterized as such by Novitskii and Mil' themselves in several places in their book. A potent material factor that motivates retirees to work is their average monthly per capita income: for 40 percent of all who work at home and 42 percent of disabled home workers it is 50-69 rubles; 35 percent of aged home workers have an average income of 39-40 rubles. Among kolkhozniki whose average per capita income is less than 30 rubles, 70 percent are pensioners; of those with 31-49 rubles, 60.5 percent are pensioners; of those with 90 rubles or more, 39 percent are pensioners (Novitskii and Mil' 1981: 116, 193).

†This respondent continues: "The question of the simultaneous receipt of earnings plus pension is extremely complicated, and the answer to it depends

fell into three groups in terms of work status: those who did not claim pensions when eligible, remaining on their jobs (13 percent); those who worked after receipt of pension (61 percent); and those who did not work after retiring (39 percent).* Of the first group, 52 percent continued to work after they claimed their pensions, thus merging into the second group; the rest became members of the third. The second group included eighty men and sixty-two women. Economic reasons—especially the family's material needs and the desire for a better standard than could be bought with pension alone—were decisive or important for all of them; these reasons are cited three times as often as psychological reasons (among which "I liked my work" and "I wanted to remain with friends in a congenial group" are given most often). Psychological reasons are important for most professionals but for relatively few skilled workers. Four fifths remained in the same work places and same jobs; only 17 percent of maximum-pension receivers changed jobs, but all below-poverty-line pensioners did so.

The nonworkers included three times as many women as men. The most frequent reasons for quitting work were psycho-social and health-related. Among the former, a desire for leisure and household duties and/or care of children predominated. Among the latter, most respondents reported "bad health" and reduced work ability. The lower the pension, the higher the proportion for whom health-related reasons were determining factors. Health played a role for only 30 percent of professionals but for 65 percent of skilled workers.

While four fifths of the respondents agree with Soviet experts that the desire to get higher pensions "stimulates" people to work harder, they point out that such stimulation is mostly effective during the last year on the job, when high earnings most affect pension calculations.

More than three quarters of all respondents maintain that pensions alone do not meet "modest needs" or meet them "barely"; the rest, that they meet them well. None of the nonworkers report a

---

on a multitude of factors." As she details only some of these factors, the complexities that emerge are almost endless.

*It should be kept in mind that the respondents emigrated before the new regulations took effect in January 1980 so that they were subject to more stringent limitations, including the two-months-a-year limitation on employment for many white-collar workers (espeically managerial and supervisory personnel). In our survey we listed four types of reasons for either continuing or discontinuing work: economic, psychological, psycho-social, and health-related.

rise in living standard; for one third, the standard fell slightly, and for nearly one half, it fell substantially. Workers were much more successful in maintaining their pre-pension standard or raising it slightly, although this was not true uniformly: the standard changed least for the two groups of lowest pre-pension earners; for the rest, the higher the pre-pension earnings, the higher the proportion whose standard fell—largely because high earnings postretirement were virtually eliminated due to pre-1980 limitations. It is difficult to say what the effect of the 1979 decree will be on these limitations since so much depends on the importance of the "character and place of work" *at a given time*—that is, at retirement.

ADMINISTRATIVE ARRANGEMENTS

The administrative apparatus has remained virtually unchanged since the 1930s for workers and employees and since 1965 for kolkhozniki.

(1) Administrative organs. The directing organs are the republic Ministries of Social Security, whose regional, district, and municipal departments parallel the republic structure. Within them are the Medico-Labor Expert Commissions (VTEK) responsible for disability determinations. Since 1955 the ministries have been "controlled" by the Union-Republic Committee on Labor and Social Questions; each ministry is also accountable to its republic Council of Ministers. Double-subordination applies to its lower organs as well: vertically, to higher echelons in the hierarchy; horizontally, to the soviet of people's deputies (Maksimovskii 1974: 90).* Normative regulations are embodied in all-union statutes; procedures, organizational forms, and operational methods are regulated by republic statutes. The fragmented nature of applicable laws—for workers and employees, labor law; for kolkhozniki, collective farm law; for war veterans and their survivors, administrative law—generate additional complications. Furthermore, ministries do not maintain earnings records of covered individuals; these must be developed at the time claims are made at individual enterprises and farms.

*Theoretically, vertical relationships bring about procedural unity in implementing legislation; horizontal relationships make possible appropriate responses to local conditions. However, according to Maksimovskii, the problems generated by the system of double-subordination—e.g. numerous directives from above about questions that are clearly within the purview of lower organs—are yet to be resolved.

The AUCCTU and the All-Union Social Security Council of Collective Farmers oversee payments of contributions and reimbursements into social security funds and act as "broadly based social organizations [that] participate in resolving . . . questions" on citizens' rights to pensions and placement of the disabled in suitable jobs (Batygin 1979: 45).* The AUCCTU works through its constituent unions, organized on a territorial basis by industry. The kolkhoz hierarchy starts with the farm council and goes up to district, region, and republic councils. The last three are required to include representatives of Ministries of Social Security and of Finance.

Persons who apply for pensions after they leave employment go to Ministries of Social Security directly. Workers and employees who apply while still at work may go either to the ministries or to a three-member committee comprised of the enterprise's bookkeeper and one representative each from union and management (the last, chairs). In kolkhozy such committees are appointed by district councils. Applications are then "presented" to ministries; if found in order, they are submitted for payment; if incorrect, they are returned to the presenters for redoing. If disagreements persist, they are reviewed by a committee appointed by the local soviet, representing the Ministries of Social Security and of Finance and unions or kolkhozy, depending on the case in question. Presentations for disabled and survivors are made in the same manner, except that the process is more complicated: disabled have to go through the VTEKs; suvivors have to establish the deceased person's status as breadwinner and often also face VTEKs.

Delays and errors in processing applications were especially numerous in the postwar chaos. Subsequent measurable improvements are attributed to automation, initiated in the late 1960s and still in progress. Many large cities are now completely automated, but in autonomous republics and smaller regional and district departments automation is still partial or nonexistent.

According to Komarova (the RSFSR Minister of Social Security), the "most urgent, acute" problems are still numerous. Half of all delays and errors in processing occur when the requisite work record is privileged; in many regions staff does little either to stimulate

---

*Batygin also lists among union functions "control" of activities of social security organs and of the correctness of expenditure of funds assigned for pensions and services to pensioners, with no explanation, however, as to how this control is exercised.

pensioners to work or to carry out the law when they do work—that is, make sure that management notifies ministries within five days after hiring a pensioner, specifying his occupation. Notifications are often delayed, and sometimes pensioners are incorrectly listed as engaged in occupations which entitle them to full pensions. All this results in large overpayments—a problem that calls for a constant "struggle." Furthermore, enterprises often ignore the law that 2 percent of jobs be reserved for the disabled; little is done to develop home work; special workshops are poorly maintained; prosthetic and orthopedic devices are of poor quality; VTEKs make many mistakes regarding degrees of disability, partly because staff and union representatives, who by regulation are supposed to attend VTEK sessions, do so only sporadically—a "vicious" practice that has become common in many places; and enterprises often ignore VTEK recommendations. Republics fail to use fully national budget allocations for the construction of institutions; many existing institutions lack essential amenities, such as central heating, running water, and sewers (Komarova 1979: 5; 1975: 5; 1981: 5-6).*

(2) Staff. Ministries have always experienced serious problems in hiring, training, and retaining qualified personnel. These problems are not as acute as they were in earlier years, but neither are they negligible. Recruitment of personnel is centered on those with training in law, accounting, bookkeeping, and medical labor. Staff is expected to do the work of ministries as well as to act as teachers, organizers, and sources of information for cooperating bureaucracies.

In varying degrees the fifteen ministries try to raise the competence of staff, chiefly through varied types of in-service training that emphasize "practical" knowledge; questioning goals and policies is not encouraged. These efforts have been successful to a degree, more so in the RSFSR ministry than in most of the others (Emel'ianova 1981:3).† There is no training that would qualify staff to deal with

---

*As the head of the RSFSR ministry, Komarova is the leader among social security ministers. In 1981 the RSFSR ministry served more than 56 percent of the country's entire pensioner contingent. In comparison with other ministries, it has at its disposal the most impressive resources, such as research institutes and training courses; it publishes the monthly journal *Sotsial'noe obespechenie*, which is the major publication in the field. In regard to overpayments, Komarova reported that during nine months of 1974 the RSFSR ministry alone had overpayments of four million rubles. No data are given on underpayments.

†In 1981 there were in the RSFSR ministry 36,000 "specialists" with higher and secondary education, a number that fulfilled 63 percent of required specialist replacements. In addition, 30,000 workers raised their qualifications during

the emotional and social needs of their clients. Occasionally staff are exhorted to be compassionate, patient, and well-mannered. In his speech to the central committee of the party at its plenum in November 1982, Premier Yuri Andropov reviewed at considerable length the accomplishments and problems of the social security system in RSFSR, with which he seemed to be thoroughly familiar. Among other things he noted the following about staff:

> When one becomes acquainted with such facts [delays, complaints, failure to take account of individual needs], involuntarily one is led to ask: how could these woebegone workers be entrusted with serving the elderly and the disabled? From everything they do there flows indifference toward people, their questions and needs. And yet quite often heads of departments exhibit incomprehensible liberalism and total forgiveness toward them.

Table 10 shows the opinions of our respondents regarding the availability and need of social services in the USSR. For the most part, the services available are delivered by activists (among them pensioners)—that is, volunteers attached to local offices. Nothing is written about the staff-activist relationship, and there is little information about the activities volunteers are empowered to undertake or the extent of their involvement. From observation, the impression is gained that what they do is at best helpful to some pensioners sporadically, often superficially. Activists are practically unknown in many rural communities.*

(3) Fair hearings. As is generally recognized, the appeals process often yields data and insights into how well or poorly a social program

---

1975-80. This is an improvement over the situation in 1976, when more than two thirds of the regional and local RSFSR social security workers lacked secondary and specialized or higher education (Azarova 1979: 48-49).

*In the Soviet Union it is thought that social security (which provides cash benefits) and social services should be integrated—that is, that both should be provided by the same agency in order to facilitate coordination and assure efficiency. Given this approach, it is from local social security departments that Soviet pensioners obtain services. As Table 10 shows, most pensioners feel that there is a need for a wide variety of services, but that this need is either largely unfulfilled or only partially fulfilled. We found that only 6 percent of our respondents were reached by social services offered by paid personnel and volunteers in social security departments. This meager assistance is not appreciably extended by what other agencies do: altogether fewer than 10 percent of the respondents received any kind of social services. In the words of one respondent, "Most pensioners know nothing about any kind of services or help from anyone"—especially, it turns out, from the social security system.

Table 10

AVAILABILITY AND NEED FOR VARIOUS SOCIAL SERVICES:
OPINIONS OF RESPONDENTS

Service	Opinions about Availability and Need (*Percent*)				
	Available and Needed	Available, Not Needed	Not Available but Needed	Not Available, Not Needed	Total
Counselling for social problems	21%	13%	45%	21%	100% (N=217)
Referral for counselling for social problems	22	8	59	11	100 (N=216)
Help with finding suitable housing	12	3	83	2	100 (N=225)
Help with finding suitable work	24	5	67	4	100 (N=226)
Arranging free vacations[a]	45	6	48	1	100 (N=226)
Arranging housekeeping services for the homebound	17	3	79	1	100 (N=224)
Arranging visiting nurse services for the homebound[b]	62	1	34	3	100 (N=225)
Arranging institutional care	47	5	43	5	100 (N=222)

[a] Arranged by unions—not by social security personnel or volunteers.

[b] Arranged by medical personnel—not by social security personnel or volunteers.

is fulfilling the purposes for which it was created. Discussion of this process, other than a ritual recitation of regulations, is meager, and statistical data are altogether absent.

Under Soviet arrangements two types of appeals are possible: the first is in regard to facts which are essential for establishing eligibility—e.g., marital status or work record; the second, in regard to decisions made on the basis of these facts. For facts the individual's first recourse is to agencies in charge of pertinent documents. If he disagrees with the facts as contained in them, he has the right (since 1966) to take his case to court. Such court cases, if they exist, have not been mentioned in the literature. Redress of decisions can be sought only via an administrative review. From a statement by Komarova and published materials, it appears that grievances center on pension amounts. That procedural violations are quite common is established by Maksimovskii (1974: 26, 35), who brands them as particularly reprehensible because the majority of clientele. are elderly, sick, or unable to work, and in addition are not well informed about their rights.

The administrative route of appeal of an old-age pensioner who is a worker or employee is to the executive committee of the district or city soviet of people's deputies, which almost routinely sends his appeal to a higher organ within the social security hierarchy. The latter has no power to reverse decisions made by the local commission for awarding pensions or to require the commission to reexamine cases; its function is only to recommend and advise. For kolkhozniki the district soviet is the final arbiter; there is no recourse to a higher authority.* Appeals from VTEKs are forwarded to higher organs in the hierarchy—reaching the ministry if the claimant persists— which reexamine the appeal and hand down a final decision.

Most of our respondents needed less than six months to get the required documentation ready; for 14 percent it took between six months and more than a year. More than four fifths found the application process reasonable and fairly simple; for the rest— mostly those with work records dating to the prewar era—this process got snarled up in "bureaucratic red tape so respectable as to be an object of envy." More than four fifths say that pension amounts were in accord with their understanding of what the law promised—a "stingy" pension. Occasionally, however, administrators tried to "nip" their rights. Although nearly all wanted to know on what basis decisions were made, only two fifths were given full and clear explanations; for 25 percent explanations were vague; one third got none.

Although more than half of the respondents judge social security workers as competent and experienced, most are unenthusiastic about their expertise. This seeming anomaly is clarified by their views on such in-service training as exists (see Table 11). Striking majorities assign major importance to the need for workers to appreciate the right of their clients to seek and receive an objective review of

*Maksimovskii notes that this limitation is in conflict with legal practice that governs appeals from administrative decisions, but "still remains to be changed after 14 years of operation" (1974: 106).

Table 11

SOCIAL SECURITY WORKER TRAINING: RESPONDENTS' VIEWS
ON AREAS REQUIRING IMPROVEMENT

Degree of Importance	Area in Which Better Training is Important *(Percent of respondents agreeing)*			
	Knowledge of Laws and Regulations	Applying Laws and Regulations to Individual Situations Correctly and Promptly	Respect for Human Dignity and Individual Differences	Appreciation for Right to Seek and Receive Objective Review of Decisions with Which Clients are Dissatisfied
Not important	3%	1%	--	1%
Fairly important	17	16	10%	7
Important	46	49	30	24
Very important	34	34	60	68
Total	100 (N=224)	100 (N=224)	100 (N=225)	100 (N=225)

decisions (92 percent) and to being treated with respect and a recognition of individual differences (90 percent). However, less than 67 percent of workers themselves assign major importance to objective review; more of them stress the need for improved expertise in applications of laws and regulations, which suggests that they are not sufficiently strong in them.

Respondents report a high turnover in workers. Almost half consider the workers' pay low or lower than that of employees with similar qualifications in other settings; nearly two thirds believe that the general public shows them less respect than (say) teachers. There is an underlying feeling among respondents that the workers' relatively low status within the community is a reflection of the low esteem in which the clientele itself is held.

Of 232 respondents, 32 percent were dissatisfied with decisions regarding their pensions (especially their amounts), but less than 7 percent complained. Four fifths of noncomplainers felt that "appeals do not receive competent, objective review—useless!"; the rest were either afraid to antagonize staff, or did not want to get involved in a drawn-out process. Of 15 complaints, 9 were lodged within the system and 6 with newspapers, local soviets, and unions.

Of 9 who complained about amounts, 3 won (their cases involved errors that were easily corrected at the workplace); of 6 who complained about procedure, some received form letters and others heard nothing. When we asked whether a pensioner dissatisfied for substantive reasons should have the right to go to court, 93 percent said "Yes," but many were skeptical about anything good coming out of court review.

In the speech referred to above, Andropov noted an unsatisfactory handling of clients' complaints and pointed out that in many areas of the RSFSR complaints were increasing—especially concerning old-age pensions and disability determinations. He attributed this to weak explanatory and propaganda work of social security organs and to "formalism" and "bureaucratism" on the part of some personnel. The 1977 Constitution contains the famous Article 58, which for the first time in Soviet constitutional practice "fixed" the right to complain: it gave citizens the right to appeal to courts not only in criminal and civil matters, but also in conflicts prompted by administrative abuses of government officials and measures of the organs of state and social organizations. This article has touched off quite a lively discussion among social security scholars and administrators, a majority being in favor of its implementation, which will require a number of changes in the system's legal structure yet to be promulgated (see Azarova 1979: 45, and 1982: 75; Maksimovskii 1974: 124-25; Tarasova 1976: 134-37, and 1981: 64; Prokopenko 1980: 12, Fogel 1972: 174-75; Gushchin 1975: 70-71).

EVALUATION OF THE SYSTEM

Soviet advances in pensions since 1917 are substantial, but so far they have not been sufficient to eliminate the discrepancy between the ideological commitments the regime considers necessary and the performance of which it is capable. Nor has Soviet policy evolved theories, forms, or methodologies for coping with poverty and insecurity that are unique and that have not been practiced or explored by Western democracies. Lengthy periods of rigidity inhibit the pension system's capacity for change and hinder its responsiveness to the needs of its clientele. It does not seem likely that policy will change in the 1980s, or that seminal new ideas will emerge or be implemented. On the contrary, as an institution in a maturing industrial society used to exerting powerful social control, the system will face a decreasing number of options—despite the modernization process of which it is part. Specifically, the following are likely in particular areas:

(1) *Extension of coverage.* Given the shortage of labor, improved administrative procedures, and Soviet experts' concern about failure to cover all people (Kolesnikov 1974: 32; Zakharov 1975: 27), coverage may be extended to most of the currently excluded by permitting them to add up their short-term jobs into work records now required for full or partial pensions.*

(2) *Levels of benefits.* It is doubtful that benefits will be significantly raised in the 1980s. Since 1966 the number of aged pensioners has risen from half to 68 percent of the system's clientele. As noted, males remain in pension life for fifteen to seventeen years, females for almost twenty-five years; projections indicate that "the proportion of the population of retirement ages . . . will be considerably larger in the year 2000 than in 1975, in the Soviet Union as a whole and in all republics and regions except Central Asia" (Baldwin 1979: 15, 130; see also Sonin 1976: 156). It will account for 19.1 percent of the population in 2000 compared to 15.4 percent in 1980. This will necessitate increases in expenditures which even at current levels are likely to be judged an unacceptable drain. If, as anticipated, the proportion of elderly who live apart from their families rises, pension levels for them will have to be raised. The call by prominent Soviet scholars and social security administrators—such as Zakharov, Pavlova, Rabkina, Rimashevskaya, Lantsev, Azarova, and Kozlov (the last a senior scientific collaborator in the Institute of State and Law in the Academy of Sciences SSSR and in 1984 a candidate of jurisprudence)—for basic readjustments in the scale of pensions gained momentum in the 1970s and 1980s. But their proposals were not incorporated into the Eleventh Five-Year Plan and so far have not been integrated into law. Lenin's dictum that benefits must equal total earnings is still a slogan.

The aging of the population, coupled with labor shortages, has sparked a discussion among scholars and social security administrators about old age and old-age pensions. Few conceptualize the former as an immovable point in time since ability to work decreases

---

*That many people engage in short-term jobs is suggested by our findings concerning recipients of sick benefits. Seventy-six percent of our respondents reported that one reason for malingering—very frequently, quite frequently, and occasionally—is that "people want extra time so they can do extra work for more income" (Madison 1981: 11, table 5).

at different ages in different people, and all agree that people ought not to be made into full-time pensioners before their time. Yet most believe that there is a "typical" age—not defined—beyond which working as before is either impossible or too demanding. Most see an old-age pension as a historical concept which changes with time. In developed socialism a pension should not be a reward for work performed in the past; rather the basis for awarding a pension should be inability to work, combined with work performed in the past. To provide for those able to work should not be the aim of pensions (Acharkan 1971: 122). However, four fifths of our respondents do not agree; they believe pensions should provide adequate minimum support at legally established ages, either as compensation or as reward for work performed in the past so that old people can take it easy.

How should the USSR control the interplay of economic, social, and political forces? The earlier pension age in the USSR, "rightly regarded as one of the major gains and advantages of the socialist system," must not be compromised by a comparison with the trend in capitalist countries toward early retirement (Pavlova, Rabkina, and Rimashevskaya 1979: 31). Even though for a majority of workers the loss of the ability to work as a result of age-related changes comes at least five years later than retirement ages fixed by law, it is argued that to simply legislate higher ages is at present unacceptable in the USSR (*ibid.*; Solov'yev 1977: 44; Smirnov 1977: 88). Rather later retirement may come indirectly as the number of pensioners remaining at work increases. Thus will nonegalitarian pension life coexist with a largely mythical egalitarian ideology.

(3) Effectiveness of work incentives. "Desirable material incentives" are judged to have produced less than effective results so far. The major deterrents to continuing work are poor health (reported by 56 percent of workers and employees and three quarters of kolkhozniki), unsatisfactory working conditions; failure of management to provide easier part-time and home work; household duties; care of grandchildren; and time needed for private plots. Among workers and employees only 3.9 percent do not work because they are "materially secure"; among kolkhozniki of pre-pension age who wish to retire, 10.3 percent (Acharkan 1971: 119; Kogan 1973: 71-76; Smirnov 1977: 89; Demidov 1977: 5; Yakushev 1976: 244; Ministerstvo 1982: 39; Novitskii and Mil' 1981: 97). Nevertheless, it is not suggested that material

---

*A study of the state of health of the urban population of the USSR showed that only 2.6 percent of men and 2 percent of women 70 years and older do not suffer from chronic illnesses (Berzhikovskaia 1982: 31).

incentives be curtailed or discontinued. On the contrary, it is proposed that kolkhozniki be paid full pensions and full earnings not only for work in agriculture, but in other sectors of the economy as well, especially in service occupations in the villages; that the circle of professions and occupations which are now privileged be broadened across the board, especially in sectors with acute labor shortages; and that the job of "consultant" be created for highly qualified "intellectual" workers and be remunerated on a privileged basis.

The nature of major deterrents and the high cost of material incentives have led many to argue that the time has come to redirect policy toward retaining pensioners at work as long as possible and making their work as effective as possible, rather than retiring them and then "stimulating" them to reenter the labor force.* To this end, "a whole series of measures must be realized: legal, economic, organizational, medical" (Novitskii and Mil' 1981: 47). Investigators are advocating mandatory medical examinations for persons reaching retirement age to help them "ascertain the state of their health and their ability to work" (p. 51);† these would be given through improved gerontological services, which, if associated with medical social work, would also help to determine the kind and amount of work these people could do. Investigators also stress the need to improve sanitary-hygienic conditions of work, lower physical norms by mechanizing difficult and time-consuming work, institute a more flexible regimen by greatly expanding part-time and home work, and address the desire of some pensioners for retraining.**

*The cost of pensions for working pensioners went up from 0.5 billion rubles in 1968 to 2.5 billion in 1975, a sum which is not much less than the amount budgeted for all improvements in the pension system during the entire Ninth Five-Year Plan (1970-75).

†The recommendation may be the result of differences between pensioners' self-evaluations of "poor health" and medical findings. The latter report that two thirds of pre-pensioners are fully able to work, for every fifth person, ability to work is limited slightly, and for only one in ten is it seriously limited (Ministerstvo 1982: 80).

**The proportion of working pensioners in skilled physical work with considerable strain is reduced from 19.5 percent prior to getting pension to 10.2 percent after receiving it, and among "intellectual" workers (who are said to experience considerable nervous-psychic strain) from 8.3 percent to 4.3 percent. However, the proportion employed as unskilled workers rises from 25.4 percent to 34.3 percent, and of those in physical work with slight strain, from 8.7 percent to 12 percent (Ministerstvo 1982: 81). According to a 1976 study, 12 percent of working pensioners who are skilled workers would like to change their profession for an easier specialization (Novitskii and Mil' 1981: 22).

Furthermore, everything that is undertaken must conform to the pensioners' work potential, individuality, professional work habits, level of education, preferences, and desires—as well as to a number of "social factors" (Novitskii and Mil' 1981: 98, 165-66, 171, 189; Ministerstvo 1982: 92).

On the organizational level, planners urge the creation of a special coordinating council that would help elderly people retain health, ability to work, and social activity. In the legal domain, normative acts regulating home work must be updated and labor agreements must be "corrected." As for increasing financial resources for the pension system, they recommend that the issue of raising enterprise contributions be reexamined, not just at specialized enterprises that employ old and disabled pensioners, but throughout the national economy (Novitskii and Mil' 1981: 22, 157, 168, 186, 189).

Clearly all this adds up to a big order. In view of managerial rigidities and negative attitudes toward employing pensioners, it will not be easy to carry out.* Nevertheless, it is probable that redirecting efforts will be intensified. If the proposed measures are humanely administered so that they do indeed respond to pensioners' preferences and desires, some of them might prompt some pensioners to remain at work—given the low pension amounts.

In the meantime, the stimulation drive postpones the need to formulate an acceptable ideological base for supplementing low benefits by the pension system. Current regulations not only act as a supplementation-through-work formula favoring the low wage earner, but also have other advantages for the government: they motivate low pension receivers to remain in the labor force, they do not discourage high pension receivers from continuing to work, and they are firmly affixed to occupations and can be manipulated to energize workers needed by the state to keep working. But there are disadvantages. For example, enterprises find it difficult to lay off unproductive pensioners, and the income of working pensioners is higher in relation to both nonworkers and younger workers—an abnormal outcome because there is no increase in the pensioners' productivity or in their consumption needs. This disparity not only conflicts with the principle of distribution according to work,

---

*Management fails to appreciate pensioners' role in labor resources and lacks interest in financing conditions of work needed to utilize their labor. In turn, pensioners do not receive adequate information concerning possible job openings, nor are they and the public made aware of "leading" experience in utilizing labor in varied settings (Novitskii and Mil' 1981: 7).

but also undermines the material incentive to raise productivity and underlines the lack of equality in earnings for equal work. Furthermore, in the future the rise in minimum and average earnings (the latter are planned to reach 190-95 rubles a month by the end of the Eleventh Plan) for workers and employees and the use of the present formula for calculating pensions will result in a single norm for the majority—55-50 percent of earnings. Pensions for higher than average earners will not be calculated in proportion to earnings, but will amount instead to the general maximum—120 rubles. For many skilled workers this may deflate the connection between pension amounts and distribution according to work, thereby reducing their productivity during the pre-pension period. Payment of pensions from social funds while recipients work goes against the principle of using these funds for providing material security to those no longer able to work. The pension-plus-wage solution, incorporating a decision not to raise retirement ages, is a response to the labor shortage which is likely to become more untenable as time goes on. Too great a share of resources is used up for the benefit of relatively few, decreasing the possibility of raising support levels for the majority who do not work and assisting the needy ineligibles.

(4) Individual equity versus social adequacy. Egalitarianism in the sphere of pensions was discarded shortly after the 1917 Revolution, and since then differentiation, broadened and deepened, has held sway. Policy became centered on resolving the conflict between individual equity and social adequacy. The former, tied to the program's insurance objective, requires that benefits be directly related to an individual's contribution to social production, as expressed in wages and salaries; the latter, tied to its welfare objective, that benefits provide a certain level of living, regardless of what the average earnings had been. From an ideological standpoint the social adequacy goal, closer to the communist ideal, should be the winner, but it is the individual equity goal—"To each according to his work"—that is the rule. To be sure, efforts to deemphasize individual equity— relying on a benefit formula weighted in favor of low earners (but only to a limited degree, in view of the low maximums), supplements for dependents, and heavily on minimums—have not been absent. But so far their impact has been too weak to move the system decisively toward social adequacy because minimums are not efficient welfare devices, supplements are stingy, and there is no indexing.

As a result of "stimulating" measures, which absolve the pension system from maximizing the social adequacy goal, benefits become as much a work incentive tool as a means to provide a decent minimum. Unremitting pressure by party and bureaucracy demands that pensions "face production"—not people. The hardest hit are the weakest and the neediest: the chronically ill, the disabled, the very old who retired some time ago, those whose occupations are unimportant for the state, and women (who, as noted, constitute nearly three fourths of old-age pensioners). That their lot will remain submerged is clear from the Eleventh Plan, which does almost nothing to improve "actual security" (*fakticheskoe obespechenie*)—that is, social adequacy.

(5) *Administrative complexity and limitation of applicants' and beneficiaries' rights.* Improvements in the quality of records necessary for establishing eligibility have reduced a number of problems to vestiges of past eras. For further improvements reliance is placed on a universally automated system, better trained staff, and the willingness of cooperating bureaucracies to recognize social security as an important social institution that must be actively assisted in achieving its goals.

A fully automated system is a matter of time. Eventually it may lead to streamlining and unification of applicable laws and their more uniform implementations, to primary dependence on trained professionals (whose higher pay and occupational status would lower turnover), and to centralized record-keeping and payments. This in turn could eventuate in an all-union ministry with direct access to top decisionmakers and equal in power with cooperating bureaucracies, which would then be more likely to acknowledge the importance of social security. In the meantime, vexing problems must be dealt with.

Differentiation—said to have been transformed by the 1956 law into "a modern type implemented according to basic criteria" (Lantsev 1976: 90)—continues complicated, creates various inefficiencies, and results in unequal treatment of persons with the same rights.* Staff is confronted with privileged and ordinary occupations

---

*Soviet analysts question the double differentiation enjoyed by privileged categories. They point out that work conditions (as well as living and climatic conditions) have already been taken into account in basic wages, that differentiation in fact applies to occupations and work settings rather than to work conditions, that valid and "scientific" criteria for decreasing the minimum retirement age and shortening the work record in relation to work conditions are lacking, that the low length of service for those working underground or under difficult conditions means that a single job may in twenty or twenty-five years provide privileged retirement benefits for two persons rather than one, and that the

which may be changed at any time to suit the needs of the economy, producing many pension-plus-earnings patterns; uninterrupted work records are defined by minute instructions about who (for how long and for what reason—"respected" or not) is entitled to leave a job and stay off it without interrupting continuity; for some occupations, work in several enterprises can be added together; for others, it cannot.

In regard to financing, there is concern about the rise in national budget subsidies—especially for kolkhozniki, for whom post-1965 improvements have had to be covered almost entirely by subsidies. Most Soviet experts urge a greater absorption of pension expenditures by general revenues for the long term. All advocate an "optimum" relationship in the development and utilization of funds allocated to wages and salaries, on the one hand, and to social funds, on the other—as yet a major unresolved problem. Administrators, required to conduct accounting operations for each fund separately, continue to press for streamlining the fragmented and complicated financial structure.

To become a more effective vehicle for pension policy, administration will have to devote much greater resources to research. So far not a single signficant study has been published that would address humanitarian issues—levels of living at which pensioners maintain themselves, their family situations, housing, cultural activities, etc. Disturbing as well is the total silence about ineligibles and the superficiality of information about institutional care.

Our respondents felt that bureaucrats with whom they had the most direct and frequent contact—the local first-line workers and union activists—were the least influential in what they could do to improve their clients' lot, and that only infrequently could pensioners generate action by the more important wielders of power—the municipal party apparatus, the republic Ministries of Social Security, or the executive committees of local soviets. More than half believed that the party and government usually ignored the needs of elderly citizens, while more than a third thought they occasionally demonstrated

---

number of persons receiving such pensions is increasing faster than the overall growth in the number of old-age pensioners—an expensive outlay for the pension system. In 1976, 7.8 percent retired at earlier ages on privileged conditions. One example of unequal treatment, cited by Lantsev, will suffice: given the same group of disability and the same former earnings, differentiation produces thirty different sizes of pensions for Group I disabled, fifty-four for Group II, and twenty-four for Group III (1976: 90-95).

a desire to meet these needs more fully; few judged that the party and government demonstrated this desire often, and still fewer believed it consistent. As for undertaking organized activity themselves, more than 90 percent were interested, but they felt that to expect results would be unrealistic because they were not a socially dangerous group, but rather "downtrodden people" (*pribitye liudi*) in whose welfare the movers and shakers of Soviet society were only mildly interested.

It is not surprising that our respondents saw the pension system as only minimally supportive of values which they believed would ensure a more genuine response to their needs, desires, and hopes. (Table 12 shows their evaluations of the system.) Half to four fifths said that the system weakened all these values.* Material well-being is of primordial importance, but being treated as respected individuals— rather than as members of an undifferentiated mass whose identicalness derives from shallow eligibility requirements—contributes importantly to satisfaction with life. The realization of these values and the right to fair hearings is not likely to measurably accelerate in the 1980s, although the potential for progress in the latter sphere has been enhanced by the 1977 Constitution.

Viewed as an income maintenance program, the Soviet pension system is still quite a distance away from fulfilling Lenin's four principles. Viewed as a social institution, its contribution to the Soviet welfare state has been restricted. The essence of the ideal at the core of a welfare state is compensation to the individual for the negative consequences of a particular organization of life. Emphasis is on the common-needs principle, rather than on the reward of individual productivity. Instead of strengthening equality and social justice—the major driving forces of the 1917 Revolution—the system sharpens inequalities and intensifies social controls, in tandem with planned failure to provide actual security that for many sacrifices the golden years to the needs of a hungry economy.

---

*Respondents' views on values are associated with their pension life experience. Thus the more often their pensions did not meet their needs, the more likely they were to say that the system eroded material well-being; the older the pensioners, the more often they judged elemental humanity weakened by the system—no doubt because older pensioners continue to receive amounts that were fixed some years ago and are excluded from sharing in a rising standard of living when it is achieved for the general population. The more often they felt that the party and government usually ignored their needs, the more often they reported that the system weakened the "one for all, all for one" value.

Table 12

EXTENT TO WHICH SOCIAL SECURITY SYSTEM SUPPORTS
SELECTED KEY VALUES: RESPONDENTS' EVALUATIONS
(Percent)

Value	System Strengthens Value	System Weakens Value	Percent Responding
Material well-being	28.1%	71.4%	83.8%
Compassion and respect for individual			
Elemental humanity	35.8	62.0	78.6
Personal worth and inviolability	23.3	75.2	80.8
Respect for privacy	36.2	61.8	65.0
Gives pensioner opportunity to influence decisions that affect him	19.3	77.0	73.1
System can be used to further equality and social justice			
Equality	18.9	79.3	70.1
Social justice	27.3	70.8	71.8
Mutual respect	32.1	65.8	79.9
"One for all, all for one"	16.5	81.3	59.4
System can be used to enhance welfare aspects of society			
Emphasis on individual human needs	27.6	71.2	69.7
Assures pensioner secure, dignified status in society	22.0	75.9	83.3
Rights guaranteed by law can be enforced	49.4	49.4	77.8

NOTE: Although respondents found these questions the most difficult to answer, a majority (ranging from 60 to 84 percent) found it possible to voice their opinions. The pattern of distribution of their responses shows unambiguously that these questions had a genuine meaning to the respondents, that they gave serious thought to their answers, and that they were not responding in an undifferentiated manner. The highest response rate is in regard to material well-being, a relatively clearcut value that affects all directly; the lowest rate is for "one for all, all for one"—perhaps a reflection of unfamiliarity with the benefit formula, which is weighted in favor of the lowest wage earner, or a conviction (voiced quite frequently) that this is merely a slogan.

REFERENCES

Acharkan, V. 1971. "Pensionnoe zakonodatel'stvo i problemy zaniatosti." *Sotsialisticheskii trud*, no. 1.

Ankudinov, A. 1962. "Slavnoe." *Okhrana truda i sotsial'noe strakhovanie*, no. 1.

Aralov, V. A., and Levshin, A. V. 1959. *Sotsial'noe obespechenie v SSSR*. Moscow: Profizdat.

Astrakhan, E. I. 1961. *Printsipy pensionnogo obespecheniia rabochikh i sluzhashchikh v SSSR*. Moscow: IUridicheskaia Literatura.

_____. 1971. *Razvitie zakonodatel'stva o pensiiakh rabochim i sluzhashchim. Istoricheskii ocherk, 1917-1970*. Moscow: IUridicheskaia Literatura.

Azarova, E. G. 1979. "O zashchite pensionnykh prav grazhdan." *Sovetskoe gosudarstvo i pravo*, no. 2.

_____. 1982. "Sotsial'noe obespechenie: Rasshirenie prav grazhdan v svete reshenii XXVI s'ezda KPSS." *Sovetskoe gosudarstvo i pravo*, no. 12.

Baldwin, Godfry S. 1979. "Population Projections by Age and Sex: For the Republics and Major Economic Regions of the USSR, 1970 to 2000." *International Population Reports*, Series P-91, no. 26. Washington, D.C.: Bureau of the Census, Foreign Demographic Analysis Division.

Batygin, K. 1979. "Konstitutsiia SSSR i rasshirenie demokratii pri osushchestvlenii sotsial'nogo obespechniia." *Sotsial'noe obespechenie*, no. 2.

Berzhikovskaia, N. V. 1982. "Zdorov'e i medico-sotstial'noe obsluzhivaniia pozhilogo naseleniia." In *Pozhiloi chelovek: Meditsinskaia i sotsial'naia pomoshch*, ed. D. F. Chebotarev. Kiev: USSR Gerontology and Geriatrics Society Yearbook.

Chapman, Janet G. 1979. "Recent Trends in the Soviet Industrial Wage Structure." In *Industrial Labor Force in the USSR*, ed. Arcadius Kahan and Blair A. Ruble, pp. 151-83. New York: Pergamon Press.

Danskii, B. G., and Komarovskii, K. A., eds. 1913. *Strakhovanie rabochikh v Rossii i na zapade*, vol. 1, 1st ed. St. Petersburg.

Demidov, Pavel. 1977. "Comrade Pensioners." *Izvestiia*, 14 June.

Dmitriev, A. V. 1980. *Sotsial'nye problemy liudei pozhilogo vozrasta*. Leningrad: Nauka.

Eason, W. 1963. "Labor Force." In *Economic Trends in the Soviet Union*, ed. A. Bergson and S. Kuznets. Cambridge, Mass.: Harvard University Press.

Emel'ianova, M. 1981. "Stabil'nost' kadrov — Zalog uspekha." *Sotsial'noe obespechenie*, no. 7.

Fogel', Ia. M. 1972. *Pravo na pensii i ego garantii*. Moscow: IUridicheskaia Literatura.

Gushchin, I. V. 1975. *Pravootonosheniia po sotsial'nomu obespecheniiu chlenov kolkhozov*. Leningrad: Leningrad University Press.

Karpukhin, D. N., and Kuznetsova, N. P. 1968. "Dokhody i potrebleniia trud-iashchikhsia." In *Trud i zarabotnaia plata v SSSR.* Moscow: Ekonomika.

Kogan, V. 1973. "Otnoshenie lits pozhilogo vozrasta k uchastiiu v obshchest-vennom proizvodstve." In *Narodnoslenie i trudovye resursy*, ed. D. I. Valentii et al. Moscow: Statistika.

Kolesnikov, A. 1974. "Aktual'nye problemy sotsial'nogo obespecheniia." *Okhrana truda i sotsial'noe strakhovanie*, no. 8.

Kolesnikov, S. 1983. "Returning to the Subject: Once More about Retired People's Labor." *Pravda*, 4 January. Reprinted in *Current Digest of the Soviet Press* 35, 1: 13 (1983).

Komarova, D. 1974. "Novoe proiavlenie zaboty o blage sovetskikh liudei." *Sotsial'noe obespechenie*, no. 1.

_____. 1975. "Invalidam—Zabotu i vnimanie." *Sotsial'noe obespechenie*, no. 6.

_____. 1979. "Za vysokoe kachestvo nashei raboty." *Sotsial'noe obespe-chenie*, no. 3.

_____. 1981. "Na blago sovetskikh liudei." *Sotsial'noe obespechenie*, no. 2.

Kravchenko, M. 1979. "Zadachi gosudarstvennykh organov sotsial'nogo obes-pecheniia v svete novoi konstitutsii SSSR." *Sotsial'noe obespechenie*, no. 4.

Krukhmalev, A. 1979. "Osnovnye napravleniia politiki KPSS v oblasti sotsial'nogo obespecheniia v usloviiakh razvitogo sotsializma." *Sotsial'noe obespechenie*, no. 11.

Krulikovskaia, V.; Kiseleva, P.; and Gorbunov, A. 1959. *Planirovanie biudzheta sotsial'nogo strakhovaniia.* Moscow: Ekonomika, Profizdat.

Lantsev, M. S. 1973. "Progress in Social Security for Agricultural Workers in the USSR." *International Labour Review*, no. 3.

_____. 1976. *Sotsial'noe obespechenie v SSSR: Ekonomicheskii aspekt.* Moscow: Ekonomika.

Lenin, V. I. 1948. *Sochineniia*, 4th ed. Moscow.

Lopata, P. 1980. "Desiataia piatiletka—Vazhnyi rubezh v razvitii sistemy pen-sionnogo obespechenia." *Sotsial'noe obespechenie*, no. 10.

McAuley, Alastair. 1982. "Social Welfare Policy." In *Soviet Policies for the 1980s*, ed. Archie Brown and Michael Kaser. London: Macmillan.

Madison, Bernice. 1973. "Soviet Income Maintenance Policy for the 1970s." *Journal of Social Policy* 2, pt. 2: 97-117.

_____. 1978. "Soviet Income Maintenance Programs in the Struggle against Poverty." Colloquium presented at Kennan Institute for Advanced Russian Studies, Woodrow Wilson International Center for Scholars, Washington, D.C., 20 June.

_____. 1981. "The Soviet Social Welfare System as Experienced and Evalu-ated by Consumers and Personnel." Presented to National Council for Soviet and East European Research, Washington, D.C., September.

Maksimovskii, V. I. 1974. *Upravlenie sotsial'nym obespecheniem.* Moscow: IUridicheskaia Literatura.

Ministerstvo Vysshego i Srednego Spetsial'nogo Obrazovaniia SSSR. Nauchno-Tekhnicheskii Sovet. Sektsiia Narodnoseleniia. 1982. Vypusk 27, *Pered vykhodom na pensiiu.* Moscow: Finansy i Statistika.

Minkoff, Jack. 1959. "The Soviet Social Insurance System since 1921." Ph.D. dissertation, Columbia University.

Namal'tsev, S. I. 1976. *Problemy raspredeleniia v razvitom sotsialisticheskom obshchestve.* Moscow: Ekonomika.

Narodnoe khoziastvo SSSR v 1922 g. . . . v 1982 g. Moscow: Finansy i Statistika.

Novitskii, A. G., and Mil', G. V. 1981. *Zaniatost' pensionerov: Sotsial'noe-demograficheskii aspekt.* Moscow: Finansy i Statistika.

Pankin, M. 1982. "Novoe polozhenie ob usloviiakh truda nadomnikov." *Sotsial'noe obespechenie,* no. 4.

Pavlova, N. M. 1976. "Notes and Letters—Differentiation of Pensions." In Russian. *Ekonomika i matematicheskiye metody,* no. 6: 1196-1200.

Pavlova, N. M.; Rabkina, N. Ye.; and Rimashevskaya, N. M. 1979. "On the Improvement of the Methods of the Planned Regulation of Old-Age Pensions." In Russian. *Ekonomika i matematicheskiye metody,* no. 4.

Porket, Joseph L. 1982. "Retired Workers under Soviet-Type Socialism." *Social Policy and Administration,* no. 3.

_____. 1983. "Income Maintenance for the Soviet Aged." *Aging and Society* 3, pt. 3 [November].

Povarov, P. 1980. "Trudovoe ustroistvo invalidov i prestarelykh." *Sotsial'noe obespechenie,* no. 12.

Prokopenko, I. 1980. "Tsenit' rabochee vremia." *Sotsial'noe obespechenie,* no. 6.

Rimlinger, Gaston V. 1971. *Welfare Policy and Industrialization in Europe, America, and Russia.* New York: John Wiley.

Sarkisian. G. S., and Kuznetsova, N. P. 1967. *Potrebnosti i dokhod sem'i.* Moscow: Ekonomika.

Sbornik Ofitsial'nykh Materialov. 1983. *Sotsial'noe strakhovanie v SSSR.* Moscow: Profizdat.

Shapiro, V. D. 1980. *Chelovek na pensii.* Moscow: Mysl'.

Shchennikova, L. 1984. "Trudovaia deiatel'nost' pozhylikh liudei i ee stimulirovanie." In *Naselenie i sotsial'noe obespechenie.* Moscow: Ministerstvo Vysshego i Srednego Spetsial'nogo Obrazovaniia SSSR, Nauchno-Tekhnicheskii Sovet, Sektsiia Narodnaseleniia, Finansy i Statistika.

Shedrova, G. 1982. "Pensii materiam." *Sotsial'noe obespechenie,* no. 1.

Simonenko, G. 1980. "Kto podlezhit sotsial'nomu strakhovaniiu." *Sotsial'noe obespechenie,* no. 7.

Slobozhanin, V. P. 1981. "Pensiia—Po trudovomu vkladu." *Sovetskoe gosudarstvo i pravo*, no. 9.

Smirnov, S. 1977. "The Employment of Old-Age Pensioners in the USSR." *International Labour Review*, no. 1.

Solov'ev, B. 1913. "Organizatsiia bol'nichnoi klassy." In Danskii and Komarovskii, eds.

Solov'yev, A. 1977. "Sotsial'noe obespechenie na sovremennom etape." *Sotsialisticheskii trud*, no. 9.

Sonin, M. 1976. "The Elderly in Family and Society." In Russian. *Sovetskaya kul'tura*, no. 2.

Sternheimer, Stephen. 1982. "The Graying of the Soviet Union." *Problems of Communism* 31, 5.

Stiller, Pavel. 1983. "Sozialpolitik in der UdSSR 1950-1980." *Osteuropa und der internationale KOMMUNISMUS* 3-4.

"Strakhovanie rabochikh ili boikom?" 1913. *Strakhovanie rabochikh*, no. 5.

Tarasova, V. A. 1976. "Okhrana sub'ektivnykh prav grazhdan v oblasti pensionnogo obespecheniia." *Sovetskoe gosudarstvo i pravo*, no. 8.

_____. 1981. "Pravovoi status grazhdan v sfere sotsial'nogo obespecheniia." *Sovetskoe gosudarstvo i pravo*.

Tsederbaum, Iu. 1980a. "Material'noe stimulirovanie rabotaiushchikh pensionerov po vozrastu." *Sotsial'noe obespechenie*, no. 3.

_____. 1980b. "Material'noe stimulirovanie rabotaiushchikh pensionerov po vozrastu." *Sotsial'noe obespechenie*, no. 6.

United States, CIA, Directorate of Intelligence. 1983. *Soviet Gross National Product in Current Prices, 1960-80*. Research paper, Sov. 83-10037, March.

V TsK KPSS, Prezidiume Verkhovnogo Soveta SSSR, Sovete Ministrov SSSR I V Ts SPS. 1981. *Sotsial'noe obespechenie*, no. 11.

Vul'f, L. 1981. "Novoe uvelichenie pensii." *Sotsial'noe obespechenie*, no. 12.

Yakushev, Lev P. 1976. "Old People's Rights in the USSR and Other European Socialist Countries." *International Labour Review*, no. 2.

Zakharov, M. L. 1974. *Sovetskoe pensionnoe pravo*. Moscow: IUridicheskaia Literatura.

_____. 1975. "Razvitie edinoi sistemy pensionnogo obespecheniia." *Sovetskoe gosudarstvo i pravo*, no. 11.

_____. 1983. *Pensii rabochim i sluzhashchim*. Moscow: Profizdat.

Zakharov, M. L., and Povarov, P. 1979. "Konstitutsiia SSSR i zadachi sotsial'nogo obespecheniia." *Sotsial'noe obespechenie*, no. 1.

A COMPARATIVE STUDY OF PENSION POLICIES IN THE UNITED STATES AND EUROPE

Martin Rein

ONE-SECTOR INQUIRY IN A THREE-SECTOR WORLD

Three themes emerge from a review of the literature on the welfare state. First, American welfare state expenditures tend to lag behind those of the leading countries, such as Sweden and the Netherlands. For example, in 1977 social security expenditures as a percent of GNP were 14 percent in the United States, as compared to 31 percent in Sweden and 28 percent in the Netherlands. Comparing the United States and twelve European countries and Canada for 1977, we find that the United States spent about two thirds as much as the other countries for social security and less than half as much (45 percent) for other cash transfers like unemployment and disability. Only in the provision of civil servant pensions does the United States spend almost as much. (See Table 1 for the comparisons.)

Second, there are different types of welfare states based on the mix of cash transfers and services. The continental model concentrates resources on transfers, whereas the British and Scandinavian model concentrates them on services.

Finally, there are different types of transfer states. Welfare states differ not only in their level of transfer expenditures, but also on the beneficiaries of these transfers. Austria, West Germany, and the United States spend about three quarters or more of total transfer money for pensions; by contrast, the Netherlands spends only a little more than half of its transfer resources for pensions. Countries also differ in their reliance on welfare or means testing. For example, the United States and the Netherlands spend about 12 percent of total income maintenance on means-tested programs, as compared with Sweden and West Germany, which spend only 3-4 percent.*

*For a discussion of these issues, see Kohl (1981). This essay contains a discussion of types of welfare states. For a review of types of transfer states, see OECD (1977); for an analysis of lag and lead countries and a review of determinants of aggregate expenditures, see Heclo (1982).

Table 1

SOCIAL SECURITY SPENDING IN THE UNITED STATES,
TWELVE EUROPEAN COUNTRIES, AND CANADA, 1977
(Mean percent of GNP)

United States			
Total social security	12.90%		
Total social insurance		6.88%	
Pension insurance			4.56%
Other social insurance			2.32
Other social security		6.02	
Government employee programs			2.13
Family allowances			--
Public assistance			3.10
Public health			0.80
Non-social security civilian government revenue	14.1		
Total civilian government revenue	27.0		
Europe and Canada[a]			
Total social security	20.37%		
Total social insurance		12.44%	
Pension insurance			7.30%
Other social insurance			5.14
Other social security		7.93	
Government employee programs			2.34
Family allowances			1.20
Public assistance			2.19
Public health			2.20
Non-social security civilian government revenue	18.97		
Total civilian government revenue	39.34		

[a]The European countries are Austria, Belgium, Denmark, Finland, France, West Germany, Italy, the Netherlands, Norway, Sweden, Switzerland, and the United Kingdom.

This discussion assumes that it is only the welfare state that provides welfare. However, in each society we may think of provisions as being organized in three sectors: a public sector, where government acts directly to administer as well as to finance pensions according to some principle of social responsibility; a personal sector, where the individual assumes primary responsibility, making use of financial institutions like banks, life insurance systems, or the real estate market, and the state plays only a minimal role; and a mixed sector, conventionally referred to as the private sector, where the state acts indirectly via its capacity to regulate, stimulate, and subsidize civil society, and the major actor is the firm serving in its role of employer.* Each society combines these sectors in different ways.

Most comparative studies of income maintenance systems, including pensions, focus on the public sector and neglect the protection provided through employee pensions in the private sector and tax-subsidized savings in the personal sector. In this chapter we shall discuss these sectors in the United States; then we shall compare Sweden, a leading welfare state, with the United States, a laggard welfare state. It will become apparent that when we aggregate across sectors, we get a very different perspective about the level of social protection in the United States relative to other countries. This finding raises new questions about the pattern of social protection in European countries as well.

By and large, the neglect of the private and personal sectors and focus on welfare state activities is not grounded in a lack of awareness of the importance of the first two sectors. In a very thoughtful essay on the development of the welfare state in Belgium, Jan Vranken offers the following observation:

> Pillarization helps to explain why up to now these organizations continue to play an important role in policy making on and in the daily administration of the welfare state provisions, even when the latter have meanwhile been subsidized, made compulsory, guaranteed or financed by the State. For Belgium, one might even argue that not the political authorities but the pillarized organizations have been the prime policy agents, and that not the State as such has been made responsible for providing the Welfare State provisions,

---

*The idea of three pillars on which social policy rests is an accepted part of the ideology of most societies. The pillars are usually defined as public, private, and nonprofit, and imply an orderly division of labor. In our distinction the state is always central, acting in a direct or indirect role.

but that it has merely been given the responsibility of enabling the organizations concerned to run the Welfare State (1986: 3).

In this interpretation, it is not the state that intrudes into civil society, but the other way around. Instead of a simple dichotomy between public and private (including religious bodies, nonprofit institutions, and market-based firms), we have at the least a purely public sector, a purely private sector, and a mixed sector (pillarization). The institutional arrangements are so intricately commingled that we cannot conceptually distinguish any pure sectors, or even the primacy of one sector over another. Yet despite the subtlety of the analysis, Vranken proceeds to analyze only the social security system administered by the state. Arrangements for civil servants who are outside of the public social security program and private sector arrangements are not included in this study. The analysis is self-referential, not to the system as a whole, but to only one of its parts—namely, the activities of the welfare state narrowly conceived. This study is typical of the modern literature on the evolution of the welfare state.

Practical and conceptual problems inhibit the development of a more comprehensive approach to the study of social protection. At the practical level, data about the private sector are in short supply. In the United States most of the information on private pension assets, contributions, and benefits before 1975 was derived from a survey carried out by the Securities and Exchange Commission (SEC); the survey was based on a very small sample concentrating on pension plans with a large number of members, supplemented by a sample of banks acting as trustees for pension funds. The Social Security Administration adjusted the SEC data to take account of unfunded pension funds and insured life insurance plans. Benchmark data provided by a Department of Labor (DOL) survey in 1977, combined with an implicit "rule of reasonableness" (for example, checking estimates of the per capita value of pension benefits), were used to further adjust these estimates. These are the official statistics on private pensions.

The weakness of these estimates became evident over time. Perhaps the essential problem was that the SEC failed to develop a sampling frame to take account of both the variety of pension plan arrangements and their changing mix over time. Hence the sample was not representative of the evolving system of private pensions. Informed reviewers believe that the SEC data were better in the early years, when the large plans that were surveyed represented more closely the universe of all plans. In recent years the diversification of plan types has reduced the validity of the SEC sample. To illustrate, multi-employer pension plans have gradually become more important, accounting in 1977 for about 12 percent of pension assets, but these plans are not included in the SEC survey.* The seriousness of the problem emerged in 1982, when the preliminary findings of the 1977 DOL survey of the financial characteristics of pension plans was published. This survey was based on data collected from a weighted sample of pension plans filing annual financial reports with the Internal Revenue Service (IRS); it provides the best information available on private pension plans in the United States.† Among other things, the survey found the following: "In 1977, the market value of total private pension plan assets not held by insurance companies was reported by the SEC at $181.6 billion, or $101.1 billion less than the $282.7 billion in non-insured assets estimated from the weighted sample of [Form] 5500 reports (United States, DOL 1981: 6).

The SEC's underestimate naturally raises questions about its past estimates of contributions and benefits, which are the main focus of this chapter. The DOL survey provides better estimates of private pension benefits for 1975, 1977, and 1978, the only years for which IRS Form 5500 was analyzed. However, even these estimates are incomplete if one wants to know total benefit outlays, because the survey was designed primarily as an enforcement tool to identify plans with potential financial difficulties. Insured pension plans financed from life insurance companies were not analyzed.** To determine total expenditures, contributions, and assets, it is necessary to piece together information from many different sources. Some information is dramatically underestimated and other information

---

*For a discussion of the problem with the SEC statistics, see United States, General Accounting Office (1982).

†Plans with one hundred or more participants are required to file IRS Form 5500, which calls for detailed data on participant and financial chracteristics of plans. Plans that have fewer than one hundred participants are required to file Form 5000C. The survey was based on a sampling of these forms (see United States, DOL 1981).

**These data are reported in the Schedule A forms submitted to the IRS but were not analyzed, partly because they were not the focus of the study, and partly because allocated and unallocated funding arrangements were not clearly separated.

is duplicative. No one puts all the pieces together; hence it is very difficult to get a picture of aggregate pension contributions and expenditures.

There is no coordinated fact-gathering in the private pension area—i.e., no central point accumulates statistical information for purposes of policy. Employer pension schemes are administered, invested, and funded through different institutional arrangements. Trusted schemes are administered through banks and trust companies or self-administered by firms and life insurance fiduciaries. Tax-deferred annuities are administered through an even more varied set of institutions. About two thirds of pensions are funneled through banks, and only 20 percent of tax-deferred annuities are administered by life insurance agencies. The fact that pension plans rely upon a mixed funding system, shuffling between investments in banks and insurance companies, or tax-free rollovers of corporate pensions into Individual Retirement Annuities (IRAs), only exacerbates the problem of getting an unduplicated count.

In principle these statistical and conceptual problems can be solved, but in practice the problems have grown. The SEC carried out its last survey for benefits and contributions in 1975 and has gathered data on assets since 1982. Its survey was to be replaced by a more comprehensive survey of participant and financial character-istics of private pension plans by the DOL. However, for budgetary reasons the DOL survey has been discontinued. Currently the only available information on aggregate expenditures for private pensions comes from a private pension forecasting model prepared for the Pension and Welfare Benefits Program of the DOL.

Despite the difficulties in acquiring information, there is a lively and growing interest in private pensions. It is stimulated by (among other things) the fiscal problems in the federal scheme, the debate about public pensions and private savings, the growth of the private pension field, the interest of conservative governments in the privati-zation of benefits, and the creation of the Employers Benefit Research Institute (EBRI). Sar Levitan observes:

> The employer community did not fully anticipate the federal regulation of private pensions. Holding steadfast to the view that pensions were within the preserve of managerial prerogatives, business organizations were late in appraising the potential impact of . . . proposed [pension regulation] legislation, and . . . exercised only modest influence on the law's content (1985: 85).

Business organizations did not intend to be caught off guard again, however. In the fall of 1978 a dozen consulting actuarial firms helped create EBRI. Life insurance companies, banks, and law firms contributed resources to EBRI to create a rather substantial budget for the main purpose of doing research on private pensions. The benefits industry was very concerned that Congress might pass new legislation to regulate it, and it was eager to get facts to protect its interests.

This brief review of the structure of knowledge in the field of private pensions raises the question of what determines which information is gathered. Perhaps it is the urgency of an issue that leads to gathering new information. During the 1970s income-support policy was almost obsessively concerned with an alleged rise in welfare dependency and whether income guarantees reduced work incentives. After extensive research on the negative income tax and the failure of Congress to reform welfare, many analysts began to feel that they were working on the wrong problem. Welfare, after all, is only a very small portion of total income-support programs. By the late 1970s and early 1980s it became clear that the major policy question concerned pensions and the financial solvency of the social security system. In this context, the importance of private-sector pensions as a substitute or supplement to public pensions became evident. Critics call attention to the weakness of the private pension system and its inability to cover more than half of the active working population and to provide benefit levels which take account of inflation.* The competing points of view stimulate controversy and nourish inquiry even in the absence of data. Despite the urgency of the issue, the flow of information has, at least for the moment, declined rather than expanded. Below we shall return to the puzzling interplay between information and inquiry.

The practical problems of gathering information about private pensions are even more severe in the European context. In some countries—for example, Austria—not only is there a dearth of information, but also the few surveys which have been conducted on pension plans and aggregate expenditures have been kept secret. There is a general apprehension that the release of such survey information would expose the comparative advantage of different classes of workers, encouraging union demands for more equitable treatment. In the Scandinavian context it is particularly difficult to

---

*See Munnell (1982). Munnell is criticized for ignoring defined contribution plans "intended to provide the retiree with inflation protection" (EBRI 1982).

gather information on contractual pensions available for civil servants; indeed the Nordic social security system excludes civil service benefits from its statistical series. In the Netherlands considerable information is available but not easily accessible. No centralized system draws together information on pensions administered through life insurance companies, civil servant and "civil servant-like" schemes, and industries and corporations.

CONCEPTUAL PROBLEMS

The distinction between public and private pension schemes poses a number of conceptual problems. At the most fundamental level, government indirectly shapes the size and character of the private sector through a variety of institutional mechanisms.* In Belgium the private sector shapes the actions of government, reinforcing the pattern of pillarization based on class, religion, and language. Yet even if we believe that all private schemes owe their origin at least in part to government action and that therefore there is no pure public or private sector but only a mixed sector, other conceptual problems arise. I have selected two conceptual problems for discussion. The first concerns the role of personal pensions, and the second concerns the boundary between public and private social protection based on contract and law.

Because the aggregate level of personal pensions is small, they do not play an important role in understanding current pension expenditures. However, with the growth of tax-deferred annuities, this form of protection may be important in the future. Moreover, these pension arrangements raise a broader question of whether voluntary asset accumulation aided by tax rebates is part of collective social protection. There is an unclear boundary between IRAs and private employer pensions which are funneled through fiduciary institutions like trust funds, banks, and life insurance companies. In the case of corporate pensions, an individual cannot withdraw the funds at will, nor can he control the investment decisions. In the case of IRAs, not only is the retirement scheme voluntary, but also an individual can (if he chooses) control where his resources are invested. There are additional forms of personal retirement savings—for example, home ownership, stocks and bonds, or liquid

---

*For a discussion of the different ways in which government shapes private initiative, see Rein (1982: 117-35).

assets invested in money funds and banks. In the United States the government has subsidized some of these savings. Should these be included as part of the private sector, or should we restrict the term *private sector* to employer pension plans administered through life insurance or funded arrangements?

The European Economic Community (EEC) insists on the importance of including all forms of social protection, regardless of the sector in which this protection is financed or administered. However, the EEC narrowly defines social protection as only that involving intervention by third parties—i.e., some party other than the individual beneficiary controls the investment of funds for protection and designates the conditions for their allocation:

> The general definition chosen for "social protection expenditure" is as follows: any expenditure involved in meeting costs incurred by individuals or households as a result of . . . the existence of certain risks, contingencies or needs, in so far as this expenditure gives rise to the intervention of a "third party," without there being any simultaneous equivalent counterpart by the beneficiary. The "third parties" intervening may be public bodies (e.g. a public enterprise) or some level of Government or private institutions (e.g. private enterprises, mutual societies, insurance companies or private social assistance agencies) (EEC 1980: 15-16).

In this definition a sharp distinction is drawn between the institutional arrangements which control personal savings and those which belong to social policy. In the personal sector an individual chooses and controls both the types of investment and the amount of his foregone consumption that is to be invested. In social policy these decisions are controlled by fiduciaries.

This conceptual issue reflects a nineteenth-century debate about the potential for asset accumulation by individuals. Proponents of state intervention argued that most low-income individuals lacked the resources for lifetime accumulation; even if they succeeded in creating an asset pool, some life cycle catastrophe could easily wipe it out. Therefore, most individuals could not forego current consumption to provide protection against risk of future interrupted income. The conventional economic liberals argued that, by and large, anyone could accumulate if the preference for present consumption were disciplined; hence government policy was not needed. The welfare state proponents won the debate, and there has been a steady growth in both the public and private

sectors of savings institutions for retirement in which the individual
has no control of the funds.

In recent years there has been a growth of hybrid institutional
arrangements characterized by both outside control (which restricts
when individuals can make use of their invested money) and some
measure of individual control over investment decisions. Government
motives for providing attractive tax incentives to encourage these
forms of personal savings are mixed. In part, there is anxiety about
capital shortage and a belief that such incentives will encourage
savings; in part, there is a desire to implement a widely shared
philosophical view about social protection. Briefly, this view holds
that the state should intervene and limit the consumption of its
citizens by taxation, that an employer has an obligation to protect
his workforce, and that an individual's autonomy and independence
are best encouraged by social policies designed to promote personal
asset accumulation. In periods of economic growth, government
encourages all three strategies. While economic policy is concerned
with how much saving a society needs, social policy is directed
toward which groups in society save.

What will be the future development of IRAs and tax-deferred
annuities? In the framework of economic policy, critics argue that such
schemes only shift the sector of savings but do not affect net savings
levels. In the framework of social policy, critics predict that without
a mechanism of control, most people—especially those with low
incomes—will not make provisions for retirement through savings.
IRAs will not grow in the future except for those who use them as a
tax loophole, which will encourage a social policy that multiplies
the privileges of advantaged groups. (The evidence is discussed below.)

The question of individual control over assets is broader than pension policy. A parallel to this debate can be found in the call for flexible
fringe benefits, where individuals choose and hence control their pack-
ages of protection. A similar issue arises in the area of home ownership.
A reverse annuity mortgage can serve as a source of income for the
elderly in light of the fact that nearly three fourths of all elderly
persons own their own homes. The importance of this hybrid area
between personal asset accumulation and conventional definitions of
social policy cannot easily be resolved. I have chosen to include it in my
definition of social protection. The amounts paid out in benefits
from IRAs are trivial, although contributions and accumulated assets
are large and growing. At this stage, the issue is largely conceptual,
but it might be important in future policy debates.

The second conceptual problem concerns the boundary between social protection arising from labor contracts and social policy originating in social legislation. The distinction between contract and law is important partly because the two systems create different institutional arrangements, which in turn give rise to a different intellectual tradition for examining questions of public policy. Labor policies pursued both by private organizations and by governments are concerned with modifying market forces by affecting wages and nonwage employee benefits—especially pensions and health, but also hours and working conditions. Social policies have traditionally been concerned with compensating for the negative effects of labor markets on the economic well-being of workers and their families. Of course not all pensions offered by firms arise from political struggle or collective bargaining. Paternalism still plays an important role, but paternalism is often another way of preempting collective bargaining.

Civil servants form an anomalous category. With them the state is not acting as a provider for the well-being of its citizens, but as an employer contracting for services. In some countries civil servants (*Beamte* in the German and Austrian systems) have a lifetime service to the state. Technically they do not retire beyond a given age (say 65); they simply no longer have an assignment. Once a person achieves the status of civil servant, he retains it for life. These programs are grounded in law and, in many countries, financed exclusively by government. Yet civil servants are also outside of the public social security program.

It is this double role of the state as both provider and employer which is a source of ambiguity in the development of a clearcut dichotomy among the sectors. A further complication is the tendency for government to subcontract its work through the private, religious, and nonprofit sectors. In the Netherlands, for example, many teachers work for the church. Indeed there is a state tax to support the work of the church. Yet these "civil servant-like" employees enjoy the same benefits as civil servants. In the United States, government acts as a contractor or subsidizer in the profit and not-for-profit sectors. In this role it pays for the labor costs of private employees. About 6–10 percent of private sector earnings is allocated for private pensions (discussed below). Thus government indirectly pays for these pensions. Yet we have no accounting system to enable us to isolate the public funding of private pension schemes.

We could argue that the government as direct and indirect employer ought to be treated within the framework of labor policy. Pension benefits would thus be classified together with contractual pensions in the private sector. To do so would provide a sharply different interpretation of the role, size, and growth of the different sectors.

A similar issue arises with war veterans and the personnel voluntarily employed in the state military. Conventionally, military personnel are thought of as employees of the state and grouped together with civil servants, but veterans are treated as a separate category. It seems reasonable to assign nonmeans veterans' compensation to the category of government as employer. While reasonable, this criterion is not without problems because family need enters into the salary of the military even when rank and years of service are held constant. Since the pension arrangements (especially in the United States) are very costly, how we think about and classify military personnel and veterans is a matter of great importance in our understanding of the public sector.

These practical and conceptual problems make an inquiry into pension arrangements frustrating. In order to approach the subject in a meaningful way, we have decided to concentrate on aggregating outlays in the three sectors of social insurance, private pensions, and personal retirement savings. We have selected 1977 as the base year for such a comparison because it provides the best information available on private pensions in the United States. Moreover, focusing on a single year provides an opportunity to explore in more depth the components of a more comprehensive approach to pension arrangements in the United States.

MULTI-SECTOR REALITY

We shall first clarify what we mean by the term *pensions* and then review the institutional arrangements for their provision. The EEC definition of social protection isolates the nature of the risk to be protected as "the decisive criterion for delimiting the field of observation" (EEC 1980: 16). Broadly speaking, the function of social protection in the area of pensions refers to the provision of cash transfer income for those who reach a certain age, who retire and are above a certain age, who are the wives and children of those who retire, who are the survivors of those who retire (widows, children, and elderly parents), or who are disabled. The program for risk of disability includes many individuals below retirement age. We believe it makes sense in a study of pensions to include only older disabled workers (above age 55) for whom the disability pension is the first transition to retirement. This restriction poses a practical problem because it requires information on both risk and age.

Cross-national statistics on pensions can be misleading if they fail to disaggregate these various programs. The task is even more demanding when both the public and private sectors are taken into account. Because we are dealing with many different programs under different systems of financing and administration, comparable information is difficult to obtain.

In discussing risk associated with pension policy and practice, we need to take account of the following:

1. Clearly, aggregate expenditures for pensions depend in part on the size of the elderly population. The proportion of persons 65 or older as a percentage of the total population varies quite sharply for different countries. There appear to be two broad patterns: a low or a high percentage of elderly. In the United States, 11.2 percent of the total population was 65 or older in 1979. The Netherlands also has a low proportion—11.4 percent in 1979. By contrast, Austria has 15.5 percent, West Germany 15.5 percent, Sweden 16.1 percent, and the United Kingdom 14.7 percent.

2. As noted, pensions are not restricted to those who retire or are disabled. In 1977 in the United States 37 percent of all social security beneficiaries were dependents or survivors of retirees. Many of these are below the age of 60. Wives and widows are eligible for benefits if they have a dependent child in their care. It appears that about 26.1 percent of the wives and 87.5 percent of the widows of retired or disabled workers who were awarded benefits in 1977 were below the age of 55.

3. The proportion of survivors and dependents who receive benefits differs sharply among countries. For example, of those who received a public pension in the Netherlands in 1972, only 14 percent were dependents.

4. Early retirement is widespread. In the United States two thirds of those who receive a public pension for the first time are between the ages of 62 and 65. Even more striking is the finding that the median age of those receiving private pensions is 62. In the public sector, benefits are payable upon retirement or after age

72. Benefits are permanently reduced for those who retire before age 65 (by 20 percent at age 62 and 10 percent at age 63½).

There is a striking secular trend of withdrawal from the labor force on the part of men between the ages of 55 and 64. In 1947, 10 percent of men in this age group were out of the labor force. By 1980 the figure had increased to 28 percent. Looking at five-year age groups, we find that in 1980, 18 percent of those aged 55-59 were out of the labor force, as compared with 38 percent of those aged 60-64. However, absence from the labor force cannot simply be equated with retirement because some of these men will return to work. Nevertheless, labor force figures signal a long-range trend toward withdrawal associated with early retirement. Many private and civil service pensions are based on years of service as well as age. Thus a combination of public employee and private programs must play an important role in the labor force participation or withdrawal of men over 55 years of age.

5. Those who retire may have earlier been entitled to a disability pension. When these men and women reach age 65, they can convert the disability pension into a retirement pension. Many European countries have a program in which older workers unemployed for a year or more become entitled to a retirement pension. As a result of these practices, the boundaries separating disability, retirement, and unemployment of older workers are becoming increasingly vague.

6. Pensions cannot be equated with retirement. In the United States benefits are conditioned on actual retirement from the labor force, and the test of retirement has been defined as substantial withdrawal from covered employment. However, over the years the definition of substantial withdrawal has been relaxed. A retired person can earn $5500 annually without loss of benefits; those above age 72 can work without any loss of benefits. Turning from rules to performance we find the following: in families headed by individuals 65 or older with an annual family income of $6000 or less, 10 percent of the income comes from earnings; in such families with incomes up to $12,000, 27 percent comes from earnings; in those with incomes of $20,000 or more, 53 percent comes from earnings. Such figures are the results of two very different patterns. In 1944, 90 percent of men aged 55-64 were in the labor force. By 1977 the proportion had declined to 74 percent. At the same time, some men beyond age 65 continue to work; this is most striking among men with the highest income levels.

PUBLIC SECTOR PENSIONS

When we turn to a review of the institutional arrangements for providing pensions in the public, private, and personal sectors, it becomes evident that a three-sector model is a simplification of reality. The more we probe the specific program content of pensions, the more difficult it becomes to decide whether a particular program should be classified as public or private, and the more we realize that the heterogeneity of public programs makes a simple classification of the public sector misleading. We propose for analytic purposes to identify three components of the public sector: government as provider, government as employer, and government as guarantor.

Government as Provider. This component consists of three separate programs: social insurance, welfare, and veterans' pensions. The largest—the social insurance program for retirement and disability—is administered by the federal government. In 1977, $84 billion was spent. Benefits are paid as a matter of statutory entitlement rather than need and are conditioned on actual retirement, not only age. Almost one third of the outlays was to dependents and survivors of retired or disabled workers; one third of disabled workers are below the age of 55. The original legislation was a means of forcing older workers out of a depressed labor market. The program is financed from employer and employee contributions and is based on the pay-as-you-go principle. Critics believe that this is misleading. They argue that benefits are based on a generation contract: "The generation that works provides the support for the generation that is retired, and mostly the former are the children of the latter" (Keyfitz 1987: 2).

In addition to social insurance, there is a means-tested welfare program. Old Age Assistance (OAA) came into existence with the passage of the Social Security Act in 1935. This program was administered by the states, with the federal government paying half the costs. In 1974 OAA was replaced by the Supplementary Security Income (SSI) program, mainly financed and administered entirely by the federal government and designed to reach needy blind, disabled, and aged persons. Although SSI is a federal program, states provide supplementary payments accounting for about 32 percent of total benefits. The SSI program is designed for those who do not qualify for social insurance or whose insurance benefits are inadequate. In 1977, $6 billion was spent on SSI, with 70 percent of the aged beneficiaries also receiving social insurance.

There is no clear distinction between the social insurance and welfare aspects of social security. The 1935 Social Security Act was governed by the principle that benefits should reflect as closely as possible the private insurance concept of an individual benefit tied directly to the amount of taxes paid. However, by 1939 the insurance system had radically departed from this concept and embraced "welfare-like" features, such as weighted benefits for low-income earners, early blanketing in beneficiaries, and benefits for survivors and dependents. Critics of these developments believe that social insurance has increasingly moved to allocate benefits on the basis of need rather than of past contributions. There is a tension between the insurance and welfare dimensions of social insurance.

Veterans' pensions are paid to a veteran or his survivors based on active duty during a war, disabilities considered permanent and total (age is considered a disability), and "countable income below established levels" (United States 1979: 829). In 1977 about one third of a total of $9.2 billion cash benefits for veterans was for pensions, with 40 percent going to survivors.

Welfare-type benefits based on need (SSI and veterans' pensions) accounted for about $9 billion, or about 9 percent of the $93 billion in pensions benefits spent by government in its role as provider.

Government as Employer. Entirely distinct from national old-age insurance are several retirement programs run by the federal government and by state and local retirement systems. Employees covered under public employment retirement systems (PERS) are not concurrently covered under social security. An abuse developed because participation in social security was not mandatory. While civil servants were excluded from social security, they could join it by holding another job either during or after retiring from their civil service work. Once they had established eligibility for full benefits—often with only a short continuous work history—they were able to get the minimum social security benefits as well as their civil servant pensions.

Under the existing law, employees of state and local governments are covered by social security only if they enter into a voluntary agreement for such coverage. In 1980 about 70 percent of all state and local government employees were covered by social security. In general, social security coverage has expanded. However, between 1973 and 1975 about 350,000 workers submitted notices of intent to terminate their coverage.

PERS can be regarded as a contractual obligation on the part of government. The Supreme Court has interpreted pensions as deferred compensation for services rendered. Thus PERS pensions are within a contractual framework which is very similar in principle to private sector pensions.

PERS pensions provide retirement, survivor, and disability benefits to career employees in the federal, state, and local governments. Many state and local retirement systems — especially those for police and firemen — offer retirement at an early age after a brief period of service, usually about twenty years. By and large PERS are financed through a funded system rather than the pay-as-you-go system of social security. In fact, only about 17 percent of government plans use the pay-as-you-go financing approach to meet their benefit obligations. In 1975 state and local pension fund investments exceeded $108 billion, and these assets have been increasing at a rate of about 16 percent annually. Federal systems total $40.4 billion. The public pension system assets are 51 percent as large as the total assets of all private sector pension plans (United States, Congress 1978: 129). However, this is clearly an underestimate because the assets are listed in terms of book value rather than current market prices.

Employee contributions play a more important role as revenue in the public employment system than in the private system. They make up about 35 percent of state and local pension plans and 16 percent of federal plans. In contrast, in private plans they total less than 6 percent (United States, Congress 1978: 135).

Veterans' compensation is similar to other government retirement schemes in principle and should thus come under the category of the government as employer. Conventionally the veterans' program is treated as a category separate from military retirement to avoid conceptual problems. There are differences between military retirement and veterans' compensation. Usually a person receives a military pension only after a twenty-year vesting period, which can be accrued by some combination of active military service and service in the reserve. By contrast, veterans' compensation for service-connected disability is available for individuals with as little as 180 days of service.

A total of $33 billion is spent under the category of government as employer. Of 5 million active federal retirees in 1975, 2.1 million were in the military retirement system. Veterans and military retirees together comprise the largest component of the federal system, in terms of both active membership and aggregate expenditures. The large majority of state and local public employees are police, firemen, and teachers.

Government as Guarantor. The government as guarantor was until the early 1980s almost exclusively a program for railroad workers and their survivors. The Railroad Retirement System is unique in the pension field. It dramatically illustrates the commingling of private and public institutional arrangements, operating on behalf of private employees but administered by the federal government. The political history of the system is a striking example of the willingness of the federal government to honor pension contracts originating in the private sector when the private sector lacked the resources to meet its commitments. The system was established by the Railroad Retirement Act in 1937 in an attempt to restore financial stability to the private railroad pension plans that were threatened during the depression years with fiscal insolvency. About 25 percent of the labor force in the railroad industry was approaching retirement age in the early 1930s, just when the industry's financial position was especially weak (Munnell 1982: 9). Organized labor, perhaps in cooperation with employers, was able to effectively convince Congress to protect the pension rights of the industry. While many other industries were also in difficulty, they were not as successful as the railways in getting the federal government to act as guarantor of their pension schemes.

The Railroad Retirement Act is particularly relevant because with the passage of the Employee Retirement Income Security Act (ERISA) in 1974, a Pension Benefit Guarantee Corporation was formed with the responsibility of guaranteeing pensions when plans terminated or firms went bankrupt. Of course the Guarantee Corporation is not a direct equivalent to the Railroad Retirement System because its resources depend upon very different sources of income: premium payments from all contributing private pension plans and the funded liability of the corporation pension plan.

In 1977 the Pension Benefit Guarantee Corporation spent $13 million on behalf of plans which were terminated voluntarily or because of bankruptcy. By 1981 this figure had increased to $57 million for single-employer trust funds and $4.3 million for multi-employer trust funds. While the money spent in 1981 is relatively small, we need to recognize that the system has not yet matured.* About 97

---

*The figures cited include benefit payments for both deferred and immediate pay status. A deferred payment is allocated but not spent until an individual becomes eligible for benefits. No information is available on the ratio between percent of the early outlays was spent on plans that had insufficient funds. Only in recent years has the Guarantee Corporation picked up the benefit obligations of large corporations in financial trouble.

In the early 1980s there were two major bankruptcies—the White Motor Company and Braniff International Airlines. The former had unfunded pension liabilities of about $60 million, while claims against the latter were projected at about $70 million (the actual cost may be closer to $40-60 million). The total premium income of the Guarantee Corporation was about $75 million in 1981. With an annual operating deficit of $189 million and a projected deficit of almost half a billion dollars in 1986, the corporation petitioned Congress to increase the premiums from $2.60 per worker per year to about $6 per worker (*New York Times*, 16 July 1982).

A good deal of attention has been focused on the bankruptcy of public social security, but little attention has been given to the potential bankruptcy of private pension plans. If a number of firms with large unfunded liabilities go bankrupt during future economic recessions, the Guarantee Corporation will find itself with substantial deficits. As the corporation continues to take over the unfunded liabilities of firms that go bankrupt or terminate their pension schemes, the government may find itself once again in the anomalous role of financing pensions in the private sector.

PRIVATE SECTOR PENSIONS

Industrial pensions have a long history in the United States. It is useful to distinguish the early period of American welfare capitalism from the postwar period of fringe benefits.* The pensions paid during the early period were usually discretionary, with the employer assuming no legal obligation to provide such benefits. Retirement plans evolved via the gratuity theory of pensions. Pensions were assumed to serve a useful purpose in the struggle for the loyalty of workers and the prevention of unionism. If employees went on strike, they ran the risk of sacrificing their future security. Because security was obviously more important for older workers, "pension plans . . . served to divide the labor movement along age lines; divided it could be conquered" (Brandes 1976: 106). A 1924 survey by the National Industrial Conference Board of a limited number of companies

deferred and immediate payments. It seems likely that this category of benefits will grow in the future.

*For an extensive discussion of the earlier era, see Brandes (1976).

showed that about 1 percent of employees was covered by pension arrangements. By 1980 private pension plans covered almost 50 percent of the labor force.

A standard textbook on private pensions attributes the development of private pensions to several factors: (a) the desire of employers to increase productivity by reducing turnover and the cost of training replacements; (b) the interest of labor in promoting pensions as a result of a 1949 Supreme Court ruling (*Inland Steel* v. *National Labor Relations Board*) that since pensions are deferred wages, they are a subject for collective bargaining; and (c) tax inducements. The Revenue Act of 1926 exempted the income of pension trusts from current taxation. Over the years tax inducements have grown more generous. In 1980 the special tax concession to private pensions resulted in a loss of income to the treasury of nearly $25 billion.

In the post-World War II era, welfare capitalism fell into disrepute and was replaced by the fringe benefit movement. In this new era the role of discretion was not eliminated, but more formal, contractual pension arrangements became common. The passage of ERISA in 1974 may be considered the landmark legislation that marks the transition. Before ERISA the IRS was under no obligation to be concerned about the actuarial soundness of private pension plans, and there were no rules for vesting. Horror stories of pension abuse were rampant and contributed to the passage of ERISA. While the full protection of pension rights of individual participants has not yet been achieved, the era of welfare capitalism has ended (see McGill 1979: ch. 2).

The modern pension movement is part of a broader expansion of fringe benefits. Table 2 shows trends in the development of these benefits in the United States, based on a Bureau of Labor Statistics study of employer expenditures for compensation. By 1976 pensions accounted for about 5.6 percent of wages and salaries (or 4.3 percent of total compensation). Expenditures by firms for private pensions still lag behind health expenditures, but they have continued to grow as a proportion of total compensation.

Munnell (1982) points out that the main expansion of today's private pension system occurred during the 1950s. During this era unions were effective in bargaining for the creation of multi-employer pension plans to cover industries containing many small companies. Pension plans continued to expand during the 1960s, but this expansion was largely accounted for by the growth of employment in firms that already had pension plans rather than through the introduction

Table 2

COMPENSATION COMPONENTS AS A PERCENTAGE OF TOTAL
COMPENSATION IN ALL U.S. INDUSTRIES: 1966, 1972, AND 1976

Compensation Component	Percent of Total Compensation		
	1966	1972	1976
Pay for time worked[a]	83.0%	80.5%	76.7%
Paid leave (except sick)[b]	5.2	5.6	6.1
Employer expenditures for retirement	5.6	7.0	8.6
Social security	3.1	3.7	4.3
Private	2.5	3.3	4.3
Employer expenditures for insurance and health benefit programs	3.5	4.7	5.8
Life, accident, health	2.1	3.1	4.0
Sick leave	0.5	0.7	0.7
Workmen's compensation	0.9	0.9	1.1
Employer expenditures for unemployment benefits[c]	1.4	1.0	1.4
Nonproduction bonuses	1.2	1.0	1.2
Savings and thrift plans	0.1	0.2	0.2
Total compensation	100.0	100.0	100.0
Wages and salaries (gross payroll)[d]	89.9	87.8	84.7
Supplements to wages and salaries[e]	10.1	12.2	15.3

Source: Sheingold (1980).

[a]Includes straight time wages, overtime, and shift differentials.

[b]Includes vacations, holidays, personal and civil leave, and contributions for holiday and vacation funds.

[c]Includes state and federal payroll taxes, severance pay, and supplemental benefit funds.

[d]All direct payments to workers. Includes wages and salaries, paid leaves (including sick), severance pay, and nonproduction bonuses.

[e]Includes employer expenditures for retirement programs, health benefits, unemployment benefits, social security contributions, holiday and vacation funds, and thrift plans.

of new pension schemes. By the 1970s the growth in pension plans had leveled off. By 1980 only 48 percent of the private, nonfarm labor force was covered by private pension schemes.

There is wide variation in coverage depending on age, employment status, tenure, industry, and size of firm. For example, about 75 percent of workers in the mining, manufacturing, and transportation industries are provided corporate pension plans, and 80 percent of workers in large firms have pension coverage. By contrast, only about 40 percent of employees working in the trade, construction, and service industries are covered, as are only 34 percent of workers in firms with less than one hundred employees. About two thirds of full-time workers over 25 years of age with at least one year of tenure are covered by pensions.

Disability benefits lag behind the development of corporate pensions. About two thirds of employees covered by corporate pensions have a disability pension as well. While all workers are eligible for disability benefits, a surprisingly large number are concentrated among older workers: a 1978 disability survey shows that 74 percent of those who receive disability benefits are 55-64 years of age. (These figures apply to all beneficiaries, in both the public and private sectors.)

Only in recent years has the number of individuals who receive company pensions increased. During 1979, 9.6 million received a pension from the mixed sector, as compared with half as many in 1970. As pension adequacy increases and investment becomes more secure and as more systems mature, we can expect the number of recipients to increase. When added to social security benefits, the combined replacement ratio for the highest three years of indexed earnings was 44 percent for married men, but only 32 percent for those without private pensions (Fox 1982: 20).

Despite the broad coverage and the growth of private pensions, public policy has not been successful in assuring that all workers receive these supplementary pensions. As a result, the President's Commission on Pension Policy recommended a mandated, compulsory private pension system to be paid for by a 3 percent tax on payroll. A change in the tax law would be needed to ease the tax burden on small firms. It is unlikely that such mandated pensions will be accepted in the United States, but the very fact that such a bill was proposed testifies to the weakness of the existing private pension schemes.

The best available source of information on the contributions, benefits, and assets of private pension schemes is the 1977 DOL survey discussed above. The survey analyzed 450,000 private pension plans that covered about 50 million workers. The highlights are worth reporting briefly. First, about 69 percent of all plan participants were covered by a defined benefit plan—i.e., one providing for the payment of definite amounts usually based upon a formula calculating benefits as a percent of earnings. (By contrast, a defined contribution plan generally provides for a fixed rate of contributions which are then allocated to individuals based on their contributions to an account after considering expenses, gains, losses, and forfeitures against the account.) Second, although the vast majority of all plans are small, it is the large plans with one hundred or more participants which cover 90 percent of all participants. In 1977 the total income for pension plans was $65.2 billion, 22 percent of which came from investment earnings. About $23 billion was spent on direct benefits. Trust fund assets amounted to $282 billion, and $43 billion was for unallocated insurance contracts, making a total of $325 billion in assets.

As noted above, these estimates cover only part of the private pension system because the primary purpose of the DOL survey was to monitor trouble spots rather than to gain a comprehensive picture of private pensions. Hence the survey focused on unallocated pension funds—i.e., those which do not designate a particular beneficiary and which are by and large uninsured. In addition to these unallocated and uninsured plans, many life insurance plans rely upon allocated funding instruments, "under which the insurer has a legally enforceable obligation to make all benefit payments for which it has received the premiums or consideration requested" (McGill 1979: 240).

The largest category of private pension plans covered and reported through life insurance companies falls under the heading of group annuities. Benefits accounted for $2.7 billion in 1978 and $4.2 billion in 1980. However, these group annuities include both allocated and unallocated pensions. It is therefore difficult to know how much of these payments should be added to the figure reported in the DOL survey.

In part unallocated funds are no longer separated because of a major change in the insurance industry. Noninsured or trusted pension funds which are not administered by life insurance companies have shown the most rapid growth in the past two decades. These funds now rank as the fourth largest financial intermediary (the middlemen between the suppliers of capital and the investors in real assets). Various factors account for the declining role of life insurance as an outlet for household savings. For one thing, life insurance companies faced increasing demands for loans against the face value of life insurance plans when interest rates increased and life agencies were forced by law to lend money at low interest. A General Accounting Office report offers another explanation for the declining role: "Where insurance had previously provided both protection and retirement income, these functions are increasingly performed by two distinct vehicles—a pension plan or savings and a term life insurance plan for protection" (United States, Comptroller General

1981: 8). These changes have led to a shift within the life insurance field away from permanent life insurance and "pension plans have become an important part of the life insurance business."

PERSONAL SECTOR PENSIONS

We turn now to that hybrid sector which lies between personal savings and conventional social policy and where resources for specified risks are controlled by third parties. In the United States the tax-sheltered IRAs are the programmatic format for retirement savings in this sector. IRAs originated with the recognition that although many individuals are technically covered by corporate pension and profit-sharing plans, many did not work long enough with an employer to earn vested rights; moreover, many profit-sharing plans do not yield a profit at the time of an individual's retirement.* In 1971 President Richard Nixon sent a message to Congress calling attention to this tax inequity and recommended that individuals be eligible to establish their own IRAs or supplement employer-financed pensions. Congress decided in 1974 with the passage of ERISA to limit the tax incentives to individuals who are not covered by employer-sponsored pension plans and to allow a relatively small sum of money to be set aside for such pensions annually—the lesser of 15 percent compensation or $1500. However, ERISA established a precedent, and in future years both restrictions were relaxed. As part of the Economic Recovery Tax Act of 1981, a new and expanded IRA program was developed. Beginning with tax year 1982, the program was universalized to anyone receiving compensation for work. Thus individuals could set up their own IRA even if they were already covered by an existing tax-qualified plan. In addition, the contribution level was increased to $2250 if an applicant had a nonworking spouse.

It would appear that the United States has launched upon an asset-formation policy. Currently this policy is not directed at reducing pressure for the expansion of social insurance programs. Rather, the rationale seems to lie in providing individuals with an opportunity to supplement existing public and private provisions. Present legislation does not attempt to develop an asset-formation

---

*The reported statistics on corporate pensions in the National Income Accounts include profit-sharing. A best estimate is that about 10 percent of such schemes are set aside for profit-sharing. Of course many individuals are entitled to both pensions and profit-sharing schemes, making it difficult to get unduplicated counts.

policy to assist those with low or modest incomes, either through a direct subsidy or a tax credit. Instead the IRA works through the mechanism of tax deduction; this favors high-income individuals because the higher one's tax bracket, the more valuable the deductions. When an IRA is created, the money paid into the plan and the earnings accumulating from the plan are deductible for income tax purposes. After retirement, when an individual is in a substantially lower tax bracket—both because his earnings are lower and because he is entitled to an exemption for age—the funds set aside for the plan as well as the earnings are taxed. If the funds are withdrawn before an individual reaches 59½ years of age, they are subject to a 10 percent penalty tax, and a 50 percent penalty tax if the individual does not use the money before age 70½. Congress hoped to encourage the use of the IRA for retirement purposes through these penalties.

The U.S. Savings League estimates assets of $13.5 billion in 1977, with life insurance companies accounting for only 25 percent of the total.

Does an asset-accumulation policy which makes use of tax incentives produce perverse income redistribution and encourage greater use by higher income earners? The Carter administration decided not to propose expanding IRAs because the participation rates of individuals with annual incomes below $20,000 was less than 5 percent, while those with incomes above $50,000 was over 50 percent. However, the issue is not settled. Ray Schmitt (1982: 11) at the Library of Congress points out that about one third (31 percent) of all IRA contributors had adjusted gross incomes of under $20,000 and 57 percent had incomes below $30,000.

It is of course too early to judge the importance of asset-accumulation policies through IRAs since the liberalization and expansion of the program did not come into effect until the end of 1982. In 1977 about $3.2 billion in payments were received from IRAs. Benefits were very small, accounting for $13 million in 1978 and $45 million in 1980.

DISAGGREGATING PENSIONS BY RISK AND SECTOR: A COMPARISON OF SWEDEN AND THE UNITED STATES

In this section we shall compare pensions in Sweden, the leading welfare state, with the United States, the laggard welfare state. Tables 3 and 4 provide a disaggregated picture of pensions by sector (public, private, and government employment) and risk (retirement, disability/handicap, and dependents/survivors). The purpose of this comparison is to see what generalizations can be drawn when we examine the institutional details of the pension system.

The first and perhaps most striking observation is that in 1977 there was only a modest difference in the percentage of GNP spent on pensions in Sweden and the United States when both the public and private sector pension arrangements are taken into account: 10.5

Table 3

PENSION EXPENDITURES BY SECTOR AND RISK: SWEDEN, 1977
(*Thousands of krona*)

Sector	Risk			
	Retirement	Disability and Handicap	Dependents and Survivors	Total
Public	K24,318	K5,819	K2,838	K32,975
Basic	15,792	3,239	1,215	20,246
Partial	412	--	--	412
Earnings-related (ATP)	6,064	2,460	1,153	9,677
Housing and Social Help	--	--	--	--
Cash	2,050	120	470	2,640
Private[a]	1,071	410	158	1,639
White-collar workers	623	71	128	822
Blue-collar workers	213	318	--	531
Consumer coop	116	12	8	136
Pension insurance societies	119	9	22	150
Civil servants	--	--	--	3,973
Central government	--	--	--	3,116
Local government	743	--	114	857
Total				38,587
GNP				367,300
Percent of GNP				10.5%

Sources: National income accounts and unpublished data.

[a]Nonstatutory, nonlegislated, collectively bargained pensions for white-collar workers and blue-collar workers employed in the cooperative sector (e.g., firms cooperatively owned by unions and other organizations).

Table 4

PENSION EXPENDITURES BY SECTOR AND RISK:
UNITED STATES, 1977
(Millions of dollars)

Sector	Retirement	Risk Disability and Handicap	Risk Dependents and Survivors	Total
Government as provider	$52.4	$13.2	$27.8	$93.4
Social insurance	48.1	9.5	26.5	84.1
Veterans' pensions	1.9	--	1.3	3.2
SSI	2.4	3.7	--	6.1
Government as employer	16.9	13.5	3.0	33.4
Federal	9.2	7.8	1.4	18.4
State and local	7.7	0.6	0.5	8.8
Veterans' compensation	--	5.1	1.1	6.2
Government as guarantor	2.3	0.5	1.1	4.03
Railway retirement	2.3	0.5	1.1	3.90
Benefit guarantee corporation	--	--	--	0.13
Private sector				25.6
Employer pensions	--	--	--	22.9
Pensions with life insurance	--	--	--	2.7
Personal sector				
IRA/Keogh and tax	--	--	--	0.17
Total				156.6
GNP				1837.0
Percent of GNP				8.5%

Sources: Same as for Table 3.

percent in the former and 8.5 percent in the latter.* This finding is very puzzling, especially when we recall that 16 percent of the population in Sweden is aged, as compared to 11 percent in the United States. One possible explanation why the leading welfare state spent only 2 percent more of GNP for pensions than the laggard is that the Swedish pension system is in transition from a flat-rate *Folkpension* to an earnings-related scheme (ATP). The legislative struggle for ATP was resolved in 1959, but it took twenty years for the system to

*ILO figures for 1977 show 9.2 percent of GDP spent on pensions. The difference between the figures we report and those of the ILO are wholly accounted for by the use of GNP rather than GDP. When the GNP figure is applied to the ILO statistics, the proportion spent on pensions is 8.8 percent. See ILO (1981: table 8 and appendix table).

mature before earnings-related benefits were paid out. As a result, partial payments began to be paid only in the early 1970s and accelerated throughout the decade. As a result, pensions increased by 113 percent between 1970 and 1980.

To explore this interpretation, Table 5 shows trends in social protection for selected EEC countries using the broader concept of social protection employed in the European Common Market. The largest increases in protection between 1970 and 1980 were 44 percent in the Netherlands and 36 percent in France. West Germany had the smallest increase—only 12 percent—and the United Kingdom and Denmark had increases of about 23 percent. Only one program more than doubled in the decade: the Dutch disability pension, which increased 136 percent. With 5.2 percent of GNP spent on disability in 1980, the Netherlands stands out for its singularly large commitment of resources for disability.* No other country reported such high levels of expenditures. Aside from the increase in the Dutch disability benefits, no other component of pensions increased as rapidly as did the Swedish pension system, which more than doubled during the 1970s.

Another possible explanation for the small difference in spending between leader and laggard is a general tendency for the Scandinavian countries to spend less on pensions. This is borne out by the Danish figures reported in Table 5: the United States spent more on pensions in 1977 than Denmark spent in 1978.

While the aggregate level of pension expenditure in Sweden and the United States in 1977 was broadly similar, the countries differed sharply in how the benefits were distributed and which sectors of the society received them. These differences raise some interesting general questions about public policy choices in the pension field. Below we shall discuss the differences in risk mix and sectoral mix.

RISK MIX

One striking difference is in dependent and survivor benefits in the two countries. Focusing on the government as provider, we find that in Sweden less than 10 percent of pensions went for dependents and survivors as compared to 30 percent in the United States. Part of the explanation for this difference lies in a philosophical commitment

---

*The Dutch disability program is very different from either the American or Swedish system. Only 44 percent of beneficiaries are 55 years or older.

Table 5

TRENDS IN SOCIAL PROTECTION BY RISK FOR SELECTED EEC COUNTRIES, 1970 AND 1980

Risk
(*Percent of GDP*)

Country	GDP	Retirement (1)	Disability and Handicap (2)	Dependents and Survivors (3)	Total Cash (4)	Benefits in Kind (5)	(1) + (2) + (3)
				1 9 7 0			
West Germany	678.7	5.8%	1.5%	3.4%	15.9%	4.6%	10.7%
France	782.6	6.0	0.8	1.3	12.6	5.6	8.1
Netherlands	114.6	6.7	2.2	1.3	16.1	3.9	10.2
United Kingdom	52.2	6.4	0.6	0.5	10.6	4.7	7.5
Denmark	118.6	5.5	1.6	0.2	11.1	8.0	7.3
				1 9 8 0			
West Germany	1488.9	6.9	1.3	3.8	18.3	9.0	12.0
France	2754.9	8.3	1.0	1.7	16.5	7.9	11.0
Netherlands	333.3	8.1	5.2	1.4	23.2	6.3	14.7
United Kingdom	231.4	7.9	0.9	0.4	14.2	6.6	9.2
Denmark	374.1	7.1	1.8	0.1	16.6	10.6	9.0
			Percent Change, 1970-1980				
West Germany		19.0	-13.3	11.8	15.1	95.7	12.1
France		38.3	25.0	30.8	31.0	41.1	35.8
Netherlands		20.9	136.4	7.7	44.1	61.5	44.1
United Kingdom		23.4	50.0	-20.0	34.0	40.4	22.7
Denmark		29.1	12.5	-50.0	49.5	32.5	23.3

Source: EEC 1980.

in Sweden to move away from the principle of family protection to that of security for each individual. In Sweden each individual is entitled to a basic, noncontributory, flat-rate pension when he reaches the age of 65. When the spouse of a retired or disabled worker gets benefits, it is because he or she is less than 65 and not yet entitled to a full pension. In the United States social insurance also provides benefits for both wives and survivors, but there is evidence that the wife supplement will decrease in importance in the future as women earn entitlement through work. Thus both systems appear to be moving away from family protection toward individual entitlement. However, the Swedish system is based on common citizenship, whereas the American is based on employment.

In Sweden widows can get benefits from the age of 36, although they receive lower benefits until age 50 if they do not have children in their care. By contrast, in the United States a widow with a child in her care can get benefits at any age, or at ages 50–59 if she is disabled. Otherwise, survivors' benefits start at age 60. When a widow gets benefits at a lower age, the benefits are actuarially reduced.

Survivors' protection is also provided in the private sector through life insurance. In Sweden in 1977 life insurance was 0.24 percent of GNP, as compared to 0.6 percent in the United States. When the public and private survivors' benefits are added together, it appears that the private sector has only about one-third of total survivor costs. With the passage of ERISA, in order to qualify for favorable tax treatment, pension plans that pay retirement benefits must offer a joint and survivor annuity as the standard plan for retirement. (Of course a worker has the option of not electing survivors' protection.) The effect of this legislation has been to increase survivors' benefits in the private sector.

While survivors' benefits in life insurance are substantially more important in the United States than in Sweden, the level of protection provided in the United States is modest. In 1977, $10.2 billion was paid to almost 3 million beneficiaries at an average of $3553 per beneficiary (American Council of Life Insurance 1979: 41). Death benefits under life insurance are typically paid in lump sum payments, with the amount depending on the amount of insurance purchased and the age at death of the policyholder.

In the United States disability expenditures account for 11 percent of social insurance and 13 percent of all public sector risks. Unfortunately we are not able to locate good information on the distribution of risks within the private sector. In Sweden disability accounts for about 18 percent of the pensions allocated by the government as provider and about 25 percent in the private sector. A recent report provides some evidence that private disability benefits in Sweden are related to plant closings. The findings suggest that firms use disability to encourage retirement when they either experience financial difficulty or are forced to close and relocate.

In Sweden about 10 percent of male disability beneficiaries are 55 years and older. In 1976 more people were retired with a disability pension than with a retirement pension. However, they received the disability pension for only a short time—two or three years—before switching to a retirement pension. Thus the disability pension was a way of lowering the age of retirement. This was borne out in 1976 when the pension age was lowered from 67 to 65 and the number of disability beneficiaries dropped sharply. However, the numbers again increased in succeeding years.

In general, we can conclude that about one third of disability expenditures in the United States and about one quarter in Sweden are not related to early retirement. Thus the inclusion of disability in pension estimates overstates the pension obligations in society.

SECTORAL MIX

The sectoral mix—i.e., the sectors which allocate pensions— is even more dramatically different than the risk mix in the two countries. In Sweden the pension system is essentially a public program: 85 percent of benefits are allocated in the public sector with the government as provider. In sharp contrast, in the United States the government as provider accounts for only 60 percent of benefits, or close to two thirds if we include the Railroad Retirement System.

We have already noted one important difference within the public sector—namely, a basic Folkpension in Sweden for all citizens over 65. America rejected a noncontributory, flat-rate pension during the stormy passage of the Social Security Act in 1935. The designers of this legislation were apprehensive that a flat-rate system would resemble the claims for universal pensions that the Townsend movement demanded.

Both Sweden and the United States have means-tested programs. Somewhat surprisingly, means testing is quite large within the public sector in Sweden, accounting for 8.0 percent of public pensions. However, this estimate does not include the traditional welfare program administered at the local level, known as Social Help. By and large, Sweden has eliminated the aged from its welfare rolls. In 1941, 18 percent of the aged received Social Help, but by 1968 the proportion had dramatically declined to 0.9 percent. In 1968, 10 percent of Social Help recipients were between 60 and 66 years of age. The proportion declined and by 1977 represented only trivial expenditures.

The Swedish means-testing program is largely within the framework of social insurance. To appreciate the Swedish test of need, we must distinguish assets, earnings, and transfer tests. The wives' means test follows the traditional test based on assets and earnings and is administered by a local commune, with some transfer income (like that of the Folkpension) exempt. By contrast, the pension supplement is only transfer tested. These supplements are a device for integrating different social insurance benefits. They were designed to prevent the growth of inequalities among already retired pensioners who had not gained entitlement to an earnings-related benefit. After earnings-related ATP was introduced, a minimum guaranteed pension was set at a higher rate than the Folkpension. Pension supplements were paid to individuals who received only the Folkpension or ATP benefits which did not raise them to the minimum guaranteed level. These supplements are thus technically income-tested, but only on the transfer income needed to bring recipients up to the guaranteed level.

In the United States less than 10 percent of public pensions is allocated through means testing of two types: since 1974 a nationally administered SSI test (with the option of state supplementation), and a very liberally interpreted means test for veterans in need (measured by ease of access and adequacy of benefits). These programs are separately administered outside of the framework of social insurance and thus follow the more traditional welfare programs.

Another major difference between Sweden and the United States is the proportion of pensions allocated to civil servants. In Sweden only 10 percent of pensions is so allocated, as compared to 21 percent in the United States. The difference is accounted for by the structure of pensions and not the size of the civil service. Indeed in Sweden civil servants account for one third of the labor force, as compared with only about one fifth in the United States. Moreover, about 70 percent of local civil servants in the United States do not receive public employment pensions because they have opted to join the social security system. The 21 percent allocation in the United States is very large considering the small proportion of eligible civil servants in the labor force.

In Sweden all civil servants receive a Folkpension and the earnings-related supplement administered through the public program. Civil servants do not receive a separate pension with more generous provisions for indexing and age of retirement as they do in the United States. However, they get additional fringe benefits similar to the supplements received by blue- and white-collar workers outside of the public program. Indeed civil servants get more than twice as much as blue- and white-collar workers combined.*

The private sector in Sweden accounts for 4.2 percent of total pension outlays, or about 5.0 percent of public pension expenditures. By contrast, in the United States private sector pensions account for 16.4 percent of total expenditures and 27.4 percent of public pensions, excluding pensions paid through the civil service.

In summary, Sweden's pension system is administered essentially through the public sector; both civil servants and private pensions play only a very small role. By contrast, social security and veterans' payments for retirement and disability account for 60 percent of the total in the United States. Both the private and civil servant sectors are much larger than in Sweden. Paradoxically, in the United States civil servants account for an even larger proportion of outlays than that of the private sector. As discussed above, a good part of the pensions of the military and from state and local governments are for individuals who retire in their late fifties or early sixties. Because these schemes promote early retirement, their integration into the social security system is difficult. Moreover, many civil servants also "double-dip"—i.e., receive both a civil servant pension and social security benefits from working part time outside of government.

CONCLUSION

We have argued that the lag-lead framework of comparing welfare states is misleading. To illustrate, we have shown that when the institutional details of risk and sector are taken into account, there is virtually no difference in the level of pension expenditures between Sweden and the United States. To explore why this fact

---

*In Sweden earnings-related pensions are paid by the employer. This would mean that the government pays for the pensions of civil servants, but the figures reported here clearly do not include these payments.

has been overlooked, we return to the theme raised above about the structure of knowledge.

We believe that a competition of interests between public and private sectors in the field of pensions generates partisanship which can yield more objective knowledge and self-reflective criticism (collective learning). This knowledge promotes understanding which can serve as a basis for change and can provide an intellectual foundation for enabling the public sector to act in a public manner, which then leads to a further redefinition of how the public, private, and mixed sectors combine. To produce partisan grounded knowledge, the sectors need to be both separate and integrated. We have no formal way of documenting our understanding about the knowledge that exists in each society.

In the pension field three main institutions generate and make use of knowledge. First, and perhaps most important, are public and private mission agencies—the DOL, life insurance companies, and firms offering private pensions—whose task is to run pension programs. The mission agencies tend to have only a small research division. The knowledge they generate is programmatic or mission-oriented, based on the information needed for purposes of financing and administration. Second, regulatory agencies monitor the mission agencies in both the public and private sectors. (Oversight research in the private sector in the United States is divided among three main agencies: the DOL, which deals with pensions as part of the labor contract; the Department of Health, Education, and Welfare, which handles the public mix exchange; and the Federal Reserve Bank, which oversees personal or private pensions and savings. This leaves the field open for independent inquiry.) Third are independent or autonomous institutions ranging from universities to research centers to partisan interests. (Here we can place international fact-gathering and research bodies like the OECD and ILO.)

The impressions we have from our preliminary review can be summarized as follows: Knowledge in the private sector is limited. Each mission agency generates restricted programmatic knowledge about its own mission. In consequence, information proliferates without a center for integration and reconciliation. When missions conflict, some mechanism is needed to reconcile the varying interpretations. Whether assimilated knowledge is generated depends on the distribution of power of the contending groups. The current structure of knowledge and ignorance in the field of private pensions sets the stage for an ideological debate along at least three lines:

(1) The impact of the public and private sectors on saving and capital accumulation. The debate is most extensive in the United States and takes the form of a conflict among autonomous researchers (e.g., Martin Feldstein at Harvard and Alicia Munnell at the Federal Reserve Bank). There is a standoff on the findings, each side holding firm to its own position.*

(2) The limits of the public and private sectors. The controversy in the public sector centers on fiscal crises due to demographic shifts and a slowdown of the economy. This leads to a debate about the reduction of benefits, as well as to a shift to the private sector. "Mounting sentiment has developed in the United States for moving some of the responsibility for retirement back to the private sector" (Munnell 1982: 1).

(3) The relationship between the public and private sectors. An integration of public and mixed sector pensions becomes critical. Knowledge of integration is limited. At issue in the United States (as well as in the Netherlands) is whether the rules of integration increase the advantages of middle and upper earners when mixed-sector pensions are available only as supplements to public pensions.

REFERENCES

American Council of Life Insurance. 1979. *1979 Life Insurance Fact Book.* Washington, D.C.

Brandes, Stuart D. 1976. *American Welfare Capitalism 1880–1940.* Chicago: University of Chicago Press.

EBRI [Employment Benefit Research Institute]. 1982. News release, 26 May.

EEC. 1980. *European System of Integrated Social Protection Statistics* [ESSPROS]. Luxembourg: Eurostat.

Fox, Alan. 1982. "Earnings Replacement Rates and Total Income." *Social Security Bulletin* (October).

*In the Netherlands the main controversy centers not on capital markets, but on the transfer of pension credits known as "pension breaks." After thirteen years of study, no action has been taken. A caretaker government took a position to break the deadlock. But knowledge about finances is a precondition for reforms which are proposed. The mission agencies have been reluctant to provide Parliament with the information it has requested. Parliament could force the issue, but not without political costs.

Heclo, Hugh. 1982. "Income Maintenance Expenditures." In *Comparative Public Policy*, ed. Arnold Heidenheimer and Hugh Heclo, 2d ed. New York: St. Martin's Press.

ILO. 1981. *The Cost of Social Security*. Geneva.

Keyfitz, Nathan. 1981. *How Secure Is Social Security?* Luxembourg: International Institute for Applied Systems Analysis.

Kohl, Jurgen. 1981. "Trends and Problems in Post-War Public Expenditure Development in Western Europe and North America." In *The Development of the Welfare States in Europe and America*, ed. Peter Flora and Arnold Heidenheimer. New Brunswick, N.J.: Transaction Books.

Levitan, Sar. 1985. "Business Lobbies in the Welfare State." Mimeo.

McGill, Dan M. 1979. *Fundamentals of Private Pensions*, 4th ed. Homewood, Ill.: Irwin Dorsey.

Munnell, Alicia. 1982. *The Economics of Private Pensions*. Washington, D.C.: The Brookings Institution.

OECD. 1977. *Old Age Pension Schemes*. Paris.

Rein, Martin. 1982. "The Social Policy of the Firm." *Policy Sciences* 14: 117-35.

Schmitt, Ray. 1982. "Individual Retirement Accounts [IRAs] : Tax Incentive for Retirement Savings." Washington, D.C.: Library of Congress, Congressional Research Service. Mimeo, 17 June.

Sheingold, Steve. 1980. "The Effect of Payroll Taxes on Total Labor Compensation." From Bureau of Labor Statistics, *Employment Expenditures for Compensation*. Mimeo, 17 June.

United States. 1979. *The Budget of the United States Government, Fiscal Year 1980*. Washington, D.C.: Government Printing Office.

_____, Congress. 1978. House of Representatives, Committee on Education and Labor. *Pension Task Force on Public Employee Retirement Systems*; 95th Congress, 2d sess., 15 March.

_____, Comptroller General. 1981. *Report to the Congress: Billions of Dollars Are Involved in the Taxation of the Life Insurance Industry — Some Corrections in the Law Are Needed*; 17 September.

_____, DOL [Department of Labor]. 1981. Labor Management Service Administration, Pension and Welfare Benefits Program. "Preliminary Estimates of Participant and Financial Characteristics of Private Pension Plans." Mimeo.

_____, General Accounting Office. 1981. *Multiemployer Pension Plan Data Are Inaccurate and Incomplete*; 25 October.

Vranken, Jan. 1986. "Report on the Post-War Development of the Welfare State in Belgium." Paper prepared for a comparative conference of welfare state development in Europe, Florence, Italy; organized by Peter Flora.

SOCIAL WELFARE AND

TRANSFER PAYMENTS

THE DISTRIBUTIVE EFFECTS OF
THE SOCIAL CONSUMPTION FUND
IN THE SOVIET UNION

Gur Ofer and Aaron Vinokur

I. INTRODUCTION

The Social Consumption Fund (SCF) is a Soviet term that encompasses all additions to household incomes—as money allowances or direct services—made by the public sector that are not strictly wages. The early foundations of the term can be found in Marx's *Critique of the Gotha Program* in the form of deductions from the total value of production prior to payment of wages for two consumption purposes: (1) "for the common satisfaction of needs, such as schools, health services, etc.," and (2) "funds for those unable to work, etc." (1966: 14). Given the necessity, during the socialist stage, to pay to workers wages that are "proportional to the labor they supply" (16), the SCF stands out as a major contributor to equality and to income maintenance.

In 1980 the total value of the SCF to families of state employees was more than 130 billion rubles—almost 70 percent of the entire net wage fund of about 188 billion rubles.* Put differently, almost 40 kopecks of every ruble (=100 kopecks) worth of consumption a Soviet family enjoys comes from this fund. In principle such a fund can be used as a major instrument of income policy, both as an equalizer of incomes and a vehicle of income maintenance. One would expect this to happen in a socialist country that is forced to maintain significant wage differentials dictated by efficiency considerations. Soviet and Western analysts have different evaluations of the contribution of the SCF to these two goals. These differences result on the one hand from the use of alternative definitions of the SCF and a variety of databases of different population segments, and on the other hand from different views on what constitutes a satisfactory contribution to equality and welfare.

*Collective farm members receive another 14 billion rubles of SCF payments and services (*NK* 1980).

251

The main aim of this essay is to describe and analyze the impact of the SCF on incomes of the Soviet urban population, based on a sample of families that emigrated from the Soviet Union during the mid-1970s. The main elements of the Soviet SCF system will be discussed, but a detailed description of the system and its regulations will not be provided. The reader who wants that is referred to Minkoff and Turgeon (1977), McAuley (1979), and Madison (1979). The primary emphasis is on macro-distributive effects rather than on effects of specific programs on specific segments of the population. Because of the sample used, the analysis concentrates on urban families of state employees from the European republics of the Soviet Union.

THE ROLE OF SCF IN SOVIET INCOME POLICY

The sum of the SCF and the (net) wage bill in any given year is equal to the amount of consumption households can claim and receive from the public sector.* Unlike in market economies, the government controls the total consumption pie, and it can determine how to slice it among different types of payment or service and the distribution of each payment or service to the population. Three major considerations have to be balanced in the program adopted. First, the system of payments must have enough allocative power and built-in incentive structure so that the allocation of labor between different jobs and the level of effort put forth on the job will approach optimality. Second, the payment structure must encourage the highest possible rate of participation in the labor force. This consideration assumes special significance at the borderline between minimum wages and welfare payments, and it has an added weight in the Soviet Union, where the maximization of growth rates has always been the goal and where growth depends on maximum mobilization of inputs, including labor. The third consideration is to increase social equality and to prevent poverty. At least in the short run, there is a conflict between efficiency, as defined by the first two considerations, and the third consideration, which clearly requires payments that are independent of wages or amount of work done. Any nonwage payment has a negative income effect against work. In addition, if the total consumption fund is fixed, as in the Soviet case, it will have a negative substitution effect because wage

---

*We shall disregard savings, the private sector, and the problem of market disequilibrium here. Also put aside is pure public consumption like administration and defense.

rates will have to go down. Both income and substitution effects are of special significance at the low-wage, poverty level, where almost any welfare payment implies a high rate of taxation imposed on those joining the work force. Finally, any injection of equality considerations into the wage structure may weaken it as an allocative instrument. Faced with such conflicts and committed to production and growth, the Soviets came up with a compromise that was significantly tilted toward the production goal. Their overall income policy can be summarized as follows:

A. Everybody who can work should work. In addition to social and ideological pressures, there are economic pressures because wages are set at levels that make it very difficult to support a family with one salary.

B. Involuntary unemployment is ruled out. This is a matter of principle, but also an outcome of overambitious plans and the control mechanism. It enables the state to avoid the problem of fixing the level and structure of unemployment compensation so as not to affect work incentives.

C. Nonwage monetary and other support is conditioned on work and as much as possible attached to wages. In addition to the holiday pay that the Soviets include in some of their SCF statistics, there are pensions of all kinds, sick pay, maternity leave, etc. Wherever possible, these benefits are structured to reduce work interruption. Other services, like housing, child-care facilities, health, and recreation, are generally provided through working places on a priority basis. When these services are not proportional to wages, they can have an equalizing role—at least among wage earners. To avoid the granting of nonwage payments, the wage structure has also been used as an income maintenance instrument, mostly through raising the minimum wage. Such a policy has made it possible to support low-income families while at the same time raising participation rates of women. The alternative of welfare payments with low minimum wage rates would have an opposite effect on participation rates. Furthermore, without raising minimum wage above the sheer subsistence floor, there is no room for "pure" welfare payments.

D. Pure welfare, like children allowances and income supplements, should be used only as a last resort and even then very cautiously and in small amounts. Many of these programs are relatively new.

The overall outcome of these policies is that family units with high dependency rates or who rely solely on pensions for income make up the majority of the poor in the USSR. The general response of the population to this income policy had been to work if possible, even if difficult (like mothers of babies or pensioners), or to reduce the dependency rate by raising fewer children. The long-term costs of very low birth rates, the "demographic problem" facing the Soviet Union, and the high cost of child-care centers combined with basic welfare considerations to bring about rather late increased allowances under maternity leave and children's programs (see Lapidus 1978, ch. 8).

Compared with money welfare payments, the Soviet Union is much more generous in the provision of free public services — education and health — and in heavily subsidizing basic needs like housing, public transportation, and (recently) food. In principle, education, health, and rental housing are allocated according to need on a universal basis to everybody, but as noted, some of these services are better provided to workers, especially to workers in priority industries. With the exception of the food subsidy, the ability to pay is not a factor in determining the amount received. All fall under the principle of the provision of basic services to the population on an equal basis at low cost. Education and health also have direct productivity implications as well as long-run income equalization effects.

A full discussion of the equalization potential of SCF payments beyond the degree of equality embodied in the wage structure is presented below. It must be obvious from the above analysis that the SCF system is not intended only to promote equality: a large part of it is linked to wages, and most other parts are distributed on a universal basis and without income tests. It will also be shown how well SCF deals with poverty.

II. THE SCF IN 1973 OFFICIAL DATA AND IMMIGRANT SAMPLES

According to the official definition, the SCF includes free educational and health services, money payments and allowances for vacation, pensions, educational stipends, sick leave, maternity leave, children and income supplementary allowances, and a list of subsidized services: rental housing, extracurricular activities for children, vacation homes, etc. (*NK* 1980: 381). McAuley (1979: 262) points out that holiday pay is probably included as a transfer rather than a part of wages because it is not strictly a payment for work done. Excluded from the Soviet definition are food subsidies, which have been growing very fast, and a number of other transfers and subsidies. Since data on food subsidies are available, they are included in Table 1 as part of the official data on SCF (Treml 1978; Kraeger 1974).

In Table 1 a comparison is made between Soviet official data on SCF for state employees and data derived from our immigrant sample made up of state employees and their families. The first four columns of Table 1 contain the official Soviet information on SCF. The figures in column 1 relate to the entire population, and those in column 2 to state employees and their families (including retired state employees). The figures in column 2 were derived by guesstimating the probable shares of state employees in each SCF component, taking into account their share of the population and the nature of the program. The share of total SCF going to state employees was made to be consistent with available Soviet data (see notes to Table 1). The figures of column 2 are then calculated per employee and per capita for the population of state employees (cols. 3 and 4).

Before turning to the data derived from the survey—the "sample" data—a few details on the survey should be presented. Two groups of Soviet immigrants who came to Israel during the mid-1970s were surveyed. One was group of 1,016 two-parent families with head in the working age and working; the second was a group of 250 "units" including retired people, one-parent families, and singles — of all age groups, working or not. Since neither group nor both together correspond to the Soviet urban population of state employees, an attempt was made to restructure the sample. The outcome of the restructuring is a population of 1,688 household units made to match as closely as possible the Soviet population of European-urban state employees. The European and urban limitations are dictated by the nature of the sample, and in these two respects the sample population is different from that of all state employees. The sample was restructured, or reweighted, to resemble the target population in terms of sex, working and retired age-groups, and employment status. The employed were further restructured according to levels of education and rank and occupational groups.* The correspondence between the restructured sample and the target population is in general quite good, but differences remain which will be noted when relevant.

*For full description of the process of restructuring and its results, see Ofer and Vinokur (1980).

Table 1
SCF ALLOWANCES: OFFICIAL DATA AND SAMPLE, 1973

| | Soviet Official Data | | | | Immigrant Sample Data | | |
| | Rubles (billions) | | Rubles per Month[c] | | Rubles (billions) | Rubles per month | |
Income Categories	Total	State Employees[a]	Per Employee	Per Capita	Total	Per Employee	Per Capita
	(1)	(2)	(3)	(4)	(5)	(6)	(7)
(1) SCF (total) A[b]	R93.0	R81.0	R69.3	R33.0	R87.7*-93.5[d]	R64.4	R40.2
(2) SCF (total) B	78.0	66.0	56.4	27.0	68.5	48.0	30.0
(3) Money transfers	40.5	34.6	29.6	14.2	38.1	28.0	17.5
(4) Holiday pay	10.8	9.2	7.9	3.8	10.0*	8.5	5.3
(5) Pensions	20.8	17.7	15.1	7.2	19.1	12.5	7.8
(6) Allowances	7.0	6.0	5.1	2.5	7.9	6.3	3.9
(7) Sick leave	4.3	3.7	3.2	1.5	5.4*	4.6	2.9
(8) Others[e]	2.7	2.3	2.0	1.0	2.5	1.7	1.0
(9) Stipends	1.9	1.7	1.5	0.7	1.1	0.7	0.4
(10) Non-money transfers	52.5	46.5	39.8	19.0	49.6*-55.4	36.4	22.7
(11) Subsidies[f]	20.1	20.1	17.2	8.2	29.7*-35.5	23.3	14.5
(12) Housing	4.4	4.4	3.8	1.8	10.5	6.9	4.3
(13) Food	15.0	15.0	12.8	6.1	19.2*-25.0	16.4	10.2
(14) Others[g]	0.7	0.7	0.6	0.3	--	--	--
(15) Free services	32.4	26.4	22.6	10.8	19.9	13.1	8.1
(16) Education	21.0	17.1	14.6	7.0	12.0	7.9	4.9
(17) Health	11.4	9.3	8.0	3.8	7.9	5.2	3.2

Sources: Column 1: NK 1973: 607, 781-82; McAuley 1979: 262, 280. Food subsidies: Treml 1978; Kraeger, 1974. Rest: As explained in notes and text.

[a] Column 2 is derived by assuming that state employees receive the following shares of the total: lines 4, 5, 7, 8, 9, 10: 85 percent; lines 12, 13, 14: 100 percent; lines 16, 17: 81.5 percent.

[b] A includes all items; B excludes food subsidies.

[c] Calculations of figures in columns 3, 4, and 5 are based on 97,466 thousand state employees and 203.6 million people in the families of state employees.

[d] All figures with asterisks are based on per employee figures; all others are based on per capita figures. Aggregate figures are sometimes mixes of both calculations.

[e] Maternity pay, children allowances, and other.

[f] Exclude food subsidies.

[g] Probably a mix of free and subsidized items.

Returning to Table 1, let us outline the methods and assumptions used in estimating the sample data on SCF expenditures (cols. 5-7):

A. The survey data are for a range of years around 1973 —mostly 1972-1974; therefore they are compared with Soviet data for 1973.

B. All the data on money transfers (lines 3-9) are presented as reported by the families after the adjustment of reweighting.

C. Data on non-money transfers (lines 10-17) are usually calculated on the basis of information given by the families on the extent of use of the services and information from Soviet or Western sources on the costs involved in supplying each service and the extent of the subsidy. In many cases information on the use of a service is available only for the group of 1,016 two-parent families, so figures for the rest of the sample had to be estimated by indirect methods. For example, estimates of consumption of meat and dairy products for the rest of the sample were derived on the basis of their reported incomes, using consumption patterns of the main sample. The values of education services received are calculated by multiplying costs given in Soviet sources by the number of children attending various types of schools or institutions. The education figure includes some of the subsidized services which the Soviets include under a different category ("Other" in the table). It does not include the value of extra-curricular youth activities. The value of the rent subsidy is calculated by multiplying the rent actually paid by two—the average rate of public support grants (*Potrebnosti* 1975: 110). The food subsidy is for dairy products and meat only. It is calculated as a product of purchases in government and cooperative stores and the rate of subsidy as given by Soviet sources. The sample survey does not have good data from which to determine the value of health services received. It is therefore assumed that each family received the per capita level of services as reported by Soviet sources, proportional to the number of days its adult members spent in the hospital during the year of the report.

D. The sample survey data are first determined on a per capita and per employee basis, and then a total annual figure is calculated by multiplying each SCF element by the number of state employees *or* the number of members of families of state employees. The total sum of each element is different when calculated by the alternative methods because the number of people per employee in the sample population is different from that in the real Soviet population of state employees. The ratio of population to state employees in the real population is 2.09 and in the adjusted sample population is 1.60. This happened despite the adjustments for two reasons: (1) while the two populations have the same proportion of active households, the sample population has more workers per household; (2) there are differences between the European-urban target population and that of families of all state employees. The latter includes rural families and families from the Asian republics, which both have higher dependency rates. One way to get the Soviet total from the sample data is to use the per employee figure when the payment is made to employees or when it depends on the family's income, as in the case of food subsidies. In doing this we correct for the higher income of the sample families resulting from more employees per capita. In all other cases per capita figures are used.

Despite these methodological problems, the comparisons of the Soviet and the sample SCF figures produce very reasonable results — that is, the sample estimates are not out of line.

Among the cash payments, the sample estimates for pensions, holiday pay, and sick leave are higher than our estimates of the official figures. The first is due to the higher proportion of employees in the sample population, and the other two to the fact that even after reweighting the sample wages are still somewhat higher than in the target population. Other allowances are similar by both estimates, and stipends are lower in the sample probably because of the absence from the sample of students living alone.

Total monthly cash transfers including holiday pay are estimated by the sample at 17.5 rubles per capita and 28.0 rubles per employee, compared with the official Soviet figures of 14.2 and 29.6 rubles respectively. The 1973 cash part of SCF allocated to state employees is about 34.6 billion rubles according to official sources and 38.1 billion rubles as estimated from the sample data. (Without holiday pay the figures are 25.4 and 28.1 billion rubles respectively.)

In the categories of free and subsidized services, the official and sample estimates for health services are similar, but the sample estimate for education is significantly lower. We were unable to estimate the value of some activities in education, but that explains only part of the difference. On the other hand the sample estimates of food and housing subsidies are much higher than those derived from Soviet sources (housing) or Western estimates (food). These differences may be due in part to the higher incomes of the sample families and to their concentration in major cities, where the housing subsidies are higher and more meat products are bought in government stores at prices below those in the collective farm markets. Because the difference in food subsidies is so great when the sample estimate is calculated on the basis of per capita figures, we also provide an estimate based on per employee figures as a possible alternative. Thus, depending on which method is used for estimating the food subsidy, the annual noncash SCF estimated from the sample data is between 49.6 and 55.4 billion rubles compared with the Soviet official figure of 46.5 billion rubles.

Finally, the per capita estimate for the total SCF based on the sample data is 40.2 rubles per month compared with 33 rubles according to the official figures; the corresponding figures per employee are 64.4 and 69.3 rubles respectively. The total 1973 SCF allowance for state employees is estimated from the sample data at 87.7-93.5 billion rubles compared to the "officially" reported total of 81 billion rubles.

The purpose of this rather tedious exercise has been to give credibility to the sample estimates of the SCF. This accomplished, we can move on to examine how the various SCF elements are distributed according to levels of income.

III. DISTRIBUTION OF SCF ALLOWANCES BY WORK STATUS AND INCOME GROUPS

The estimates presented in this section are mostly for two populations: the entire sample population, which has been adjusted to resemble the Soviet European-urban population, and the "active" population, a subsection of the sample comprising all households with heads working in the public sector. A weighting system was also applied to this subsample to make it very similar in its main characteristics to its Soviet counterpart. In this section we examine the distribution of SCF allowances across a range of incomes where the basic ordering criterion used is public sector earnings per household member. Public earnings rather than total income were used as the ordering income criterion to emphasize the impact of SCF on the distribution of income generated by public net earnings. Since this is the distribution that the authorities most likely consider when they plan any intervention, private incomes were also excluded. In all the following tables, *per capita* earnings are used rather than household incomes despite the fact that the distribution is for entire *households*. Per capita income represents better than total household income the real economic position of the family. When public earnings are the ordering criterion, all non-active families fall by definition to the bottom of the distribution. There are 180 such families who make up almost exactly the lowest decile of the total population (169). In Table 2 we present data on the household characteristics and SCF distribution by work status for the entire sample population and two subsections: active and non-active populations. In Table 3 we present similar data for the active population only by income deciles.

Table 2 provides data on the relative size of the SCF compared with the total public wage bill. Even without holiday pay, SCF comprises almost one-third of all public sector transfers to households; with holiday pay, SCF reaches 36 percent, compared to 64 percent in the form of wages. SCF clearly has significant potential for affecting the levels of income equality and poverty. The most important aspect of Table 2 is the comparison of SCF allowances between active and non-active households. The different characteristics of the two groups of households are readily apparent. Non-active households are smaller, with many singles and couples, virtually all of whom are retired; only the levels of education of the two groups are similar. Correspondingly, the levels and structures of income of the two groups, including incomes from SCF, are different. By definition virtually all the public income of non-active household comes from SCF. Of the total of R128 per household per month, almost two-thirds comes from retirement pensions, and the remaining third is mostly in the form of food and housing subsidies and free health services. Active families receive less from SCF overall, but still get R83.5 per month (R98.6 including holiday pay)—about two-thirds the amount received by non-active households. Obviously most of this support comes in the form of subsidies and free services, including education, and much less in the form of money transfers. Money transfers are concentrated in work-related payments, such as holiday and sick pay, and to a lesser extent in children-related transfers—stipends and various children allowances. While it is clear that SCF narrows the income gap between the two groups, it is interesting to note that only 13.4 percent of all SCF transfers go to the non-active population—just slightly above its share of the entire household population. (On a per capita basis, however, the

Table 2

HOUSEHOLD CHARACTERISTICS, SCF ALLOWANCES, AND INCOME BY POPULATION GROUPS

	Entire Population		Active Population		Non-Active Population	
	(1)	(2)	(3)	(4)	(5)	(6)
Household characteristics						
(1) Number of households	1688		1508		180	
(2) Household members	2.53		2.66		1.42	
(3) Earners	1.58		1.77		0.02	
(4) Children	0.48		0.54		--	
(5) Age of head (years)	45.1		42.6		66.2	
(6) Education of head (years)	10.0		10.0		9.9	
	Rubles	Percent	Rubles	Percent	Rubles	Percent
Income categories (per month)						
(7) Public income	R285.1	100.0%	R303.7	100.0%	R129.7	100.0%
(8) Public earnings	196.8	69.0	220.2	72.5	1.5	1.2
(9) Holiday pay	13.5	4.7	15.1	5.0	0.4	--
(10) SCF (total)	88.3	31.0	83.5	27.5	128.2	98.8
(11) Money payments	30.8	10.8	24.7	8.1	82.3	63.4
(12) Retirement pension	14.3	5.0	6.4	2.1	80.8	62.3
(13) Nonmoney income	57.5	20.2	58.8	19.4	45.9	35.4
(14) Subsidies	40.4	14.2	40.5	13.3	39.6	30.5
(15) Education	3.5	1.2	4.0	1.3	--	--
(16) Housing	10.9	3.8	10.6	3.5	13.5	10.4
(17) Food	25.9	9.1	25.9	8.5	26.1	20.1
(18) Free services	17.1	6.0	18.3	6.0	6.3	4.9
(19) Education	8.9	3.1	9.9	3.2	--	--
(20) Health	8.2	2.9	8.4	2.8	6.3	4.9
Reference (per month)						
(21) Public money income (8 + 11)	227.6	79.8%	244.9	80.6%	83.7	64.5%
(22) Private income	43.4	15.2	45.1	14.9	27.6	21.3
(23) SCF including holiday pay (10 + 9)	101.8	35.7	98.6	32.5	128.6	98.8

equalization impact is much stronger.) We discuss distributive effects in greater detail below.

Turning to the active population, the data presented in Table 3 show the two primary sources of differentiation among the income deciles: household characteristics and earning capabilities (see Kuznets 1982: 697). Families in higher deciles are generally smaller, and while the number of earners per household starts to go down past the sixth decile, the number of earners per household *member* rises throughout and the dependency rate declines. The negative association between income per capita and family size causes income inequality to be wider for income per capita as compared with income per household. In addition to the demographic factors, income differentials are also increased by differences in earning capacity as manifested here by the strong association between the level of education of the family head and the rank of the income decile.

The main elements of the distribution of SCF transfers among households at different deciles are the following:

A. Without holiday pay, total SCF per household declines from near R100 in the lower deciles to about R75 in the top deciles (line 9). With holiday pay, however, the absolute difference narrows to between R105–108 at the bottom to close to R100 at the top decile. Under both definitions, however, the relative importance of SCF in total public income declines as the decile rank rises. SCF makes up half the public income of households in the lowest decile but only 18.5 percent for households in the top decile. (With holiday pay the proportions are 54 and 24 percent respectively.)

B. Money transfers per household (without holiday pay) are the most progressive elements of SCF. They decline over the income range from R37.8 in the lowest decile to R19.2 in the top decile and from 19.3 to 4.8 percent of public income. This progressivity is made up by an interplay of the various allowances included. While pensions are concentrated in the bottom decile and then rise from very low levels in lower deciles to a high level in the top decile, sick pay allowances increase and then decline, while other transfers are very progressive. In each case the pattern is determined by the number of recipients of a specific allowance and the size of the allowance. There are relatively more receivers of pensions in the lowest decile, but a few high individual pensions increase their relative importance for the top decile. More sick people are concentrated among the lower deciles, but the rate of

SCF ALLOWANCES AND SERVICES PER HOUSEHOLD IN ACTIVE POPULATION BY DECILE GROUPS

	Deciles of Households[a]											
	Low 1		2		4		6		9		High 10	
Household characteristics												
(1) Household members	3.14		3.28		2.93		2.89		2.28		1.75	
(2) Earners	1.31		1.78		1.94		1.95		1.86		1.49	
(3) Children	0.89		0.76		0.72		0.66		0.33		0.23	
(4) Age of head (years)	50.6		43.7		44.6		41.9		44.9		42.8	
(5) Education of head (years)	7.6		8.6		8.1		10.0		11.3		12.6	
Income categories	Rubles	Percent	Rubles	Percent	Rubles	Percent	Rubles	Percent	Rubles	Percent	Rubles	Percent
(6) Public income	195.4	100.0%	256.3	100.0%	292.6	100.0%	338.2	100.0%	374.8	100.0%	402.2	100.0%
(7) Public earnings	96.0	49.1	158.6	61.9	200.1	68.4	251.1	74.2	300.7	80.2	327.8	81.5
(8) Holiday pay	6.6	3.4	11.2	4.4	12.6	4.3	17.3	5.1	23.7	6.3	23.5	5.8
(9) SCF (total)	99.4	50.9	97.7	38.1	92.5	31.6	87.1	25.8	74.1	19.8	74.4	18.5
(10) Money payments	37.8	19.3	37.4	14.6	27.8	9.5	25.2	7.5	18.7	4.9	19.2	4.8
(11) Retirement pension	20.8	10.6	3.8	1.5	1.6	0.5	9.4	2.8	7.3	1.9	17.3	4.3
(12) Nonmonetary services	61.5	31.5	60.4	23.6	64.7	22.1	61.9	18.3	55.4	14.8	55.3	13.7
(13) Education[b]	17.6	9.0	17.2	6.7	18.1	6.2	17.5	5.2	8.1	2.1	7.6	1.8
(14) Health	8.5	4.3	10.5	4.1	9.1	3.1	8.5	2.5	8.2	2.2	6.1	1.5
(15) Housing subsidy	13.4	6.9	9.2	3.6	10.1	3.5	9.9	2.9	12.5	3.3	11.6	2.9
(16) Food subsidy	22.0	11.3	23.5	9.2	27.4	9.4	26.0	7.7	26.6	7.1	30.0	7.5
Reference (per month)												
(17) Public money income (6 + 10)	133.8	68.5	196.0	76.5	227.9	77.9	276.4	81.7	319.4	85.2	347.0	86.3
(18) Private income	115.1	58.9	39.6	15.5	56.5	19.3	30.9	9.1	41.9	11.2	29.7	7.4

[a] Deciles are defined by monthly public earnings per household member (see text).

[b] Part in the form of subsidy, part as free service (see Table 2). Stipends are included under money transfers.

sick pay is higher for those with high earnings. Stipends for higher education are available to families with children from the lower deciles, but children from higher income families are more likely to go to universities. Holiday pay, which rises at a faster rate than earnings, is the only SCF element in public income (if included) that is regressive. It contributes 3.4 percent to the income of families in the bottom decile but 5.8 percent to the highest incomes.

C. Nonmonetary subsidies and services as a whole decline only very moderately as income rises. The bottom decile receives R61.5 per month, and the next several deciles receive almost that much or more. Only for the top two deciles do the allowances decline – to about R55. The progressiveness of these allowances is maintained, however: they make up almost one-third of the incomes of the lowest decile, but only 13.7 percent of incomes for the highest decile. The outcome is a result of varying tendencies among the different elements. The most progressive element is the support for education (excluding university stipends), and the progressivity is determined mostly by the fact that poorer families tend to have more children. (When stipends are included, the progressivity declines only slightly.) It should be noted that the absolute amount of the allowance to education starts to decline only after the sixth decile despite a consistent decline in the number of children per household, implying that the allowance per child is rising with income to that point.

Health services and housing subsidies are fairly constant per family at all income levels. Only the top decile receives less than the average in health services, due mostly to the smaller household size. At the lower income end, smaller household size is "compensated" for by higher use of medical services due to older age. Health services are thus distributed progressively.

Subsidies for housing show somewhat higher support at the bottom and top income levels. The distribution of residential apartments for rent is managed by government and municipal agencies, and the family size is a major formal criterion governing it. The somewhat higher subsidy for non-active families may reflect historical needs – i.e., when their families were larger. The higher subsidy for the lowest decile of families is probably due to their larger families, but the higher subsidy to top decile families is less easily explained. Not only are they smaller families, but also a higher proportion among them own cooperative apartments, which we assume are not subsidized. If the estimate is correct, it may point to a preference in practice in the wrong direction.* Even so, housing subsidies are distributed in a progressive manner.

The general principle that more affluent families with higher consumption levels receive larger amounts of consumption subsidies is true also in the Soviet Union. Among active families, based on their own reports, those in the lowest decile receive R22 per month in food subsidies while families in the highest decile get R30. As we shall see, the gap is even wider on a per capita basis (see Table 4). The inequality would be greater but for the relatively large purchases of meat by affluent families in the nonsubsidized, collective farm markets. The only exception to this general pattern is the food subsidy received by the non-active segment of the population (see Table 2), which is higher per household (and even more so per capita) than the subsidy for the higher deciles in the active population. This may reflect the better ability of non-active people to purchase subsidized items in government stores by having more time to wait in lines and screen more stores. Even so, the distribution of food subsidies to households is still progressive. These subsidies contribute 20.3 and 11.3 percent respectively to the incomes of the bottom non-active and active deciles respectively compared with 7.5 percent to the income of the top decile.

So far attention has been focussed on SCF allowances per household. But as noted earlier, because lower income households are typically bigger, a higher allowance per household may not necessarily mean a higher allowance per household member. (This distinction is important only when *absolute* size allowances are discussed since the *relative* importance of any transfer to income is the same whether total income or per capita income is considered as long as the ordering of the families is unchanged.) The data for allowances per household member for the entire and active population are presented in Table 4. It is notable that for a number of categories, with some exceptions of the non-active decile, absolute SCF allowances per household member are larger for the rich than for the poor. Thus while total SCF transfers (holiday pay excluded)

*The preference shown here to the affluent may be an indication that many of them have larger apartments than they are entitled to and are paying higher rent than they should (McAuley 1979: 288-89). On the other hand, if a high percentage of high income families own cooperative apartments, then among those who rent the bias in favor of the affluent is greater than shown by the figures.

Table 4

SCF ALLOWANCES AND SERVICES PER HOUSEHOLD MEMBER BY DECILE GROUPS
IN ENTIRE AND ACTIVE POPULATIONS

	Deciles of Household Members[a]											
	Entire Population						Active Population					
Income Categories	Low 1	2	3	5	9	High 10	Low 1	2	4	6	9	High 10
(1) Public income	R97.8	R72.1	R80.3	R116.5	R167.1	R249.2	R72.6	R79.5	R109.6	R120.8	R172.0	R258.3
(2) Public earnings	--	31.6	50.0	71.4	128.5	199.9	31.2	48.4	68.1	87.0	134.1	206.3
(3) Holiday pay	--	2.1	3.5	4.8	9.8	13.1	2.1	3.4	4.3	6.0	10.4	13.4
(4) SCF (total)	97.8	40.5	30.3	45.1	38.6	49.3	41.4	31.1	41.5	33.8	37.9	52.0
(5) Money payments	62.4	17.7	11.6	17.6	8.3	13.2	18.2	12.4	17.3	11.5	8.9	13.1
(6) Retirement pension	57.3	11.0	1.2	1.1	3.2	4.8	11.4	1.3	0.3	5.9	2.4	5.4
(7) Non-money payments	35.4	22.8	18.7	27.5	30.4	36.0	23.2	18.6	24.2	22.3	29.0	39.0
(8) Education[b]	--	4.6	4.3	4.8	2.5	2.2	4.5	4.6	5.2	5.5	2.5	2.2
(9) Health	4.3	2.9	3.4	3.1	4.0	3.7	2.9	3.4	3.3	3.1	4.1	3.7
(10) Housing subsidy	10.2	5.3	3.0	4.3	7.5	8.1	5.5	3.0	3.3	3.4	7.2	9.0
(11) Food subsidy	20.9	10.0	7.9	13.7	16.4	22.1	10.3	7.6	12.4	10.3	15.2	24.1

[a]Deciles are defined by monthly public earnings per household member.
[b]Part is subsidy and part is free services (cf. Table 2).

are at least twice as high per non-active member than any active member, they are higher for members of top income active households than for lower income active households. The top decile members receive R49.3 per month as compared with R40.5 for second decile members or R30.3 for third decile members. When holiday pay (where transfers per member rise steeply with income) is added to the SCF total, the advantage of the rich increases significantly. In non-money transfers, top income members receive not only as much as the non-active decile, but much more than members of active households with lower incomes. The only SCF category that gives more to the poor, active or non-active, on a per capita basis is total money transfers. But even here, the rise of sick pay is partly due to increasing support with income, starting from the third decile. The positive association between support per capita and income levels underlines one aspect of the Soviet support system noted above: it is tied very strongly to earnings and levels of consumption and is not attentive enough to family size.

IV. THE EFFECT OF SCF ON POVERTY AND INCOME DISTRIBUTION

The two main distributional motivations behind the provision of SCF are (1) to assure a minimum level of income and of specific services to poor families and (2) to intervene in the distribution of income in the direction of greater equality. While the two goals are highly complementary, the first affects primarily the lower deciles of the population while the second can affect everyone.

The degree to which SCF in the Soviet Union is directed toward the poor is reflected in Tables 5 and 6, which provide data on overall income and SCF distribution in the Soviet Union. Among other things, Table 5 shows how SCF transfers help to reduce the numbers of poor families, while Table 6 shows what proportions of the total SCF and its different elements are devoted to the various income groups. But before examining the data in these tables, we need a definition of who is poor.

The Soviet definition of the poverty line is an absolute level based on a calculation of minimum needs, usually for a family of four. Two such levels were defined in 1967—one for the "current period" and another for "nearest perspective." The first was set at a net money income of R51.4 per month per household member, and the second was set at R66.6 (Sarkisyan and Kuznetsova 1967; Karpnkhin and Kuznetsova 1968). For 1973 we use both definitions, rounded respectively to R50 and R75. The lower level is still used for 1973 because the Soviet government in 1974 set the level of eligibility for the new program of income supplements at R50 per capita. The higher level takes account both of the recognition by Soviet scholars that the minimum must be raised and a degree of hidden inflation in Soviet consumer prices. With these two yardsticks at hand, we can see from Table 5 that, on the basis of public earnings alone, 26.1 percent of the entire population and 17.4 percent of the active population belong to the poor according to the more conservative Soviet definition. When R75 is the poverty line, the percentages increase to 47 and 40.7 respectively. When SCF money transfers are included, the proportions of poor in the two populations decline substantially to 11 and 8.4 percent respectively according to the official Soviet poverty line and to 37.2 and 32.9 percent according to the more liberal definition. It is interesting to note that while more than half the potentially poor by official Soviet standards are pushed out of poverty by SCF money transfers, only about one-fifth of those with earnings below R75 per household member are pushed above that level by such transfers. A major part of the push above the poverty line, especially the R50 line, is provided by retirement pensions, but other money transfers also play a role.

On the basis of the crude calculation that non-money SCF transfers to the poor are about R25 per capita, Table 5 provides data for estimating the proportion of poor households remaining after all SCF is accounted for. For the entire population, the proportion is 39 percent (all with *total* public income of up to R100), and for the active population it is 37.5 percent, higher proportions than those calculated before. In the same way it can be observed (by comparing relevant figures in lines 1 and 5 on the one hand and lines 4 and 8 on the other) that the impact of SCF transfers in reducing poverty according to this definition is even smaller than that calculated above.

Elsewhere we have shown that the proportion of poor estimated from the sample may be somewhat too low for the target population (Ofer and Vinokur 1980: 11-13). On the other hand, the calculations above are based on public income only and disregard all private sources of income. Our estimate of private income is much higher than the Soviet government's, but even in Soviet official statistics there is some private income from private agricultural plots and other sources (*NK* 1973: 632). Since the two biases are in opposing directions, we can ignore this issue here. But even if a small distortion remains, the composition of the poor as estimated from the sample

Table 5

DISTRIBUTION OF HOUSEHOLDS BY INCOME PER HOUSEHOLD MEMBER

(In percent)

Income Category	Income Bracket[a]					
	Up to 50 Rubles	51-75 Rubles	76-100 Rubles	101-125 Rubles	126-150 Rubles	150 Rubles and Over
Entire Population						
(1) Public earnings	26.1%	20.9%	27.0%	10.5%	7.9%	7.7%
(2) Public money income	11.0	26.2	27.5	14.4	7.9	12.9
(3) Public money income and subsidies	4.3	12.4	27.4	21.1	13.9	21.0
(4) Total public income	2.8	9.6	26.6	21.6	15.8	23.6
Active Population						
(5) Public earnings	17.4	23.3	30.2	11.7	8.8	8.6
(6) Public money income	8.4	24.5	28.9	14.9	8.8	14.5
(7) Public money income and subsidies	4.0	11.0	27.4	20.5	14.2	22.8
(8) Total public income	2.8	8.0	26.7	20.8	16.3	25.5

[a] According to money income categories.

is close to the mark for the Soviet European-urban population. We also show elsewhere that almost half of all the poor are retired units, and nearly a quarter of them are working-age, one-parent (woman) families. Put differently, while constituting only 8.4 percent of the households, the poor include 30 percent of all retired people, 20 percent of all one-parent families, but only 3.4 percent of two-parent, active families. A higher than proportional share of children is found only in the next income group of per capita income of 50–75 rubles per month. So while the SCF payment in 1973 did allow about 14 percent of all households to move from the lowest income bracket (up to R50) to the next higher one, there were still 10–15 percent of urban families who lived below this level and who were getting from the government SCF cash payments of no more than 12.4 rubles per capita per month (not counting holiday pay for employees). This reflects both the low level of pensions and an unwillingness to provide enough support to units with high dependency ratios (see Ofer and Vinokur 1980: 24–28; McAuley 1979: chs. 4, 11, 12).

Turning to Table 6, we can see that of the total SCF received by the entire population (again not including holiday pay), the lowest decile of households receive just over 15 percent of the funds and the lowest quintile just over a quarter—that is, 50 percent and 25 percent more than their respective proportions in the population. On the other end the top quintile received 17 percent and the top decile 8.1 percent of all funds—just slightly below their respective population shares. When only the active population is considered, the preference given to the low income households is even smaller.

In line 12 of Table 6, there are data on the distribution of the population across the household deciles which enable us to evaluate the distribution of SCF on a per capita basis. In only one instance— that of the two lowest deciles of the entire population—does SCF distribution reflect significantly more attention to the poor on a per capita basis. Here a quarter of the total SCF fund is devoted to only 18 percent of the population, and 15.2 percent of the fund to the poorest 5.6 percent. In all other cases the per capita distributions point to lack of attention to the poor and to consideration of equality in general. Thus the poorest 24.1 percent of members of active households receive less than their proportion in the population—only 23.6 percent of all SCF transfers. On the other hand the affluent segment of the population consistently receives slightly more than its proportional share. All this demonstrates either that the distribution of SCF is influenced to some extent by considerations

Table 6

DISTRIBUTION OF SCF AMONG GROUPS OF HOUSEHOLDS

(In percent)

	Households Belonging to Percentile Group[a]								
	Entire Population					Active Population			
	Lowest			Highest		Lowest		Highest	
Income Categories	10 Percent	20 Percent	50 Percent	20 Percent	10 Percent	20 Percent	50 Percent	20 Percent	10 Percent
(1) All SCF	15.2%	25.8%	56.8%	17.1%	8.1%	23.6%	54.0%	17.6%	8.7%
(2) Money allowances[b]	27.9	39.4	66.7	12.8	6.5	30.4	59.0	15.2	7.6
(3) Subsidies and free services	8.3	18.5	51.4	19.4	8.9	20.7	51.5	18.8	9.4
(4) Subsidies	10.2	19.2	50.7	20.7	9.4	19.2	49.5	20.5	10.2
(5) Education	--	9.2	51.2	8.8	1.4	17.6	48.3	21.7	11.4
(6) Housing	12.9	24.3	52.7	21.9	9.4	21.3	49.6	22.5	10.7
(7) Food	10.5	18.5	49.7	21.8	10.5	17.6	48.3	21.7	11.4
(8) Free services	3.8	16.5	53.2	16.2	7.7	24.0	57.3	14.6	7.0
(9) Education	--	15.3	55.1	14.3	7.8	25.4	60.1	12.6	6.9
(10) Health	8.0	17.9	51.4	18.2	7.7	22.5	54.0	17.0	7.2
(11) Holiday pay	--	2.3	28.3	32.4	17.0	11.5	37.5	29.4	14.9
(12) Percent population	5.6	18.0	53.1	16.0	7.2	24.1	55.9	15.2	6.6

[a] According to public earnings.
[b] Holiday pay not included.

unrelated to distribution or that the policies for distribution are not very effective.

Table 6 also shows how each SCF element is distributed. It can be seen that, from the distributional point of view, the most effective programs are the money allowances (other than holiday pay), where 40 percent of all disbursements are directed to the two lowest deciles. Among the non-money elements only the housing subsidy pays more than the proportional share to the poor of the entire population. For the active population, education and health services also slightly favor the poor households, but not when people are counted. The least helpful to the poor is of course holiday pay.

The effects of SCF allowances on the overall distribution of incomes depends on three factors: (a) the weight of the element in total income, (2) the size distribution of the element itself, and (3) the degree of correlation between the distribution of the individual element and total income.* These effects are estimated here for a number of commonly used inequality measures, and the results for the size distribution of income per capita for the population of households are presented in Table 7.

All measures of inequality show significant movement toward equality when SCF transfers are added. The Gini coefficient goes down from 0.357 to 0.240 for the entire population and from 0.281 to 0.240 for the active population. The most significant equalizing contribution for the entire population is rendered by money transfers, which reduce the Gini coefficient to 0.270. In the case of the active population, however, the equalization impacts of the money and non-money transfers are about the same. The SCF impact is seen in a similar fashion in the decline of the various dispersion measures (cols. 2–5). As an illustration, the decile ratios decline from 3.6 to 2.7 for the active population and from technical infinity to 2.7 for the entire population (col. 5). Finally the same impact is seen through changes in a number of Lorenz measures – the percent of income received by segments of the population. For example, the share of public earnings earned by the bottom 20 percent of the active population is only 4.7 percent, but its share of total public income after SCF transfers rises to 11.3 percent. Correspondingly, the income shares of the richest 20 percent of the population decline in the process from 31.6 to 27.1 percent (col. 9). It is interesting that the distribution of all public income for the

*In the calculation of the Gini coefficient, the total effect is exactly the product of these three elements (see Lerner and Yitzhaki 1984).

Table 7

SELECTED MEASURES OF THE IMPACT OF SCF ON INCOME INEQUALITY

		Measures of Dispersion[a]				Income Shares Received by Percentile Groups					
						Households				Household Members	
						Lowest			Highest	Highest	Lowest
						10 Percent	20 Percent	50 Percent	20 Percent	10 Percent	10 Percent
Income Categories	Gini	P_{98}/P_2	P_{95}/P_5	P_{90}/P_{10}	P_{50}/P_{10}						
	(1)	(2)	(3)	(4)	(5)	(6)	(7)	(8)	(9)	(10)	(11)
Entire Population											
(1) Public earnings	0.357	--	--	--	--	--	4.7%	31.5%	31.6%	16.5%	--
(2) Public money income	0.270	8.3	5.3	3.3	1.7	3.8%	9.5	36.4	29.0	15.1	6.6%
(3) Public money income and subsidies	0.252	7.4	4.3	2.9	1.6	4.8	10.9	38.5	27.8	14.2	8.2
(4) Total public income	0.240	6.6	3.9	2.7	1.6	4.7	11.3	39.2	27.1	13.9	8.2
Active Population											
(5) Public earnings	0.281	7.7	5.5	3.6	2.0	4.4	11.5	38.1	28.3	14.6	3.4
(6) Public money income	0.263	7.5	4.5	3.1	1.7	5.5	13.4	40.2	27.0	13.9	4.8
(7) Public money income and subsidies	0.281	6.5	4.5	2.9	1.6	6.1	14.2	41.5	26.0	13.4	5.4
(8) Total public income	0.240	5.8	4.1	2.7	1.5	6.5	14.8	42.5	25.4	13.0	5.7

^{a}P_i/P_j is a ratio of incomes received by households or household members with incomes higher than i and j percent of the population.

entire population is more equal than that of public earnings for the active population. Compare the Gini coefficient of 0.240 (line 4) with that of 0.281 (line 5). Similarly, it is interesting to note that the overall inequality of total public income is equal for the entire and the active population. This means that SCF transfers have incorporated the non-active part of the population without widening the income gaps of the entire population. This is due mostly to the pension system but also partly to the fact that a full third of all retirement age heads-of-households keep jobs in the public sector and continue to work.

V. COMPARISONS AND CONCLUSIONS

In order to make the sample findings comparable to some of the results published by Soviet scholars of the field, it will be necessary to make some more reweighting and adjustments in our sample. In many cases even these will not help because the exact structures of the Soviet samples are not specified. A detailed comparison with all the available sources is now being prepared, and final judgment will have to be postponed. In general it can be stated that most of the studies relating to the 1970s obtain results that are in the same ball park as ours.

In general it seems that studies that are based on samples that do not include, or underrepresent, retired (non-active) units find that total SCF transfers are higher for high income than for low income families (see, e.g., Mamontova 1975: 298). When retired units are included in a sample, poor families get more SCF per capita (*Potrebnosti* 1975: 113), as in our sample.

All the studies we have examined show (or claim without showing) a rise in the money payments of SCF across the income range (Mamontova 1975: 198; *Potrebnosti* 1975: 114). Our findings show that this results from the behavior of holiday and sick pay. Our sample that includes the same proportion of retired units as in the Soviet urban population probably shows higher money payments to households in lower income brackets. One wonders why Soviet studies fail to take notice or advantage of such a "positive" phenomenon.

On free services, especially education, all studies but one (Gerasimov 1978: 82) show or claim that low-income families get larger values of services mostly because they have more children (see Mamontova 1975: 296; *Potrebnosti* 1975: 114) In this connection Gerasimov (1978: 77-78) points out that the level of health services provided to workers is somewhat higher than that for non-working people. If true, it raises doubts that low-income families enjoy a higher level of health services per capita.

Turning to findings on the distribution of subsidies, most studies reach the conclusion that high-income families collect more value from this source. This is the case with respect to food and rent subsidies (Mamontova 1975: 297; Gerasimov 1978: 82, 102). Only one study finds equal absolute amounts of subsidies for all income groups (*Potrebnosti* 1975: 114). Though food subsidies were not included, this is nevertheless somewhat surprising.

One study based on a survey in one industrial city of the Russian Republic comes to the conclusion that through SCF, inequality—actually "incomes difference"—was reduced by 40 percent and the share of low-income families declined by a factor of 1.5 times (*ibid.*, 115). Direct comparisons with this study are impossible at this point, but while the decline in the share of low-income families seems reasonable, a 40 percent decline in the decile ratio (provided this is what is meant by "incomes difference") seems a little too optimistic.*

Three points can be made by way of summary. First, the entire Soviet SCF program has quite a significant effect on the level of income equality—especially when the entire (urban) population is considered. The impact on the active population is less impressive. When the distributive impact of SCF is evaluated, one must take into account that Soviet income policies are geared to achieve very high labor participation rates, that the distribution of earnings is already somewhat more equal than in market economies due mostly to the elimination of most property incomes (see Bergson 1984), and that the tax system is not nearly as progressive as in many other countries.

Second, through SCF payments a significant proportion of families with no earnings or with low earnings was pushed above the Soviet poverty line. But relatively low pensions and the reluctance to significantly raise the level of pure income maintenance leave many retired, one-parent, and large families below the poverty line. A significant proportion of retired people manage to stay above the line by continuing to work. Other families try to stay at reasonably low dependency ratios by limiting the number of children.

Finally, if the Soviet Union has a higher level of income equality and a lower incidence of poverty (at least when defined in relative

*A number of other comparisons between our findings and those of Soviet studies can be found in Ofer and Vinokur (1978: 31-40).

terms) than Western societies, it is only partly the outcome of the
distribution of SCF. Partly, or perhaps mainly, it is a result of a
much broader range of policies.

REFERENCES

Bergson, A. 1984. "Income Inequality under Soviet Socialism." *Journal of Economic Literature* 22: (December) 1052-99.

Gerasimov, N. V. 1978. "Obshchestvennye fondy potreblennia neobkhodimost sushchnost napravlenie razvitiia, Minsk 'Nauka i Teknika.'"

Karapetian, A. Kh., and Rimashevskaia, N. M. 1977. *Differentsirovannii balans dokhodov i potreblennia naseleniia.* Moscow.

Karpnkhin, D. N., and Kuznetsova, N. P. 1968. "Dokhody i petrebleniye trndgashchikhsya." In *Trad i zarabotraya plata v SSSR.* Moscow: Ekonomika.

Kraeger, Constance B. 1974. "A Note on the Size of Subsidies on Soviet Government Purchases of Agricultural Products." *ACES Bulletin* 16, 2 (Fall): 63-69.

Kuznets, Simon. 1982. "Children and Adults in Income Distribution." *Economic and Cultural Change* 30, 4 (July): 697-738.

Lapidus, Gail W. 1978. *Women in Soviet Society.* Berkeley: University of California Press.

Lerner, R. I., and Yitzhaki, Sh. 1984. "A Note on the Calculation and Interpretation of the Gini Index." *Economic Letters* 15: 363–68.

Madison, Bernice Q. 1968. *Social Welfare in the Soviet Union.* Stanford: Stanford University Press.

_____. 1979. "Trade Unions and Social Welfare." In *Industrial Labor in the USSR*, eds. A. Kahan and B. Ruble, 85-115. New York: Pergamon Press.

McAuley, A. 1979. *Economic Welfare in the Soviet Union: Poverty, Living Standards, and Inequality.* Madison: University of Wisconsin Press.

Mamontova, T. I. 1975. "Vliianie obshchestvennykh fondor potrebliniia na differentsiatsiih v urovne zhizni robochikh i sluzhoshchikh." *Sotsialisticheckii obraz zhizni i narodnoe blagocotoenie.* Sarotovskovo Universiteta.

Marx, Karl. 1966. *Critique of the Gotha Program.* Moscow: Progress Publishers.

Minkoff, Jack, and Turgeon, Lynn. 1977. "Income Maintenance in the Soviet Union in Eastern and Western Perspective." In *Equity, Income and Policy*, ed. J. L. Horowitz, 176-191. New York: Praeger.

NK [*Narodnoe Khozyaistvo SSSR*] . 1973. Moscow.

_____. 1980. Moscow.

Ofer, Gur, and Vinokur, Aaron. 1980. "The Distribution of Income of the Urban Population in the Soviet Union." Unpublished ms.

Potrebnosti dokhodi potreblenie mitodologiia analyiza i prognozirovaniia narodnovo blagololtoianiaa. 1975. Moscow.

Sarkisyan, G. S., and Kuznetsova, N. P. 1967. *Potrebnosti i dokhod semi.* Moscow: Ekonomika.

Treml, Vladimir G. 1978. *Agricultural Subsidies in the Soviet Union.* U.S. Bureau of the Census, *Foreign Economic Report,* no. 15.

THE GROWTH OF SOCIAL PROTECTION IN THE
UNITED STATES: 1929-1979

Lee Rainwater

The United States is well known as a "welfare state laggard." Its level of social security spending in relation to gross national income is roughly equivalent to that attained by a country like Germany or France in the mid-1950s. Yet we have a welfare state crisis—indeed the term *welfare state* was first popularized here, and not in Western European countries with far higher levels of social spending. Over the last few years we've seen a steady rise in commitment by political elites to cut the size of this country's puny welfare state.

The principal purpose of this essay is to lay out the details of the pattern of growth of social protection expenditures in the United States over the past fifty years. We will see that the United States is less a laggard in some areas than others (cf. the paper by Martin Rein below). By social protection, I follow the definition of the European Community to refer to a range of institutional mechanisms—public, private, and in-between—through which people receive resources "intended to relieve households of the financial burden created by . . . certain risks or needs, without there being any simultaneous equivalent counterpart provided by the beneficiary" (Eurostat 1980: 84)—social benefits, in short. This is a definition by convention rather than theoretical rigor. By convention, some income is considered transfers, and other income payment for services. In the United States, employee welfare benefits are considered "compensation"; benefits from government are considered "transfers." Employer contributions for social insurance are also considered employee compensation, yet social insurance benefits are considered social transfers. The distinction between the

I have benefitted greatly from discussion of these issues over the years with Gosta Esping-Andersen, Frieder Naschold, and Martin Rein.

concept of pay for services and transfer works poorly in the modern world where the simple cash nexus—a day's pay for a day's work—is sharply attenuated. Thus Richard and Nancy Ruggles (1981:77ff), in their integrated economic accounts for the United States, argue that employer welfare contributions should not be counted as part of households' income, but rather as part of enterprise expenditure providing employees with benefits in kind.

An even more general critique of the concept of transfers has been undertaken by Robert Eisner, who notes several problems in the definition of "transfer payments to persons" in the National Income and Product Account (NIPA): "Income payments to persons, generally in monetary form, for which they do not render current services. It consists of business transfer payments . . . and government transfer payments" (USDC 1981:xi). Eisner observes:

> Examination of this definition, however, may quickly suggest several problems: (1) Why the restriction "generally in monetary form"? (2) What are "services" and what are "current services"? (3) Why restrict transfer payments to persons to business transfer payments and government transfer payments? . . . Are the transfer items included in NIPA adequate to inform us how transfers affect work, saving and the income distribution? (1985).

The issue of monetary form plagues both systematic treatment of American data and comparative research on welfare state expenditures. What are we to make of the fact that, in the United States, Medicare is treated as a cash transfer, but Medicaid is treated as a government-provided service? In this analysis of the development of welfare state spending in the United States, I've tried to include the most important services along with cash transfers.

I don't have a way of dealing with a much more basic issue that Eisner raises with respect to the concept of "current services":

> Slowing of economic activity, it is widely believed, brings substantial labor hoarding, in which firms continue to pay employees at their previous rates, even though fewer (if any significant) services are being performed. The excess of such payments over the value of current services might well be viewed as transfer payments, if their definition is to be taken literally.

Indeed Eisner says that if one takes literally the current services criterion for transfers, one might be required to define interest and dividends as transfers. The issue is not merely a dry question of definitions for statistical series, but goes to very basic issues of the normative grounds on which some people are allowed to derive their current consumption from sources other than current labor. As he observes, "An elderly person with substantial interest receipts may be just as reluctant to work for a current wage or salary as one receiving Social Security benefits."

While NIPA transfers amounted to $194 billion in 1966, Eisner's additional transfer payments amounted to $743 billion. In addition to government services (at $436.7 billion), business provided media consumption services, health and safety services, interest, and dividends. Insurance and pension funds paid "transfers" of $68.8 billion. This expanded definition of transfers increases their size so that the grand total amounts to some 55 percent of GNP rather than the conventional measure of social security transfers of around 13 percent. A sociologist has to applaud such an adventurous project on the part of economists because it highlights the role of government in social stratification (Coleman and Rainwater 1978: 311-13).

Because of the conceptual complexity of dealing with a very broadly expanded definition of transfers, in this essay I will expand the conventional definition (the NIPA definition) only very slightly, by adding government-provided medical services and social work services and private employee welfare benefits. This modestly expanded definition, however, increases social protection from the 10 percent represented by government transfers to persons to about one-sixth of GNP, which corresponds rather closely to that of "social protection benefits" as defined by the European Community.

What are the "certain risks and needs" which social protection benefits respond to? The conventional list of risks and needs recognized by the European Community is as follows: sickness, old age, death and survivors, disability, physical or mental infirmity, industrial injury and occupational disease, unemployment, parental responsibility, personal injuries suffered by acts of war, vocational training of adults, and housing. For the latter two, only cash income and rent supplements are included.

It is apparent that most of these needs have to do with an actual or threatened disruption in the normal flow of income to a family — the only exceptions are parental responsibility and housing subsidies. Social protection programs assume a world in which persons are for most of their lives expected to be doing one of three things: to be growing up (in which case their proper place is in school), to be at work earning money, or to be keeping house for a worker who provides the means of support. The history of the welfare state is the history of the progressive institutionalization of programs designed to provide income for families and individuals who cannot acquire their livelihood through being a child in the parental home, a worker, or a housekeeper. Differences in the size, completeness, and "generosity" of the welfare state can be expected to have to do with the processes by which institutionalization of new roles is established. Two new roles are those of retirement and disability (temporary or permanent). Indeed in the early part of the development of social protection institutions, the two were seen as essentially the same in that older people needed pensions because they no longer had the capacity to work. It is only relatively recently, and incompletely, that a separate normal role of retirement as a reward for a lifetime of work has begun to be institutionalized.

Social protection programs have to be understood as social control institutions established through a process of struggle on the part of governments, employers, employees, and social movements. It is not always clear what the point of these struggles is. The main thrust has certainly been that of decommodifying labor in the sense that the livelihood of individuals is not to be completely dependent on the current sale of labor power (Esping-Andersen 1981).

Thus the object of social control has most often been the employer. In that sense, the development of the welfare state needs to be understood in the context of the development of labor relations institutions more generally. It may be also the case that a less obvious struggle has gone on in which a variety of organizations (employers, unions, governments) have intervened to control the consumption of individuals by controlling the initial distribution of their "compensation" into categories of take-home pay, fringe benefits, and payroll taxes.

On the surface, social protection programs seem to make employers and government responsible for providing social security to individuals and families. But it's clear that all but a small portion of the cost of social security comes out of the pay of the currently productive workers in the society. So one can also say that social protection involves a very heavy element of protecting individuals against themselves—against the likelihood of their failure to operate in the fully rational way that the life-cycle model of how individuals should handle the earnings stream requires. The welfare state might be regarded as the institutional outcome of what Thomas Schelling has called "the intimate contest for self-command" (1980:94ff).

Two broad types of resource-distribution politics have gradually evolved in most Western nations reflecting the results at any particular time of various contending forces as they impact on citizens. *Labor politics*, pursued by private organizations of workers and owners and by governments, is concerned with regulating the terms of labor contracts. *Social protection politics* has traditionally been concerned with compensating for negative effects of labor markets on the economic well-being of workers and their families.

Labor policies seek to modify market forces by affecting wages, nonwage employee benefits, hours, and working conditions through collective bargaining and political bargaining in a corporatist framework. Social policies in turn seek to circumvent market forces by providing money, goods, and services on bases other than current, day-to-day labor force participation.

The past thirty years have seen an enormous elaboration of policies in these areas both through private-sector collective bargaining and contractual arrangements and through political bargaining and legislation in the public sector. The degree of intervention in market forces determining economic resources and working conditions has increased, but there has been very little systematic and comparative study about the effects of this intervention.

The traditional split between concerns of "economic policy" and "social policy" is reflected in the separate traditions of industrial relations and social welfare as fields of study. Both fields tend to focus very heavily on the structure of subsystem institutional arrangements (e.g., inputs such as collective bargaining systems) rather than on the effects of these arrangements on the living conditions of their supposed beneficiaries (e.g., outputs such as wages) or on other aspects of society. This generalization appears less true of European industrial relations research than British and American, but nowhere has research on outputs, and on the connections between institutional arrangements and outputs, received the attention it deserves.

An understanding of the distribution of economic well-being in modern welfare societies requires analysis of both the institutions of the labor contract and of welfare-state provision for its citizens. Some twenty-five years ago Jean Marchal observed that "the distinction between incomes due to production and incomes due to transfers becomes obscured and is no longer usable. . . . What is needed is a theory of the total income of labor, a theory of wages in the widest sense" (1957).

Marchal's observation and quite similar arguments by Richard Titmuss were largely ignored by social scientists concerned with these issues until recently. The social turmoil of the late 1960s and the economic troubles of the 1970s have brought the question of the interaction of state and economy, industrial relations and politics, strongly to the fore:

> Recent developments . . . have made clear the enormous role politics and governmental policy have in determining the success and failures of those who meet around a bargaining table. Two examples suffice to demonstrate this point: incomes policy and welfare policies. . . .
>
> By increasing resources, growth made it easier for labor and management in some countries to achieve relative satisfaction of their goals in both politics and in collective bargaining. Both parties were able therefore to accept a separation of the agenda of politics from that of industrial relations, and had little reason to push demands from one arena to the other.
>
> Economic difficulties burst this bubble. . . . Incomes policy, wage-price controls, and tripartite or neo-corporatist arrangements clearly link politics and the industrial relations systems. . . .
>
> Similarly, the expansion of the welfare state has also had marked effects on the character of bargaining. . . . By providing services through the government which workers would otherwise have to acquire directly, these policies encourage bargaining peace. Effective national health insurance policies, for instance, may alter the structure of demands for fringe benefits at the labor-management bargaining table. At the same time, welfare state policies may exacerbate industrial conflict. Unemployment compensation may reduce the effectiveness of market "discipline" on worker demands (Gourevitch, Lange, and Martin 1981).

Much research in the fields of social stratification, economic resources, and social policy highlights the importance even in advanced welfare societies of those social arrangements that produce income and other resources through work. The rights acquired by workers to particular levels of current income and to particular kinds of fringe benefits and other kinds of job rewards continue to be central to the question of economic well-being in modern society and to related issues of poverty, low income, gender discrimination, minority rights, etc.

The field of comparative social policy has attracted increasing interest over the past decade. The various mechanisms of government-based social policy have been studied comparatively either in their totality or from the point of view of technical issues of particular programs (for example, health policy). But if one asks how most people meet the needs that various social programs are designed to meet, one discovers that even today those needs are met by families principally through the rights and rewards conferred on their employed members by virtue of their work (including the right to work-related social security).

Also, for most resources traditionally considered part of "social security" or "social protection," one can observe comparable resources conferred as part of remuneration for employment—that is, as part of the labor contract. By the same token, most resources received by workers as part of their remuneration can also be received through social protection programs.

The major exception seems to be the resource of "leisure." Although governments could pay for vacations, weekly days of rest, and holidays, they do not. Leisure time is not a government social insurance program. Instead, governments may regulate or mandate its provision by the employer at his own expense, as well as regulate the length of the work day and treatment of overtime.

The provision of other kinds of resources may come from either or both the employer and government, as the following listing shows:

Social Provision	Work Remuneration or Condition
Taxes (negative)	Earnings (positive)
Public assistance payments	Job creation and minimum wage
Unemployment insurance	Termination pay
Family allowances	Pay variation by family size
Sickness insurance	Sick pay
Maternity benefits	Maternity leave with pay
National health service or insurance	Private health insurance
Disability insurance	Private disability insurance
Survivor's insurance	Group life insurance
Retirement insurance	Private pensions
Social services	Industrial counselling
Workmen's compensation	Preventive occupational health and safety

For almost all "needs," there are parallel employer and government programs. But by and large, discussion of social policy tends to underemphasize the role of provisions derived from the employment link and to ignore the complex institutional interactions around the workplace. Ignored also are the political dynamics by which "voluntary" employee benefits become legally mandated and therefore as universal as social insurance benefits.

The implementation of the desire for social protection has produced a bewildering variety of programs in different countries along with a bewildering variety of eligibility criteria, benefits, and kinds of regulation. This complexity tends to distract from the rather simple functions of these programs. As noted, all of the money spent on social protection can be thought of as dealing with problems of incapacity to work, unavailability of work, or inadequacy of income even though there is a family provider. We can say that there are two basic kinds of eligibility—one having to do with being affected by a specific definable risk involving health or unemployment, and the other having to do with actual or threatened income inadequacy. We can call the first kind of eligibility "problem-tested eligibility." The programs deal either with the incapacity of the individual to continue to earn or with the fact that his services are no longer needed—that is, his exclusion from participation. The income adequacy standard may be phrased in absolute or relative terms, such as a family equivalence scale. (In addition to the two basic kinds of eligibility criteria, there may be specific eligibility criteria based on membership, contributions, working history, or whatever for determining who is entitled to benefits.)

The benefits provided can conveniently be thought of as of two kinds. Most simply, cash is provided. In this case, consumption is not directed by the program to particular goods, and the beneficiary is free to spend the money however he or she wishes. Other benefits, however, are directed to certain kinds of consumption—either through cash reimbursement for expenditures on particular goods or, more importantly, through the direct provision of goods.

Combining these two sets of categories, we have the sociologists' magic tool—the fourfold table. Figure 1 presents a listing of various kinds of social benefits in a variety of countries classified in four categories. (So far I have not been able to identify a social program that will not fit in the fourfold table, but there may be one.)

There are, of course, other important dimensions in understanding who is eligible for the programs and exactly how consumption is

Figure 1

CLASSIFICATION OF SOCIAL PROGRAMS BY PURPOSE AND DIRECTION OF CONSUMPTION

	Type of Consumption Supported	
Definition of Purpose	Directed (*Cash reimbursement and services*)	Undirected (*Unrestricted cash benefits*)
To remedy: Problems associated with specific, definable conditions (RISK)	Medical insurance and services Other in-kind benefits tied to ill health or death (e.g., homemaker services) Job retraining Social services Institutions (e.g., nursing homes) Funeral benefits	Sickness insurance Maternity leave with pay Widows and orphans insurance Disability insurance Unemployment insurance Job retraining allowances and stipends Occupational injury and disease insurance
Actual or threatened inadequacy of income relative to a standard (NEED)	Housing allowances Food stamps Periodic cash welfare (clothes, appliances) Initial job training Free school books School buses School lunches The poorhouse	Pension insurance Public assistance to healthy householders Child allowance FIS (England) Earned income tax credit Allowance to newly married couples or at the birth of a child Advanced maintenance payments

directed. Thus, in all four of the boxes, programs can be subject to income- or means-tests. They may also be income-related in the sense that benefits increase as a function of normal earnings. In fact, in the directed-consumption category, benefits tend to be the same for all covered persons. It is only in the case of cash benefits that one finds benefits increasing as a function of normal earnings.

Because there are different kinds of social protection programs, it can be misleading to look only at their total. While it's understandable that the pioneers of research on the development of the welfare state have looked primarily at overall social spending levels, the next phase of research will have to become much more subtle in charting the development of programs associated with different risks as well as of programs grouped together in terms of other categories, such as the degree of decommodification in eligibility or the degree to which consumption is decommodified through the provision of services versus cash (Esping-Andersen 1981).

Indeed, as we shall see below, across a range of countries there is not a high degree of correlation among different areas of social provision. We may have to shift from the search for a single index of rank in welfare state development to a concern with profiles of welfare state development.

AMERICAN SOCIAL PROTECTION IN COMPARATIVE PERSPECTIVE

We began with the observation that the United States is a welfare state laggard. This is apparent in Table 1, which tabulates the proportion of GNP devoted to social security benefits according to a standardized set of definitions developed by the International Labor Organization for its Cost of Social Security studies published periodically since 1948.

We see that in 1977 the United States was the lowest spender of the fourteen countries listed.* The United States also ranked at

---

*I am interested in comparing the United States to countries of West European cultural heritage, and therefore have excluded Japan from the set of eighteen democratic countries used by such researchers as Korpi (1980) and Esping-Andersen (1981). I have not included Australia, New Zealand, and Ireland because I am interested in comparisons with 1950, and complete data were not readily available. However, the inclusion of these countries would not change our picture of the United States as a welfare state laggard in the post-World War II period.

Table 1

SOCIAL SECURITY EXPENDITURES AS A PERCENT OF GNP IN SELECTED WESTERN COUNTRIES

Country	1977	1950	1933
Sweden	29.70%	8.81%	3.52%
Netherlands	26.60	6.47	2.49
Belgium	23.70	10.00	6.09
Denmark	23.30	7.49	6.17
France	22.50	10.82	3.75
Germany	22.40	11.68	11.40
Italy	20.50	6.38	1.61
Austria	20.10	10.13	7.00
Norway	19.10	4.61	4.13
Finland	18.70	6.43	0.25
United Kingdom	16.30	8.64	7.04
Switzerland	15.90	5.45	4.47
Canada	14.20	5.88	—
United States	12.90	4.00	4.37
Mean	20.37	7.63	4.79

the bottom in 1950, which makes it all the more interesting that in 1933 the United States was near the middle of the distribution of countries. In the early 1930s, Germany stands out conspicuously as the highest spending welfare state: the social democracy of the Weimar period had built upon a social security foundation that had grown slowly since Bismarck. However, a great deal of the growth in the late 1920s and early 1930s was in the form of means-tested programs (poor relief and unemployment assistance) rather than social security.

United Kingdom, Austria, Denmark, and Belgium were quite similar by 1933 in spending 6 to 7 percent on social security. Another cluster of countries, in the 3.5 to 4.5 percent range, included the United States, Switzerland, Norway, France, and Sweden. At the opposite end, social security spending was practically nonexistent in Finland and very low in Italy (where state workers were the primary beneficiaries of what little there was).

Thus one could not have foreseen in 1933 that by 1950 the United States and Switzerland would become welfare state laggards or that Sweden, Norway, and France would become welfare state leaders. (Although the United States was spending as much as several of the other countries, the nature of its programs was different. It had only one social insurance program—workmen's compensation—while many of the others had a range of social insurance programs covering at least portions of the working population.)

Poor relief and unemployment assistance in one form or another represented a large proportion of social protection expenditures in many of the countries, particularly Norway, Sweden, Belgium, and Switzerland. The United States was distinctive for its veterans' programs, which represented a quarter of its expenditures. These, together with public assistance, accounted for fully 60 percent of U.S. expenditures. With the exception of Norway, the United States seems to have spent more on medical benefits than any other country.

The significance of veterans' pensions in the development of American thinking on social welfare has recently been analyzed by Theda Skocpol and John Ikenberry (1983). They quote Isaac Rubinow's estimate that in 1912 "every second native white man over 65 was receiving a pension," amounting to perhaps two-thirds of those men who were not Southerners. Their figures suggest that veterans' pensions amounted to about 0.75 percent of GNP in 1900. By the time of the ILO survey in 1933, veterans' benefits had increased to approximately 1.1 percent of GNP. Veterans' benefits, along with public assistance and health and hospital programs, accounted for more than 3 percent of GNP in 1933. Thus these three programs alone consumed a higher proportion of GNP than the total social spending of the Netherlands, Italy, and Finland. In terms of welfare state effort, though not philosophy, the United States did not enter the Depression years as a laggard. Given its transformation from welfare state moderate in 1933 to welfare state laggard in 1950, careful research on exactly how American social protection institutions developed during the 1930s and 1940s is badly needed.

That inertial growth accounts for the range of welfare state expenditures we find in the late 1970s is clearly falsified when one examines the correlations of proportion of GNP spent on social security at different times. The correlations for the thirteen countries for which we have data for all three years are .51 from 1933 to 1950, .47 from 1950 to 1977, but only -.02 for the whole period from

1933 to 1977. Clearly, then, little of the variance in expenditure levels even over the shorter periods of time is accounted for by proportionate growth for all nations.

Indeed there is a surprising lack of association for the fourteen countries between spending measures for 1950 and for the late 1970s. Thus we find a correlation of only .29 for civilian government expenditures as a proportion of GNP. The correlations are somewhat higher for cash transfers (.52) and civilian government consumption (.43), but even these correlations suggest that the level and pattern of government expenditures in the late 1970s were primarily a product of social and political factors that operated after 1950 and only to a very small degree a product of social forces that kept the countries in the same niches over the whole period.

For social security programs in particular, the picture is much the same. I find the following correlations for the major categories of social expenditures provided in the ILO series:

Type of program	Correlation of 1977 benefits with 1950 benefits (as a percent of GNP)
Government employee programs	.72
Pensions	.34
Other social insurance programs	.43
Family allowances	.50
Public assistance	.50
Public health	.54
All medical expenses	.36

The relatively high correlation for government employee programs only tells us that countries which had special programs for government employees in 1950 are still likely to have them in 1977. But the other correlations tell us that similar patterns of growth can account only for from 10 percent to a high of 25 percent of the variance in 1977 benefits.

Much earlier writing has suggested the importance of working class mobilization as a factor in accounting for welfare state expenditures (for example, the summary of the relevant literature up to 1980 by Shalev 1983). It is all the more surprising, then, that a measure of working class mobilization (Korpi 1980) explains less than 5 percent of the variance in four types of social security programs (government employee programs, pensions, other social insurance, and family allowance), less than 20 percent of the variance in public assistance, some 25 percent of the variance in medical and other in-kind programs, and 43 percent of the variance in public health programs.

If we use the ILO data to develop a measure of cash social security (undirected consumption in the formulation of Figure 1), we find that only 4 percent of the variance in this measure is accounted for by working class mobilization. On the other hand, if we look at the relationship between civilian government consumption (by subtracting transfers from total civilian government expenditures), we find an extremely robust relationship. Working class mobilization correlates .82 with civilian government consumption in the late 1970s. Strong working class movements do seem to cause governments to alter the balance between government consumption (and government-directed consumption in the private sector) and undirected private consumption.*

The intercorrelations for these fourteen countries among the different social programs suggest that disaggregation of social security is necessary if we want to better understand the dynamics of growth. Public health expenditures and public assistance expenditures actually have a negative correlation with all other social insurance programs (except for each other—these two correlate .66).

Programs for government employees do not correlate very highly with any other programs (ranging from .32 to .52), and pensions have a low correlation with other social insurance programs (.24). However, there is quite a high correlation (.80) between family allowances and nonpension social insurance. This suggests that we ought to search separately for the social and political dynamics that explain the variance across countries of at least four kinds of programs—pensions, social insurance for the non-aged and child allowances, public health and public assistance programs, and programs for government employees.

Because the United States does not have family allowance programs, it is clearly a laggard in that area. It is also at the bottom for cash social insurance for the non-aged and next to the bottom (after Canada) for pensions. It is also at the bottom for medical

---

*If one were to add the four countries which I have excluded, the relationship would be slightly stronger.

programs. On the other hand, it has a middling position on programs for government employees, and ranks third (after Denmark and Sweden) for public assistance programs. (The principal reason for the negative correlation between cash social insurance programs and public health and public assistance is that expenditures for the latter are both high in the Nordic countries and quite low in the Continental core countries of France, Germany, Austria, and Belgium.)

With this understanding of where the United States has stood earlier and today in relation to other welfare states, let us turn to a more detailed consideration of the growth of social programs in the United States. First, we will consider data that cover the period from 1929 to 1979 and then finer grain data that are available for the period 1952 to 1978.

THE GROWTH OF AMERICAN SOCIAL BENEFITS FROM 1929 TO 1980

I have tried to assemble data from the national accounts in such a way as to chart the growth of both government social benefits and private sector fringe benefits in the spirit of the European Community definition of "social protection" benefits which does not make a distinction between putatively private and public payment of benefits. (Appendix A specifies in detail what programs are included in this definition.) Let us look at the results for the latest year for which all the data are available—1978—as reported in Table 2, which shows the percent of GNP spent on benefits from employee welfare programs, veterans' programs, government em- for Britain (Eurostat 1980). By 1980 these proportions had climbed to the population-at-large as opposed to the special categories of employees, veterans, and government employees. I have classified the benefits into seven types which are reasonably self-explanatory.

We find that, in the United States, one-sixth of GNP is channelled through these various forms of "social wage." This compares with an average in 1977 of about one-quarter of GNP for the continental European Community nations and 19 percent for Britain (Eurostat 1980). By 1980 these proportions had climbed slightly both on the Continent and in Britain (Eurostat 1982).

Overall, we find that almost a quarter of social benefits are provided as employee welfare benefits, and an additional 10 percent are in the form of fringe benefits for government employees, making

Table 2

SOCIAL PROTECTION BENEFITS IN THE UNITED STATES AS A PERCENT OF GNP: 1978 AND 1952

Type	Sector				
1978	Employee Welfare Benefits	General Social Benefits	Veterans' Benefits	Government Employee Benefits	Total
Pension, survivors, and group life insurance	1.24%	4.42%	0.50%	1.51%	7.67%
Medical insurance and public health	1.84	3.45	na	*a*	5.29
Unemployment and readjustment	0.07	0.41	0.14	0.01	0.63
Employment injuries	na	0.33	na	0.10	0.43
Sickness pay and insurance	0.66[b]	0.03	na	*a*	0.69
Public assistance	na	1.40	na	na	1.40
Social services	na	0.46	na	na	0.46
Total	3.81	10.50	0.64	1.62	16.57
1952					
Pension, survivors, and group life insurance	0.27	0.75	0.87	.35	2.24
Medical insurance and public health	0.42	0.77	na	*a*	1.19
Unemployment and readjustment	na	0.31	0.19	na	0.50
Employment injuries	na	0.20	na	0.06	0.26
Sickness pay and insurance	0.44	0.02	na	*a*	0.46
Public assistance	na	0.74	na	na	0.74
Social services	na	0.10	na	na	0.10
Total	1.13	2.89	1.06	0.41	5.49

Sources: USDC 1981: Tables 3.11, 3.16, 3.17, 6.15; USBLS 1983. See Appendix A.

[a] Included with employee welfare benefits

[b] Estimated from labor force statistics and national accounts

a total of about one-third of all social benefits that come to individuals as part of their labor contracts. With another 4 percent of the benefits for veterans only, less than two-thirds of benefits are directed toward the general population via the government.

As in all countries, benefits for old-age and survivors and medical care benefits consume most of the money—not quite 80 percent. This proportion would be lower in most other welfare states, of course, because the United States does not have a family allowance program. In the European Community, family allowances account for about 10 percent of total benefits. Similarly, the United States does not have a national sickness insurance program. Five states have temporary disability insurance, but this amounts to only 0.03 percent of GNP. Using the *Handbook of Labor Statistics* (as well as the national accounts), I have estimated that sick pay probably amounts to about 1 percent of the total compensation of workers or 0.66 percent of GNP. This too is low by European standards, where average sick pay and sickness insurance is closer to 1.5 percent of GNP (about 6 percent of total benefits).

It is interesting to note that, although government workers account for only about one-fifth of employed persons, more money is spent on their old-age and survivors' benefits than for workers in the private sector. To some extent this may be due to the fact that many government workers are not covered by social security, but it still seems that government workers fare better in old age than those in the private sector.

Over the period 1929 to 1979, we find two kinds of programs with cyclical patterns--unemployment and veterans' benefits. Unemployment benefits began in 1937, rapidly increased in the late 1930s, decreased during the war years, and then began a pattern of ups and downs which has continued to the present (with a slight upward trend). They reached their highest point in 1975 at 1.08 percent of GDP.

Veterans' benefits follow a different cyclical pattern—tending to rise sharply at the end of each war and then decline steadily until the next war. Veterans' benefits were over 2 percent of GDP in 1946 and 1947, and again in 1950 because of a sevenfold jump in life insurance payments at the beginning of the Korean War.

Government employee benefits have shown a reasonably steady increase over the fifty-year period from 1929. From the 1950s the rate of increase has risen sharply; from the 1950s to the 1980s it is about double that from the 1930s to the 1950s. This increase has taken place despite the fact that the proportion of the labor force employed by government has changed very little since the late 1930s.*

The series for general social benefits breaks at 1952. Before that we do not have data on expenditures for health and hospitals or medical and social services. Since the addition of these benefits increases the percent of GNP for benefits by almost one half, earlier estimates are not at all comparable with those after 1952.

We see a very slow rate of growth in social benefits after 1933. If medical and social services had been included in this early period, it would probably have made the growth of total general social benefits essentially flat through the 1930s, down during the war, and up slightly after the war. (Workmen's compensation was also excluded from the data before 1950.) Using the ILO data to estimate general social benefits at the middle of the Depression, we arrive at a figure of roughly 3 percent of GNP. Taking these kinds of benefits as the best index of welfare state commitments, this indicates an essentially flat level of monetary commitment to social purposes through government in the United States over the twenty-year period beginning in 1933.

During this time we see shifts, with some decline in public assistance and gradually rising spending for social security. However, it was not until the early 1950s that spending for social insurance programs exceeded that for public assistance programs.

The period of sustained growth in general social benefits seems to have begun in the mid-1950s. It was set off by a spurt of growth in social security benefits and continued growth in other programs at various points afterwards. Until 1970, public assistance showed an essentially flat, slightly declining trend, while social security programs showed steady increases.

The U.S. proxy for private fringe benefits—other labor income— shows only modest growth from 1929 until just after World War II. Then a very steady period of growth began which exceeded that of social security. In the late 1950s other labor income was at about the same level as social security, which had been the more rapidly growing of the two. From then on, however, old-age, survivors, and disability insurance (OASDI) grew more slowly than other labor

---

*We are underestimating the level of government employee fringe benefits because we cannot separate health insurance and sick pay benefits into government and private sectors.

income. Even if we include Medicare in the later years, its rate of growth is not as great as that in private fringe benefits. All this emphasizes the point that employee benefits in both the government and private sectors have been as dynamic a factor in the growth of social protection in the United States as social security programs, although the latter have attracted much more attention from political commentators and policy analysts.

Stepping back from precise comparisons of rates, it is perhaps more useful to say that by and large the public and private sectors have grown at roughly similar rates in the United States. Table 3 gives a schematic picture of the phases of growth of the major

Table 3

PHASES OF GROWTH OF MAJOR SOCIAL PROTECTION
PROGRAMS IN THE UNITED STATES TO 1978

Type of Program	Percent GNP 1978	First Passed One-Half 1978 Level	First Passed One-Quarter 1978 Level
Employee welfare benefits			
Pensions, etc.	1.24%	1962	1954
Medical insurance	1.84	1961	1954
All benefits	3.81	1961	1954
Government social benefits			
Pensions, etc.	4.42	1959	1954
Medical insurance and public health	3.45	1967	1956
Public assistance	1.40	1932	1931
All benefits	10.50	1961	1949
Government employee benefits			
All benefits	1.62	1964	1952

categories of social protection listed in Table 2. It shows the proportion of 1978 GNP devoted to each of the types of benefits, then indicates the year the proportion surpassed one-half its 1978 level, and then the year it surpassed one-quarter of that level. With the exception of the OASDI, all the types of benefits were in existence in 1929 (when the data series starts), although they were often funded at minuscule levels, and new programs were added to most categories. Private benefits were probably only about 0.2 percent of GNP in 1929. Public health and charity medical programs would certainly have been larger, on the order of 0.66 percent, and public assistance in that prosperous year amounted to about 0.14 percent of GNP.

Table 3 shows that government medical programs have been the most dynamic in growth due to heavy investments in health and hospitals beginning in the mid-1950s and continuing with the introduction of Medicare and Medicaid in the late 1960s.

Returning to Table 2, we see that, overall, 5.49 percent of GNP went to social protection benefits in 1952. These benefits almost tripled from 1952 to 1978. We find small shifts in the margins for type and sector over this period. Fringe benefits accounted for slightly less of total social protection in 1952 than in 1978, and veterans' benefits accounted for more with the accumulated claims of one ongoing and one recent war. But overall the sector proportions appear not to have shifted dramatically over this time.

There are somewhat greater changes in the distribution by type of program. Old age accounted for less total spending in 1952, and medical expenses accounted for markedly smaller amounts, while public assistance accounted for more.

What about the distribution of effects on the total growth in social benefits from 5.49 percent to one-sixth of GNP? Table 4 shows the effect of each type/sector combination on the total growth. Overall we see that 86 percent of the growth is due to the growth in either old-age or health areas. Public assistance, which receives such a large share of attacks on social spending, accounts for about 6 percent of the growth (or 9 percent if one includes social services).

Employee welfare benefits for private and government employees combined account for one-third of the growth in social protection, and the balance falls to general social benefits.

It is an oft-commented-upon irony that the eight years of Democratic administrations in the 1960s produced a relatively modest 11 percent increase in government social protection as a percentage of GNP while the succeeding eight years of Republican administrations increased the proportion of GNP spent by government on social protection by over 50 percent. During the succeeding four years of a Democratic administration, the proportion of GNP spent on social protection began to drop.

The rate of growth of most benefits seems to have tapered off

Table 4

PERCENT CONTRIBUTION TO TOTAL CHANGE IN SOCIAL PROTECTION
AS A PERCENT OF GNP: 1952-1978

Type of Benefit	Sector				
	Employee Welfare Benefits	Government Social Benefits	Veterans' Benefits	Government Employee Benefits	Total
Pension, survivors, and group life insurance	8.75%	33.12%	-3.34%	10.47%	49.01%
Medical insurance and public health	12.82	24.19	0.00	0.00	37.00
Unemployment and readjustment	0.63	0.90	-0.45	0.09	1.17
Employment injuries	0.00	1.17	0.00	0.36	1.53
Sickness pay and insurance	1.99	0.09	0.00	0.00	2.08
Public assistance	0.00	5.96	0.00	0.00	5.96
Social services	0.00	3.25	0.00	0.00	3.25
Total	24.19	68.68	-3.79	10.92	100.00

in the late 1970s. Private fringe benefits peaked in 1976 and then declined a bit. Programs for government employees seem to have reached a plateau from 1976 to 1979 from which they have fallen as a result of cuts in government employment in the 1980s. Veterans' benefits have declined reasonably steadily since the Vietnam War. OASDI reached a peak in 1976, public assistance reached a peak in 1975 and has declined very sharply since, and all government health programs combined hit a plateau by 1976. Overall the late 1970s were a period of sharply reduced growth or no growth at all.

From the perspective that there was a welfare state crisis in the United States in the late 1970s brought about by too much social spending, social programs appeared as a "flabby hodge-podge, funded without policy consistency or rigor, that increasingly looks like a great social pork-barrel" (David Stockman; quoted in Skocpol and

Ikenberry 1983). If there is a social pork-barrel, it seems to consist primarily in old-age, survivors, and disability programs and medical care programs—fully 85 percent of the increase of government-provided social protection has been in these two areas. As the current administration has learned to its sorrow, little dent can be made in the size of this social pork-barrel without attacking social security programs themselves. And that is perhaps the political challenge of the 1980s: how to bring about a reduction in social security as a proportion of the national income without losing popular support.

Let us shift now to a rough estimation of the impact of the growth of benefits on the distribution of incomes. We will have to bypass services and directed cash benefits (with the exception of food stamps) and focus solely on cash income. Cash represents only about 60 percent of total social protection, but it is possible to chart the impact of cash transfers on income distribution from the mid-1950s to the present period.

FAMILY INCOME PACKAGING AND THE ROLE OF TRANSFERS:
   1954 TO 1979

Let us consider some very early and tentative results from a historical study of changing income packaging and distribution since 1954. We have assembled a Family Income over Three Decades (FITD) dataset by combining several Surveys of Consumer Finance conducted by the University of Michigan in the 1950s and 1960s with the Panel Study of Income Dynamics, also conducted by Michigan. Included in Appendix B are tabulations from the FITD dataset for total income, taxable income, and transfer income for the full sample and for five family types of particular interest at five-year intervals.* These are (1) couples aged 25 to 64 with

*In order to make comparisons between years easier, I have divided all the income amounts of each year by the mean family income for that year and then multiplied by 1,000, which makes the mean total income for each year $1,000. Means of other income sources can be thought of as percentages of the mean total income. The tables in Appendix B report the weighted (by household size and sample weight) sample size, the percent of households receiving a particular income source, the mean amount received from that source before taxes, the standard deviation before tax, the mean amount received after tax, and the standard deviation after tax. Where appropriate, some tables indicate the mean percentage of the family's before and after tax income that comes from a particular source. Finally, some tables indicate the proportion of the sample who are

children, (2) female heads aged 25 to 64 with children, (3) married couples 65 and over, (4) female heads 65 and over, and (5) male heads 65 and over.

Unfortunately we are not able to distinguish the types of transfer income included in the transfer category. (Eventually we will be able to do so from 1959 on.) Therefore our transfer category includes public transfers, private pensions, and interfamily transfers. Even so, the results are of interest as a first approximation. We find that from 1954 to 1979 the overall distribution of income probably changed very little. This is apparent from an examination of the standard deviations.

There is no striking change in the proportion of persons categorized as poor. It seems to rise very slightly through 1969 and declines slightly afterwards, but given that these are different surveys with somewhat different questions, I'm not sure we are justified in concluding anything other than that there are about the same number of poor families in all six surveys.

When we examine the results by family type, however, we find that there do seem to be changes in the distribution of total income. It would seem that for couples 25-64 years of age with children, income may have become more equally distributed—there being a downward trend in the coefficient of variation—but there does not seem to be much change in the distribution for female heads with children. There seems to be a trend toward increasing income of couples over 65 relative to the average household, but not for single heads over 65.

Shifting now to taxable income, we find overall a slight decline in the proportion of family income that is taxable, as would be expected given the rise in transfer income. The distribution of taxable income seems to have become more unequal over time, which appears to indicate that the lack of change in the inequality of income distribution for all households is due to compensating trends—increasing inequality in taxable income and an increasing proportion of transfer income. We note that in the 1950s over 90 percent of income was taxable on average; by 1979 average taxable income had declined to 82 percent.

---

poor based on after-tax taxable income only or total income. I have defined poverty as a family-size-adjusted income of less than half the median income (adjusted for a family size of four); see Rainwater (1974) for a discussion of this definition.

When we compare different family types, we find it is primarily among the old that the reliance on taxable income has declined. For married couples with children, there doesn't seem to be much change in the proportion of family income that comes from taxable sources, and there is a fairly clear trend for the taxable income distribution to become more equal over time.

For female heads with children, there is perhaps a very slight trend toward less reliance on taxable income, but in the main the proportion of income from taxable sources seems to have changed little. However, for older people there have been dramatic changes. In 1954 an average of almost 80 percent of the income of couples over 65 came from taxable sources, but by 1979 only 40 percent came from these sources. Somewhat the same pattern is apparent for the two categories of single heads over 65.

The number of recipients of transfer income has increased dramatically from 22 percent of all households in 1954 to 52 percent in 1979. For those households receiving transfer income, however, there has been very little change in the proportion of income that comes from transfers. Transfer income, on average, represents slightly less than half of total after-tax income. So the transfer revolution has been mainly one of an ever-widening circle of recipients of transfers rather than an overall increase in dependence by transfer recipients. Thus we find that transfer-receiving households received an average of about 20 percent of the mean family income in all of the survey years.

The increase in receipt of transfers has occurred in all family types but most dramatically among the old. In 1954, 13 percent of couples 25-64 with children received transfers; by 1979, 30 percent were recipients. For female heads 25-64, the increase was from around 60 percent to over 85 percent. By 1979 almost all households with heads over 65 were transfer recipients, whereas in 1954 the range had been from 55 percent of couples to 68 percent of single female heads. But within these family types there do not seem to have been any marked increases in dependence among transfer recipients. Neither the old nor the younger families seem to have become more dependent on transfers once one controls for family types and recipiency. Overall, in all periods, about 20 percent of the income of couples with children has come from transfers, about half of the income for female heads with children, and from 65 to 75 percent for different types of aged families.

To what extent, then, has the role of transfers in moving people out of poverty changed over the period 1954 to 1979? Table 5 summarizes the results derived from the tables in Appendix B. The first row in each subsection shows the proportions of individuals in poor families based on total income at five-year intervals; the second row shows the proportions who would have been poor if they had to rely solely on their taxable incomes; the third row shows the proportions of those in the second row who were moved from poverty by transfers.

We find that, for the total sample, transfers have been necessary to move an increasing proportion of persons from poverty during the twenty-five-year period. If there had been no transfers, the proportion of poor would have increased by 50 percent. That it did not increase at all has meant that while in 1954 only about a quarter of poor families were "saved" from poverty by transfers, by 1979 about half of poor families required transfers to escape poverty.

Among couples with children, there have been declining proportions of poor based on either total or taxable income. But because the former has declined more rapidly than the latter, an increasing proportion of couples with children is being moved out of poverty by transfers. In the 1950s perhaps 20 percent of the pre-transfer poor were moved out by transfers; by the 1970s that proportion had doubled.

For female heads with children, there is no clear trend in the proportion poor either before or after taxes and therefore no clear trend in the proportion of pre-transfer poor moved out by transfers. The move from poverty by transfers seems to be on average about 40 percent.

Among older people, we find dramatic increases in the importance of transfers. For all older couples there has been a decline in the proportion who are poor on the basis of total income, although that decline seems to have been significantly greater for couples than for single heads, perhaps as much because the couples are younger as anything else. An increasing proportion of older couples would have been poor had they had to depend on their taxable income alone. Thus we find that a third of pre-transfer poor older couples were moved out of poverty by transfers in 1954, whereas by 1979 almost 80 percent of the larger group of pre-transfer poor were moved out of poverty by transfers.

The trends are less dramatic for single older people, but there we find that while some 20 percent of the pre-transfer poor were moved from poverty by transfers in 1954, by the 1970s about

Table 5

PERCENT POOR ON BASIS OF TOTAL AND TAXABLE INCOME BY FAMILY TYPE AND YEAR: 1954-1979

Family Type	Year					
	1954	1959	1964	1969	1974	1979
Total Sample						
Total income	14.4%	15.2%	15.2%	16.5%	13.8%	13.8%
Taxable income	18.7	22.9	24.0	26.4	23.6	27.1
Percent moved from poverty by transfers	23.0	33.6	36.7	37.5	41.5	49.1
Couples 25-64 with Children						
Total income	8.8	7.5	7.1	4.4	2.8	2.7
Taxable income	10.2	10.4	8.4	6.4	4.6	4.6
Percent moved from poverty by transfers	13.7	27.9	15.5	31.3	39.1	41.3
Females Heads 25-64 with Children						
Total income	20.3	39.7	29.1	38.1	29.5	31.2
Taxable income	39.1	59.0	52.7	57.7	50.4	50.1
Percent moved from poverty by transfers	48.1	32.7	44.8	34.0	41.5	37.7
Couples 65 and Over						
Total income	34.9	27.5	31.3	25.6	19.2	14.3
Taxable income	51.5	57.1	63.9	57.7	60.7	64.7
Percent moved from poverty by transfers	32.2	51.8	51.0	55.6	68.4	77.9
Female Heads 65 and Over						
Total income	55.3	53.0	49.4	62.6	41.5	43.2
Taxable income	69.5	74.0	74.7	85.7	75.6	78.2
Percent moved from poverty by transfers	20.4	28.4	33.9	27.0	45.1	44.8
Male Heads 65 and Over						
Total income	46.4	60.5	45.0	55.1	35.8	33.5
Taxable income	56.0	84.3	85.0	76.1	80.5	72.4
Percent moved from poverty by transfers	17.1	28.2	47.1	27.6	55.5	53.7

45 percent of the single men and 55 percent of the single women were moved from pre-transfer poverty by transfers.

We can conclude, then, that despite its status as a welfare state laggard, in the United States the development of social protection mechanisms has become increasingly important over the last three decades to the benefit of a wide range of American families. These mechanisms do not, however, seem to have produced a significant shift toward greater equality in income distribution because of an increasing inequality in factor income distribution, which is produced by a complex interaction between changes in wage distribution, changes in patterns of labor force participation (particularly by wives), and changes in family living arrangements. A significant challenge for understanding the changing role of the welfare state comes from the necessity to understand how welfare state programs interact with changing conceptions of family, gender roles, and the role of work.

REFERENCES

Coleman, Richard, and Rainwater, Lee. 1978. *Social Standing in America.* New York: Basic Books, Inc.

Eisner, Robert. 1985. "Total Income Systems Accounts." *Survey of Current Business* 65, 1 (January): 24-48.

Esping-Andersen, Gosta. 1981. "The Welfare State as System of Stratification." Paper prepared for European Consortium for Political Research. April.

Eurostat [Statistical Office of the European Community]. 1980. *Social Indicators for the European Community: 1960-1978.*

_____. 1981. *European System of Integrated Social Protection Statistics: Methodology, Part I.*

_____. 1982. *Social Protection Expenditures, Notes Rapides.* December.

Gourevitch, Peter; Lange, Peter; and Martin, Andrew. 1981. "Industrial Relations and Politics: Some Reflections." In *Industrial Relations in International Perspective,* ed. Peter Doeringer. London: Macmillan.

Korpi, Walter. 1980. "Social Policy and Distributional Conflict in Capitalist Democracies: A Preliminary Comparative Framework." *West European Politics* 3, 3 (October).

Marchal, Jean. 1957. "Wage Theory and Social Change in Groups." In *Theory of Wage Determination,* ed. John Dunlop. London: St. Martins.

Rainwater, Lee. 1974. *What Money Buys.* New York: Basic Books, Inc.

Rein, Martin, and Rainwater, Lee, eds. 1986. *Public/Private Interplay in Social Protection: A Comparative Study.* Armonk: M. E. Sharpe, Inc.

Ruggles, Richard, and Ruggles, Nancy D. 1981. *Integrated Economic Accounts for the United States: 1947-1980.* Working Paper No. 841 (revised). Institution for Social and Policy Studies, Yale University. November.

Schelling, Thomas. 1980. "The Intimate Context for Self Command." *Public Interest.*

Shalev, Michael. 1983. "Class Politics and the Western Welfare State." In *Evaluating the Welfare State*, eds. Shimon E. Spiro and E. Yuchtman-Yaar. Orlando: Academic Press.

Skocpol, Theda, and Ikenberry, John. 1983. "The Political Formation of the American Welfare State in Historical and Comparative Perspective." *Comparative Social Research* 6: 124-25.

USBLS [U.S. Bureau of Labor Statistics]. 1983. *Handbook of Labor Statistics.* U.S. Department of Labor, Bulletin 2175. December.

USDC [U.S. Department of Commerce]. 1981. Bureau of Economic Analysis. *The National Income and Product Accounts of the United States, 1929-76. Statistical Tables.* September.

_____. 1982. Bureau of Economic Analysis. *The NIPA of the United States, 1976-80.* July.

Appendix A: DATA SOURCES AND DEFINITIONS

In assembling data for a time series, one finds areas in which compromises have to be made and incomplete data accepted.

The national accounts (USDC 1981, 1982) provide data on benefits paid by private pension and welfare funds from 1952. By combining pension and profit-sharing and group life insurance payments, I have arrived at the category for private old-age, survivors, and disability benefits (OASDI). Group health insurance is straightforward enough, as is supplemental unemployment. For the period before 1952, we can index the development of employee welfare benefits by the overall figures for other labor income, which involves contributions to funds rather than benefits paid by the funds. The contributions have always been greater than the benefits paid, principally because of the buildup in pension funds.

The national accounts provide data on government transfer payments to persons from 1929. As different kinds of social security programs have been established, one finds figures on expenditures phased in. The categories provided are reasonably straightforward. To make the general old-age category, I have combined OASDI and railroad retirement. For veterans' old age, I have taken the pension and disability category and veterans' life insurance. For government employees, I have combined federal civilian retirement, military retirement, and state government pensions. For the health category, I have combined Medicare from the government transfer payments table, medical care from the tables on federal and state and local government expenditures by type and function, and health and hospitals from the same table. Medical care thus combines social insurance, means-tested welfare benefits for medical care, and public health activity by government. (I inadvertently omitted veterans' hospitals, but these expenditures amounted to only .002 percent of GNP in 1978.) In the case of unemployment insurance, the categories are straightforward: I combined railroad and general unemployment insurance into one category; federal employees have a separate insurance fund; for veterans I combined readjustment and unemployment benefits. For employment injuries, I have used workmen's compensation from benefits paid out by private funds. I have classified this as a general government social benefit since it is a mandated program. In addition, there is a separate workmen's compensation fund for federal, state, and local government employees.

As noted in the text, I have estimated sickness pay as a fringe benefit for both private and government employees.

Under public assistance, there is a variety of programs, the largest of which are food stamps, supplemental security income, general assistance, and aid to families with dependent children (AFDC).

I have omitted two categories included in the government transfer to persons category. One is described as consisting of "mustering out pay, terminal leave pay, and adjusted compensation benefits" for veterans, the other as consisting "largely of payments to non-profit institutions, and aid to students."

Finally, from the tables on government expenditure I have included purchases of goods and services for the "welfare and social services" function. I have not included some expenditures that in conceptual terms ought to be included—namely, housing subsidies and job retraining allowances—because the necessary detail is not available in the national accounts. However, these omissions would affect the data only in the third decimal of the percentage of GNP measures.

COMPONENTS OF U.S. SOCIAL PROTECTION AS PERCENT OF GDP: 1929-1979

Year	Private Pensions	Private Medical Insurance	Private Unemployment Insurance	Old-Age and Survivors Insurance	Medicare and Medicaid	Temporary Disability	Unemployment Insurance	Govt. Employee Workers Compensation	Public Assistance	Government Workers Pensions	Govt. Workers Unemployment Insurance
1929									.14	.12	
1930									.21	.15	
1931									.35	.20	
1932									.70	.29	
1933									1.16	.34	
1934									1.28	.33	
1935									1.44	.32	
1936									.90	.30	
1937				.04			.46		1.01	.29	
1938				.13			.48		1.27	.32	
1939				.14			.53		1.25	.32	
1940				.15			.29		1.16	.31	
1941				.17			.22		.96	.25	
1942				.16			.04		.72	.21	
1943				.15			.03		.53	.19	
1944				.16			.21		.48	.19	
1945				.20			.54	.05	.51	.23	
1946				.26			.36	.05	.66	.35	
1947				.28		.01	.33	.05	.83	.31	
1948				.31		.01	.72	.05	.99	.29	
1949				.37		.01	.51	.05	.97	.33	
1950	.24	.31		.44		.01		.05	1.06	.34	

Year											
1951	.25	.38		.66		.01	.27	.05	.74	.33	
1952	.27	.42		.75		.01	.31	.06	.74	.35	
1953	.30	.46		.94		.01	.29	.06	.71	.38	
1954	.34	.52	.01	1.13		.02	.61	.06	.72	.41	.01
1955	.36	.55	.03	1.37		.02	.37	.06	.70	.42	.01
1956	.40	.34	.19	1.49		.02	.35	.06	.66	.46	.01
1957	.44	.70	.10	1.80		.02	.42	.06	.68	.50	.02
1958	.49	.76	.11	2.05		.02	.91	.07	.74	.55	.01
1959	.52	.79	.15	2.26		.02	.55	.07	.72	.57	.01
1960	.55	.86	.11	2.38		.03	.58	.07	.71	.61	.01
1961	.61	.93	.10	2.59		.03	.81	.07	.73	.64	.01
1962	.65	.97	.06	2.71		.03	.54	.07	.69	.66	.01
1963	.68	.99	.06	2.73		.04	.49	.07	.68	.70	.01
1964	.71	1.06	.07	2.68		.04	.41	.07	.67	.74	.01
1965	.75	1.10	.09	2.78		.04	.33	.07	.66	.75	.01
1966	.80	1.06	.06	2.78	.13	.04	.24	.07	.67	.81	.01
1967	.86	1.06	.06	2.81	.54	.04	.27	.07	.74	.87	.01
1968	.91	1.21	.07	2.98	.64	.04	.24	.07	.78	.87	.01
1969	.96	1.30	.15	2.96	.69	.04	.23	.07	.85	.92	.00
1970	1.01	1.49	.17	3.34	.71	.04	.39	.07	1.11	1.03	.01
1971	1.07	1.53	.12	3.58	.73	.04	.53	.07	1.28	1.10	.01
1972	1.11	1.53	.05	3.63	.73	.04	.47	.08	1.28	1.17	.01
1973	1.10	1.50	.17	4.01	.73	.03	.32	.08	1.24	1.21	.01
1974	1.16	1.63	.20	4.21	.87	.03	.46	.08	1.45	1.33	.01
1975	1.21	1.72	.07	4.46	1.00	.03	1.08	.09	1.65	1.47	.02
1976	1.20	1.90	.06	4.54	1.07	.03	.84	.10	1.65	1.52	.02
1977	1.20	1.79	.07	4.54	1.13	.03	.61	.10	1.51	1.51	.01
1978	1.24	1.84		4.42	1.15	.03	.41	.10	1.40	1.51	.01
1979				4.43	1.21	.03	.38	.11	1.38	1.53	.01
Mean:	.7383	1.0681	.1002	1.9094	.8108	.0240	.4284	.0700	.9044	.6061	.0096

COMPONENTS OF U.S. SOCIAL PROTECTION AS PERCENT OF GDP: 1929-1979

Year	Veterans' Pensions	Veterans' Unemployment Benefits	Workmen's Compensation Total	Total Employee Benefits	Other Labor Income	Total Government Expenditures	Total Government Compensation	Total Government Purchases	Total Government Transfers	Total Govt. Workers Benefits	Other Govt. Expenditures	Nonsocial Government Purchases	Govt. Medical Services	Social Services
1929	.43				.51	9.94	4.91	3.62	.25	.64	.52	3.62		
1930	.51				.57	12.21	5.85	4.63	.33	.79	.62	4.63		
1931	.72				.62	16.25	7.12	5.31	.49	2.23	1.09	5.31		
1932	.99				.71	18.26	8.82	5.45	.90	1.58	1.52	5.45		
1933	.83				.60	19.19	9.53	5.24	1.35	1.28	1.79	5.24		
1934	.60				.63	19.70	9.59	5.75	1.42	.97	1.96	5.75		
1935	.57				.61	18.46	9.26	4.81	1.57	.94	1.88	4.81		
1936	.51				.64	19.42	9.78	4.92	1.01	2.55	1.16	4.92		
1937	.47				.60	16.54	8.54	4.71	1.14	.91	1.24	4.71		
1938	.52				.64	19.75	10.01	5.47	1.93	.91	1.42	5.47		
1939	.53				.63	19.31	9.36	5.49	1.89	.89	1.68	5.49		
1940	.50				.63	18.42	8.74	5.41	1.87	.83	1.57	5.41		
1941	.38				.56	23.00	8.39	11.55	1.44	.65	.96	11.55		
1942	.30				.54	40.39	10.31	27.44	1.15	.52	.98	27.44		
1943	.26				.56	48.56	14.07	32.18	.83	.45	1.03	32.18		
1944	.33				.72	48.90	16.01	30.05	.82	.64	1.38	30.05		
1945	.57	.07			.84	43.64	17.30	21.68	1.03	1.62	2.00	21.68		
1946	.91	1.32			.93	21.72	10.81	2.32	1.56	3.61	3.43	2.32		
1947	1.03	1.12			1.02	18.25	8.02	2.91	1.65	3.13	2.54	2.91		
1948	.95	.88			1.05	19.46	7.61	4.71	1.81	2.28	3.04	4.71		
1949	1.00	.88			1.14	22.96	3.52	6.34	2.26	2.28	3.56	6.34		
1950	1.85	.60	19	.55	1.28	21.90	8.23	5.91	2.20	2.82	3.82	5.91		

Year														
1951	.94	.37	.19	.63	1.40	23.94	9.19	8.98	1.83	1.69	2.25	8.98	.03	.10
1952	.87	.19	.20	.69	1.49	26.98	9.96	11.76	1.94	1.54	1.78	10.91	.04	.10
1953	.85	.13	.20	.77	1.60	27.69	9.68	12.82	2.06	1.46	1.67	11.98	.05	.11
1954	.87	.17	.20	.86	1.67	26.45	9.83	10.82	2.58	1.54	1.68	9.93	.05	.10
1955	.83	.18	.19	.92	1.76	24.49	9.51	9.24	2.55	1.51	1.68	8.38	.05	.11
1956	.80	.19	.20	1.05	1.91	24.77	9.64	9.19	2.61	1.49	1.84	8.28	.06	.11
1957	.80	.17	.20	1.17	2.04	25.96	9.70	9.84	3.03	1.50	1.82	8.86	.06	.11
1958	.84	.16	.21	1.44	2.09	28.38	10.42	10.71	3.85	1.57	1.83	9.65	.07	.12
1959	.81	.12	.20	1.41	2.17	26.85	10.06	9.94	3.67	1.49	1.68	8.85	.08	.13
1960	.81	.08	.21	1.52	2.22	26.93	10.41	9.39	3.83	1.49	1.81	8.27	.11	.13
1961	.87	.05	.21	1.70	2.25	28.42	10.74	9.80	4.30	1.57	1.93	8.68	.14	.14
1962	.78	.03	.21	1.73	2.31	28.40	10.72	10.17	4.12	1.47	1.92	8.95	.15	.14
1963	.78	.02	.22	1.78	2.34	28.12	10.85	9.87	4.10	1.51	1.79	8.60	.16	.14
1964	.72	.02	.22	1.83	2.47	27.64	11.00	9.36	3.98	1.48	1.84	8.03	.16	.16
1965	.70	.01	.21	1.90	2.58	27.18	10.91	9.11	3.99	1.45	1.72	7.76	.17	.17
1966	.62	.02	.21	1.93	2.63	28.25	11.25	9.74	4.06	1.45	1.76	8.31	.21	.19
1967	.65	.04	.22	2.01	2.71	30.32	11.79	10.75	4.62	1.56	1.60	9.16	.28	.21
1968	.61	.06	.22	2.19	2.89	30.81	12.07	10.72	4.92	1.54	1.57	8.94	.38	.23
1969	.62	.08	.23	2.32	3.02	30.38	12.26	9.85	5.02	1.63	1.62	7.96	.42	.26
1970	.63	.14	.25	2.66	3.27	31.57	12.98	9.19	5.87	1.79	1.73	7.06	.50	.30
1971	.62	.19	.24	2.76	3.40	31.74	13.00	8.80	6.45	1.90	1.59	6.51	.57	.33
1972	.60	.22	.24	2.76	3.63	31.34	12.91	8.44	6.44	1.98	1.58	6.03	.61	.36
1973	.55	.23	.25	2.66	3.68	30.55	12.55	7.83	6.61	1.99	1.57	5.36	.63	.38
1974	.56	.25	.27	2.96	3.89	32.07	12.64	8.56	7.31	2.13	1.43	5.91	.81	.41
1975	.56	.36	.29	3.12	4.16	34.49	12.97	8.97	8.64	2.39	1.52	6.14	.80	.44
1976	.55	.29	.31	3.17	4.42	33.47	12.67	8.40	8.49	2.36	1.54	5.59	.82	.45
1977	.53	.19	.32	3.06	4.64	32.53	12.25	8.32	8.16	2.23	1.57	5.55	.82	.46
1978	.50	.14	.33	3.15	4.74	31.62	11.88	8.18	7.80	2.16	1.61	5.44	.80	.46
1979	.48	.11			4.91	31.20	11.51	8.12	7.81	2.13	1.64	5.40	.80	.45
Mean:	.6887	.2520	.2296	1.8859	1.9293	26.6297	10.5135	9.4536	3.3245	1.6177	1.7203	8.5520	.3419	.2388

COMPONENTS OF U.S. SOCIAL PROTECTION AS PERCENT OF GDP: 1929-1979

Year	Govt Health & Hospital Expenditures	Total Pension Benefits	Total Health Benefits	Govt Total Health Benefits	Total Unemployment Benefits	Total Social Benefits	Total Govt Employee Benefits	Total Veterans' Benefits	Total Social Security Benefits	Total Social Protection Benefits	Total Workmen's Compensation
1929		.55				.14	.12	.43	.69	.69	
1930		.67				.21	.15	.51	.87	.87	
1931		.93				.35	.20	.72	1.27	1.27	
1932		1.28				.70	.29	.99	1.98	1.98	
1933		1.18				1.16	.34	.83	2.34	2.34	
1934		.93				1.28	.33	.60	2.20	2.20	
1935		.90				1.44	.32	.57	2.34	2.34	
1936		.82				.90	.30	.51	1.72	1.72	
1937		.80				1.05	.29	.47	1.81	1.81	
1938		.97			.46	1.86	.32	.52	2.70	2.70	
1939		.98			.48	1.87	.32	.53	2.71	2.71	
1940		.96			.53	1.85	.31	.50	2.65	2.65	
1941		.81			.29	1.42	.25	.38	2.06	2.06	
1942		.68			.22	1.11	.21	.30	1.62	1.62	
1943		.60			.04	.73	.19	.26	1.18	1.18	
1944		.60			.05	.68	.19	.34	1.21	1.21	
1945		.69			.28	.92	.23	.64	1.79	1.79	
1946		1.51			1.86	1.46	.39	2.23	4.08	4.08	.05
1947		1.62			1.47	1.48	.36	2.14	3.98	3.98	.05
1948		1.55			1.21	1.63	.33	1.83	3.80	3.80	.05
1949		1.70			1.60	2.08	.38	1.88	4.34	4.34	.05
1950		2.88	.31		1.13	2.21	.40	2.45	5.05	5.60	.24

1951	.72	2.19	.38	.75	.64	1.88	.39	1.31	3.58	4.20	.25
1952	.71	2.25	1.17	.75	.49	2.87	.41	1.06	4.33	5.02	.26
1953	.71	2.48	1.21	.75	.41	2.99	.44	.98	4.41	5.18	.26
1954	.74	2.76	1.30	.78	.77	3.57	.48	1.04	5.09	5.95	.26
1955	.71	2.98	1.32	.76	.56	3.51	.49	1.01	5.01	5.93	.25
1956	.74	3.15	1.43	.80	.55	3.63	.53	.98	5.14	6.19	.26
1957	.81	3.55	1.57	.87	.63	4.10	.57	.97	5.64	6.81	.26
1958	.88	3.93	1.70	.94	1.27	4.99	.63	1.00	6.63	8.07	.28
1959	.89	4.15	1.76	.96	.78	4.85	.65	.93	6.42	7.82	.27
1960	.91	4.35	1.85	.99	.78	5.04	.69	.89	6.61	8.13	.28
1961	.95	4.72	1.99	1.06	1.03	5.57	.73	.92	7.22	8.91	.29
1962	.95	4.81	2.06	1.09	.69	5.42	.74	.81	6.97	8.70	.29
1963	.98	4.90	2.12	1.13	.62	5.43	.78	.81	7.01	8.79	.29
1964	1.01	4.85	2.23	1.17	.50	5.35	.82	.74	6.91	8.74	.29
1965	1.01	4.97	2.28	1.18	.40	5.37	.82	.71	6.90	8.80	.28
1966	1.04	5.01	2.44	1.38	.33	5.50	.88	.64	7.02	8.95	.28
1967	1.10	5.19	2.98	1.92	.41	6.20	.94	.70	7.83	9.85	.29
1968	1.16	5.37	3.40	2.19	.38	6.69	.94	.67	8.30	10.49	.29
1969	1.22	5.46	3.63	2.33	.39	6.90	1.00	.70	8.60	10.93	.30
1970	1.33	6.01	4.03	2.54	.69	7.96	1.11	.76	9.83	12.49	.31
1971	1.39	6.37	4.21	2.68	.90	8.68	1.18	.81	10.67	13.43	.31
1972	1.44	6.51	4.30	2.77	.82	8.79	1.25	.82	10.86	13.62	.32
1973	1.46	6.88	4.33	2.83	.61	9.07	1.29	.78	11.14	13.80	.33
1974	1.53	7.25	4.74	3.11	.90	9.96	1.42	.81	12.18	15.14	.36
1975	1.59	7.70	5.11	3.39	1.66	11.35	1.57	.92	13.85	16.97	.38
1976	1.54	7.81	5.33	3.43	1.22	11.26	1.64	.83	13.74	16.91	.41
1977	1.50	7.78	5.24	3.44	.88	10.91	1.64	.72	13.26	16.31	.42
1978	1.50	7.67	5.29	3.44	.63	10.49	1.63	.64	12.76	15.91	.43
1979	1.46	6.45	3.48	3.48	.50	10.15	1.64	.60	12.39	12.39	.11
Mean:	1.1160	3.3620	2.7716	1.8633	.6986	4.2151	.6575	.8665	5.7392	6.8115	.2659

Appendix B

INCOME PACKAGING TABLES

Table B-1

TOTAL INCOME OF FULL SAMPLE BY YEAR

Year	Weighted Sample Size	Mean Amount Before Tax	SD Before Tax	Mean Amount After Tax	SD After Tax	Percent Poor
1954	2,150	$1,000	715	$886	575	14.4%
1959	2,565	1,000	691	892	565	15.2
1964	1,496	1,000	701	875	555	15.2
1969	1,981	1,000	714	887	580	16.5
1974	3,043	1,000	702	885	566	13.8
1979	3,894	1,000	747	859	562	13.8

Table B-3

TRANSFER INCOME OF FULL SAMPLE BY YEAR

Year	Weighted Sample Size	Percent Recipients	Mean Amount Before Tax	SD Before Tax	Mean Percent Before-Tax Income	Mean Percent After-Tax Income
1954	2,150	22.4%	$182	165	43.0%	43.5%
1959	2,565	32.8	211	184	45.7	46.3
1964	1,496	34.5	209	167	49.8	50.5
1969	1,981	39.8	227	191	51.4	52.2
1974	3,043	40.9	208	189	43.4	43.9
1979	3,894	52.3	213	202	45.7	46.2

Table B-2

TAXABLE INCOME OF FULL SAMPLE BY YEAR

Year	Weighted Sample Size	Percent Recipients	Mean Amount Before Tax	SD Before Tax	Mean Amount After Tax	SD After Tax	Mean Percent Before-Tax Income	Mean Percent After-Tax Income	Percent Poor If Taxable Income Only
1954	2,150	95.1%	$1,002	716	$881	573	94.1%	93.9%	18.7%
1959	2,565	93.5	992	705	876	577	90.5	90.3	22.9
1964	1,496	92.5	1,003	719	868	572	89.5	89.3	24.0
1969	1,981	91.3	997	735	874	598	87.1	86.9	26.4
1974	3,043	94.2	971	731	849	591	87.3	87.1	23.6
1979	3,894	92.3	963	780	810	587	82.5	82.2	27.1

Table B-4

TOTAL INCOME BY FAMILY TYPE AND YEAR

Family Type	Year	Weighted Sample Size	Mean Amount Before Tax	SD Before Tax	Mean Amount After Tax	SD After Tax	Percent Poor
Couples 25-64 with children	1954	993	$1,116	711	$1,001	558	8.8%
	1959	1,202	1,187	679	1,065	548	7.5
	1964	646	1,196	662	1,053	520	7.1
	1969	736	1,266	653	1,123	523	4.4
	1974	1,035	1,326	697	1,163	536	2.8
	1979	1,141	1,396	726	1,174	511	2.7
Female heads 25-64 with children	1954	54	668	428	634	384	20.3
	1959	91	596	436	559	383	39.7
	1964	55	667	430	614	364	29.1
	1969	92	608	385	573	344	38.1
	1974	174	653	372	628	350	29.5
	1979	225	597	416	567	376	31.2
Couples over 65	1954	167	735	589	593	494	34.9
	1959	226	699	629	658	533	27.5
	1964	147	678	660	627	536	31.3
	1969	213	757	719	703	591	25.6
	1974	226	779	602	737	511	19.2
	1979	327	798	694	743	543	14.3
Female heads over 65	1954	79	409	475	380	415	55.3
	1959	116	374	334	356	295	53.0
	1964	93	446	577	408	446	49.4
	1969	144	303	274	290	243	62.6
	1974	177	381	275	372	259	41.5
	1979	372	387	324	375	290	43.2
Male heads over 65	1954	47	663	674	597	580	46.4
	1959	45	355	381	343	357	60.5
	1964	40	474	800	424	600	45.0
	1969	53	445	559	415	471	55.1
	1974	53	535	639	506	533	35.8
	1979	96	521	556	489	456	33.5

Table B-5

TAXABLE INCOME BY FAMILY TYPE AND YEAR

Family Type	Year	Weighted Sample Size	Percent Recipients	Mean Amount Before Tax	SD Before Tax	Mean Amount After Tax	SD After Tax	Mean Percent Before-Tax Income	Mean Percent After-Tax Income	Percent Poor If Taxable Income Only
Couples 25-64 with children	1954	993	99.7%	$1,096	709	$ 980	556	97.8%	97.7%	10.2%
	1959	1,202	99.2	1,164	687	1,041	554	96.6	96.5	10.4
	1964	646	99.5	1,182	665	1,037	523	97.5	97.4	8.4
	1969	786	99.2	1,243	664	1,099	534	96.9	96.8	6.4
	1974	1,035	99.6	1,303	706	1,140	544	97.0	96.9	4.6
	1979	1,141	99.5	1,362	739	1,138	521	95.7	95.4	4.6
Female heads 25-64 with children	1954	54	93.2	530	404	493	345	76.3	76.0	39.1
	1959	91	90.2	469	406	428	347	74.6	74.2	59.0
	1964	55	87.3	555	449	493	375	72.2	71.5	52.7
	1969	92	75.2	529	374	483	322	76.6	76.0	57.7
	1974	174	89.2	504	382	476	356	67.3	66.9	50.4
	1979	225	84.7	495	407	460	365	69.8	69.3	50.1
Couples over 65	1954	167	78.3	632	635	581	530	78.7	78.8	51.5
	1959	226	73.3	632	702	576	590	65.4	65.2	57.1
	1964	147	74.8	559	717	496	573	56.6	56.4	63.9
	1969	213	83.6	577	741	517	602	55.9	55.5	57.7
	1974	226	89.3	497	641	449	535	48.0	47.6	60.7
	1979	327	86.0	474	683	411	505	40.5	40.1	64.7
Female heads over 65	1954	79	61.8	434	496	388	423	71.1	70.6	69.5
	1959	116	65.2	307	334	279	286	59.2	58.7	74.0
	1964	83	66.3	388	691	331	526	51.6	50.8	74.7
	1969	144	62.6	230	300	210	257	46.6	46.2	85.7
	1974	177	66.5	281	293	268	272	49.6	49.3	75.6
	1979	372	70.3	250	343	234	299	39.6	39.3	78.2
Male heads over 65	1954	47	76.9	701	698	615	593	80.3	79.9	56.0
	1959	45	56.9	311	445	291	416	53.0	52.6	84.3
	1964	40	55.0	485	1,057	394	785	46.3	45.6	85.0
	1969	53	56.8	441	658	389	542	50.7	49.9	76.1
	1974	53	64.7	371	390	326	452	43.0	42.3	80.5
	1979	96	70.5	355	542	310	420	39.7	39.1	72.4

Table B-6

TRANSFER INCOME BY FAMILY TYPE AND YEAR

Family Type	Year	Weighted Sample Size	Percent Recipients	Mean Amount Before Tax	SD Before Tax	Mean Percent Before-Tax Income	Mean Percent After-Tax Income
Couples 25-64 with children	1954	993	12.8%	$137	148	15.8%	16.2%
	1959	1,202	19.5	157	167	20.8	21.2
	1964	646	15.6	124	122	19.0	19.7
	1969	786	14.7	219	240	26.1	26.9
	1974	1,035	19.5	146	148	17.3	17.9
	1979	1,141	29.6	142	165	16.4	17.1
Female heads 25-64 with children	1954	54	61.0	267	272	44.8	45.2
	1959	91	58.1	298	236	56.2	56.9
	1964	55	78.2	234	186	47.3	48.1
	1969	92	74.7	281	222	56.6	57.3
	1974	174	86.0	237	154	46.5	46.9
	1979	225	87.4	203	155	46.8	47.3
Couples over 65	1954	167	55.2	240	175	68.7	69.0
	1959	226	74.1	312	178	69.4	69.6
	1964	147	86.4	301	179	66.7	67.3
	1969	213	98.0	293	176	56.8	57.6
	1974	226	89.9	374	232	63.6	63.9
	1979	327	96.1	406	242	67.8	68.2
Female heads over 65	1954	79	67.7	183	121	76.8	77.1
	1959	115	83.7	204	127	72.6	73.0
	1964	83	91.6	207	124	71.9	72.4
	1969	144	97.8	162	94	72.4	72.7
	1974	177	96.2	201	106	69.6	69.8
	1979	372	98.2	215	123	73.5	73.7
Male heads over 65	1954	47	61.7	178	149	60.2	60.7
	1959	45	93.3	195	86	76.5	76.8
	1964	40	95.0	218	165	78.5	78.9
	1969	53	97.0	201	81	73.4	73.9
	1974	53	98.2	301	222	73.5	74.0
	1979	56	98.7	274	175	72.9	73.4

THE CITIZEN AND THE

WELFARE BUREAUCRACIES

THE GOVERNOR

A man who has grown old in the State service—in his own opinion, a smart official. He wears an air of dignified respectability, but is by no means incorruptible. He speaks to the point, generally avoiding extremes, but sometimes launches into an argument. His features are harsh and stern, like those of a *chinovnik* [bureaucrat] who has worked his way up from the lowest rank. His coarse and ill-educated nature causes him to pass with rapidity from fear to joy, and from servility to arrogance.

—Nikolai Gogol, *The Inspector-General*

THE CLERK AKAKY AKAKYEVICH

During all the years he had served in that department many directors and other high officials had come and gone, but he still remained in exactly the same place, in exactly the same kind of work, to wit, copying official documents. Indeed, with time the belief came to be generally held that he must have been born into the world entirely fitted out for his job, in his civil servant's uniform and a bald patch on his head. Outside this copying nothing seemed to exist for him.

—Nikolai Gogol, "The Overcoat"

UNEQUAL ENCOUNTERS:
THE CITIZEN AND THE
SOVIET WELFARE BUREAUCRACIES

Zvi Gitelman

Western social scientists have recently begun to investigate the routine bureaucratic encounters between citizens and government officials. Political scientists have come to appreciate that policy outputs and their application are an important part of the political process, that policy is made as much by its executors as by its formulators (see Eisinger 1972; Katz et al. 1975; Jones et al. 1977; Vedlitz et al. 1980; Mladenka 1981; Sharp 1982; Thomas 1982; Goodsell 1981). The political significance of the bureaucratic encounter is especially great in the Soviet Union for two reasons. First, the physical and psychological distances between the top elite and the mass of citizens are greater there than in most other systems— due in part to the size of the country, to Russian traditions of physical, cultural, and political separation between rulers and ruled, to a distrust of the masses growing out of Leninist fears of "spontaneity," and to the multi-layered hierarchical organization of every aspect of life. Since the Soviet politician's career depends not on electoral success, but on bureaucratic politics, he is not compelled to "go to the people" or "press the flesh" except on a few carefully orchestrated occasions. On the other hand, in the absence of a significant private sector outside agriculture, the government controls many of the basic desiderata of life—jobs, housing, higher education, for example—which in other systems are only marginally or indirectly affected by the state. Therefore, government-citizen contacts are much more frequent than they are in the American system. These contacts are most often between citizens and lower-level employees of the various branches of the state administration, which makes the

This paper is based on research done with the financial assistance of the Ford Foundation, the National Council for Soviet and East European Research, and the Sapir Development Fund (Israel). Research assistance was provided by Konstantin Miroshnik, Wayne DiFranceisco, and Yury Polsky.

local officials "the target for citizen demands which in another regime might be handled by non-political subsystems" (Friedgut 1978: 462; see also Oliver 1969). Thus the Soviet citizen's most frequent and most meaningful contact with the political system is as a client, indeed a supplicant, making demands and requests of lower-level officials representing the state.

The second reason for the political importance of bureaucratic encounters is that they may well be the most meaningful political activities of many, perhaps most, citizens. As we shall see, evidence from recent Soviet emigrés strongly suggests that citizen participation on the "input side" (demands and supports) are so highly ritualized that they are not taken seriously as ways of exerting political influence. Another type of participation is citizen-initiated contacts with people presumed to have influence on inputs—deputies to soviets, newspaper editors, party members and officials, officials of government executive committees (*ispolkomy*). These contacts are not public-oriented activities designed to influence general policy, but rather private initiatives launched for private ends. In general, they are made to seek personal benefit rather than to affect the system as a whole. The type of participation that may be the most "political" is the bureaucratic encounter—not with policy-makers but with those implementing it, wherein citizens seek to have policy implemented in the way most favorable to themselves. The encounter with the official administering policy is far more important to the individual than the rituals surrounding the ostensible making of policy. He has no real say in policymaking, so his political activity becomes focussed on its implementation.

A COMPARATIVE VIEW OF BUREAUCRATIC ENCOUNTERS

Are there systematic differences in the forms of bureaucratic encounters in different nation-states? There are four major influences on the style of bureaucratic encounters: structural, political, economic, and cultural. These influences may work differentially within states, especially in federated states with significant economic and cultural variations among regions, but they surely vary from state to state.

Structural or organizational factors determine how much authority the official has, how much discretion he can exercise, and hence how immediately responsive he can be to his citizen client. Structure also determines how many officials must be encountered to obtain a final decision. One of the most frequent complaints about bureaucracy is that "they send you from one clerk to another." The structural features of the Soviet administrative system include a very high degree of centralization and a dual subordination of officials—vertically to their superiors in the state apparatus and horizontally to Communist Party organs. There are some weak legal-constitutional restraints on official power and a few legal resources for the citizen to mobilize against officialdom, but the official's considerable power vis-à-vis the citizen enables him to compensate for his limited power within the system by lording it over the defenseless client. If one views the bureaucratic encounter as an "exchange relationship," as Hasenfeld does (1978; see also Hasenfeld and Steinmetz 1981), it appears at first glance that the exchange is a very uneven one in the USSR, with the official greatly advantaged. In Hasenfeld's terms, the Soviet bureaucracy has little need for client resources, the client has no right to much information about the organization's procedures and rules, and the organization does not depend on either income from the clients or utilization of its services as a justification for budgetary allocations (the centrally devised plan actually specifies in advance what utilization shall be). Moreover, there is likely to be a low level of trust between the organization and the client because of the confrontational relationship between rulers and ruled, the past use of coercion to force compliance, and the apparent mistrust of the masses by the elite. (How else explain the rigid censorship and suppression of embarrassing information seventy years after the Revolution?) The lack of trust between the parties in a bureaucratic encounter makes it more of a confrontation, and Western observers often get the impression that a mutual challenge is being thrown down. It is as if the official tells the client: "You try to get what you want, and I'll try to stop you."

John Armstrong and others point out another characteristic of Soviet administration which undoubtedly imposes a great burden on the citizen. The desire for political control leads to a deliberate confusion in the allocation of authority, with a multiplicity of overlapping jurisdictions blurring the lines (Armstrong 1965: 644). This may serve the needs of the political leadership, but it creates enormous frustrations for the citizen, who "has no place to go" because another structural characteristic of the Soviet system is its monopolistic control of the economy and of welfare services.

The second major influence on the bureaucratic encounter is the political system, which establishes the posture of the state toward the citizen. Is the citizen to be treated as subject or object? Does the state exist to serve the citizen, or is it the other way around? The American ethos, at least in the private sector, is nominally that "the customer is always right," but ever since Lenin's strictures against "tailism"—where the proletarian masses attempt to dictate policy to the historically conscious political leadership—the Soviet position has been that the party is right, by definition, and the citizen must subordinate himself to it. Ironically it was Trotsky who told the thirteenth Party Congress in 1924 that

> In the last instance the party is always right, because it is the only historic instrument which the working class possesses for the solution of its fundamental tasks. . . . I know that one ought not to be right against the party. One can be right only with the party and through the party because history has not created any other way for the realization of one's rightness (quoted in Deutscher 1965: 139).

The presumption of authority extends from the party to the state administration as well. A former Communist prime minister of Hungary describes the attitude of officials toward their clients as follows:

> The "client" is conceived as some kind of strange outsider, or even some downright malevolent person, over whom the administration, as the representative of the whole society, holds power. . . . This mystified social interest represents a much greater power for the individual official than it did for a king ruling by divine right or any capitalist company. And to make the situation more grotesque and complicated, this tendency to make a derived power absolute often penetrates much more deeply into the lower ranks of the hierarchy than into the upper ones. The lower ranks are inclined to take out on the client their lack of a substantial deciding voice in the administrative system (Hegedus 1976: 25).

In the 1977 Soviet constitution a new provision, Article 58, gives citizens the right to lodge complaints "against actions of officials and of state and social organizations." This right has existed previously in Soviet law (though it is not mentioned in the 1936 constitution), but it is limited by the constitutional proviso that "complaints must be reviewed in a manner and within time limits established by law." Like a 1968 edict "On the Procedure for Considering Proposals, Applications, and Complaints of Citizens," this article is seen by most Western scholars as "not having the desired effect of making Soviet bureaucrats more responsive to citizen complaints and opinions" (Barry 1979: 13; see also Uibopuu 1979 and Barry 1978). When a Soviet citizen tried to lodge a complaint against the KGB based on Article 58, he was promptly arrested. A new law to go into effect in 1988 has been proposed to enable citizens to appeal officials' decisions in the courts.

The Soviet administrative system is not shielded from political interference as it would be in some democratic societies. Indeed what in American eyes would be seen as "interference" would be perceived by Soviet officials as "guidance." To them, intervention by political authorities in administrative actions to serve the aims of the regime is not only justified but desirable.

Political influence on the bureaucratic encounter also derives from decisions about the priorities of various sectors. An agency's resources depend on its priority. Nine years after Sputnik was launched, clerks and clients in many Soviet post offices were still filling out forms on rough paper with pens dipped in inkwells. Westerners have often remarked on the poor quality of clerical facilities and office machinery in Soviet agencies:

> Office space is limited and poorly arranged, with file cases crowding the corridors even in such a high-level agency as the . . . Ministry of Foreign Affairs. Relatively simple items . . . such as typewriters and carbon paper, are in short supply and poor in quality. More important, the ratio of secretaries, typists and file clerks to administrators is very low (Armstrong 1965: 647).

Politically determined priorities also affect the recruitment and training of personnel. Especially in the Soviet case, where manpower allocation is centrally planned, political decisions directly affect the number and quality of officials that a citizen will encounter in a particular agency.

The third main influence on bureaucratic encounters is economics because, even if it is given high priority, an agency's personnel, equipment, and services may be of poor quality if there are only meager resources to allocate. Political decisions about the relative position of an agency are made within a context of economic realities. In wealthy countries, low priority agencies enjoy greater capital and human assets than high priority agencies do in poor countries.

Fourth and finally, bureaucratic encounters are heavily influenced by cultural norms. In certain cultures deference and humility are the approved postures for clients, while in other cultures aggressive behavior and even violence are seen as both appropriate and effective. Different groups in the same country will display different styles, complicating the question of how officials should respond to their clients (Eilam 1978). Officials also develop different styles. These are partly functions of rank and personality (compare Gogol's descriptions of the governor and the clerk Akaky Akakyevich above), but also of the general culture, which provides cues as to whether an official should be haughty or pleasant, distant or friendly, and so on. It has been suggested that the stratification of American society predisposes public officials to discriminate among the strata in dealing with them (Stone 1980), and this is undoubtedly true even in the "classless" society of the USSR.

BUREAUCRATIC ENCOUNTERS IN THE SOVIET UNION

In the exchange relationship between Soviet officials and citizens, the latter seem quite disadvantaged in comparison with their counterparts in the United States. On all four factors influencing bureaucratic encounters, the Soviet client seems to come out behind the American one. Structurally the Soviet system is so centralized that often the resolution of a citizen's case is pushed up to higher echelons where he is an abstract case, not a real person standing before the official. Under the Soviet political system the client's individual interests are weakly protected by law, and he is expected to subordinate them to the collective good. The Soviet Union's tremendous economic growth has been felt least in the services and agricultural sectors, and both continue to suffer relative deprivation. For the client of bureaucracy this means long lines and waits (the *ochered*, or queue, is an entrenched institution), harassed officials, inefficient procedures, and a lack of modern equipment. Finally, the cultural heritage of tsarism and the Soviet political culture have produced patterns of bureaucratic relations favorable to the officials (White 1979a; Pintner and Rowney 1980). It is not surprising, therefore, that former Soviet citizens have a generally negative view of most agencies about which they were questioned.

It is important to emphasize that the citizen is not completely without resources in his dealings with government agencies, and the exchange is not as uneven as might be supposed. In exploring the Soviet bureaucratic encounter from the perspective of the client, we shall raise three questions: (1) How do former Soviet citizens evaluate some Soviet service agencies and their personnel? (2) How did they "work the system"—i.e., what strategies and tactics did they employ to extract what they wanted from the system? (3) Do different groups of people deal with the bureaucracies in different ways? In other words, do views of the bureaucracies vary significantly by republic, sex, age, education, occupation, or other variables? Perhaps the bureaucracies operate differently in different republics, which would indicate that the Soviet system is less monolithic and its administrative practices less uniform than is often assumed in the West.

Two methodological problems must be addressed. The first concerns terminology.

> Bureaucracy is a word with a bad reputation. If you ask people to supply an adjective to go along with the noun, their choices will almost inevitably be pejorative. . . . Complaints about government bureaucracies have probably been commonplace at every period of history and in every country (Weiss 1979: 7-8).

But people do not inevitably give a negative assessment when asked to evaluate a public bureaucracy in the light of their own experience. In fact a major study of interactions between citizens and American public bureaucracies found that two-thirds of the respondents were satisfied with what they judged their most important "bureaucratic encounter." Private agencies were generally seen more favorably, and people had more positive pictures of the way *personal* experiences were handled by them, and more negative *generalized* attitudes toward government agencies (Katz et al. 1975: 14-15, 120; Nelson 1981: 27). Soviet emigrés also have differentiated attitudes toward bureaucracies and, despite a generalized hostility, are prepared to speak favorably about individual experiences. One woman recalls several instances of Soviet officials being kind and extending themselves even after she had been identified as an intended emigré and hence a traitor to the motherland:

> It became beautifully clear to me that in every bureaucrat somewhere there sits a human being, and you have to be able to find him. . . . There's only a very small group of people who have become petrified, become completely hard and unreachable in the process of serving the Soviet Union. . . . But . . . there aren't many such people. In most others a soul still shines through (personal interview 1980).

In addition to the fact that people's views of bureaucracy are not uniformly negative, differentiations of outlook are more likely if they are asked to compare bureaucracies with each other. Even where there is generalized hostility to bureaucracy, people can be induced to differentiate among degrees of hostility.

The second methodological problem concerns the use of emigré informants as substitutes for Soviet citizens, who of course cannot be systematically interviewed by Western scholars. The problem of using emigrés as sources of information about the Soviet system has been dealt with extensively elsewhere (Inkeles and Bauer 1968), and, in my opinion, successfully. Whether or not one can use an emigré sample to generalize to the Soviet population as a whole, in this study we shall be comparing relative differences *within* an emigré group. Furthermore, as Inkeles and Bauer pointed out twenty years ago, it is likely that "comparable groups in the Soviet population will stand in the same relationship to each other as do members of our sample" (*ibid.*, p. 27).

Strictly speaking, it cannot be claimed that the results obtained from an emigré sample are generalizable to the population in the Soviet Union because the emigrés are not only demographically different from the population as a whole, but presumably their attitudes and assessments are different as well. It is reasonable to assume that, having chosen to leave the USSR, they were less satisfied with the system than those who stayed behind. While accepting the inadmissibility of generalizing freely from the emigré to the general Soviet population, the assumption of emigré bias can be questioned. First, the emigration is demographically unrepresentative not because only Jews, Armenians, and Germans have chosen to leave the USSR while others have chosen to remain, but because under Soviet policy of the last decade only those groups have been allowed to leave. Therefore the ethnic imbalance of the emigration is as much a product of Soviet emigration policy as it is of feelings of social alienation on the part of those who have left. Second, when questioned about their emigration, the respondents cited a wide variety of reasons, many of them having little or nothing to do with the Soviet political system. Thus 23 percent gave as their primary reason for leaving the fact that they had relatives abroad or that they were following spouses, parents, or children who had decided to leave. Many of these "secondary migrants" left reluctantly, and some resent having been pulled along by the decisions of others ("I did not want to leave, but my children did, so what could I do?").

Another 23 percent cited their desire to live among people of their own ethnic group (among the Germans, 51 percent cited this reason). Despite the likelihood that many may have thought the interviewer was eager to hear about their dislike of the USSR, overall only 15 percent cited "political reasons" or "hatred of the Soviet system" as their reason for leaving. There was little variation on this score among the immigrants to Germany (12 percent), Israel (13 percent), or the United States (17 percent). Nearly one-fifth of the respondents gave such varied answers as to defy classification under common rubrics. These included such responses as: "Soviet life had become boring"; "My sister in Israel fell ill, and I felt I had to come and help her"; "I thought the Israeli climate would be good for my daughter's asthma"; "Everyone was going, so we went too"; "I was looking for something new in my life." While some of these reasons may seem trivial or frivolous, it should be remembered that travel abroad is nearly impossible for most Soviet people, and emigration becomes the only choice for people who in other countries would have other options. In sum, lacking reliable data on the Soviet population's attitude toward the system, it cannot be assumed that the attitudes of the emigrés are significantly more hostile than the general populace, and in our sample at least, alienation from the political system was by no means the primary reason for leaving the country.

THE SAMPLE

A total of 1,161 ex-Soviet citizens, almost all of whom had left the USSR in 1977-1980, were interviewed between April 1980 and March 1981. The interviews were conducted in Israel (N=590), the Federal Republic of Germany (N=100), and the United States (N=471). The sample was purposely drawn in line with some preliminary hypotheses so that a certain distribution by age, sex, education, nationality, and republic of residence could be achieved. Six hundred women and 561 men were interviewed, the youngest being 22 (to ensure that respondents would have had at least some personal dealings with Soviet bureaucracies). Most had reached maturity in the Stalinist and post-Stalinist eras.

Table 1

PERIOD OF BIRTH OF RESPONDENTS

1893-1917	1918-1929	1930-1939	1940-1949	1950-1959
173	195	259	320	214

About 40 percent of the Soviet immigrants to Israel and the United States have claimed some form of Soviet higher education, and this is reflected in the educational profile of our sample—47 percent of whom had higher education, with 38 percent having secondary schooling and 15 percent elementary schooling only. With regard to nationality, 77 percent (N=889) had been registered as Jews on their internal Soviet passports. (All Soviet citizens are classified officially by their ethnic group or "nationality.") There were 129 registered as Russians, 98 as Germans, 18 as Ukrainians, and 27 as other nationalities. The areas in which the respondents lived most of their lives are shown below:

Table 2

RESPONDENTS' AREA OF RESIDENCE IN USSR

RSFSR	Ukraine	Moldavia	Baltic[a]	Georgia	Central Asia[b]
330	247	120	174	120	165

[a]Latvia = 99; Lithuania = 49; Estonia = 26.

[b]Uzbekistan = 87; Kazakhstan = 39; Kirghizia and Turkmenistan = 25; Tajikistan = 14.

The men and women are quite evenly distributed by age and region, but males dominate the blue-collar professions and females the white-collar ones, despite very similar educational levels (48 percent of the men and 46 percent of the women have higher education). As might be expected, there are more young people from Georgia and Central Asia, where birth rates are higher, than from the other regions. Educational levels are highest among those from the RSFSR (69 percent have higher education—as do 72 percent of the ethnic Russians), followed by people from the Baltic, Ukraine, and Georgia. Those from Moldavia, where Jews are less urbanized than in any other European area, and from Central Asia have the lowest educational levels (23 percent of the Moldavian Jews and 18 percent of the Central Asians have higher education). They also have the lowest proportion of Communist Party members, although among ethnic Germans, where only 16 percent have higher education, there is only one ex-party member.

The respondents were interviewed in Russian or Georgian by native speakers. There were remarkably few refusals to be interviewed, though the average interview lasted between two and three hours. In addition to the standard questionnaire administered to the entire group, over forty "in-depth" interviews were conducted with people who themselves had been officials of the Soviet government agencies we investigated, or who seemed to have unusual *savoir-faire* and knowledge of how things were done in their respective republics.

GENERAL EVALUATIONS OF THE SOVIET BUREAUCRACY

Not surprisingly, the emigrés interviewed have a somewhat negative view of Soviet bureaucracy in general. Two-thirds think that most Soviet government offices do not "work as they should." They take a somewhat more charitable view of the workings of government offices in the countries to which they have immigrated.* Their most frequent complaints about bureaucracy in general focus on both structure and personnel; the main problems are said to be waste of time caused by the procedures, being shuffled back and forth among offices, and officials who do not want to understand them.† But it is not a strictly rational bureaucracy that they prefer. When asked whether they prefer the government official who treats everyone equally or the one who "treats each case individually, taking account of its special characteristics," over 60 percent preferred the latter in all circumstances, and the proportion among young people was even higher. The Europeans are most in favor of individualized treatment, while only slightly more than a third of the Central Asians prefer it. This preference is highly correlated with higher education. Because they are confident of their ability to deal with bureaucrats and to manipulate the system, the more highly educated prefer a more flexible system, whereas the less educated want equal treatment guaranteed to all, probably correctly assuming that they are not as likely to be treated well by a bureaucracy with room for maneuver as are their more educated counterparts.

Nine sets of seven adjectives, each ranging from a very positive to a very negative quality, were presented to the respondents, who

---

*Of those in Israel, 60 percent think government offices do not work as they should; of those in the Federal Republic of Germany, 38 percent; and of those in the United States, 25 percent (47 percent of the Americans expressed no opinion). In all cases, the more educated the immigrant, the more critical he is of the immigrant country's government offices. This is also true regarding the Soviet bureaucracy, except that those who were themselves its employees are more sympathetic to it than the (less educated) manual workers.

†Understandably, the less educated are most bothered by the necessity of filling out forms, while the most educated are most disturbed by the waste of time and failure of officials to understand them.

were then asked to indicate which adjective in each set they would use to describe "the majority of government officials in the USSR." From every set of adjectives, more people — though not a majority in all cases — favored terms near the negative end of the scale, though the modal response was in the middle.

In a further probe of generalized attitudes toward officialdom, respondents were asked to evaluate eleven occupations, including four kinds of officials. Employees of the Communist Party were ranked lowest of all the occupations, and officials of offices which assign housing were next lowest. Pension officials were seen more favorably, and those in charge of admissions to higher education were evaluated even more positively — outranking brigadiers and ordinary workers. Older, less educated people and Central Asians evaluated the officials more positively, and it was the Germans by far who took the dimmest view of Soviet officials.* As we shall see, among the agencies we have focussed on (which do not include the party), those dealing with housing were seen most negatively.

Thus while the overall disposition of the ex-Soviet citizens toward Soviet officials is generally negative, it is not undifferentiatedly so. People do distinguish among bureaucracies, and different groups of emigrés evaluate the bureaucracies differently. We shall explore this further by examining evaluations of particular bureaucracies and the methods Soviet citizens use to deal with them.

EVALUATING INDIVIDUAL AGENCIES

The emigrés were questioned in some detail about their experiences with certain Soviet bureaucracies, including agencies dealing with housing, employment, pensions, admission of students to institutions of higher learning, and assignment of jobs to them upon graduation.

The agencies which provide housing, most frequently the *zhilotdel* [housing department] of the local soviet, are evaluated most negatively, and those providing pensions, in almost all cases the *gorsobes* or *raisobes* [local or district social security administrations], are evaluated most positively. Understandably, a poor evaluation of an agency goes hand in hand with resorting to informal and even

---

*Thus 67 percent of the Germans rate housing officials negatively compared to 43 percent of the Jews; 87 percent of the Germans are negative on party officials compared to 45 percent of the Jews. Even pension officials are rated negatively by 61 percent of the Germans, but by only 34 percent of the Jews.

illegal methods of obtaining the services the agency is supposed to provide. Why does the housing sector get the worst marks and the pension agencies the best? In the absence of any evidence that employees in the housing field are less educated or less skilled than those in the pension area (what little information there is points in the opposite direction) or that the housing agencies are more poorly organized than the pension agencies (again the evidence points in the opposite direction), we must assume that it is the chronic housing shortage which makes for fewer satisfactory outcomes in the encounters between citizens and housing officials. As Henry Morton (1980) points out, despite the fact that since 1957 the USSR has been building 2.2 million housing units annually, in the mid-1970s the average per capita living space in urban areas was only eight square meters (ten in Moscow). An estimated 30 percent of urban households still shared apartments, and it is not uncommon for people to wait as long as ten years to get an apartment. Even getting on the waiting list is a problem because only those with less than a certain minimum living space (it varies from city to city) are eligible. (Twenty percent of our respondents had been on a waiting list for an apartment.) There are significant disparities in housing space across the republics, especially if measured on a per capita basis (Nechemias n.d.: 30-31). In the southern areas, particularly Central Asia, housing is a less critical problem, partly for climatic reasons. In addition, Central Asian houses, often privately owned, are built around courtyards, which increases the amount of space that can be used by a household. As Michael Rywkin points out, *per family* space is much higher in Uzbekistan than in the RSFSR, though per capita space is lower, and "a six-person family does not need exactly double the space of a three-person one" (1979: 5). Among our respondents, 86 percent of the Europeans had less than 60 meters of living space per household, whereas 64 percent of the Asians had more than 60 meters, and 36 percent had more than 100 meters. In Georgia, 74 percent had more than 60 meters! These differences probably explain why the Asians and Georgians are more kindly disposed toward housing officials than the Europeans, rating them higher on efficiency, fairness of treatment, and the efforts they make on behalf of clients.

Whereas housing is probably the most difficult thing for the typical citizen to obtain from the state, getting a pension seems to be a very routine procedure. Soviet pensions are not very generous, but people can retire earlier in the USSR than they can in most

Western countries, and some privileged groups—military officers, members of the Academy of Sciences, high party officials—receive handsome pensions (Madison 1968; Von Beyme 1981: 90; Matthews 1978). A Soviet observer points out that because the clientele of social security organs—the aged, sick, and disabled—are less able to defend themselves and frequently know less about their rights than younger and healthier citizens, social security employees need to have special sensitivity, conscientiousness, tact, and knowledge of legal intricacies, but that these qualities are often lacking (Maksimovskii 1974: 35). Other Soviet commentators are highly critical of social security employees and commiserate with their clients.* Our respondents take a much more benign view of the social security organs (70 percent of those who had dealings with them received old-age pensions, 21 percent disability pensions, and the rest other types of pensions). It is possible that old age, lack of education, and the realization of dependence induce a willingness to settle for whatever the state will provide, whereas the struggle for housing is carried on by younger people who are still trying to "make it" in society. But the contrasts in the evaluation of the two bureaucracies are too great to be strictly a function of different groups' stages in life. Pensions are simply granted more routinely than housing, and less informal manipulation is required to obtain a pension.

In Table 3, which shows overall evaluation by our respondents of five types of agencies, housing agencies clearly rank lowest of the five.

Respondents were also asked specific questions about their treatment by three agencies and their impressions of their operations and personnel. Had they been treated with respect? Did they think

---

*See, for example, Azarova (1979), who notes that more than two-thirds of district and city social security inspectors in the Russian Republic have no specialized education. She strongly criticizes red tape, "illegal acts of employees," and the process whereby citizens appeal the size of their pensions. She implies quite clearly that the administration of pensions in the USSR is inferior to that in other socialist countries, citing specific examples.

Similar criticisms are presented by Tarasova (1976) and Tosunian (1981: 11). Tosunian describes pension officials in this way: "For some, rudeness and caddishness are the way they treat all visitors. Others are polite, well-mannered, speak softly to everyone, but they are nevertheless capable of confusing the simplest cases. Many experienced employees are well-versed in the nuances of their job, but they use their knowledge, however strange it may sound, not to benefit but to harm their clients."

Table 3

OVERALL EVALUATION OF HOW AGENCIES
HANDLED RESPONDENTS' CASES
(*By percent*)

	Type of Agency				
Handling of Cases	Housing (N = 196)	Pension (N = 231)	*Raspredelenie*[a] (N = 314)	Jobs[b] (N = 832)	Admissions Committees in Higher Education (N = 597)
Very well	4.1%	8.2%	11.1%	9.4%	9.3%
Well	30.1	74.0	61.5	78.4	75.0
Poorly	48.5	14.7	18.2	8.4	12.0
Very poorly	17.3	3.0	9.2	3.8	3.7

[a]Job assignment to graduates of higher educational institutions.

[b]Jobs obtained other than through raspredelenie.

the agency operated efficiently and fairly? Was everyone treated equally? In Table 4 their responses are combined and compared.

On nearly every dimension, housing agencies rank lowest and pension agencies highest, with a very wide gap between the two. Perhaps it is inevitable that when an agency cannot satisfy the demands of most clients it will be thought of as inefficient, unfair, and biased. Whether or not the harsh judgment of the housing agencies is "objectively" justified is of little importance for our purposes, because we are dealing with the perceptions and evaluations of the clientele. Unsatisfactory outcomes breed negative images of the

Table 4

CHARACTERISTICS OF THREE AGENCIES AS SEEN BY RESPONDENTS

	Type of Agency		
Treatment	Housing	Raspredelenie	Pensions
Respectful	51% (N = 309)	80% (N = 299)	78% (N = 241)
Efficient	1% (N = 304)	53% (N = 277)	75% (N = 236)
Fair treatment given	10% (N = 296)	34% (N = 282)	NA
All are treated equally	9% (N = 257)	NA	74% (N = 171)

NOTE: The same questions were not asked about the other agencies in Table 3.

operation of an agency, and it is likely that even if the agency's operation and personnel could be objectively assessed, as long as it did not produce the hoped for results, clients would tend to blame the agency rather than the material constraints or high-level policy decisions (or both) that are chiefly responsible for the unsatisfactory outcomes.

In an attempt to make the respondents distinguish between a bureaucracy and its personnel, they were asked to broadly characterize those employed by the different agencies. Only 5 percent spoke of the housing personnel in explicitly positive terms. Another 10 percent observed that there were "all kinds of people" in the housing offices, but 23 percent spoke of them in strongly pejorative terms. The majority (54 percent) used expressions such as "ordinary bureaucrats," "usual Soviet employees," and other terms with mildly negative connotations. The pension officials were seen more positively, with 38 percent using explicitly positive adjectives to describe them and only 11 percent explicitly negative ones. But one-third did use mildly negative characterizations. Pressed to recall their personal experience with the officials, over 60 percent insisted that housing officials had done nothing at all for them or less than they were supposed to, whereas only 17 percent said that of pension officials. (Seventy-eight percent said the pension people had done just what was needed.) Not surprisingly, 86 percent thought the pension officials had been fair, but only 45 percent said that of housing officials. The great majority believe that *blat* [influence and favoritism], personal connections, and even bribery are the means by which the housing officials operate.

WORKING THE BUREAUCRACIES

Our interviews revealed that formal participation on the input side was regarded as having no effect on policy. Those who displayed less knowledge of the Soviet system were more sanguine about their ability to influence policy. The less educated are more likely to accept at face value what they are taught about how the system works (Gitelman 1982: 7-13; DiFranceisco and Gitelman 1984). Those who initiated contacts with the political authorities were no different from the others in their attitude toward the system as a whole. The contacts were made solely to secure private, individual benefits, not to influence policy, and did not signify a more positive evaluation of the Soviet system.

The form of political participation that primarily concerns us here is attempts by citizens to influence policy implementation by bureaucrats. We found three categories of administrative agencies: (1) bureaucracies toward which citizen initiative is unnecessary, because the agency is likely to produce the desired outcome with no special effort by the client (pension agencies), or useless, because the agency will not respond (the military); (2) agencies about which opinion is divided as to the best way to achieve the desired outcome (e.g., some suggested that traffic police could be persuaded by bribes, whereas others thought this would not work); (3) agencies whose routine workings were unlikely to produce the desired result without a special push by the citizen, which might involve illegal or semilegal methods (higher education admissions committees, housing agencies, hiring departments of enterprises, job assignment commissions [*raspredelenie*]).

How Soviet citizens attempt to influence the implementation of policy seems to vary primarily with their education and with the particular agency involved. Regional differences are not as great as might be supposed. Sex and age are not important in differentiating styles of confronting and dealing with the bureaucracy.

Respondents with higher education tend to be more assertive in the family, at school, and in the workplace than others with less education, but they do not present themselves as more assertive personalities (more self-assured, more decisive, preferring to be the boss, etc.). Thus higher education is linked to greater confidence in social situations, but not to more aggressive personalities. Self-confidence in social situations enters into bureaucratic encounters as well, as we saw when noting that those with higher education preferred individualized, not standardized, bureaucratic treatment. Seventy-four percent of the highly educated, but only 37 percent of the elementary school graduates, preferred individualized treatment. As an engineer from Kharkov expressed it: "Taking each case on its own merits means that the opportunity to use blat or *znakomstvo* [connections] is present, and that's the only way to survive in the USSR. In the United States, on the other hand, I prefer that state employees treat everyone the same." In the country of immigration, in other words, the engineer felt disadvantaged vis-à-vis the rest of the population and no longer had confidence in his ability to swing things his way in bureaucratic encounters. Less educated people defer to the status conferred on the official by his position, making no judgments about the person and hesitating to challenge the position.

The educated look at the person and calculate they can handle him because they are better educated.

However, this does not mean that the less educated will meekly accept whatever fate, speaking through the bureaucrat, ordains. Many people, irrespective of their educational background, try to influence the implementation of policy and the decisions of administrators. But the tactics of the highly and less educated differ. Less educated people are more inclined to bribery, while highly educated ones will pull strings and use personal connections to extract what they want from a bureaucracy. Obviously the highly educated are more likely to know people in high places, how to get to them, and how to approach them. This tactical difference has probably been the pattern in Russia and elsewhere for centuries; the best the peasant could do to gain the favor of the all-mighty official was to bring him a chicken or some moonshine, whereas the educated and the wealthy were more likely to mix socially with the official and, probably, his superiors.

Reading the Soviet press one gets the impression that bribery and corruption are concentrated in the southern and Central Asian republics. It is well known that corruption reached such proportions in Georgia and Azerbaizhan, involving the highest echelons, that in the 1970s the first secretaries of the party in each were purged, along with perhaps hundreds of associates. One might assume that in bureaucratic encounters in those areas there is perhaps a greater tendency to use illegal means than in other areas of the country.

Our data do not support this assumption. To be sure there are differences in style among people from different regions. Europeans are twice as likely as Georgians and Central Asians to initiate contacts with official bodies for the satisfaction of various claims. Georgians and Central Asians seem more passive and are more persuaded of the fairness of officials generally. Perhaps because of their lower educational levels, the political cultures of their regions, or both, the Central Asians and especially the Georgians place more emphasis on money and the role it can play in bureaucratic transactions. When asked what is the most important factor for success in the USSR, 12 to 18 percent of the Europeans and 21 percent of the Central Asians identified money, but 48 percent of the Georgians did so. Three-quarters of the Georgians thought it possible to bribe a policeman to forget a minor infraction, but only 51 percent of RSFSR residents thought so. Central Asians, Balts, and Moldavians resembled each other very closely on this question—about 64 percent of each thought a bribe would be possible—and those from Ukraine gave replies similar to the RSFSR group.

However, there was no significant variation by region in answer to the question of what proportion of Soviet empoyees take graft, nor was there any such variation in the responses to seven hypothetical situations in which respondents had to choose a course of action that they thought would have been effective. The possible actions included legal steps, appeals, looking for connections, bribery, and so on. In no situation was there a tendency for a particular regional group to recommend a course of action different from the other groups.

What emerges very clearly is that different agencies evoke different kinds of behavior on the part of the clients, probably not because of differences in the agencies themselves so much as in the nature of the services they provide. Let us look at some of the strategies used by citizens for particular agencies.

The scramble to obtain housing is a fairly general experience, and quite a few short stories, feuilletons, and even novels have been written on the subject (e.g., Plekhanov 1979: 12; Ianovskii 1967; *Pravda* 1979; *Sovetskaia rossia* 1979; Voinovich 1977). Small wonder that highly imaginative tactics are devised to obtain even the most modest apartments. An informant who worked in two housing administrations in Moscow in the late 1940s and 1950s, when housing was especially short, notes that bribery to obtain an apartment was so widespread that "people did not ask each other 'did you give?' but only 'how much?'" Party officials, those with "resonsible posts," those who had other favors to trade, and those who simply had relatives and friends working in the housing administration were advantaged in the struggle for a dwelling. Though the situation has improved markedly in recent decades, nearly two-thirds of our respondents report that they tried to advance their position on the waiting list either through appealing to a higher Soviet organ or, less frequently, using illegal tactics. The intervention of one's supervisor at work is often sought. Of those who went through the appeal process, just over half report that the appeal was successful and got them an apartment. Those who do not appeal successfully use other tactics, entering what Morton calls the "subsidiary housing market" (private rentals, cooperatives, exchanges of apartments and private houses).* Exchanging apartments is the remedy most often prescribed for those who have been unsuccessful in getting one from the official

*For colorful descriptions of how these operate, see Morton (1980: 242ff).

lists, but bribery is the second best. The official list is quite "flexible," as Soviet sources explain. "Too often the decisive factor is not the waiting list," *Pravda* commented, "but a sudden telephone call . . . after which they give the flats to the families of football players and the whole queue is pushed back" (16 February 1973; quoted in Morton 1980: 250). Even to purchase a cooperative apartment involves waiting lists.

Special types of bribery may be required in some cases. When a "Bukharan" Jewish woman from Tashkent applied for a co-op, the Uzbek clerk, who could not read Russian well, asked her to fill out an application and have it typed:

> When I brought the typed version I put a bottle of vodka on the desk. He didn't take money, only vodka. Uzbeks don't take money. They are very humane people. He took vodka because, as an Uzbek, he is not allowed to drink. He can't go into a store to buy vodka because the clerks are Uzbeks and it would be embarrassing. So they get vodka from us, the "foreigners."

Getting a pension rarely involves this much chicanery, although the press reports numerous instances of bureaucratic snafus connected with pensions, and there are occasional reports of pension officials making money from "dead souls" in the Gogolian tradition (*Trud* 1980). But some pensioners also monkey with the system, especially since many pensions are very low. (There are reports from Central Asia of pensions as low as 24 rubles a month, and many instances in the European USSR of pensions around 60 rubles, the latter being roughly one-third the average urban wage in the 1970s.) A bookkeeper from a small town in Moldavia explained that, because pensions are based on average salary in the last years of employment, "sometimes to help out a worker who was going on pension the administration would promote him to a vacancy with a higher pay scale, even if he was not qualified for the job." Bonuses and overtime pay would also be calculated into the figures for average salary in order to inflate the pension—all of which was assumed to be legal.

Getting into higher education is a far more complicated matter, especially for Jews in the periods 1945-1958 and from 1971 to the present. Though some respondents indicate that blat rather than bribery is used to gain entrance to higher education, two former members of admissions committees recall the widespread use of bribery, and one woman from the Ukraine frankly said that she was admitted only because her mother paid a 3,000 ruble bribe.

Another person who was on the admissions committee of a poly-technic institute in Leningrad reports that in his institution the bribes ran about 500 rubles, but into the thousands for the pediatric faculty and the First Medical Institute in Leningrad.

Other forms of chicanery are more prevalent. A Georgian Jew paid 100 rubles in Kulashi to have his nationality changed from Jew to Georgian so that he would be admitted to the pediatric institute in Leningrad. The trick having worked, he returned as a pediatrician to Kulashi, but when he tried to change his nation-ality back to Jew ("Everyone knew me there, and it was silly to be registered as a Georgian"), "the boys" demanded 200 rubles explaining that since the Jews were getting out of the country, it was now worth more to be a Jew! A Leningrad informant, who had been helped in getting into the school of his choice because he was a basketball player, reports that athletes and residents of Leningrad were favored for admission, as were children of faculty. Admissions committee members in Leningrad were instructed not to admit anyone to the journalism faculty without recommendations from the party *raikom* [district committee], and certain specialities, even in the philological faculty, were explicitly closed to Jews. In such cases, bribery, connections, and other tactics will work only very rarely, and excluded people learn quickly to give up on these institutions.

The other side of the coin is an "affirmative action" program designed to increase the number of natives in a republic's higher educational institutions. Prikhodko and Pan assert that "it is under-stood that in socialist societies objectively there can be no discrimi-nation against any national group. Soviet educational practice knows no such examples." At the same time, they say that "it must be assumed that the more the proportion of a nationality in higher education corresponds to its proportion in the population as a whole, the more the system of higher education lives up to the democratic ideal of equal educational opportunity for all people irrespective of nationality," and to achieve this "one can permit . . . conditional influence of a variable such as the nationality of an individual" on admissions decisions (1974: 70, 61). Indeed infor-mants from two cities in Moldavia report that in the 1970s they were told quite openly not to bother applying to Kishinev Poly-technical Institute because that was being reserved for ethnic Mol-davians. Central Asian respondents portray admissions officials desperately trying to fill ethnic quotas, and one woman draws a perhaps exaggerated picture of Uzbek officials scouring the country-side for young Uzbek women who could be persuaded to attend a pedagogical institute training music teachers for elementary schools. Other informants report that in the Ukraine and Moldavia rural students were favored for admission to institutes and were eagerly recruited, and this is confirmed by official sources.

For those departments and schools which are open to Jews, the way in is not always a direct one. A common practice is to hire a tutor for the applicant—not so much to prepare the applicant as to prepare the way with the admissions committee. Often the tutor is a member of the faculty, and he will see to it that his student gets in, sometimes by turning over some of his fees to his colleagues (reported in Moscow, Kharkov, Leningrad). One tutor told parents: "I'll get your child into the institute for 1,000 rubles. Give me 300 now and the rest only if he gets in." The advance was used to bribe clerks to put the child's name on the list of those admitted, bypassing the admissions committee, and then the rest was pocketed by the "fixer." One admissions committee member admitted frankly that he gave high-er admission grades to students who had been tutored by his friends.*

If citizens and members of admissions committees fool with the system, so of course does the party. A woman who taught in several pedagogical institutes reports that at the final meeting of the admis-sions committee a representative of the party raikom and another of the *obshchestvennost'* [public] (usually someone working with the party) would come and express their opinions freely. They would ensure that certain ethnic distributions were achieved and that certain individuals were admitted or turned down. In Kharkov, it is claimed, there are three lists of applicants: those who must be admitted, those who must not be, and the rest. The party does not directly participate in the admissions process, but does so indirectly by approving members of admissions committees, making up the aforementioned lists, and providing guidelines for admission policies.

The Soviet press does not hide the fact that the struggle for admission to higher education is a fierce one, and that all kinds of means are employed in it:

---

*Corruption is involved in admissions even to military schools. *Krasnaia zvezda*, in reporting a case where a general got his relatives admitted despite their poor grades, acknowledges it is not an isolated case: "When applications to the military school are being considered the admissions committee is besieged with phone calls. . . . There are really two competitions for admission: the regular competition and the competition of relatives" (Filatov 1980).

Every summer when the school graduates boom starts and the doors of *vuzy* [higher educational institutions] are blocked by lines of applicants, ripples of that wave sweep over editorial staffs as well. Parents and grandparents of school graduates call up and come in person (the person who failed the exams never comes). With great inspiration they tell what profound knowledge their child has, how diligent he was, how well he replied to each question, but the perfidy of the examiner was beyond all expectations. . . . The majority of complaints are quite just (Loginova 1980: 11).

The intelligentsia is especially anxious to have its children obtain higher education. In Azerbaizhan none other than the first secretary of the republic party organization, later a member of the Politburo, Gaidar Aliev, complained that in the law faculty of the local university "the overwhelming majority of the students are children of militia, procurators, judges, law professors, and employees of party and state organs . . . [raising] the threat of nepotism and 'patrimonialism' within the administrative organs." He also complained about the "fashion" in the 1960s of senior officials arranging to receive higher degrees, alluding sardonically to a popular saying that "A scholar you might not be, but a *kandidat* you surely must become."*

When a student graduates from an institute or university, a raspredelenie commission will normally assign the graduate his or her first job. Very often this is an undesirable position in an even less desirable location. For example, it is common practice to assign teachers or physicians (many of whom are single women) to rural areas in Siberia and Central Asia. To avoid such assignments, some take a job outside their fields, others arrange fictitious marriages with spouses who have residence permits in desirable locations, and many appeal the assignment and try to get a "free diploma"—that is, a diploma without a specific job assignment, which leaves them to their own devices. In only one instance were we told of a bribe being used (in the West Ukraine) to get a good assignment. Several informants reported being assigned to jobs in Central Asia only to find upon arrival that there was no need for them, the local institutions had not requested them, and the local authorities were not eager to have non-natives take jobs there. Despite the inconvenience, such contretemps were welcomed because they freed the person

*Interview in *Literaturnaia gazeta*, 18 November 1981, p. 10.

from the assignment. In 1979 nearly 30 percent of assigned jobs were not taken (*Uchitel'skaia gazeta* 1980), and in some rural areas the proportion of those who did not show up to their assignments was especially high.* Of course some graduates try to use blat to pull strings with the job assignment commission, and this is reported to work fairly well. The other use of blat is to get some "big boss" to specifically request the graduate as an employee of his institution.

Getting nonprofessional jobs is less complicated. The most frequent way of finding a job is through a friend or relative and, as in the United States, there are instances of three generations employed in the same factory. However, payoffs are sometimes involved. A former teacher from Transcarpathian Ukraine, who later worked in construction, found a teaching job in a small Ukrainian city, but the principal made it clear that a "tax" would have to be paid to him and other officials. (The tax was paid but returned within days because the "higher-ups" did not want the teacher employed under any circumstances.) For a construction job that paid 190 rubles a month, one man had to pay 260 rubles in advance, which was shared by the director, chief engineer, supplies chief, and other bosses in the *kombinat* [group of enterprises]. Thereafter a small sum was automatically deducted from his monthly pay which everyone understood was going to "the kombinat." This kombinat also had some "dead souls" on the payroll whose salaries went to people very much alive. When the man moved to Siberia, he found that practices were quite different. Money bribes were not needed in labor-hungry Siberia, and appreciation was expressed with a bottle of vodka at most.

Ethnicity is often a factor in employment. A former polytechnic instructor in Kharkov reports that in the school's personnel department he saw a list with each employee's nationality color-coded for quick recognition: red for Russians, green for Ukrainians, blue for Jews. In many regions people try to hire others of their own ethnic group. A Jewish dentist from Kokand (Uzbekistan) reports that because the dental polyclinics there were heavily staffed by Armenians and Jews, there was special pressure to hire Uzbeks. Only by pulling

---

*In Orel province in 1979 only 179 of 323 graduates of agricultural institutes showed up to their assigned jobs. Some "'signed in' only to vanish immediately afterward. . . . In all fairness it must be said that not all farm managers create proper conditions under which young specialists can work. . . . In other cases they simply 'forget' to provide them with apartments . . . leave them on their own to solve all the problems of everyday life" (Troian 1980).

strings did he get hired, and then only for a half-time job. He did not object, however, because under a *khozraschet* [cost accounting] system he was paid for full time; moreover, he could make substantial sums in private practice. As he put it: "Over there when you find a job you don't ask 'what will my salary be?' but 'how much will I have on the side?'" The likelihood of substantial illegal income made him avoid party membership, for which he was recommended, because a party member would have to be on his good behavior. So he claimed that his grandfather was fanatically religious and would not allow him to join the party. Significantly, this excuse was immediately accepted in Central Asia, where patriarchal family and religious traditions are more familiar than in the European areas.

Party membership can enter the picture in an important way. Party members are favored for employment in the First Departments [cadres] of enterprises, which work closely with the secret police, because they are considered "more reliable, unable to hurt the Soviet power, more suitable." However, for less skilled or less responsible jobs, party membership is irrelevant.

From our interviews and from Soviet official sources we learn that the same kinds of tactics are used by Soviet citizens interacting with bureaucracies other than those discussed here. Some agencies, like pension and military hierarchies, seem relatively immune to extra-legal and informal procedures, but with other agencies, bribery and especially the use of blat and *protektsiia* [influence] are so widespread that they are regularly condemned in the press. Protektsiia is said to be objectionable because it violates the socialist principle of "from each according to his capabilities, to each according to his work." On the practical level, it is said to reward the incompetent, discourage hard work and initiative, allow people to make buying and selling favors their profession, and promote calculations of self-interest "incompatible with communist morality" (Kiselev 1981: 152). The resort to protektsiia arises, it is suggested, because social norms are not well defined and because of the "underdevelopment of certain branches of the economy." The law is said to be too vague for curbing its use; unlike bribery, using it is not generally considered a crime unless "substantial harm is done to state or public interests, or to the rights of individuals" (154; see also Buachidze 1975: 12).

As this discussion implies, the use of protektsiia—and under certain circumstances, even of bribery—is socially acceptable and in line with age-old traditions in many areas of the USSR. In Georgia, birthdays, weddings, mourning rituals, the departure of young men to the army, and even funerals can be occasions for trading influence and subtle forms of bribery (Dzhafarli 1978: 72; Verbitsky 1981). Soviet authors decry such "survivals of the past," which are said to contradict "socialist morality and way of life." Some Western observers see not just "survivals" but a Soviet failure to resocialize the population to Marxist-Leninist norms. Thus one student of Soviet political culture asserts that "'New Soviet man,' in short, does not yet exist; Soviet citizens remain overwhelmingly the product of their historical experience rather than of Marxist-Leninist ideological training" (White 1979b: 49; 1979a). This is an exaggeration—there has been successful resocialization in many areas of life—but it is true that pre-revolutionary styles and practices survive in certain spheres, even among third- and fourth-generation Soviet citizens. The relationship between the government official and the citizen closely resembles pre-Communist forms in the USSR and other socialist countries. Kenneth Jowitt is correct in asserting that

> in their attempt to critically redefine society, Marxist-Leninist regimes simultaneously achieve basic, far-reaching, and decisive change in certain areas, allow for the maintenance of pre-revolutionary behavioral and attitudinal political postures in others, and unintentionally strengthen many traditional postures in what for the regime are often priority areas (1974: 1176).

Jowitt shows that in Romania, *pile* [pull, connections] is no less prevalent than blat in the USSR. These practices "obstruct the development of a political culture based on overt, public, cooperative, and rule-based relationships. Instead they reinforce the traditional community and regime political cultures with their stress on covert, personalized, hierarchical relationships involving complicity rather than public agreements" (1183; see also Christian 1982; Black 1960; Simmons 1955).

The prevalence of blat should not be attributed to some mystical staying power of pre-revolutionary political culture. Rather it is supported by present-day structural factors which are themselves continuations of tsarist practices. The highly centralized and hierarchical administrative structure of tsarist days has been continued and reinforced by its heirs, so the kind of tactics used to ameliorate the harshness of tsarist administration are well suited to the present day as well. In the absence of rational-legal authority and effective interest groups in both historical periods, the average citizen is without influence over policymaking and has little legal protection against administrative arbitrariness or even the mindless application of what is construed as the law. He is left to devise individual strategies and tactics which will not change the law but will, he hopes, turn its implementation in his favor. Each person is reduced to being a special pleader—not with those who make the rules but with those who are charged with applying and enforcing them.

CONCLUSION

In his encounters with the state welfare bureaucracy, the Soviet citizen seems to be at a disadvantage compared with his American counterpart. It is the bureaucrat who seems to be favored by the structure, laws, politics, economics, and culture of the system. But the citizen is not the helpless plaything of the bureaucrat. The citizen is sometimes able to marshal powerful resources to influence the implementation of policy if not the making of policy. So perhaps it is understandable that ex-Soviet citizens have fairly positive recollections of their personal experiences with the bureaucracy— more positive than their recollections of ritual participation on the input side. In fact the greater the number of bureaucratic experiences, the more positive the evaluation of the agencies involved (Gitelman 1982: 48). However, this evaluation is not transferred to the system as a whole (44ff). A cumulation of favorable experiences with agencies that deliver some of the most important goods and services does not lead to a positive attitude toward the Soviet political system. People do not judge a system solely by what they have obtained from it in the way of basic material necessities, or education, or employment. Perhaps the perception that approved forms of citizen political participation are a charade contributes to skepticism about the system as a whole.

Soviet people concentrate their efforts on the output side of the political equation—on the implementation of policy. Jerzy Wiatr, the Polish social scientist and party activist, suggests that Almond and Verba, in *The Civic Culture*, err in their "tendency to explain discrepancies between normative standards of democracy and political reality in terms of psychological deficiencies rather than structural conditions within the system" (1980: 116-17). Wiatr says that political apathy in Western democracies may reflect critical evaluations of the system, not personal deficiencies of the citizens. The point seems equally applicable to the Soviet

Union and other socialist countries. Rational political behavior in the USSR will involve pro forma participation in the system's rituals, occasional contacting of approved agencies in approved ways to influence policy implementation in individual cases, and more frequent transactions with officials charged with policy implementation. Ritualistic participation is rational not because it influences policy, but because it protects one against charges of nonconformity and "antisocial attitudes." For some it may provide emotional satisfaction, but for others the effect is to emphasize the gap between rhetoric and reality and to reinforce political cynicism.* Despite the Khrushchevian rhetoric of the "state of the whole people" succeeding the "dictatorship of the proletariat," only the formal franchise has been broadened in the last decades. Most citizens' ability to influence policy decisions, even indirectly, is practically nil. They do have some ability to influence the implementation of policy, but this can be done only on an *ad hoc* and *ad hominem* basis, so that no systemic effects and changes are felt. As Verba and Nie comment in their analysis of political participation in America:

> Particularized contacts can be effective for the individual contactor but they are inadequate as a guide to more general social policy. . . . The ability of the citizen to make himself heard . . . by contacting the officials . . . represents an important aspect of citizen control. Though such contacts may be important in filling the policy gaps and in adjusting policy to the individual, effective citizen control over governmental policy would be limited indeed if citizens related to their government only as isolated individuals concerned with their narrow parochial problems. The larger political questions would remain outside popular control. Therefore, though electoral mechanisms remain crude, they are the most effective for these purposes (1972: 113).

---

*Aryeh Unger's interviews with forty-six former Soviet political activists of the party and Komsomol lead him to conclude that "they did not believe their own participation to be effective. . . . The combination of compulsion and formalism which characterizes participation in the Komsomol and party arenas clearly provides no scope at all for the development of a sense of efficacy. Indeed, one may well hypothesize that it has the opposite effect, that the induction of the individual into the 'spectacle' of Komsomol and party activities impresses upon him the utter futility of his participation and in consequence produces not a sense of efficacy but of inefficacy, not subjective competence but subjective incompetence" (1981).

For the foreseeable future the "larger political questions" will remain the domain of the *verkhushka* [top elite]; it is left to the citizen to grapple as best he can with those "smaller" questions of daily life which he and those who administer the system must solve together.

REFERENCES

Armstrong, John A. 1965. "Sources of Administrative Behavior: Some Soviet and Western European Comparisons." *American Political Science Review* 59, 3 (September).

Azarova, E. 1979. "O zashchite pensionnykh prav grazhdan." *Sovetskoe gosudarstvo i pravo* 2.

Barry, Donald D. 1978. "Administrative Justice and Judicial Review in Soviet Administrative Law." In Barry et al., eds., pt. 2.

_____. 1979. "The Development of Soviet Administrative Procedure." In Barry et al., eds., pt. 3.

Barry, Donald D.; Feldbrugge, F. J. M.; Ginsburgs, George; and Maggs, Peter, eds. 1978-9. *Soviet Law after Stalin.* Alphen aan den Rijn: Sijthoff and Noordhoff.

Black, Cyril E., ed. 1960. *The Transformation of Russian Society.* Cambridge, MA: Harvard University Press.

Buachidze, Tengiz. 1975. "Protektsiia." *Literaturnaia gazeta*, January 12.

Christian, David. 1982. "The Supervisory Function in Russian and Soviet History." *Slavic Review* 41, 1 (Spring).

Deutscher, Isaac. 1965. *The Prophet Unarmed.* New York: Vintage.

DiFranceisco, Wayne, and Gitelman, Zvi. 1984. "Soviet Political Culture and 'Covert Participation' in Policy Implementation." *American Political Science Review* 78, 3 (September).

Dzhafarli, T. M. 1981. "Izuchenie obshchestvennogo mneniia—neobkhodimoe uslovie priniatiia pravil'nnykh reshenii." *Sotsiologicheskie issledovanie* 1.

Eilam, Yitzhak. 1978. "Shimush bekoakh etsel olai Maroko ve'etsel olai Gruzia" [Use of force among Moroccan and Georgian immigrants]. *Megamot* 24, 4 (August).

Eisinger, Peter. 1972. "The Pattern of Citizen Contacts with Urban Officials." In *People and Politics in Urban Society*, ed. H. Hahn. Beverly Hills: Sage.

Filatov, V. 1980. "Plemianniki: K chemu privodit protektsiia pri priëme v voennoe uchilishche." *Krasnaia zvezda*, November 12.

Friedgut, Theodore H. 1978. "Citizens and Soviets: Can Ivan Ivanovich Fight City Hall?" *Comparative Politics* 10, 4 (July).

Gitelman, Zvi. 1982. "Politics on the Output Side: Citizen-Bureaucrat Interaction in the USSR." Paper delivered at the annual meeting of the American Political Science Association, Denver.

Goodsell, Charles T., ed. 1981. *The Public Encounter: Where State and Citizen Meet.* Bloomington: Indiana University Press.

Hasenfeld, Yeheskel. 1978. "Client-Organization Relations: A Systems Perspective." In *The Management of Human Services*, eds. Rosemary Sarri and Yeheskel Hasenfeld. New York: Columbia University Press.

Hasenfeld, Yeheskel, and Steinmetz, Daniel. 1981. "Client-Official Encounters in Social Service Agencies." In Goodsell, ed.

Hegedus, Andras. 1976. *Socialism and Bureaucracy.* New York: St. Martins.

Ianovskii, Ia. 1967. " O sudebnoi praktike po grazhdansko-pravovym sporam mezhdu grazhdanami i zhilishchnostroitel'nymi kooperativami." *Sovetskoe gosudarstvo i pravo* 1.

Inkeles, Alex, and Bauer, Raymond. 1968. *The Soviet Citizen.* New York: Atheneum.

Jones, Bryan, et al. 1977. "Bureaucratic Response to Citizen-Initiated Contacts: Environmental Enforcement in Detroit." *American Political Science Review* 71 (March).

Jowitt, Kenneth. 1974. "An Organizational Approach to the Study of Political Culture in Marxist-Leninist Systems." *American Political Science Review* 68, 3 (September).

Katz, Daniel, et al. 1975. *Bureaucratic Encounters.* Ann Arbor: Institute for Social Research.

Kiselev, V. P. 1981. "O povyshenii deistvennosti prava v bor'be s protektsionizmom." *Sotsiologicheskie issledovanie* 1.

Loginova, N. 1980. "Chervi kozyri." *Literaturnaia gazeta*, January 23.

Madison, Bernice. 1968. *Social Welfare in the Soviet Union.* Stanford.

Maksimovskii, V. I. 1974. *Upravlenie sotsial'nym obespecheniem.* Moscow.

Matthews, Mervyn. 1978. *Privilege in the Soviet Union.* London.

Mladenka, Kenneth. 1981. "Citizen Demands and Urban Services: The Distribution of Bureaucratic Response in Chicago and Houston." *American Journal of Political Science* 25, 4 (November).

Morton, Henry W. 1980. "Who Gets What, When and How? Housing in the Soviet Union." *Soviet Studies* 32, 2 (April 1980).

Nechemias, Carol R. n.d. "Welfare in the USSR: Health Care, Housing and Personal Consumption." Unpublished.

Nelson, Barbara. 1981. "Client Evaluation of Social Programs." In Goodsell, ed.

Oliver, James H. 1969. "Citizen Demands and the Soviet Political System." *American Political Science Review* 63, 2 (June).

Pintner, Walter, and Rowney, Don Karl. 1980. *Russian Officialdom*. Chapel Hill: University of North Carolina Press.

Plekhanov, B. 1979. "Order na kvartiru." *Literaturnaia gazeta*, July 25.

Pravda. 1979. "Fiancees with Dowries." January 20. [Translated in *Current Digest of the Soviet Press* 31, 3 (February 14).]

Prikhodko, D. N., and Pan, V. V. 1974. *Obrazovenie i sotsial'nyi status lichnosti: tendentsii internatsionalizatsii i dukhovnaia kultura*. Tomsk: Izdatel'stvo Tomskogo Universiteta.

Rywkin, Michael. 1979. "Housing in Central Asia: Demography, Ownership, Tradition. The Uzbek Example." Kennan Institute for Advanced Russian Studies, Occasional Paper Number 82.

Sharp, Elaine B. 1982. "Citizen-Initiated Contacting of Government Officials and Socioeconomic Status: Determining the Relationship and Accounting for It." *American Political Science Review* 76, 1 (March).

Simmons, Ernest J., ed. 1955. *Continuity and Change in Russian and Soviet Thought*. Cambridge, MA: Harvard University Press.

Sovetskaia rossia. 1979. "Discussing an Urgent Problem: An Apartment for the Newlyweds." February 14. [Translated in *Current Digest of the Soviet Press* 31, 8 (March 21).]

Tarasova, V. A. 1976. "Okhrana subiektivnykh prav grazhdanin v oblasti pensionnogo obespechniia." *Sovetskoe gosudarstvo i pravo* 8.

Thomas, John Clayton. 1982. "Citizen-Initiated Contacts with Government Agencies: A Test of Three Theories." *American Journal of Political Science* 26, 3 (August).

Tosunian, Irina. 1981. "Vot dozhivëm do pensii." *Literaturnaia gazeta*, September 30: 11.

Troian, S. 1980. "They Never Arrived for Their Assigned Jobs." *Izvestiia*, June 11. [Translated in *Current Digest of the Soviet Press* 32, 23 (July 9).]

Trud. 1980. "Embezzlers." October 16. [Translated in *Current Digest of the Soviet Press* 32, 42 (November 19).]

Uchitel'skaia gazeta. 1980. January 15. [Translated in *Current Digest of the Soviet Press* 32, 6 (March 12): 9.]

Uibopuu, Henn-Jüri. 1978. "The Individual in Soviet Administrative Procedure." In Barry et al., eds., pt. 3.

Unger, Aryeh. 1981. "Political Participation in the USSR: YCL and CPSU." *Soviet Studies* 33, 1 (January).

Vedlitz, Arnold, et al. 1980. "Citizen Contacts with Local Governments: A Comparative View." *American Journal of Political Science* 24, 1 (February).

Verba, Sidney, and Nie, Norman. 1972. *Participation in America*. New York: Harper and Row.

Verbitsky, A. 1981. "Vziatki, vziatki, vziatki." *Novoe russkoe slovo*, August 4.

Voinovich, Vladimir. 1977. *The Ivankiad.* New York: Farrar, Straus and Giroux.

Von Beyme, Klaus. 1981. "Soviet Social Policy in Comparative Perspective." *International Political Science Review* 2, 1.

Weiss, Carol H. 1979. "Efforts at Bureaucratic Reform." In *Making Bureaucracies Work*, eds. Carol H. Weiss and Allen H. Barton. Beverly Hills: Sage.

White, Stephen. 1979a. *Political Culture and Soviet Politics.* New York: St. Martins.

_____. 1979b. "The USSR: Patterns of Autocracy and Industrialism." In *Political Culture and Political Change in Communist States*, eds. Archie Brown and Jack Gray. New York: Holmes and Meier.

Wiatr, Jerzy J. 1980. "The Civic Culture from a Marxist-Sociological Perspective." In *The Civic Culture Revisited*, eds. Gabriel Almond and Sidney Verba. Boston: Little, Brown.

CLIENT-ORGANIZATION ENCOUNTERS
IN THE U.S. SOCIAL WELFARE SECTOR

Yeheskel Hasenfeld and Mayer N. Zald

Within the immense diversity of programs and services in the social welfare sector in the United States there are enormous variations in client-organization relations, ranging from encounters with federal programs such as social security to private services such as psychotherapy. This diversity is increased by the heterogeneity of the citizens using the social welfare sector, who not only have a wide range of different problems and needs but also highly varied socio-demographic characteristics—all of which influence the encounters. Rather than attempt to describe all the many forms of bureaucratic relations, we shall present a general framework for analyzing client-organization encounters and apply it to major components of the social welfare sector—social security, public assistance, and mental health. Although our framework is used here to analyze bureaucratic-client encounters in the United States, it can also be applied to encounters in the Soviet Union and elsewhere.

There are two distinct approaches to the study of client-organization relations leading to opposing conclusions. One approach views social welfare services as "street-level bureaucracies" in which demand for services far outstrips supply, giving low-level staff considerable discretion in handling their clients (Lipsky 1980). Relying on case studies of selected organizations and encounters, studies using this approach emphasize inequities, favoritism, and alienation in client-organization encounters (Prottas 1979).

In contrast, studies which rely on surveys of clients and their perceptions of encounters present a different picture: clients are generally satisfied with their bureaucratic experiences and evaluate the encounters favorably. To quote Katz et al.:

Our data . . . contradict certain stereotypes about service bureaucracies. One of these commonly held beliefs is that bureaucratic encounters tend to be unpleasant and that clients are typically dissatisfied. Our results pointed in a more positive direction, with three-fourths of the respondents expressing satisfaction with their most important encounter (1974).

Both approaches have limitations. The street-level bureaucracy perspective is inherently antibureaucratic, and its case study methodology tends to seek out and magnify incidences of discord between clients and bureaucrats. The survey research methodology assumes that the bureaucracies are rational and guided by universalistic norms, and relying on client perceptions and attitudes may overstate their satisfaction. The framework we develop attempts to account for some of the differences in the two approaches, but we rely more heavily on the survey results because they permit us to compare responses across different components of the social welfare sector.

In Sections I and II below, we discuss a theory of bureaucratic encounters based upon social exchange—particularly power-dependence concepts. This theory assumes that bureaucratic control or power over clients is related to the control of vital goods or services which cannot be obtained elsewhere. To the extent that the client has alternative ways of procuring these goods or services, or controls resources (including enforceable legal rights) that can be brought to bear on the bureaucrat, the client gains control or power in relation to the bureaucrat. The bureaucratic encounter occurs in an organizational and societal context. Section II spells out the contextual variables that impinge upon power-dependence relations.

In Section III we show how these theoretical distinctions work themselves out in three sector areas—social security and pension programs, AFDC and public assistance, and mental health. Section IV briefly takes up the issue of citizenship rights and bureaucrats. Ever since T. H. Marshall wrote about the evolving nature of citizenship rights, we have been aware that the emergence of the welfare state ties the issues of citizenship and rights. We will want to examine, although briefly, how changing conceptions of enforceable rights in America impinge upon bureaucratic encounters.

I. POWER-DEPENDENCE IN CLIENT-ORGANIZATION RELATIONS

The nature of bureaucratic encounters of clients with welfare programs and services in the United States is shaped by the unique organizational characteristics of the American welfare state (Gronbjerg, Street, and Suttles 1978). First, it is a highly decentralized and fragmented system composed of disparate programs and services designed for special client groups. Second, it includes a mixture of means-tested and universal programs which are only loosely coordinated at the federal, state, and local levels. Third, it has multiple, often conflicting organizational arrangements for providing services, ranging from strictly public bureaucracies to private for-profit providers. Fourth, it is legitimated by the institutional norms of individualism and self-reliance.

In such a context, bureaucratic encounters can best be understood from a power-dependence perspective which acknowledges that their nature and outcomes are in part a function of the ability of citizens to mobilize power resources when dealing with bureaucrats. That is, client-organization relations in the U.S. welfare state can be seen as a series of transactions through which resources and services are exchanged. Both clients and organizations seek to obtain the resources or services in a manner which optimizes their payoffs and minimizes their costs. (When the conditions of the encounter are coercive, as in prisons, the coerced party can only attempt to minimize the costs as much as possible.) The ability of the client to obtain a favorable outcome is a function of the power-dependence relations between the client and the bureaucrat. Following Cook and Emerson (1978), we define the dependence of the client on the organization as a direct function of the desirability of the resources and services controlled by the organization and an inverse function of their availability elsewhere. Similarly, the dependence of the organization on the client is directly proportional to the organization's need for the client's resources and inversely proportional to their availability elsewhere.

In many service areas—for example, public assistance—the organization has a considerable power advantage over its clients because it monopolizes the services they need. Clients have few or no alternatives while the organization has many more potential clients than it can serve.

The power advantage human service organizations enjoy enables them to exercise considerable control over the recipients of their services. Moreover, they use this power advantage to shape staff-client transactions in such a way that the outcomes enhance their legitimation, flow of resources, and power. Put differently, when the service provision process is important to the political and economic life of the organization, it will attempt to use any power advantage over clients to promote its interests. For example, the organization may attempt to select clients who will enhance its reputation and facilitate legitimation and the mobilization of resources (Greenley and Kirk 1973). In the case of public assistance, it has been shown that during civil unrest or economic prosperity, it is in the interest of the organization's elite to expand the welfare rolls and relax application procedures. During economic decline, however, the elite will seek to reduce the rolls and tighten and restrict application procedures (Ritti and Hyman 1977). Professional groups within the organization may use the power advantage so that the outcomes of their transactions with clients confirm their professional ideologies and buttress their status (Freidson 1970). Finally, street-level bureaucrats may use the power advantage to improve their working conditions (Prottas 1979).

Clients who have a power advantage over the organization as a result of the resources they possess can similarly use it to control transactions with the organization to optimize their interests. In particular, such clients will be in a better position to make their personal goals more congruent with the organization's objectives and to control the transfers of resources and the outcomes of exchanges. For example, both the study by Clark (1956) of the adult education program and that by Zald and Denton (1963) of the YMCA indicate that as these organizations increased their dependence on income generated by clients, program changes occurred that more closely reflected clients' preferences. Rushing (1978) found that clients with greater resources were less likely to be committed involuntarily to mental hospitals. Similarly, patients from higher socioeconomic backgrounds tend in general to have access to better medical care than lower-class patients (Krause 1977). Powerful clients can also influence the patterns of their relations with the service providers: they tend to have access to better-trained staff and receive more prompt attention (Schwartz 1975).

One measure of the power advantage of a human service organization over its clients is the degree of discretion it has in making decisions about their lives (Gummer 1980; Handler 1973). Everything else being equal, the greater the discretion of the service providers to select courses of action on the basis of their own judgments, the greater their power over clients. Herein lies the essence of professional power. Their exercise of discretion permits the service providers, while attending to the needs of clients, to make decisions that promote their own interests, which may not be consonant with those of the client.

Where there is a power advantage, it is likely to be used as long as additional benefits can be obtained, but internal and external constraints help to limit the use of power in exchanges. Internal constraints emanate from the norms upheld by the organization that governs the exchange relations (Cook and Emerson 1978). The organization, for example, may uphold norms that stress fairness and equity, commitment to the needs of the client, and respect for the client's rights — norms typically embodied in a professional code of ethics. These restrain officials from using their power advantage beyond prescribed boundaries, and occasionally even lead to suspensions of rules in favor of the client. In a study of appeals to the Israeli Customs authorities, Danet (1973) found that while 70 percent of the clients were treated fairly, in a universalistic fashion, 29 percent received favorable judgments even though their claims lacked legal justification. These were immigrants who were seen as "underdogs" and powerless, but the authorities "gave them a break" to uphold a norm of helping immigrants integrate into Israeli society.

External constraints, particularly on the organization, are imposed through laws, statutes, and administrative regulations designed to protect the rights of clients. The Mental Health Code for the State of Michigan, for example, contains a Patient's Bill of Rights that is aimed at ensuring that patients receive appropriate and humane care. However, the protection of clients' rights is problematic (Handler 1979). First, clients who are mistreated must be aware of the legal remedies available to them, must anticipate that the benefits will outweigh the costs, and must have the resources to pursue them — obviously difficult for many clients. Second, administrative monitoring requires the formulation of explicit standards for the provision of services and effective information-gathering, both of which are problematic in human service organizations. Formulation of standards is not possible for many service technologies, and the discretion of line staff prevents collection of valid and reliable information. Third, the relations between monitoring agencies, service organizations, and clients are such that organizations have considerably more resources with which to influence the agencies and possibly coopt them.

II. THE CONTEXT OF CITIZENS' ENCOUNTERS

The power-dependence relations between clients and officials are shaped by the context in which they occur. The context refers to the macro-social structural conditions of a particular welfare sector which define the boundaries of the exchange relations and determine the amount of power each party can mobilize. We discuss four contextual variables: (a) social correlates of the demand, (b) structure of the welfare sector, (c) administration of the service delivery system, and (d) norms of the exchange.

A. SOCIAL CORRELATES OF DEMAND

The social correlates of the demand for specific welfare services define the characteristics of the publics initiating contacts with welfare programs and the personal resources they can mobilize. By demand we mean the goods and services deficit as defined by both clients and service providers. The incidence, frequency, and severity of the demand for various services is correlated with different socio-demographic characteristics of the potential recipients. Thus the socio-demographic characteristics associated with poverty define the potential recipients of public assistance or Supplemental Security Income. Overwhelmingly these are likely to be female heads of households, elderly, disabled, and minorities. In contrast, the demand for social security is obviously correlated with persons over the age of 65, but less with other social characteristics.

Second, expression of demand will be a function of citizenship rights and entitlements for the services of a welfare sector. Extension of citizenship rights and entitlements reduce class differences and reliance on personal resources, giving clients more power in the welfare sector. One measure of entitlement in the United States is the extent to which potential recipients perceive that they contribute to finance the services they seek. Hence persons seeking social security benefits perceive themselves to have greater entitlement than persons seeking public assistance, while persons seeking mental health services cannot claim entitlement unless they pay for them directly or through insurance.

Third, expression of demand is a function of public awareness. Greater public awareness of the services of a welfare sector increases the demand for them and improves the ability of clients to negotiate for them.

B. SECTOR STRUCTURE

The structure of the welfare sector determines the availability and accessibility of the services to the public. First, the *domain* and *mandate* given to the sector (which reflects its political legitimation) prescribes who "deserves" its services. To the extent that the sector defines a segment of the population needing its services as "undeserving," as in the case of public assistance, they are stripped of power in their bureaucratic encounters (Roth 1972).

Second, the *scarcity* or *munificence* of the services will influence the degree of public dependence on them. The greater the scarcity of the services, the greater the dependence of the public on the sector.

Third, the *centralization* or *decentralization* of control over the distribution of the services determines the ability of citizens to negotiate with the service providers. When the control is highly centralized, as in the case of social security, citizens have little if any room to negotiate with officials, and variation between officials is limited. When the control is highly diffused and fragmented, as in the case of mental health services, citizens have considerable room to negotiate, and the nature and quality of services they receive varies significantly with their ability to mobilize power and command resources.

C. SECTOR ADMINISTRATION

The aspect of sector administration we are interested in is the amount of discretion granted to officials: the greater their discretion, the greater their potential power advantage over clients. A key determinant of their discretion is the nature of the service technology. The more routinized the service technology, the less discretion officials have. For example, because the technology of determining social security benefits is highly routinized as compared to the technology of psychotherapy, the discretion of social security officials is minimal compared to the discretion granted to mental health workers.

Human service organizations have relied on professionalization to curb the potential abuses of discretion. Professional norms are assumed to protect the welfare of the clients and constrain officials from using their power advantage for personal or organizational gains. At the same time, the professionalization of staff increases their power over clients by virtue of their control over expertise and knowledge. Hence, although professionalization helps to ensure equity and fairness in the norms of the exchange, it also increases clients' dependence.

D. NORMS OF EXCHANGE

The norms of the exchange relations institutionalized in the welfare sector determine the extent to which power advantages or disparities can be exploited by either officials or citizens. First, to the extent that norms of equity and fairness are enforced in the sector, both officials and citizens are constrained in using their power advantages (Kroeger 1975). Second, to the extent that the norms of exchange stigmatize or degrade clients, they are put at a power disadvantage. Norms of exchange result in degradation when they impute moral inferiority to those seeking the service, as in the case of applicants for public assistance.

III. THE FRAMEWORK APPLIED: ENCOUNTERS
IN THREE SECTORS

Let us apply the framework developed above to encounters in three different sectors. We shall briefly review the nature of encounters within social security (OASDI), public assistance (AFDC and general assistance), and the mental health system. Figure 1 schematically locates program sectors on the contextual dimensions as discussed above.

Figure 1

A TYPOLOGY OF WELFARE SECTORS

Context	Welfare Sector		
	OASDI	Public Assistance	Mental Health
Social Correlates			
Class correlates	Low	High	Some
Citizenship rights	Full	Partial	Limited
Public awareness	High	Some	Low
Sector Structure			
Domain and mandate	Universal	Selective	Highly selective
Service scarcity	Low	High	High
Control over services	Centralized	Semi-centralized	Decentralized
Sector Administration			
Officials' discretion	None	Some	High
Professionalization	Low	Low	Varies
Norms of Exchange			
Equity and fairness	High	Partial	Minimal
Stigma	None	High	High

A. SOCIAL SECURITY ENCOUNTERS

Old Age, Survivors, and Disability Insurance (OASDI) is a bedrock program of the welfare state. It comes the closest of any welfare program to the ideal of universal coverage. It is given as a matter of "earned right." Financed by compulsory taxes on employees and employers, it covers about 95 percent of the civilian employed labor force (SSA 1980: 58). Self-employed domestic workers and farm workers were excluded in the early years, but the general trend has been to increase the range of populations covered. Sixty-three percent of retired Americans aged 65 and over say that social security benefits are their largest source of income (Harris and Associates 1981: 87).

For our purposes, the key points are that beneficiaries automatically qualify if they have a sufficient work-contribution history. The amount of benefits is fixed by formula and is somewhat redistributive. Workers with low earnings receive a higher benefit relative to their contribution than workers with higher earnings. There is no bureaucratic discretion in the allocation of amounts, nor is there state and local variation.

In short, the context of citizens' encounters with social security is such that it gives them considerable power vis-à-vis officials. Social security is only minimally class-differentiated, and citizens have high awareness of their full entitlement rights. The domain and mandate of the program is universal, and while there are projections of resource scarcity, citizens do not as yet experience any. Control over the program is highly centralized. The norms of exchange enforce a high degree of equity and fairness and include no stigma.

The "earned right" language and "insurance" metaphor of social security have led to a sense of citizen deservingness, of proper entitlement. It is not considered "welfare"—a dirty word. We do not know if the American public distinguishes "earned rights" from insurance, or if the majority recognizes that their contributions are not invested to return at time of retirement, but actually pay next year's beneficiaries. We do not know if the sense of entitlement is based on congressional guarantees, on citizens' perceptions of "forced" savings, or on bureaucratic behavior and the routine delivery of benefits.*

*For a discussion of the use of the insurance metaphor in institutional mythmaking in the Social Security Administration, see Cates (1983).

We do know that the system has large support and that clients in contact with the social security system are much more satisfied than clients in contact with public assistance. One clear indication of the accessibility of social security, and the power citizens feel in interacting with its officials, is the exceptionally high utilization rate. In contrast, Supplemental Security Insurance, which was federalized in 1972 as part of the Social Security Administration, has a considerably lower utilization rate—67 to 73 percent (Drazga, Upp, and Reno 1981). It has been suggested that the perceived stigma attached to the program, its means-test procedures, and lack of awareness of its existence contribute to the lower rate. So far, studies attempting to identify barriers to SSI utilization are inconclusive.

A study by Goodsell (1980) comparing client responses to social security, public assistance, and unemployment compensation clearly shows that citizens rate the quality of their encounters with social security to be superior to those with other programs by several indicators (see Table 1). These findings are replicated in

Table 1

PERCEPTIONS OF CLIENTS OF SUCCESS AND
PROGRAM RESPONSIVENESS

	Type of Program		
Proportion of Clients Who:	Social Security	Public Assistance	Unemployment Compensation
Achieved what they came for in encounter	85.0%	70.0%	68.8%
(Number)	(80)	(80)	(80)
		$[X^2 = 6.9, p = .03]$	
Argued with office personnel during encounter	2.5%	6.3%	11.3%
(Number)	(80)	(80)	(80)
		$[X^2 = 5.0, p = .08]$	
Agree that by and large government serves the public well	69.4%	45.7%	60.3%
(Number)	(72)	(70)	(73)
		$[X^2 = 8.3, p = 0.2]$	
Agree that the little man often gets pushed around by government	58.2%	73.6%	77.0%
(Number)	(67)	(72)	(74)
		$[X^2 = 6.6, p = .04]$	
Expect to remember something "really unpleasant" about the encounter	29.3%	50.9%	60.0%
(Number)	(41)	(53)	(40)
		$[X^2 = 8.2, p = .016]$	

Source: Goodsell (1980).

every study of citizens' evaluations of their experiences with social security. For example, in a study of a random sample of households in the Detroit SMSA conducted by Hasenfeld and Zald in 1983, respondents having bureaucratic encounters with either social security, unemployment compensation, or public assistance were asked to evaluate their experiences. The results are shown in Table 2, confirming Goodsell's earlier findings. Generally applicants perceive their experience with social security much more favorably than with public assistance, while unemployment compensation is rated in-between.

This is not to suggest that citizens' encounters with social security are devoid of difficulties. The complexity of the program is such that citizens may experience delays or errors in the processing of their claims, or they may try to manipulate officials by withholding certain information. Like all other welfare programs, social security regularly terminates benefits for a variety of reasons, such as remarriage or divorce, changes in disability status, death, and the like, and this results in occasional disputes. Nonetheless the program generally has widespread acceptance and legitimation.

B. PUBLIC ASSISTANCE ENCOUNTERS

Public assistance has been one of the most controversial and vilified welfare programs in the United States. Its critics on the

Table 2

PERCEPTION OF CLIENTS OF PROGRAM EFFECTIVENESS
(*By percent*)

	Type of Program		
Clients who agree:	Social Security	Public Assistance	Unemployment Compensation
Too much paperwork	31.6%	76.6%	41.9%
Clear rules and regulations	73.8	55.3	84.3
Office is well run	82.2	44.2	59.5
It took too much time	33.2	74.9	76.0
Officials made mistakes	15.0	61.0	47.6
Too much effort to get response	18.6	64.3	44.7
Officials are sincere	89.2	64.0	68.7
Reveal private information	17.0	68.8	19.2
Embarrassing to deal with	4.6	61.7	29.0
(Number)	(23)	(40)	(45)

Note: For all items, differences among programs are significant at .05 level or better.

right have seen it as a "haven for the chiselers and ripoff artists," while its critics on the left have viewed it as the vehicle of oppression of the poor, women, and minorities. In contrast to social security, entitlement rights are partial at best. Citizens must demonstrate "deservingness" and accept loss of personal liberties as preconditions for receipt of welfare. There is considerable public awareness of public assistance, but it tends to be negative, and public opinion polls persistently indicate that most citizens grant it reluctant legitimation and perceive it as an undue burden on the taxpayers.

Public assistance is targeted exclusively at the lowest socioeconomic groups. It is selective in the distribution of its services, making sure that only the "deserving poor" have access to them. Public assistance has always operated under conditions of extreme resource scarcity, which are particularly manifest at times of economic decline. Although control over the program has become more centralized, with the federal government setting elaborate national standards, state and local governments can still exercise considerable discretion in its administration. Several studies suggest that levels of AFDC grants as set by the states vary significantly and are influenced by both economic and political variables, including state wealth, education, population growth, minority populations, and racial insurgency (Tropman and Gordon 1978; Iams and Maniha 1980; Isaac and Kelley 1981). Efforts have been made to routinize the administration of public assistance (Pilliavin, Masters, and Corbett 1979); nonetheless, officials still exercise significant discretion, particularly in special grant components of public assistance.

Finally, while efforts have been made to increase the equity and fairness in the administration of public assistance, these have been partial at best. The program continues to stigmatize its recipients—a stigma reinforced by the mass media.

These contextual characteristics of public assistance foster conflict-ridden encounters between officials and recipients. The power-dependence relations are such that officials have considerable power over the recipients which can be used to intimidate and discourage potential and actual recipients. Although the use of public asssistance has risen dramatically in the 1970s (the number of recipients increased from 3 million in 1960 to over 10.3 million in 1979), numerous studies suggest that less than half of all persons eligible for public assistance actually receive it (Prottas 1981; Bendick 1979). The stigma attached to public assistance and the only partial granting of entitlement rights undoubtedly play a critical role in the underutilization of public assistance. As Hasenfeld and Steinmetz (1981) and Prottas (1981) argue, officials can use their power to establish numerous barriers to citizens' encounters. These include long waiting, public disclosure of intimate and private information, inability to comprehend bureaucratic procedures, and control over information. Bendick and Cantu (1978), for example, note that while 75 percent of all welfare applicants have reading skills no higher than eighth-grade level, only 11 percent of all welfare applications and documentation were accessible to persons with eighth-grade level education. Several case studies of client encounters with welfare officials suggest that officials may give preference to clients who are perceived as cooperative and nondemanding, and to clients who have significant bureaucratic experience (Prottas 1979).

Nonetheless, the power advantage of officials is checked. It is controlled by bureaucratic norms which stress universality and fairness. These norms, reinforced by legal protection of clients' rights, ensure that the potential abuse of discretion is minimized, albeit not eliminated. Hence Kroeger (1975) found that public assistance officials tend to adhere to these norms and avoid discrimination among their clients.

The ambivalence and potential conflict in these exchanges can be noted in studies of perceptions of clients and officials toward each other. Goodsell (1980) found that welfare officials attribute significantly less honesty to their clients than social security officials do (see Table 3). Studies of clients' perceptions of welfare officials (Katz et al. 1975; Goodsell 1980; Nelson 1979; Hasenfeld 1985)

Table 3

STAFF PERCEPTIONS OF CLIENTS' HONESTY
(*In percent*)

Degree of Clients' Honesty	Type of Program	
	Social Security	Public Assistance
Almost all honest	21.4%	10.7%
A majority honest	72.9	57.9
None honest	5.7	22.1
Few honest	0	7.1
Almost none honest	0	2.1
(Number)	(70)	(140)

Source: Goodsell (1980).

suggest that in comparison to social security officials, clients express less satisfaction with and perceive less helpfulness and less fairness by welfare officials (see Table 4). The difference in expression of complete satisfaction with social security as compared to welfare is approximately 20 to 35 percent; the differences in expression of helpfulness and fairness range from 15 to 20 percent.

The importance of the context of the program on its evaluation is well exemplified in the changes of clients' perceptions when old age assistance, aid to the blind, and aid to the permanently and totally disabled were replaced by SSI. As reported by Tissue (1978), feelings of stigma have declined significantly (from 22 to 9 percent in the case of old age assistance and from 34 to 14 percent in aid to blind and aid to disabled), and perception of responsiveness increased slightly.

Table 4

CLIENTS' PERCEPTIONS OF OFFICIALS
(In percent)

Perception	Program/Survey					
Satisfaction	Social Security			Welfare		
	Hasenfeld	Goodsell	Katz et al.[b]	Hasenfeld	Goodsell	Katz et al.[b]
Very satisfied	51.5%	68.4%	64.2%	15.3%	46.8%	27.2%
Fairly satisfied	30.8	16.5	29.7	33.1	24.7	34.0
Somewhat satisfied	15.7	6.3	3.5	23.3	6.5	18.4
Very dissatisfied	2.8	8.9	2.9	28.4	22.1	9.7
(Number)	(28)	(79)	(173)	(39)	(77)	(103)

Helpfulness	Social Security		Welfare	
	Goodsell	Nelson	Goodsell	Nelson
Very helpful	74.3%	75.3%	67.1%	59.6%
Some help	17.6	15.7	21.9	25.0
No help	8.1	9.0	11.0	15.4
(Number)	(74)	(223)	(73)	(188)

Fairness	Social Security			Welfare		
	Nelson	Katz et al.[b]	Goodsell[a]	Nelson	Katz et al.[b]	Goodsell[a]
Very fair	78.3%	87.3%	74.7%	58.2%	67.0%	61.3%
Somewhat fair	14.6	2.3	19.0	28.8	5.8	28.8
Unfair	7.1	4.6	6.3	13.0	23.3	10.0
(Number)	(212)	(45)	(79)	(184)	(103)	(80)

Source: Goodsell (1980); Katz et al. (1974); Nelson (1979); Hasenfeld (1985).
[a]Treated courteously.   [b]"Don't know" responses not included.

One might have expected that the differences noted in these studies would be even more pronounced given the personal duress of welfare clients and the presumed omnipotence and social control function of welfare officials. Of course it is quite possible that the initial expectations of welfare clients are considerably lower than clients of other social programs, thus muting the differences. Yet one should not underestimate the importance of the norms of universalism and fairness exercised by most welfare officials in controlling these exchange relations.

C. MENTAL HEALTH ENCOUNTERS: A SEMI-BUREAUCRATIC SYSTEM

We have included a discussion of client-bureaucratic encounters in the mental health system because it provides a sharp contrast with bureaucracies offering largely cash benefits. Services are diffuse, the total life-space of the client may be the focus of the services, and the nature and efficacy of the services it delivers are widely debated and rapidly changing.

Several features of the mental health system are worthy of note. First, it is highly decentralized and fragmented. Most states have departments of mental health and institutions that provide residential care, but until the passage of the Comprehensive Community Mental Health Center Act of 1963, the federal government had no role in the provision or regulation of local mental health services.

Second, a variety of public, not-for-profit, and private practitioners and agencies have provided overlapping mental health services, often in collaboration with or as alternatives for other institutions in the society—police, church, school systems—which deal with troubled people and proffer services to the same clients.

Third, in the area of mental health and illness, what should be treated, by whom, and with what techniques have been subjects of continuing debate, modification, and differentiation.

Finally, the mental health system historically has been heavily class-segmented. On the one hand, large public institutions were the reservoir for lower-class clientele and for the long-term treatment of the elderly; on the other hand, a private practice grew up to handle the middle and upper classes. Even within agencies outside hospitals, services have been allocated on a class basis, with the poor receiving lower quality services while upper-class clientele were treated by more experienced and prestigious therapists.*

*The classic work on class factors in the delivery of mental health service is Hollingshead and Redlich (1958).

Several trends can be observed in this area that bear on issues of client-bureaucratic encounters. Beginning in the 1950s, with the development of psychotropic drugs and the growth of an anti-institutional ideology, state mental hospitals have changed their function. They are used much less as holding facilities for the chronically mentally ill. Nursing homes and homes for the aged have absorbed the elderly from the mental hospitals, and community-based shelters provide care for the chronically mentally ill. As a differential set of institutions developed, the average number of patients in mental hospitals at any one time declined, while the total number of patients in hospitals during a year increased. Stated another way, more people are now being serviced in mental hospitals for shorter lengths of time.

The growth of medical insurance for psychiatric treatment that covers hospitalization and short-term care, and the rise in federal and state funding of community mental health centers and psychiatric beds in general hospitals, have led to an increase in local utilization. Table 5, which *excludes* the extraordinary growth of private treatment by individual practitioners, shows the enormous growth of non-institutional mental health treatment. There has been a vast increase in general hospital beds, outpatient clinics, and community mental health centers as auspices for the treatment of psychiatrically related problems since the 1950s (Kramer 1977).

Table 5

DISTRIBUTION OF INPATIENT AND OUTPATIENT CARE EPISODES
IN MENTAL HEALTH FACILITIES BY TYPE OF FACILITY:
UNITED STATES, 1955 AND 1973

Type of Facility	Year/Percent	
	1955	1973
State and county mental hospitals	49%	12%
Veterans' hospitals	5	4
Private mental hospitals	7	3
General hospital inpatient psychiatric units	16	9
Outpatient psychiatric units	23	49
Community mental health centers	N.A.	23
Total	100%	100%
(Number of episodes)	(1.7 million)	(5.2 million)

Source: Kramer (1977).

During the same period that this complex formal mental health system has emerged, the laws have changed so that citizens can now resist involuntary assignment in the system. The courts have restricted the ability of police and family to commit citizens to hospitals when they object. It is much more difficult to arrange an involuntary commitment today than it was through the 1950s.

The loosely defined nature of mental illness means that the state-supported mental health agencies regularly have responsibility for a range of problems of social and family behavior that defy precise legal definition. More than in any other area, the bureaucratic encounter here is subject to professional (as contrasted with legal) definition, and the services rendered are determined by the context of the agency. Client and workers interact around a problem or diagnosis. What they do in any specific instance is related to the agency's position in a network of local service agencies, including the state mental health system, as well as professional ideology and client readiness and interest. Table 6 indicates that outpatient settings

Table 6

DISTRIBUTION OF PATIENT CARE EPISODES
IN INPATIENT AND OUTPATIENT PSYCHIATRIC FACILITIES
BY SEX: UNITED STATES, 1971

Diagnosis	Inpatient Services		Outpatient Services	
	Males	Females	Males	Females
	Number of Episodes			
All disorders	933,316	759,436	1,111,260	1,205,494
	Percent Distribution of Episodes			
All disorders	100.0%	100.0%	100.0%	100.0%
Mental retardation	3.0	2.5	4.3	2.3
Organic brain syndromes	9.1	9.6	3.0	2.1
Schizophrenia	31.7	31.7	14.0	17.3
Depressive disorders	11.9	27.8	9.1	16.8
Other psychoses	1.3	2.0	0.9	2.0
Alcohol disorders	19.9	5.6	8.8	2.3
Drug disorders	5.1	2.7	3.2	1.1
All others[a]	15.0	16.2	45.0	44.6
Undiagnosed	3.0	1.9	12.7	11.5

Source: Kramer (1977).

[a]Includes paranoid states, neuroses (excluding depressive neurosis), personality disorders, sexual deviations, psychophysiologic disorders, transient situational disturbances, behavior disorders of childhood and adolescence, special symptoms not elsewhere classified, and social maladjustments without manifest psychiatric disorders.

handle an enormous range of personal troubles. Indeed it is clear that historically most people have used resources outside the formal mental health system when they were in need of help.

There are few good data at the national level about patterns of utilization and responsiveness of mental health resources. One exception is the national surveys on mental health in America reported by Veroff, Kulka, and Douvan (1981). They compared the readiness of Americans facing a nervous breakdown to seek and use professional help in 1957 and 1976. Over the two decades there was a substantial increase in the readiness to use formal help, suggesting that some of the barriers such as stigma and limited financial resources have been eased (*ibid.*, p. 79). Nonetheless, over 44 percent of the respondents in 1957 and 36 percent of the respondents in 1976 were unlikely to use formal help. The decline in resistance to use of professional help is evident in the findings presented in Table 7. Persons experiencing impending nervous breakdown were more likely to use mental health professionals in 1976 than in 1957. Ability to pay and availability of mental health resources were still significant factors in self-referral, but their importance declined somewhat in 1976. Per capita expenditures and facilities for mental

Table 7

SOURCES OF PROFESSIONAL HELP USED BY PEOPLE WHO FELT IMPENDING NERVOUS BREAKDOWN, 1957 AND 1976
(In percent)

Type of Professional Help	Year of Interview	
	1957	1976
Clergy	3%	3%
Doctor	77	52
Psychiatrist or psychoanalyst	4	18
Marriage counselor	--[b]	--
Other mental health source	3	10
Social service agency	--	--
Lawyer	1	--
Other	11	17
(Number)[a]	(231)	(227)

Source: Veroff et al. (1981: 137).

[a]Does not include 233 people in 1957 and 245 in 1976 who had felt an impending nervous breakdown but did not use any professional help.

[b]Less than one-half of one percent.

health care in the counties of residence were positively correlated with formal help-seeking behavior. Women, young people, and persons with higher levels of education were more likely to use formal help. The perceptions of helpfulness of professional help are shown in Table 8. In general, people tend to view professional help favorably, but those who went to marriage counselors and other mental health professionals were least approving of the help they received. Clergy and doctors remain the most favorably perceived helpers, but psychiatrists/psychologists were viewed as more helpful in 1976 than in 1957 and clergy as less helpful.

What can we say about citizenship and class as it affects this encounter between individual and agency? First, there is some evidence that the growth of community mental health centers and the private insurance funding of outpatient centers has made noninstitutional settings more available to the working classes and the poor. To put it differently, the availability of professional services for the nonpsychotic is greatly increased. Second, public mental hospitals remain the repository for long-term lower-class patients. Third, family resources make an enormous difference in the kinds of services received (Rushing 1978). Finally, the deinstitutionalization movement which has swept the country (Lerman 1982), coupled with the voluntary nature of the system, has led to an enormous range of services for the deinstitutionalized mental patient. On the one hand, some of these programs represent the best of the welfare state, aiming for the fullest inclusion of disabled people in the life of the community and helping them to function at their highest potential. On the other hand, because many communities resist the establishment of halfway houses in their neighborhoods, and provide inadequate resources for community-based programs, other groups of citizens are subject to the terror of encounters with one of our most vulnerable disorganized communities. A strange paradox has been created. The deinstitutionalization movement increases citizens' rights, decreases coercion, and increases the provision of humane programs, but it is also possible that it enables the state to abrogate its responsibilities to a poor and dependent population (Aviram and Segal 1977).

Overall it is difficult to generalize about bureaucratic encounters in the mental health system. There has been enormous growth, and new service technologies have emerged under a variety of auspices (public, private, not-for-profit). Citizen access has increased, coercion decreased. Yet the mental health system serves as a system of

Table 8

PERCEPTION OF HELPFULNESS OF TREATMENT BY SOURCE OF HELP, 1957 AND 1976

Perceived Helpfulness	Source of Help															
	Clergy		Doctor		Psychiatrist/ Psychologist		Marriage Counselor		Other Mental Health Source		Social Service Agency		Lawyer		Other	
	1957	1976	1957	1976	1957	1976	1957	1976	1957	1976	1957	1976	1957	1976	1957	1976
Helped, helped a lot	65%	58%	64%	64%	49%	62%	25%	25%	34%	46%	50%	42%	43%	43%	44%	55%
Helped (qualified)	13	22	12	15	13	14	8	24	27	25	36	26	33	29	29	24
Did not help	18	11	14	9	23	20	67	51	30	21	14	21	14	14	20	8
Don't know	--[a]	1	1	2	5	3	--	--	3	4	--	--	--	--	2	--
Not ascertained	4	8	9	10	10	1	--	--	6	4	--	11	10	14	5	13
Total	100%	100%	100%	100%	100%	100%	100%	100%	100%	100%	100%	100%	100%	100%	100%	100%
(Number)	(144)	(226)	(99)	(124)	(60)	(167)	(12)	(49)	(33)	(113)	(14)	(19)	(21)	(14)	(41)	(38)

Source: Veroff et al. (1981).

[a] Less than one-half of one percent.

social control for "troubled" people. Subtly, without clear legal mandate sometimes, it operates to serve people in need and people other agencies (juvenile courts, families, school systems) want it to serve. Since its technologies are obscure, it would be a mistake to assume that clients always get what they want or need. It would also be a mistake to assume that its officials and professional staff do not have broad discretion.

IV. LEGAL RIGHTS, ADMINISTRATIVE TASKS, AND CITIZENSHIP

The pattern of client-organization encounters is partly linked to legislative and judicial extensions of rights and entitlements. However, between broad constitutional provisions and legislative pronouncements about the rights of citizens and the duties of the state and the actual transaction of agencies with citizens lies a vast chasm. The extent to which the chasm is bridged in any specific policy area depends upon the interpretation of legislative enactments, adequate funding, administrative competence, court interpretations, and citizenship empowerment.

At least since T. H. Marshall (1965) wrote about it, sociologists have seen the extension of citizenship rights to the social welfare sector as part of the evolution of the modern state. But the extension and legalization of rights in America presents us with a crazy quilt. There are some dominant trends in the extension of rights, but they are uneven, and there are times in which we seem not to be extending rights but to be restricting them.

As legal commentators viewed the events of the 1960s, they began to discuss the "new property"—government entitlements which gave people claims on government services (Reich 1964, 1965). Under the Reagan administration, many of these entitlement programs have come under attack, and if not eliminated, have been curtailed. First, in the institutional sector of the welfare state—mental hospitals, institutions for the retarded, prisons, even schools—the courts have intruded deeply into the day-to-day functions of public facilities. For those institutions where clients are not of potential harm to society, the courts have moved to make the involuntary commitment and retention of clients more difficult. It is more difficult now than it was twenty years ago to deprive the noncriminal of his liberty. Second, the courts have mandated that citizens deprived of liberty by the state, or under the beneficent auspices of institutions, have not lost other civil liberties (rights of privacy, access to lawyers, freedom of religion, protection against use of unreasonable restraints, etc.). Finally, but to a lesser extent, the courts have imposed a positive burden on public institutions: not only must they provide minimum standards of care, but they must have programs to help clients achieve reasonable levels of social functioning. Mental hospitals are prohibited from overdosing clients; institutions for the mentally retarded are expected to teach them skills to enable them to function at higher levels. In some cases the courts have mandated specific plans for specific institutions.

Although changes in the court-interpreted legal doctrines protecting the rights of institutionally dependent populations are clear, no one knows how much these changes in law have led to "real" changes in the behavior of staff toward clients and in the outcomes for clients. While reports can be found on the impact of particular court decisions on the immediate case and parties involved, their impact as precedents in other jurisdictions and institutional settings will unfold over decades. It is probable that formal rights are more protected, but since courts do not control state and local government allocations, and since these governments have often been faced with budgetary deficits, the overall result may actually be a widespread deterioration in levels of service. For instance, in one case in Michigan we have followed, the Department of Mental Health was under court mandate to raise the number of staff at an institution for the adolescent retarded. It complied by transferring staff from other institutions that were not part of the original litigation, thereby weakening the programs at the other institutions.

A second trend involves the development of mechanisms of appeal in cases where clients have property rights in government programs. At one time, government grants were treated in law as gratuities, under the discretionary control of officials. Handler (1979) argues that the courts first treated government subsidies and licenses to business and professions as implied contracts. Thus businessmen and professionals had property rights, and therefore legal protection of due process as government agencies administered these entitlements. In *Goldberg* v. *Kelly* (1970) the Supreme Court extended these rights to social welfare programs. *Goldberg* v. *Kelly* and related cases have two major implications for the administration of social welfare programs. First, citizen rights are protected so that local administrative agencies cannot abrogate entitlements on grounds irrelevant to the specific legislative intent. For instance, citizens entitled to AFDC or food stamps cannot be cut off during the harvesting season because the local community wants to force workers into the fields. (States *can* set up workfare programs if they so desire.) Similarly, local agencies cannot abrogate civil liberties, such as rights to privacy, without following the due process procedures governing illegal searches and seizures (as used to occur during "midnight raids" looking for a man in a household receiving AFDC support).

Not only are agencies enjoined to protect the civil rights and civil liberties of citizens, but they must also provide for an appeals procedure against their decisions. Clients must have redress if they believe they are wrongfully being denied entitlements. The forms of those appeals vary enormously, including direct complaints to supervisors, legal-adversarial hearings in which witnesses are called, appointment of ombudsmen, class-action suits, and so on. Moreover, as Handler notes, the development of managerial controls may be encouraged to strengthen the hand of central officials in enforcing rules and limiting the discretion of line bureaucrats. The systems of appeal and enforcement vary in how active clients must be in order to protect their claims.

Handler argues that the protection of rights entitlements is easiest where eligibility is clear-cut (e.g, social security eligibility) as opposed to broadly defined (e.g., disability payments, where diagnosis is difficult), and where the good or service is easily divisible (e.g., social security) as opposed to difficult to divide (e.g., housing) (*ibid.*, pp. 44-45). In the case of housing, citizens are entitled to be placed upon waiting lists and to have the lists properly maintained, but not to housing itself. (Theoretically, housing is as divisible as social security. The real issue is not divisibility in this case, but how much of the good or service the state provides and what, if any, minimum amounts it requires. For example, if the states switched from providing housing to providing a housing subsidy, it would switch from a slightly divisible program to a fully divisible program. It would still have to face the question of how much subsidy to provide and at what cutoff point to allocate it.) Handler also argues that rights are better protected where clients have greater resources and are less dependent on officials; they are then more likely to use appeals procedures.

A final issue in understanding the interpenetration of citizenship rights and the welfare state in the American context concerns the interplay of racial and ethnic status as they affect the allocation of goods and services in universal and selective programs. Ethnic and racial statuses serve as both *de jure* and *de facto* citizenship markers. On the one hand, residents who have different de jure citizenship status because of legal or illegal entry have different claims upon welfare entitlement, whether or not they have paid taxes. In earlier times local jurisdictions have used race and class as de facto criteria for including or excluding groups on the welfare rolls. On the other hand, programs have been defined on a dimension of inclusiveness—roughly from universalistic entitlements to group-need definition of entitlements to individual means-tests. Since many programs vary widely in local and state administration (e.g., some states do not have AFDC-U programs, payment levels of AFDC programs vary greatly between states), and since states differ substantially in ethnic-racial composition, wide variations in the experience of bureaucratic encounters are inevitable. In one state a significant group of residents—Hispanics, for instance—may avoid the state apparatus for fear of being deported, while in others their own children have access to public schools.

It is clear that the leading monetary growth areas of the welfare state have been programs for the aged, and these programs have been universalistically administered and treated as full property rights. On the other hand, as the welfare state expanded in the 1960s to include a wide set of means-tested goods and services, issues of citizenship and property rights intersected with problems of distribution because of limited funding, which has led to a new set of conflicts over the nature of entitlements in the welfare state.

CONCLUSION

Bureaucratic encounters in America and elsewhere must be seen in the context of power-dependence relations. These relations are shaped by the structure of the law, the alternatives available to clients, the decentralization and centralization of bureaucratic functioning, the discretion or lack of discretion inherent in the delivery of the product, and factors affecting citizenship rights.

The "quality" of the bureaucratic encounter is a function of the ability of the welfare state to allocate goods and services (the social surplus generated through the political process) and the inclusiveness of citizenship claims. By inclusiveness we mean the range of functional responsibilities the state assumes and the universality of its coverage of these functions. But the state cannot deliver everything. Even if it funds a program, the link between program services and program goals may be obscure. There are limits to the effective delivery of services, and the attempt to mandate ambiguous services leads to Leviathan, even if it is a well-intentioned Leviathan.

Our analysis of power-dependence relations can be applied to bureaucratic relations in any sector, in any society. If admissions committees in hospitals or in higher education have discretion over decisions that allocate scarce goods, the power-dependence model should apply, whether in Cambridge, Massachusetts, Cambridge England, or Moscow. If the criteria for allocating housing are ambiguous and housing is in scarce supply, clients will distrust the system and attempt to manipulate the rules and the decisions to their advantage. In most societies, clients with more education and personal resources will be better able to work the system to their own advantage. In many ways our analysis cross-cuts those presented in other chapters in this volume. They have largely been concerned with the development and operation of specific social welfare systems. Here we have been concerned with the more abstract issue of the nature and quality of the bureaucratic encounter across such systems.

The mixed social welfare system of the United States almost always presents a large portion of its citizens with alternatives — the state is rarely the monopoly provider. For example, public housing is a small fraction of the housing market, public support for mental health is growing but is still a small portion of the total, and, as private pensions grow, social security provides a declining percentage of the income of the population over 65.

We suspect that for all the complaints about bureaucracy made by Americans, the welfare-state bureaucracy does not loom as large in the average American's life as it does in that of the average Western or Eastern European. Having said that, it is clear that different parts of the welfare state vary widely in their acceptance and their makeup. Consider social security and public assistance. The latter is stigmatized — the beneficiaries are the undeserving poor; the former benefits all of us. The quality of bureaucratic encounters is then a behavioral-policy manifestation of citizenship rights. When the polity is loath to grant those rights, we can see the political manifestation of conflicts of class, race, and ideology.

A central point of our argument has been that in none of the three areas we have examined can a static encounter be seen. Shaped by demographic trends, by transformations of technology, and by changing social policy, the bureaucratic encounters are a micro-manifestation of large social processes. They must be linked to the political economy of specific policy arenas and to larger trends in citizenship and the state.

REFERENCES

Aviram, U., and Segal, S. 1977. "Exclusion of the Mentally Ill: Reflections on an Old Problem in a New Context." *Archives of General Psychiatry* 29 (July): 126-31.

Bendick, Marc. 1979. "Why Do Persons Eligible for Public Assistance Fail to Enroll?" Washington, D.C.: The Urban Institute.

Bendick, M., and Cantu, M. G. 1978. "The Literacy of Welfare Clients." *Social Service Review* 52: 56-68.

Cates, J. 1983. *Insuring Inequality: Administrative Leadership in Social Security, 1935-54.* Ann Arbor: University of Michigan Press.

Clark, Burton R. 1956. *Adult Education in Transition.* Berkeley: University of California Press.

Cook, K., and Emerson, R. H. 1978. "Power, Equity and Commitment in Exchange Networks." *American Sociological Review* 43: 721-39.

Danet, B. 1973. "Giving the Underdog a Break." In *Bureaucracy and the Public*, eds. E. Katz and B. Danet, pp. 329-37. New York: Basic Books.

Drazga, L.; Upp, M.; and Reno, V. 1981. "Low Income Aged: Eligibility and Participation in S.S.I." *Social Security Bulletin* 44: 3-21.

Freidson, E. 1970. *Profession of Medicine.* New York: Dodd, Mead and Co.

Goodsell, Charles T. 1980. "Client Evaluation of Three Welfare Programs." *Administration and Society* 12: 123-36.

Gordon, L. K. 1975. "Bureaucratic Competence and Success in Dealing with Public Bureaucracies." *Social Problems* 23: 197-208.

Greenley, J. R., and Kirk, S. A. 1973. "Organizational Characteristics of Agencies and the Distribution of Services and Applicants." *Journal of Health and Social Behavior* 14: 70-79.

Gronbjerg, Kirsten; Street, David; and Suttles, Gerald D. 1978. *Poverty and Social Change.* Chicago: University of Chicago Press.

Gummer, Burton. 1980. "On Helping and Helplessness: The Structure of Discretion in the American Welfare System." *Social Service Review* 54: 59-75.

Handler, Joel. 1973. *The Coercive Social Worker.* Chicago: Markham.

_____. 1979. *Protecting the Social Service Client: Legal and Structural Controls on Official Discretion.* New York: Academic Press.

Harris, Louis, and Associates. 1981. *Aging in the Eighties: America in Transition.* Washington, D.C.: The National Council on the Aging.

Hasenfeld, Y. 1985. "Citizens' Encounters with Welfare State Bureaucracies." *Social Service Review* 59: 622-35.

Hasenfeld, Y., and Steinmetz, D. 1981. "Client-Official Encounters in Social Service Agencies." In *The Public Encounter*, ed. C. Goodsell, pp. 83-101. Bloomington: Indiana University Press.

Hollingshead, August, and Redlich, F. 1958. *Social Class and Mental Illness.* New York: John Wiley & Sons.

Iams, Howards, and Maniha, J. Kenneth. 1980. "The Welfare Threat Replicated, 1970-1975." Paper delivered at the annual meeting of the American Sociological Association.

Isaac, L., and Kelley, W. 1981. "Racial Insurgency, the State and Welfare Expansion." *American Journal of Sociology* 86: 459-89.

Katz, Daniel; Gutek, Barbara; Kahn, Robert; and Barton, Eugenia. 1974. *Bureaucratic Encounters: A Pilot Study in the Evaluation of Government Services.* Ann Arbor, MI: Institute on Social Research.

Kramer, M. 1977. "Psychiatric Services and the Changing Institutional Scene, 1950-1985." National Institute of Mental Health, Analytical and Special Study Reports, Series B., No. 12. Washington, D.C.

Krause, E. A. 1977. *Power and Illness.* New York: Elsevier.

Kroeger, N. 1975. "Bureaucracy, Social Exchange, and Benefits Received in a Public Assistance Agency." *Social Problems* 23: 182-96.

Lerman, Paul. 1982. *Deinstitutionalization and the Welfare State.* New Brunswick, NJ: Rutgers University Press.

Lipsky, Michael. 1980. *Street-Level Bureaucracy.* New York: Russell Sage Foundation.

Marshall, T. H. 1965. *Class, Citizenship and Social Development.* Garden City, NY: Doubleday & Co., Anchor Books.

Nelson, Barbara J. 1979. "Clients and Bureaucracies: Applicant Evaluation of Public Human Service and Benefit Programs." Paper presented to the American Political Science Association annual program meeting, Washington, D.C.

Pilliavin, I. S.; Masters, S.; and Corbett, T. 1979. *Administration and Organizational Influence on AFDC Case Decision Errors.* Madison, WI: Institute for Research on Poverty, University of Wisconsin.

Prottas, Jeffrey J. 1979. *People Processing: Street-Level Bureaucracy in Public Service Bureaucracies.* Lexington, MA: D. C. Heath.

_____. 1981. "Cost of Free Services: Organizational Impediments and Access to Public Services." *Public Administration Review* 41: 526-34.

Reich, Charles. 1964. "The New Property." *Yale Law Journal* 73: 133.

_____. 1965. "Individual Rights and Social Welfare: The Emerging Legal Issues." *Yale Law Journal* 74: 1245.

Ritti, R. R., and Hyman, D. W. 1977. "The Administration of Poverty: Lessons from the Welfare Explosion, 1967-1973." *Social Problems* 25: 157-75.

Roth, J. A. 1972. "Some Contingencies of the Moral Evaluation and Control of Clientele: The Care of the Hospital Emergency Service." *American Journal of Sociology* 77: 839-56.

Rushing, William. 1978. "Status Resources, Societal Reactions, and Mental Hospital Admission." *American Sociological Review* 43: 512-33.

Schwartz, B. 1975. *Queuing and Waiting.* Chicago: University of Chicago Press.

SSA [Social Security Administration]. 1980. *Social Security Bulletin: Annual Statistical Supplement, 1980.* Washington, D.C.: U.S. Department of Health and Human Services.

Tissue, Thomas. 1978. "Response to Recipiency under Public Assistance and SSI." *Social Security Bulletin* 38: 3-15.

Tropman, John E., and Gordon, Alan L. 1978. "The Welfare Threat: AFDC Coverage and Closeness in the American States." *Social Forces* 57: 697-712.

Veroff, Joseph; Kulka, Richard; and Douvan, Elizabeth. 1981. *Mental Health in America: Patterns of Help-Seeking from 1957 to 1976.* New York: Basic Books.

Zald, Mayer N., and Denton, Patricia. 1963. "From Evangelism to General Services: The Transformation of the YMCA." *Administrative Science Quarterly* 8: 214-34.

A SUMMARY VIEW OF

SOCIAL WELFARE

RETHINKING SOCIAL WELFARE:
THE UNITED STATES AND THE USSR
IN COMPARATIVE PERSPECTIVE

Alex Inkeles

INTRODUCTION

Late in November 1982 some ten experts on social welfare in the Soviet Union met with their opposite numbers who studied comparable issues in the United States and Europe to share their knowledge and experience. Everyone now recognizes that questions about the adequacy and the cost of social welfare are of crucial concern in all of the more industrialized countries. Social welfare, therefore, provides one of the best grounds for a comparative analysis of the United States and the Soviet Union—the two great national societies which dominate the world, but are served by political and economic systems so profoundly different that scholars are often discouraged from undertaking any systematic comparison of their institutions and their functioning.

The conference served the purpose of providing both comparison and contrast. By way of *similarity*, one could learn that the Soviet Union provides its citizens little that is innovative in the standard array of programs such as old-age pensions, disability payments, and the like. Another echo of something quite familiar to those knowing the demographic composition of poverty in the United States is the report that one-fourth of all the Soviet household units living below the poverty line were "working age, one parent, female-headed families" (Ofer and Vinokur 1988).* By way of *contrast*, a careful

*In the United States in 1982, about 46 percent of all households with incomes below the poverty level were in the category "families with female householder, no husband present." Many of these were, however, households of older women living alone. Making an adjustment for that fact, it seems likely that at least a quarter, perhaps one-third, of the U.S. households below poverty

The Russell Sage Foundation provided generous support in the final stages of the preparation of this report. Ms. Chikako Usui gave intelligent and effective research assistance.

listener would discover the rather notable fact that unemployment insurance is nonexistent in the USSR, excused by the fiction that there is no unemployment in that nominally socialist country.* And he would learn, perhaps to his surprise, that the USSR has in recent years spent only about 4 percent of the gross national product to run its health maintenance system, whereas in the United States in the same period, expenditures for medical care rose to almost 11 percent of the GNP, with per capita outlays in dollar terms at least fourteen times that spent in the Soviet Union.†

Going through the papers presented at this conference it is apparent, as it is in almost any other collection of its kind, that we have no end of numbers. What seems in short supply, however, are systematic conclusions about what the numbers mean. But one will not for very long work toward developing answers before realizing that the more fundamental problem resides in how we ask our questions to begin with. Moreover, the utility of the questions themselves depends on how we have conceptualized the realm we purport to be studying. Asked to present a summary of the conference, and to respond to the explicit and implicit challenge it raised, I found five issues of central importance. Most fundamental, we must

would fall in a category comparable to that referred to by Ofer and Vinokur as "working age, one parent, female-headed families" (see USDC 1985: 455, 458, t759, t765).

*Since there is no official recognition of unemployment in the Soviet Union, there is no way to determine how many persons are not employed but would be willing to work at jobs appropriate to their skill levels—a reasonable definition of unemployment. However, on any day in the Soviet Union there are large numbers who quit their jobs and others who are fired for various reasons. During the time these people are seeking other assignments, they are surely unemployed in the sense in which that term is used in other countries. The percent in this category at any moment, given the size and complexity of the Soviet labor force, can hardly be less than 1 percent. People who refuse to work at the job they have been assigned are called "parasites" in the Soviet Union, but they would be considered unemployed elsewhere. Finally, there are those who have asked to emigrate and are removed from their jobs—perhaps for years. They are also not considered unemployed in the USSR, although they would be so classified elsewhere.

†In 1982, according to Davis (1988), the per capita expenditure for health care in the USSR was 75 rubles. In the United States the figure was $1,365. At the official exchange rate of R1 = $1.26, the 75 rubles would equal $94.50. A more realistic rate of R1 = $0.70 puts the Soviet expenditure at $52.50. On that basis U.S. per capita expenditures were not fourteen but rather twenty-six times the Soviet.

more precisely delineate the realm we are exploring, providing a clearer conception of what is, or should be, meant by social welfare. Second, since we deal not with technical imperatives, but with social policy, we need to understand better how societies explain their policies—in short, we need to explicate the ideological justification mobilized for the adoption or neglect of given programs. Third, we need somehow to demystify the term *transfer*, so important in discussions of welfare, so that we know more fully who is exchanging what, with whom, for what, and when. Fourth, we need to be more aware of what we are doing when we create those ubiquitous measures of national "effort" as indicators of how far countries seem to exert themselves for their social welfare programs as against their other national goals. And, fifth, we need to clarify the degree and way in which welfare programs meet standards of equity, justice, and humanity.

A lack of sensitivity to these issues, and the failure to resolve them adequately, has led to misunderstanding and confusion in communication, and even to some distortion and misrepresentation in the presentation of factual material by otherwise objective and unprejudiced observers. To do anything like full justice to these issues would require a statement many times the length and complexity of what can be attempted in this report. But even a brief foray into this territory may contribute to identify its broad contours more accurately, and suggest the general direction in which one should go to map the territory in its full depth and breadth.

I. WHAT IS WELFARE?

When we deal with formal institutional arrangements, we become prisoners of history and hostages of convention. Almost all discussions of social security and social welfare programs refer back to Bismarck's first Prussian social insurance legislation in 1883. As other countries adopted similar programs, and as the coverage expanded from work injury to sickness and maternity benefits, and then old-age and survivors' insurance, the scope and scale of this activity attracted more attention from both governments and scholars, who came increasingly to identify a special realm of activity referred to as "social security programs," which in turn were taken to summarize "social welfare." Two elements of this outcome should be noted.

First, a major semantic confusion developed and became almost immutable. That confusion resided in the use of the term *social* to modify *welfare*. Actually all of the programs usually grouped under this heading were directed to changing the situation of the individual, not the community.* Unlike a program which might give a park to a community or build it a road, these programs gave individuals money to compensate for injuries or loss of wages, or gave them services, such as those of a doctor. Thus the programs were "social" and improved the community only in the sense that summing benefits across individuals expresses the condition of the community as a whole.†

Second, welfare came to be increasingly identified with government programs. What nongovernmental institutions and individuals did to advance welfare was systematically excluded, or at least was not regularly included, in the accounting that was increasingly done on a large scale. Of course it is important to know what role government is playing in the process of ensuring the individual's welfare, but the most fundamental need is for information about the sum total of the welfare-generating inputs each individual experiences. Once that was in hand, it would be possible to distinguish the sources for each element in the total flow of benefits enjoyed by each person.

There exists a wide, and indeed bewildering, array of definitions of social welfare and of the welfare state which presumably brings about the condition of individual well-being. Some of these conceptions include only certain elements while excluding others which the next analyst considers very important. Some analysts stress one or another mechanism purportedly designed to achieve a given welfare outcome, but fail to measure the outcome itself; others focus on the outcome, and largely *assume* the path leading to it. In general, it may be said that much more attention has been given to the structural and ideological roots of the welfare state, or to variations in the subprograms stressed in one or another

*In the German origin of the term *social insurance (sozial versicherung)*, "social" was not understood in the common English sense, but rather referred to a status group—for example, workers—which was being insured against specific risks, such as job-related injury, frequently run by that group. Some analysts argue that social refers to the provider of the service, not the recipient.

†Whatever the target and whoever the provider of welfare programs, there is no doubt their consequences include major effects on patterns of social life and political action (see Wilensky 1975, esp. ch. 5).

country, and much less to the effect all this spending has on real welfare.*

James Meade, for example, says that by social welfare he means "the taxation of incomes of the rich to subsidize, directly or indirectly, the incomes of the poor" (quoted in Wedderburn 1965: 128). By this criterion societies with a high degree of income equality, such as Sweden and the Soviet Union, would not be welfare states.† In those societies, what is quite properly called the welfare system acts in large part not so much to redistribute income as it does to manage for individuals, through taxation, their access to services, such as medical care, which they might otherwise be obliged to arrange on their own or through some collective but nonstate agency. Redistribution of income may certainly be a path to increased welfare, but a full-scale welfare state apparatus can exist in which redistribution of wealth is not a central feature.

A more common way of conceiving of welfare programs is to think of them as insurance against the unscheduled calamities which inevitably arise in the course of living. Thus Wedderburn speaks of the welfare state's commitment "to protect individuals against the hazards of incapacity for work arising through sickness, old age, and unemployment" (1965: 128). Rainwater, summarizing the European Community's definition of "social protection," characterizes it in similar terms, saying of most of its programs that "they have to do

---

*This point was made in a private communication from Harold Wilensky, whose own work constitutes one of the important exceptions to the characterization presented above. In a similar vein, Lee Rainwater notes that the research tradition of those working on both economic policy and social policy focusses mainly on institutional arrangements "rather than on the effects of these arrangements on the living conditions of their supposed beneficiaries." He goes on to note with approval Jean Marchal's statement: "What is needed is a theory of the total income of labor, a theory of wages in the widest sense" (1988: 283). Other efforts by Rainwater, Schmitter, Korpi, and Esping-Anderson to delineate and measure the effects of welfare programs on real welfare are discussed in Wilensky et al. (1985).

†Income equality is, of course, a relative measure. Income distribution may be more equal in the Soviet Union than in the United States, but there are still marked differences in income. It is not difficult for even the casual observer in the Soviet Union to meet persons who earn the minimum wage of 70 rubles per month and others who earn 700. In addition, perquisites such as automobiles and access to scarce goods can increase the effective spread further. Famous writers, actors, etc. may earn amounts which even by Western standards would be classified as "fortunes."

with an actual or threatened disruption of the normal flow of income to a family" (1988: 281).

This conception also omits a great deal which others include in their definitions of welfare programs; moreover it fails to describe accurately the very programs it purports to characterize. Unemployment insurance and sickness pay do replace lost income, but the largest part of the medical care provided by social welfare programs is not a substitute for any normal flow of income. It provides rather a general service, and the largest expense is often for the elderly, who are no longer working. Family allowances, often an important element of government welfare programs, are also not connected with any disruption of income, or indeed with any special hazard, unless the arrival of a child be so conceived. Neither is education a special hazard or an unexpected risk, yet in the view of many it is arguably the most important welfare service offered by the state. Certainly it is the most widespread.

In still another conception, welfare programs are viewed not as designed to ensure minimum standards but rather to achieve equality. In this perspective welfare programs are meant to ensure "that all citizens without distinction of status or class are offered the best standards available in relation to a certain agreed range of social services" (Asa Briggs; quoted in Wedderburn 1965: 128). Such a principle of equal treatment has obvious appeal in the case of medical care, and is more or less effectively embodied in the structure of those systems which are true national health services. The more populist democratic societies are more likely to uphold this principle with regard to education as well. Beyond medicine and possibly education, however, even the most notable of welfare states do not seem inclined to press for this principle in other realms such as housing, where the insurance of a "minimum" rather than the "best" standard is more often the goal of government welfare programs.

Whether the emphasis is on hazards, minimums, or standards, welfare outcomes need not be the exclusive responsibility of the state. Many of these same goals may be attained by other institutions, notably by employer corporations and enterprises, and they may also be achieved by the collective or cooperative activity of groups of individuals, as through trade unions or associations of consumers.* In addition, although the idea is anathema in some

---

*In a personal communication responding to this passage, Harold Wilensky writes: "I do not know of any serious student of the welfare state who fails to recognize that these government programs often have their counterpart in cash

quarters, protection against hazards and the assurance of minimum standards can be attained by individuals taking out privately purchased insurance—as people do to protect against fire and as a support in case of accidental or sudden death. Finally, there is some role to be played by personal savings as a cushion against interrupted flows of earnings, illness, and other hazards of living. This approach is of less appeal in the consumerist societies such as the United States, but is more or less the norm in Japan.

In our view, welfare cannot be estimated by looking at government programs only. It must take account of other institutions outside government, and weigh in the collective and personal resources people can bring to bear on their condition. Otherwise we are confusing the means to achieve welfare with the level of welfare actually achieved in a society. Indeed it is an anomaly that after one hundred years of struggle by organized labor to achieve a more nearly adequate wage has been more or less crowned by success, so many analyses of the workers' situation focus not on the basic wage this struggle has won, but concentrate rather on the 20 or 30 percent of labor's income which it gets through public or government welfare programs.

Our attention should not be limited to situations of crisis, important as these may be as a special case, but should also take account of the availability of necessary and desirable goods and services provided in the normal course of events. Furthermore, the goods and services considered should not be limited by one or another arbitrary convention, but should be as broad as possible. Social welfare, then, might be represented and expressed by the total supply of goods and services sustaining and enhancing life which is available to the typical citizen of a given society at a particular time.

This view is not the conventional one. It is, however, one also espoused in other quarters. For example Wolfgang Zapf, a leading German student of comparative welfare systems, has said:

> I am thinking of welfare as being, basically, a consumption concept, meaning the objective and subjective (perceived) need satisfaction

or services delivered by corporations, unions, and voluntary associations, and families." His point can be granted, but such awareness does not ensure that in their analyses scholars will include nongovernmental sources of support when calculating the total package of welfare-generating resources available to each individual. In any event the passage is meant not as a judgment of work already done, but rather to propose a more inclusive concept of welfare to guide future efforts.

that one gets out of the input of goods and services. It is not necessarily an individualistic concept, because it also makes sense to speak of the "state of the nation" or the "health of a neighborhood". . . . Welfare production, instead, refers to the providers of those goods of which the welfare state is one very prominent unit. . . . Suffice it to say that the very notion of welfare comprises a decent supply of goods as well as its positive cognitive and affective evaluation as well-being (1980).

What a measure of welfare so conceived would be like presents a challenge to which we shall return at a later point.

II. IDEAS AND IDEOLOGIES

Answers to the question "What is social welfare?" are likely to reflect an ideological position. Social scientists weave these ideologies into the theoretical frameworks they elaborate, and international civil servants build them into the measurements they make for UNESCO or the World Bank. Such ideologies may be publicly enunciated by political philosophers and by governments and their official spokesmen. The latter may espouse them in policy directives, enshrine them in constitutions, or embed them in the preambles of major legislation. As for ordinary citizens, they may share and internalize the justifications offered in the official ideology, or they may hold rather different views as to what welfare should be in theory and actually is in practice. Moreover, both officials and citizens may present in public views which differ from those they hold in private. In short, there are always overt and covert ideologies.

The participants in the Berkeley conference gave relatively little attention to the formal ideologies of social welfare enunciated in the United States and the USSR. Perhaps they were guided in this by a professional skepticism based on their awareness that these formal ideologies are not very good guides to what is actually practiced. The U.S. Constitution and its appended Bill of Rights, even as progressively amended, gives no hint of the vast welfare apparatus that has been built up under its authority. The Soviet Constitution, for its part, proclaimed in 1936 that "citizens . . . have a right to material security in old age, as well as in the event of sickness and loss of ability to work." However, no provision was made for an objective review of the grievances of those whose right was seriously eroded by administrative practice. It was not until the 1977 Constitution that such aggrieved persons gained the right to a court review of their complaints, and as of 1987 this right had not yet been implemented by any practical measure to make possible such court action.

Constitutions and proclamations aside, both societies have developed broadly the same array of programs to ensure their citizens' welfare. Although there are important differences in how the programs are financed and administered, many of those features may also be described as broadly comparable. Moreover, where there are notable contrasts in the programs provided, the dominant overt ideology of each country would be of little help in predicting the differences between the two systems. Consider, for example, the American emphasis on individualism and the responsibility each citizen has to provide for himself, and contrast that ideology with the Soviet system's claim to be the prime protector of the interests of the working class. Given this contrast, one would hardly predict that it is the United States which provides extensive benefits for the unemployed worker whereas the USSR does not allow the Soviet worker even one day of unemployment insurance pay.

We would be equally hard put to explain the absence of a general family allowance program in the United States. Such programs were adopted by fifteen of twenty leading industrial nations by 1950, and by 1979 by nineteen of them, leaving only the United States outside the club. Some have sought to explain this by claiming it expresses an American ideology. It is a matter of principle with Americans, they say, that no welfare program will be funded except on the basis of special need (as in the case of disabled children) or on the basis of some form of prepayment (as in the case of unemployment insurance). Yet if such an ideology were really operative, it would not be the case that every child in the United States, without any test of means or proof of special need, can lay claim to a basic education and have that claim validated by statute and by the extension of constitutional guarantees.*

*In his analysis of how ideas relate to welfare policy in five leading Western democracies, Anthony King (1973) recognizes the challenge to ideological explanations posed by America's deep commitment to public education. The main explanation for the allegedly limited degree of social welfare in the United States, he argues, lies in the suspicion of government and the feeling it should be a referee but not a manager. To explain the society's commitment to schooling for all children, he falls back on a second value—equality—but this raises a new challenge. If U.S. citizens believe so much in equality, why do they not approach other welfare realms beyond education in the same spirit?

This is not to say, however, that unspoken rules and *covert* ideologies do not play a considerable role in deciding which programs are adopted, and perhaps even more important, how the rules governing eligibility and the extent of coverage are written and interpreted. In this connection, Bernice Madison's (1988) analysis of the operation of the Soviet pension system is revealing. She notes that the Soviet government's formal ideology claims that the individual's right to welfare is a special boon provided by his citizenship in a socialist society. Indeed, Article 43 of the current Soviet Constitution affirms that right.* Despite this formal ideology, Madison suggests, the structure of the Soviet welfare system is best understood as reflecting the present regime's marked "tilt toward the production goal," and its operating principle is that "everybody who can should work." Implementing this principle means that voluntary unemployment is ruled out, that monetary and other supports are made conditional on work, and that pure welfare can be given only as a last resort. Faced with a persistent and severe shortage of labor, the regime has fashioned a welfare system mainly designed to keep the population at work and working. Such a system, Madison notes, will show relatively less interest in the totally disabled and the very old, and will concentrate its medical care, above all other groups, on those capable of work.†

In the American case, the contrast between an expressed ideology and unexpressed practical considerations can be illustrated by the old-age security system. The original social security legislation affirmed the right of Americans to a dignified old age, and said nothing about the importance of solving the problem of mass unemployment. Yet many interpretations of the practical politics of the period argue that at the time the social security legislation was adopted, it was in good part a response to the difficulty the American economy was having in providing jobs for the unemployed. One partial solution was to retire older workers, supporting them through

*In the language of the 1977 Constitution, which is similar to that of 1936, citizens have "the right to maintenance in old age, sickness, and in the event of complete or partial disability or loss of the breadwinner."

†It should be noted that Davis (1988), in his analysis of the Soviet health care system, reaches conclusions very much like those of Madison. In similar fashion, Ofer and Vinokur sum up Soviet policy in the following set of principles: "Everybody who can work should work; involuntary unemployment is ruled out; nonmonetary and other support should be conditioned on work and as much as possible attached to wages; pure welfare, like children allowances and income supplements, should come only as a help of last resort" (1988).

social security, and ensuring they would stay out of the overburdened labor market by making their receipt of social security benefits contingent on not working.*

Governments have their ideas and ideologies, and the people have their own, and the two are not necessarily congruent. Thus Soviet ideology, as noted, treats old-age pensions as a "gift"—a reward for carrying out the duty to work—but not as a "payment for work done." Soviet citizens evidently perceive the situation quite differently. As Madison (1988: 176) noted in her interviews with former Soviet citizens, 91 percent were convinced that they had paid for their pensions in advance, both by receiving low wages over many years of hard work and by the taxes they had paid over those same years.

There is a comparable difference of perception in the United States concerning old-age social security benefits. The government and virtually all economists recognize that the social security system is not truly a funded insurance program, and that pensions are financed mainly out of current taxes or as a general obligation of the state. However, the typical U.S. citizen, having made mandatory social security payments through most of his working life, tends to see his pension as analogous to an annuity he might have bought by some alternative arrangement—for example, by regular payments to an insurance company. This illusion was evidently shared, perhaps contributed to, by President Franklin Roosevelt, who said of the system he did so much to create: "We put those payroll contributions there so as to give the contributors a legal, moral, and political right to collect their pension and employment benefits. With those taxes in there, no damn politician can ever scrap my social security program" (quoted in Peters and Heisler 1983: 182).

These examples indicate that we have much to learn about the ways in which formal and informal ideologies held by politicians, bureaucrats, and ordinary citizens interact with the making of policy

---

*Rita Ricardo Campbell offers this explanation: "Social security began in the 1930s when the nation was in the Great Depression. At that time, labor union leaders believed that if more individuals retired, there would be more jobs available for the unemployed. Administration economists believed that an excessive personal savings rate (i.e., one larger than the investment rate) was one of the obstacles in the path to full employment and economic recovery. Compulsory savings under a social security program, they reasoned, would in the future reduce voluntary private savings by reducing individual responsibility to save or otherwise provide for retirement. Less saving and thus more spending was to stimulate the economy" (1977: xiv).

concerning social welfare programs, and with the implementation of such programs as are enacted. A theory about special interests and a methodology for studying interest articulation in the political process should surely be elements of our analysis, but it also requires sensitivity to the role of values, of concepts of what is just and fair, of ideas about the social contract, and of the social memory as they express themselves in public action.

Some significant efforts have been made to bring a number of these perspectives to bear on explanations of the similarities and differences in national approaches to welfare policy. Anthony King, for example, tried to weigh the simultaneous influence of elites, the nature of popular demands, the role of interest groups, and the resistance of institutions in shaping the welfare policies of five leading industrial democracies. He found U.S. policy to be distinctive, and concluded that it was none of these factors but rather "differences in *belief* and *assumptions* that accounted for the American pattern" (1973: 422-23; italics added). Basing his views on the results of a systematic comparison of public opinion survey data, Harold Wilensky challenges this conclusion, arguing that in the face of the evidence "the myth of American exceptionalism crumbles" (1980: xi). Richard Coughlin, author of the study on which Wilensky bases his conclusion, is more cautious. He indeed finds that "the structure of public attitudes, beliefs, and opinions concerning the principles and programs of social policy is broadly similar" in the eight rich countries he studied, but he also finds numerous exceptions to the general agreement. These, he feels, might be explained by the interaction of national ideological climates with historically shaped political and economic factors. Such interactions can produce distinctive policy outcomes with regard to specific welfare programs in different national societies (1979: 32-33). They merit more systematic investigation of the sort pioneered by Wilensky (1976, 1983, 1985).

III. ON THE FORMS AND CONTENT OF WELFARE "TRANSFER" PAYMENTS

I have urged that the starting point for an analysis of welfare be to recognize that it is best expressed by summing up the complete "basket" of goods and services available to each individual in a society throughout the life cycle. In my view the content of this basket should be observed independently of how it got there. For example, in considering the welfare of the aged, we should sum the money income of each older person and the value of all the goods and services available to him or her from whatever source. Social security payments from the government would, of course, be a large part of any cash income received by most elderly persons. Additional sources might include funds from current earnings, from returns on earlier savings, and from personally purchased retirement annuities. Likely more important would be funds from an insurance scheme run by the individual's former employee or union. In judging cash income, moreover, we would be well advised not to forget the differential impact of taxation, which takes so large a share of income in the welfare state. Thus, in the case of the aged in the United States, social security checks were totally exempt from income tax until 1984, while after that date taxes were collected on only one-half of the payment and then only from individuals above a certain income level.* Given that for the majority of retirees their social security payments are by far the largest component of their total retirement income, this tax forgiveness makes a significant contribution to increasing the welfare of the aged.†

We would add to cash income the value of noncash benefits and privileges. In many cities, senior citizens ride the public transportation system at fares often half the regular charge. Moreover, similar benefits are offered them by the private sector as well, as in movie theatres. These particular benefits might be dismissed as small ticket items, but that certainly could not be said of Medicare and Medicaid, or of food stamps for those eligible to receive them.

Money sources tend to be easier to track and weigh than the nonmonetary. Thus, sorting out the sources contributing to the welfare of any given child, we can readily estimate its share of money income through dividing the parents' income by either the

---

*It should be noted that social security pensions in the USSR are totally exempt from income tax.

†In the median case, the proportion of retirement income which a married couple's social security and pension receipts represented in 1982 was 52 percent before taxes were taken into account and rose to 59 percent on an "after-tax" basis (Fox 1982: 17, t9). Of course someone else has to pay more taxes to make up for the income tax the retired elderly do not pay on their social security pension. This forgiveness of tax, therefore, represents a transfer from one group of the population to another as much as it represents the transfer of a welfare benefit from government to individuals. For further discussion of this issue see the section on "transfers" below.

number of household members or the number of dependent children. In the case of very poor children, we can obtain the money value of aid to dependent children available to them. But most calculations we make are not likely to take account of the cost of that child's education received in a public school. They are even less likely to set a price on the value of the services which the father and mother provide the child, despite the fact that such nonpaid work may be equal in value to something like one-third of the family's money income.*

The inadequacy of our measures of the total resources made available to each person, which constitutes society's contribution to that person's general welfare, stems from certain conventions which became established in the early days of systematic thinking and study of the wide realm of social insurance. The key term used was *transfer payments*. In the welfare state the greatest of all transfer payments are those which individuals and productive enterprises make when, through taxes or other mechanisms, they turn over to the state some fraction of the value of what they have produced but will not have available to consume—at least not before it has passed through the hands of government, which will then allocate it, consuming some itself, investing part in capital construction, and distributing the remainder to various services and to selected individuals and groups. In many—indeed one might say in the standard—discussions of welfare, attention was focussed mainly on those distributions which moved from government to individuals and families, and within that set, attention was concentrated on *monetary* transfers.† Yet it is now compellingly clear that to assess individual welfare comprehensively we must consider nonmonetary transfers in the form of goods and services.** In addition we must broaden our conception of the set of key actors, recognizing that the transferrers are multiple, and include nonstate institutions, associations, households, and finally other individuals.††

*It has been estimated that work in "home production" by men and women, combined with the value of volunteer work, would, if correctly priced, be equal to 38 percent of the U. S. gross national product (Morgan et al. 1966).

†There were of course important exceptions in earlier work, some of which are discussed in Wilensky (1958).

**A summary of more recent efforts to assign prices to goods and services is found in Page (1983); see also Moon (1984).

††The classic study of contributions by individuals of nonmonetary goods is that of Titmuss (1971).

I propose that we consider a transfer to have occurred when any resource of which the holder is rightful owner or legitimate recipient is turned over to a second party (a) by direct payment, (b) through indirect payment, as in the forgiveness of a tax due, (c) through payment to a third party on behalf of the recipient, or (d) by the direct provision of a service. Transfers may be voluntary, as in charity or gifts to children, or involuntary, as in the case of government-mandated action. The key element in transfers is that they are redistributive. If government merely acts as administrative agent for a given program, much as an insurance company might, paying out to recipients amounts in proportion to what they earlier paid in, then there is no redistribution and no transfer.

It would help keep clear what goes on in this very complicated process if we had some way to distinguish actions which merely recycle resources back to those who originally contributed them from those actions which redistribute and hence are, in the sense in which I use the term, true transfers. Under the rule I have proposed, social security benefits for which the recipients have paid by earlier contributions to specific special funds would probably not be considered transfers. On the other hand, when a segregated fund does not cover the actual outlays, those who provide the money to meet current payments above what is available in the fund have transferred part of the resources over which they would otherwise be rightful possessors. Thus the way the U.S. social security system actually operates, the current working population is, through its social security deductions, transferring income to that part of the population now retired and not working.* In this case the transfer is essentially cross-generational, but unlike gifts from parents to children, or vice versa, this cross-generational transfer is not voluntary. It is rather mandated and administered by the government.

In the case of the U.S. social security system, the transfer element is clear. In other instances, however, it will inevitably be obscured. Thus if there is no specific tax to finance medical services, and they are paid for out of the general revenue, it is very difficult to say whether any transfers are occurring, or whether we are dealing with an instance of recycling. With great effort one can measure the

---

*Juanita Kreps characterizes the method the United States adopted to fund its social security pensions as one in which "income claims against the nation's total output are transferred from persons at work and consumers in general. . . to retirees. . . . Transfers thus reallocate the annual output between workers and nonworkers" (1978: 32-33).

extent of transfer through general taxes by comparing for all households at a given level of income the parallel contribution they make to taxes, on the one hand, and, on the other hand, the benefits they receive in the form of "free" education and health protection, as well as housing, food, transportation subsidies, and so on. Families who get back more than their tax contribution then become net beneficiaries of the transfer process, while those who pay out in taxes more than they receive in benefits become net transferrers. The Berkeley conference was presented with a heroic effort by Ofer and Vinokur to assess this process for Soviet families at different levels of income.* Using double-entry accounting to measure separately the sources of funds and their expenditure, Robert Lapman (1984) has analyzed in detail the network of income transfers made in cash for health, education, food, and housing in the United States, separating the sources of the funds coming from government, insurance, pension funds, philanthropy, and interfamily gifts.

Even if we were to limit ourselves to the action of the state alone, it is clear that to deal adequately with transfers we need a much more fully elaborated conceptual framework than is commonly used. One dimension along which we should distinguish the state's role in transfers is that of the "direct" vs. the "indirect." It is along this dimension that some of the more striking contrasts between the Soviet and the American case will be observed.

At the top of the scale are those services which are provided directly by the state and by personnel on the public payroll. The Soviet health service, a vast system for delivering medical care to the Soviet population, epitomizes this pattern (see Davis 1988). Apart

---

*Ofer and Vinokur (1988) concentrate mainly on the value each household and its individual members receive from the Social Consumption Fund (SCF). Here we note only that they calculate transfers to families separately for education, health, housing, food subsidies, and so on. Unfortunately they do not take account of what each household pays out in taxes, except for noting that Soviet income taxes are not very progressive. In the case of families not on pension, they observe the anomalous fact that the amount of noncash transfer directed to high-income households tends to be about equal to the amount directed to low-income households. Moreover, since the high-income households tend to have fewer members, the result is that on a per capita basis individuals in high-income Soviet families get considerably more in subsidy value from the SCF than do those in poorer households. What makes this anomalous is that a similar phenomenon occurs in, and is often thought to be characteristic of, capitalist countries. There is some progressivity in the distributions, however, because SCF support becomes a declining proportion of total income as one goes up the earnings scale.

from formalities of registration and the like, Soviet citizens get their complete medical care through this system, with minimal specific payment on their part. Their doctors and all the institutions operating in support of the medical personnel who treat them are part of one huge apparatus designed to provide the direct health service which the government undertakes, much as it undertakes to run the defense establishment. The cost is mainly financed as part of the general state budget. Since there is no specific tax for medical services, we cannot say whether total expenditures for medical care represent a transfer from one tax category to another. For any given individual, it would also be difficult to say how far the taxes he paid actually covered the cost of the medical care he may have received over time.

In the United States, direct provision of medical services by the state in a manner analogous to the Soviet pattern is not unknown, but the eligible population is very limited. The president and a few of the highest officials of the U.S. government enjoy such services, as do all those in the military and those eligible for treatment in veterans' hospitals. There are of course other special cases at both the federal and state levels, but the vast majority of Americans obtain their medical care, even when it is linked to government programs, in a manner quite different from direct provision by the state.

This is not to say, however, that direct provision of a service by the state on a large scale is unknown in the United States. On the contrary, there is a close analogue in the American system of public education, especially at the primary and secondary levels. As a direct service by government, albeit mainly local, the U.S. system of primary education is administered in much the same way as that in the Soviet Union.

While remaining the prime mover, the state can act less directly in adding to individual welfare by paying a third party to provide a service which is sometimes entirely free to, and sometimes partially paid by, the recipient. In this realm there are a number of variants. In housing, for example, the state may itself build housing, or arrange for other agencies to build it, but in either case some charge will be placed on the users of the housing. Where this charge is below the cost, the state is providing a subsidy, although generally hidden from the view of the user.

Housing for Soviet citizens and their food and recreation costs are heavily subsidized.* In the United States only a small amount of

*The rent paid by urban residents of the Soviet Union covers only one-third of the cost of providing that housing; the government subsidizes the remaining

housing is provided on a comparable basis. It can be argued, however, that the tax deduction for interest on home mortgages provides an analogous housing subsidy for the 60+ percent of American house-holders who own their own homes. Probably the most important examples of the U.S. government's provision of services through third parties are Medicare and Medicaid, which account for a large part of all medical expenditures, private and public, in the United States. School lunches are another example of this sort of service, as are federal subsidies for urban transport. In both of these cases there is no direct service provided by the state (in this instance, the federal government): it simply gives funds earmarked for a specific purpose or recipient, and some other agency, public or private, provides the actual service. The consumer may or may not be aware of the extent of the subsidy. In the case of school lunches, often served without any charge, it is easy to assume that the service is free to the recipient. In the case of transport subsidies, however, the consumer pays a fare and so may fail to recognize that the service is being provided below cost with the difference made up by govern-ment subsidy.

Instead of subsidizing a service which the individual enjoys only by using a particular source—as in public housing or a school cafeteria—the state may put the subsidy directly into the hands of the consumer and let him or her decide from which vendor to obtain the subsidized goods or services. But even when put directly in the hands of the consumer, the subsidy may be in nonmonetary form and therefore highly restricted in the uses to which it can be put. In the United States, food stamps fit in this category, as would proposed vouchers for education. To my knowledge such "chit" or voucher systems are not much utilized in the USSR, if at all, although the USSR relies heavily on special stores in which select individuals can purchase products not available to the general public.

By contrast, in both the USSR and the United States, that form of subsidy is utilized which puts money directly in the hands of citizens without any restrictions on the service purchased or the vendor who provides it. Characteristic of such unrestricted, direct money transfers are those paid out as part of the standard programs for disability, especially for work-related injuries, and aid to depen-dent children. In the case of old-age pensions, which are the main

two-thirds. One-fifth of recreation costs are government-subsidized, and meat and dairy products are also heavily subsidized (Ofer and Vinokur 1988; U.S. Senate 1981).

form in which the state makes unrestricted cash payments to individuals, there is, as we have noted, some ambiguity as to their status as transfers or as repayments of sums previously paid into funds by the recipients.

All of the examples given so far involve the transfer of resources already in the hands of the state. But welfare may also be effected by the state through its power to require that resources not in state hands be transferred to individuals or groups by entities not formally defined as part of the state apparatus. In Germany, for example, health service is provided to almost all its citizens, but the government neither runs the medical system directly, as in the USSR, nor makes third-party payments, as with Medicare and Medicaid in the United States. Instead, in Germany the government obliges the creation of, and general participation in, special funds which provide medical services through nongovernmental institutions, although they operate under government control.

The government may also oblige other institutions to be direct providers of a service. For example, the state may require all factories to provide housing or health services of various kinds for their workers. While such requirements placed by the Soviet government on its production enterprises are very extensive, they are much less common in the United States. One example is a requirement in many states that women employees must be provided a separate room to lie down in if they are indisposed.

Such facilities are on the borderline between the usual kind of transfer and the type of expense employers may be put to in meeting state regulations concerning workers' health and safety, such as requirements for dust catchers in spinning mills, ventilators in chemical laboratories, and the like. In the United States this type of state-mandated health and safety regulation is probably at least as much elaborated as in the Soviet Union, and the level of enforcement is almost certainly much higher. Whether such work-safety and ecology-protecting measures should be included in the sum of welfare services provided to individuals is an interesting open question. We might note in this connection that congressionally mandated pollution-control "scrubbers" for coal-fired plants in the United States are estimated to add $3 billion per year to the cost of running those plants. The companies transfer this cost to the consumers, who share in the health benefits resulting from cleaner air, but by present accounting methods this amount is not added to the sum total American society is credited with spending to ensure the health and well-being of its citizens.

The government's mandating of welfare-creating actions which must be taken by nongovernmental organizations extends to requiring even more indirect forms of providing services. Indeed, in contrast to the Soviet pattern, the U.S. preference is mainly for such indirect provision. Thus if the U.S. government were to require every major employer to provide medical services to its employees, it would be unlikely to require each enterprise to have its own clinic staffed by company employees. Instead it would probably require each employer to provide medical *insurance* only, so that employees could obtain medical care elsewhere than at work and from providers other than those on the company payroll.

The last step in the chain of government mandates comes where it obliges one individual to accept responsibility for the welfare of another individual or set of individuals. Thus the United States and the USSR both have laws requiring parents to support their children, and, reversing the order, in Communist China the national constitution obliges children to support their aged parents. Soviet law creates the same obligation.

SEPARATING WELFARE AND ITS SOURCES

I have proposed that to assess how far and how well a society provides for the welfare of its citizens we should develop a profile of the total array of resources, including directly and indirectly provided services, made available to sustain and enhance the life of each individual, of each household, and of appropriate social categories such as children under five or adults over sixty-five as well. These profiles could then be compared across individuals and groups within the same nation or cross-nationally. Such comparisons would be greatly facilitated if those services which are directly provided could be reduced to monetary terms, recognizing that in such translations one might blur important qualitative distinctions.* Indeed if we could

---

*Wilensky (1975: 94) made a pioneering effort to assess the impact of in-kind transfers on the total effective income of families at different economic levels in Great Britain for the year 1970. The most important of the transfers were for pensions, education, and health. Since taxes paid offset benefits received by households, they were also taken into account. The outcome showed the impact of such transfers to be considerable and to serve a notably redistributive role. After taxes and benefits, the effective income of the poorest households had been augmented by 726 percent of their original cash income. A comparable study of Germany for 1960 showed a net gain to the poorest households of 576 percent of their original income.

express the value of "free" services in monetary terms, we would be in a good position to carry our analysis of the welfare-generating basket of goods and services one step further. In this ultimate step we could, for each good and service received by each individual or household, trace the sources which made the consumption possible. Thus for food or rent we could say what part was paid for in cash, what part of that cash came from wages or other income, what proportion of the value consumed was in the form of subsidy, and what part of the value made available came as direct service without any shared payment.

This basic idea about how to assess the amount and the source of welfare-generating resources would be a marked departure from the conventional way of analyzing social welfare expenditures, although it is in accord with thinking among some economists. Thus in their discussion of the way "government growth impinges on the well-being of individuals in society," Geoffrey Brennan and Jonathan Pincus propose that we develop a matrix of the distribution of the total product of society among different individuals. In this matrix will be all the items each individual consumes, and these in turn

> constitute in principle, everything from which the individual derives satisfaction and include all those items purchased directly in markets, those acquired by barter, and those distributed by the state. Protection from foreign aggression, protection from crime, street lighting, education and health are included . . . along with food, clothing, entertainment, leisure activities, and electricity (1983: 34-35).

Agreement on what should be included in the basket of goods and services received by individuals and households would not come easily. For example, most analysts of social welfare would not agree with the idea of including the per capita share of defense costs. Moreover, the sheer technical task of reconstructing the typical basket of all goods and services received by characteristic individuals and households would obviously be a formidable one. It would be even more so if we sought to identify the different sources of support and their differential contribution to each element in the entire basket.

Although they did not provide quite the assessment described above, Ofer and Vinokur did present some relevant and revealing data on social welfare in the USSR to the Berkeley conference. First, they called attention to the fact that official Soviet statistics report on the size and composition of what they call the Social Consumption Fund (SCF). In this category the Soviets include more than the usual welfare transfers for those unable to work by virtue of age, disability, and the like. Most important for our purposes, they add the value of all sums spent "for the common satisfaction of needs" dealt with prior to or independent of the payment of wages. Included is everything spent by the state for schools, hospitals and other forms of medical service, housing, child care facilities, and recreational facilities. Defense expenditures are not included. Curiously, neither are food subsidies.

Ofer and Vinokur note that by putting together the net wage bill, on the one hand, and the sums in the SCF, on the other, one obtains a total for any given year "equal to the amount of consumption [Soviet] households can claim and receive from the public sector."*

It is a reflection of the character of the Soviet system that the total value of the SCF in 1980 was equal to almost 70 percent of the fund from which all wages and salaries for state employees was paid. Put another way (as proposed by Ofer and Vinokur), of every ruble spent for the maintenance and welfare of the average Soviet citizen, somewhat more than 60 kopecks would have come to him through wages and just under 40 kopecks in the form of payments from the government's pool of nonwage funds. Furthermore, of those 40 kopecks made available by nonwage transfers, a large share—between one-half and two-thirds—is paid out not in cash, as exemplified by pensions, but in directly provided services or in subsidies to the prices paid by Soviet citizens.†

---

*In assessing what is actually available to the household, even this sum would have to be supplemented by income from savings, which many will be surprised to learn are a significant factor for the Soviet population. More important would be income from the work individuals perform in the so-called "private sector." This encompasses such activity as that of a government-employed doctor who sees some patients on a private basis for a fee, or that of a state-employed carpenter who puts up shelves in people's apartments on a private basis. Such income is not included in the wages fund and generally escapes official calculations.

†Calculations based on official Soviet breakdowns of the SCF assigned 44 percent to cash transfers and 56 percent to nonmoney transfers. Included in the cash transfers, however, were outlays for paid holidays, which many analysts feel are more appropriately treated as an element of wages. Excluding the holiday pay from consideration yields the result that nonmoney payments were 64 percent of the residual SCF. The importance of subsidies and directly paid

It is essential to recognize that such proportions tell us nothing about the absolute size, the quality, or the composition of the basket of consumables which the Soviet citizen receives. They also tell us nothing about the relation between the value of the total product individuals produce by their labor as against the value of the basket of goods and services they consume. This is so because the government has siphoned off not only money for defense, but also funds for running its vast bureaucratic enterprise and for investment and other purposes not convertible into individual consumption.

What these figures tell us is that the typical Soviet citizen has sharply limited direct control over whatever will be spent for his total welfare and highly restricted choices as to how it will be spent. With regard to up to one-fourth of the basket of goods and services received by the Soviet citizen, the state says in effect that it knows best how much to allocate for different purposes and where and from whom the goods and services selected will be obtained by the citizen.*

To evaluate just how restricted the Soviet citizen may be in deciding how to allocate what is spent by and for him, we should compare similar breakdowns for other countries. Unfortunately, the papers prepared for the Berkeley conference do not include an analysis for the United States or Europe parallelling that by Ofer Vinokur for the USSR.† We can assume, however, that the Soviet pattern would be roughly matched in a country such as Sweden, where the public provision of services is emphasized, and where the

---

services varied according to the status of the household, especially between "active" or employed and "inactive" or retired. Ofer and Vinokur's sample survey makes it possible to estimate those variations. For those in the inactive retired status, virtually everything they received in "public" income — 99.1 percent according to Ofer and Vinokur — came out of the SCF. Of this total, 63 percent came in the form of money payments; the remainder was in subsidies, as for food and housing, and indirect services, such as for health care. In the households of the active population, the public income profile was different: 72.5 percent came through public earnings and 27.5 percent through the SCF. The largest part of what came through SCF — equal to 19.4 percent of their public income — came in nonmoney forms, such as services for education and medical care or subsidies for food and housing.

*Taking the wages fund at 100 and the SCF at 70 percent of that, we have a base total of 170. If 63 percent of the SCF was in noncash form, that yields noncash outlays of 44.1, which is 25.9 percent of the base total of 170.

†A variety of attacks on the problems of measuring and valuing transfers in the United States will be found in Moon (1984).

narrow ILO category of social security spending accounted for 32 percent of the gross domestic product in 1980. The United States would fall at the other end of the scale because it leaves more personal income in the citizens' hands, and what it provides is mainly in the form of payments whose allocation among different needs is left to the individual. France and Germany would fall in between.* More precise and detailed accounts than this would clearly be desirable, and would surely be revealing.

IV. THE DEGREE OF NATIONAL EFFORT TO ENSURE INDIVIDUAL WELL-BEING

If we lived in the most primitive, or less pejoratively the most simple and least elaborated, condition of human existence, then communal and collective responsibilities beyond those undertaken by families or households could be kept to a minimum. There would have to be some group action for defense, and some types of deviant behavior would call for controls not available to the family or household unit. Some religious ceremonies might require numbers of participants or degrees of specialization beyond what a family or single household could provide. But apart from a few such activities, it would be possible, at least in principle, for the family or household unit in such societies to provide the full range of goods and services required by individuals for their sustenance. But most of us have long since left that world behind, perhaps forever. The societies we live in are extraordinarily complex. One of their main characteristics is the interdependence they create, so that no individual or household or small community can long survive alone. Instead we are intimately dependent, for almost everything which sustains and enriches life, on collaborative interaction with others in elaborate networks of interchange resulting from the extensive specialization and division of

*This characterization is based on the proportion of GDP spent on social insurance as calculated by the ILO (see Table 1 below). The standings of the governments are somewhat different if the percent of payroll paid out as taxes to support social security programs is considered. By that criterion, in 1981 the Netherlands led by taking an astonishing 57.7 percent of total payroll outlays for social security purposes; Italy followed closely, taking 55 percent; France weighed in at 47.6 percent. The United States took about a third as much of payroll for this purpose—i.e., 18 percent; Switzerland, 17.7 percent; Canada, only 8.4 percent. All these percentages combine the tax contribution of the employer and the employee (see U.S. Senate 1981: 13).

labor which permeates modern large-scale societies. Increasingly it has become the responsibility of the state to orchestrate and manage that complexity. The state more and more regulates, controls, and channels activity, prescribing and proscribing what individuals, households, enterprises, and other corporate groups do. Beyond such control and regulation, the modern state more and more takes charge of offering services once left to individuals and households to develop, purchase, or arrange for themselves. Observing this process we can easily lose sight of the distinction between a welfare-*generating* society and a welfare-*conferring* state.

A. VARIABLE NATIONAL APPROACHES TO PROVIDING INDIVIDUAL WELFARE

Societies, nations, and states vary in the degree to which they are sensitive to and concerned about the material and the mental or spiritual well-being of the individuals who make up the larger community. Moreover, whatever the apparent level of concern, communities vary further in how far they exert themselves collectively to ensure such welfare as they accept nominal responsibility for. A religious community of hermit ascetics might provide the outside limit for exhibiting least collective concern for material welfare. Indeed such a community might also treat spiritual salvation as mainly a matter of individual rather than communal concern, however intensely that salvation might be sought. Near the other end of the scale are variants on the modern welfare state, where public responsibility for the individual, as the popular view would have it, begins at the cradle, continues to the grave, and is extended to include mental well-being as well as physical. In the case of some Israeli kibbutzim, such communal principles were carried so far as largely to eliminate the family as either a production or consumption unit, leaving it only the function of reproduction and a limited role as a focus of affection.

Communal sensitivity to or concern about an issue may, but will not necessarily, be expressed in the taking of collective responsibility, and the taking of such responsibility may, but will not necessarily, be expressed in communal action. Thus while Americans for a long period struck Europeans as being not just sensitive about, but almost obsessed with, what was euphemistically called "plumbing" as a contributor to personal well-being, public toilets are rare in the United States despite the quality of the facilities found in private quarters. It is in France that one finds public facilities in abundance, sometimes it seems on every street corner. Similarly, taking nominal responsibility for a social guarantee may have little or no connection with its actual implementation. Thus many millions of children without access to schools live in countries where the constitution or the law, or both, affirm the right of every child to an education.

Speaking in the broadest terms, a comparison of the United States and the Soviet Union on these dimensions suggests the following: Throughout most of its history, the society developed in the United States has been intensely occupied with the elaboration of individual well-being, but it has seen the role of the state as limited to creating the general conditions which permit individuals, operating in a more or less free and competitive market, to strive by their own means to maximize their individual and household welfare. The direct provision of services by the government has been kept to a minimum, and subsidization has been viewed as a distortion of the natural process of the market.* By contrast, the Soviet system, especially in the Stalinist period, emphasized individual welfare less than national development and the growth of the economy. Whereas in most countries personal consumption tended to rise in tandem with the growth of the nation's total product, in the period from 1930 to the end of the Stalinist era Soviet total product rose almost twice as fast as personal consumption. In so far as the Soviet system concerned itself with individual welfare, it showed a marked preference for the direct provision by the state of goods and services. It also favored providing welfare through subsidies built into services selected by the state rather than putting funds in the hands of its citizens and leaving them to select the services and providers they preferred, even within the very restricted market the USSR provided.

More recently, both the Soviet Union and the United States have gradually moved away from their respective original models in ways which have brought them somewhat closer together. In the United States, since the Franklin Roosevelt/New Deal era, the state has accepted much more responsibility for building structures which assure individual welfare outside the operation of the market, increased its role in transferring income between groups, greatly expanded the degree to which it subsidizes the cost of some goods

---

*The American idea that government should play a minimal role in shaping the individual's life, and be referee rather than manager, is elaborated in some detail by King (1973) and contrasted with the dominant ideology in France and Germany.

and services, and even moved to provide some services directly to consumers. For its part, the Soviet system, at least since the end of the Stalin era, has come to acknowledge more fully the legitimacy of claims for individual consumption as against "socialist construction." As a result the rate of growth of personal consumption, which previously had lagged far behind the rate of growth in total product, gradually came more in line with the pattern shown in other industrial countries. Thus from 1951 to 1978 the rate of growth in real consumption per capita in the USSR was similar to the rate in Italy and actually somewhat greater than that for the United States. Despite this higher rate of growth, the share which consumption accounted for in the total national product was much lower in the USSR than in other leading industrial countries.* Moreover, while allowing the absolute amount of consumption to increase, the Soviet regime did not move to lessen the role of the state in fulfilling those aspirations. Indeed much of the system's accommodation has come about unofficially through the efflorescence of the so-called "second economy." Outside state control, on a private basis, an elaborate network of arrangements has evolved to provide goods and services which the state apparatus cannot deliver, or which it produces in quantity and quality far below popular expectation.

The United States also has developed a large "underground economy." This second economy is stimulated not by shortages of goods and services in the legal economy, as is its Soviet equivalent, but rather by the desire to avoid regulation and above all to escape taxation. Whatever drives it, this underground economy is evidently very large, with some estimates putting its total value at one-fifth of the nation's officially described GNP (Brennan and Pincus 1983: 46).[†]

Despite the movement toward a more common ground, however, the provision of welfare to individuals and families in the two countries continues to involve marked contrasts which reflect the underlying philosophies of national development characteristic of

---

*Over the total period 1951-78, the average annual rate of growth in real consumption per capita was: USSR, 3.7 percent; U.S., 2.3 percent; Italy, 3.8 percent. The Soviet rate was, however, lower than that in the countries experiencing an economic "miracle," specifically West Germany, where consumption grew at 4.8 percent per year, and Japan, where it grew at 6.5 percent. In 1976 the combination of spending by households plus government expenditures for education and health yielded a total share for "consumption as a percent of national product" of 71 percent for the U.S., 70 percent for Italy, 69 percent for the U.K., and only 54 percent for the USSR (see U.S. Senate 1981: 25, 26).

[†]Most analysts suggest a lower estimate of 10 to 15 percent of GNP.

the two nations. Several of the more notable of these differences will be discussed below.

B. THE UNITED STATES AS WELFARE LAGGARD

Social policy and social writing are replete with assertions that the United States is a welfare laggard. Thus Lee Rainwater began his contribution to the Berkeley conference with the statement: "The United States is well known as a 'welfare state laggard.'" It is encouraging that he went on to show that it is less a laggard in some areas than others, but in the end he repeated the general conclusion that the United States is a welfare state laggard. In applying this label he was only one more in a long line of experts on social welfare who have characterized the United States in these terms. In his extensive contributions to the analysis of welfare in the wealthiest capitalist countries, Harold Wilensky has consistently referred to the United States, along with some other rich countries, such as Japan, as a "welfare state laggard" (1975: xiv; see also foreword to Coughlin 1980). From a more leftist point of view, this characterization takes more extreme forms. Thus Wedderburn placed America "outside the mainstream of capitalist societies so far as welfare state provisions are concerned." Summarizing its deficiencies further, she asserted: "It is questionable how far the phenomenon of the welfare state can be said to exist in the U.S.A." (1965: 130).*

This image of the United States as welfare laggard substantially misrepresents the actual situation. It is, however—at least in most quarters—not the result of a deliberate campaign to diminish the world standing of the United States by spreading misinformation, but is the product of a state of mind, a particular world view which, once embodied in standard statistical measures, became authoritative, indeed more or less official and absolute, when it should have been recognized as partial and tentative.

If there is substance to what I am saying, and validity in the data to be presented below, we have to wonder why so many people

---

*Wedderburn's characterization of the United States can be understood as ideological hyperbole, but it makes little sense when examined statistically or analytically. By her own definition, the welfare state commitment was characterized as intended "to protect individuals against the hazards . . . arising through sickness, old age, and unemployment." In 1965, 94 percent of employed persons in the United States were covered by a public retirement program such as social security, and 79 percent were covered by unemployment insurance (see USDC 1980: 400, t8/10).

have described the United States as a welfare laggard. At the same time we might ask why the Soviet Union enjoys so pervasive an image as a society in which the insurance of social welfare is more or less the chief raison d'être of the system.

The bedrock on which these misconceptions rest is a series of studies published since 1948 by the International Labor Office (ILO) which focussed on the cost of social security (ILO: 1981). Two features of that series were critical in shaping conceptions about the level of welfare in the United States. First, it limited itself to measuring expenditures on only certain types of social security programs, which came by sheer inertia of convention to define social welfare activity as a whole. Thus while public health expenditures were included, those for education were not.* Perhaps even more influential in shaping the image of different countries' welfare efforts is the fact that the ILO limited itself to measuring expenditures which were compulsory by law and were administered either by governments or by public, semi-public, or "autonomous" agencies. Thus a pension secured through a national, government-operated system was counted, but one paid out by a corporation or insurance company was not, unless the corporation was mandated by legislation to pay for pensions by turning money over to a public agency. In the words of the ILO, it "does not cover benefits paid directly by employers in respect of sickness, maternity, retirement, etc." (1981: 2), no matter what agreement may be reached between employers and workers, *and even when the agreement is required by law.* This meant, for example, that the ILO would not take into account expenditures for health such as those of the General Motors Corporation, which in 1984 processed 40 million medical claims for 2.1 million employees and their dependents at a total cost of $2.3 billion (*New York Times*, 1/5/86).

By this means a seemingly simple and innocent statistical convention became a powerful, almost magical wand which converted the United States from its actual role into a welfare laggard.[†] The

---

*The ILO's calculations follow the ILO Social Security (Minimum Standards) Convention of 1952, which defines nine branches of social security, including benefits for (1) medical care, (2) sickness, (3) unemployment, (4) old age, (5) employment injury, (6) family allowances, (7) maternity, (8) invalidity, and (9) survivors' benefits (for details, see ILO 1981).

[†]The ILO statistical convention does not have the force of law, of course, and a number of scholars have studied the relation of private to public expenditures for pensions seeking to test some of the hypotheses set out by Wilensky

percentages of social security spending of various countries between 1965 and 1980 on the ILO scale are shown in Table 1. Two things are especially notable in this listing. First, those countries such as Sweden and the Netherlands which absorbed more and more welfare-generating activity directly into the government budget, or directed it to government-chartered agencies, became welfare-spending leaders. Other societies, such as the United States and Canada, which also acted to increase individual well-being over the period, but did not insist it be done through expenditures incorporated in the national budget or mandated by law, became welfare-spending laggards. Rainwater showed this process at the Berkeley conference though his historical calculations based on the ILO procedures. He showed how Holland moved from spending 1.56 percent of its GNP for ILO-type social security in 1930 to 26.6 percent in 1977 whereas the United States, starting at about the same level, moved over the same span of time from spending 1.46 to only 12.9 percent of its GNP on social security.

These data permit us to conclude that the share of GNP spent directly by government or by public bodies mandated by law, rather than by individuals and nongovernmental or nonpublic agencies, for the limited package of social security measured by the ILO went up twice as much in Holland as it did in the United States. However, they do *not* permit us to assume that welfare, broadly conceived, increased over that span of time at twice the rate in Holland that it did in the United States. Nor do they provide a basis for arguing that in 1977 Dutch citizens enjoyed twice the welfare enjoyed by American citizens. From these data one can only conclude that the government's role as a direct controller of money to be spent on individual welfare was more than twice as great in Holland as in the United States. How much welfare, even of the limited social security kind, was actually enjoyed by the comparable citizens of each country cannot be determined.

A second notable (but seldom noted) fact revealed by Table 1 is that if the figures in the table are taken as a measure of how much governments exert themselves to provide social security to their populations, then the USSR is in much the same range as the United States. According to the ILO, in 1977 the United States spent

as early as 1975. In a private communication in 1986, Wilensky expressed the view that "the state of the evidence remains: [after] adding private to public spending for pensions, etc., . . . big public spenders remain big and the rank order of effort (spending/GNP) remains roughly the same."

Table 1

SOCIAL SECURITY AND SOCIAL PROTECTION SPENDING
AS A PERCENT OF GROSS DOMESTIC PRODUCT,
1965-1980

Country	According to International Labor Office			According to European Community		
	1965	1977	1980	1965	1977	1980
Industrialized Countries						
Australia	8.3%	14.3%	12.1%			
Belgium	16.1	25.5	25.9	16.7%	26.2%	27.6%
Canada	9.4	14.5	15.1			
Denmark	12.2	24.0	26.9	--	25.4	28.7
Finland	10.6	19.3	18.6			
France	15.6	25.6	26.8	18.3	23.9	25.9
Germany (West)	16.6	23.4	23.8	20.0	27.4	28.7
Ireland	10.3	18.3	21.7	--	--	22.0
Italy	14.8	22.8	18.2	17.5	23.1	22.8
Japan	5.1	9.7	10.9			
Luxembourg	15.1	24.3	24.1	16.2	25.8	25.6
Netherlands	15.5[a]	27.6	30.5	17.3	28.8	30.5
Norway	10.9	19.6	20.3			
Sweden	13.6	30.5	32.0			
Switzerland	8.5	16.1	16.6[b]			
United Kingdom	11.7	17.3	17.7	--	19.7	21.4
United States	7.1	13.7	12.7	--	16.6[d]	--
Centrally Planned Countries[c]						
Czechoslovakia	18.2	19.0	18.9			
Poland	9.3	11.8	15.7			
USSR	11.6	13.4	14.1			

Sources: ILO (1981 and 1985): table 2); Eurostat (1980: 105; 1983: no. 2, p.1).

[a] 1966 data used for 1965.

[b] 1977 data used for 1980.

[c] Social security spending is expressed as percentage of net material product.

[d] Calculated by Rainwater (1988) for the year 1978 based on GNP, not GDP.

13.7 percent of its gross domestic product (GDP) for social security while the USSR spent 13.4 percent of its "net material product." If the Soviet data were expressed as a percent of GDP, which is generally used elsewhere in the ILO analysis, the Soviet investment in social security would look even smaller.* While these facts have been available to all in a long series of ILO reports, they somehow have been apparent to very few.[†] The ILO calculations which have been repeatedly cited to show that the United States is a welfare laggard have almost never been used to show that the USSR is at least as much a welfare laggard as the United States.

In developing their own assessment of a nation's effort to ensure the welfare of its citizens, the statisticians of the European Community avoided some of the limitations built into the ILO's measures. The most critical change was to take account of payments for social needs and services made by the private sector in addition to those made by government or through a government agency. In particular they take into account so-called "voluntary schemes" for pensions, and for medical or other services, when provided by employers either on their own initiative or through union contract (ILO 1981: 3). The European Community uses the term *social protection* to describe this package of measures and actions. As can be seen in Table 1, among the continental European Community members, the outlay for social protection benefits in 1977 was generally 25 percent of gross domestic product. The United Kingdom, at the bottom, spent close to 20 percent of GDP for social protection (Eurostat 1980: 105). By 1980 the proportions had gone up considerably everywhere in the almost universal and seemingly inexorable expansion of spending on social welfare.

Unfortunately the EC made these calculations only for its own members. To make possible a comparison with the United States, Rainwater followed the conventions utilized in the European

*The "net material product" used by the Soviet Union and the other Communist countries excludes the value of personnel services in those sectors of the economy not directly concerned with production. Thus it excludes the cost of nonmaterial outlays for defense, medicine, etc. It is therefore much smaller than the gross domestic product used as a base in calculating social security expenditures in other countries. Thus allowing the USSR the exception of calculating its percentage of welfare expenditures on the basis of net material product exaggerates the proportion of national income the USSR actually spends on social security.

[†]Among the exceptions, Wilensky noted as early as 1976 that the USSR fell in his group of welfare state laggards.

Community's reports to calculate for the Berkeley conference the equivalent estimates of spending on social protection in the United States. He arrived at a figure of close to 17 percent for the year 1978.*

The broader definition of welfare spending adopted by the European Community results in their estimates of spending as proportion of GDP being rather consistently higher than the figures given by the ILO. This comes largely from the inclusion of company pensions, group medical insurance plans, and the like. The effect of considering programs not mandated by law, but still clearly identifiable as social welfare spending, also improves the standing of the United States in relation to the welfare leaders of the European Community. In terms of the ILO's scheme, the U.S. "effort" for social welfare was only 50 percent of that of the Community's leader—the Netherlands. According to the Community's scheme, the U.S. effort for welfare was about 58 percent of that in the Netherlands. This improvement is obviously modest, and the reason continues to be the relative narrowness of the criteria for determining what should be included in welfare spending. Thus the EC formula does not take account of purely individual, nongroup insurance. Nor does it consider direct payment by individuals out of current earnings for services such as medical care, or payments out of personal savings for the cost of living in retirement. Moreover, the European Community's measure of social protection, like the ILO's, does not consider the society's investment in education, even though education is one of the most fundamental and costly of the social services governments provide.

We could satisfy our desire for a more appropriate measure if we had data on the total expenditure by government, by organizations, and by individuals for each of a set of basic ingredients important in generating personal welfare, such as health, education, pensions, unemployment, and aid to the injured and dependent. Such a measure could be constructed from the national accounts used to describe the components of GNP. An approximation of the desired measure is available for the United States in calculations made for the Social Security Administration. They include four domains—

---

*We should keep in mind that Rainwater's estimate was 16.57 percent of GNP, whereas the ILO's figures and those of the EC were based on GDP, making the two measures less comparable than one might wish. In addition, Rainwater's estimate was based on U.S. data for 1978, but 1977 data were used for the European Community in Table 1.

income maintenance, health, education, and welfare services. For each they estimate both public expenditures and private expenditures. In 1976, the last year in which such a breakdown was provided, the public part of expenditures was predominant—in most realms accounting for 86 percent or more of all expenditures, except for health, where it provided only 42 percent of all outlays. Taken together, expenditures in these four domains, public and private combined, accounted for 27.5 percent of GNP, with almost three-fourths of that coming from public sources.*

I know of no effort to construct a similar measure for the other industrialized nations. A very rough approximation can be made using the European Community reports, with some adjustments to make their calculations more like those used by the Social Security Administration. This results in a further marked reduction in the gap between the United States and the leaders in social welfare within the European Community. We obtain 1977 figures of 37.1 percent of GNP spent for social welfare in Denmark, 31.5 percent in France, and 35.1 percent in West Germany—compared to 27.5 percent in the United States—and the U.S. effort for welfare now rises to 74 percent of that in Denmark, 78 percent of that in Germany, and 87 percent of that in France.[†]

Of course it would be preferable to have a more strictly comparable assessment. Such an assessment is within the technical means of the major social security and welfare agencies, but it would no doubt be difficult getting agreement on what to include in a summary measure of welfare. For example, a strong case could be made for

*These calculations were made by Skolnik and Dales (1977). Unfortunately, comparable calculations made by the Social Security Administration for years after 1976 do not give the same detail concerning the contribution of the private sector. It would be instructive to compare the Skolnik and Dales calculations with those of Lapman (1984), whose analysis focuses on what he calls "secondary consumer income," which includes all income transfers outside of wages. Among these nonwage transfers are cash benefits, health care, education, and services. He estimated secondary consumer income in 1978 to equal 27.6 percent of GNP.

[†]Two additions must be made to the European Community reports to make them more comparable to the estimates of the Social Security Administration. First, to the figures for Europe one must add the proportion of GNP spent on education (see Table 2). Second, allowance must be made for contributions from the private sector included in the SSA estimates but not usually included in EC calculations. Thus after the percent of GNP spent on education is added to the social protection estimate of the EC, an arbitrary, but generous, 10 percent is added to the new total for the selected European countries.

including housing and/or food supplies. A spirit of accommodation might enable us to develop some reasonable alternative definitions.

In the absence of an overall measure, we may be able to get some meaningful comparisons by looking one at a time at some important realms which have been systematically studied, such as the education and health sectors.

Christopher Davis (1988) has reported to the Berkeley conference his estimate of total expenditures on health services in the USSR. We should note that his estimate takes account of items in both the state budget and "nonstate" budgets, since using the former only would have been another instance of how statistical conventions can show a nation at a misleading disadvantage.* Davis's calculations, based on official Soviet sources, yielded a figure of 4 percent of GNP spent for health services, which remained fairly steady from 1965 through the early 1980s. In the developed countries of the West, the share of GNP from all sources going to health ranged from 8 to 12 percent by the early 1980s. The United States was in the middle of that range at 10.5 percent—a figure generating much concern, even alarm, among many American policymakers because it seemed to be rising so rapidly.

We should particularly note that using this total expenditure measure, which weighs both personal and government outlays, shows the United States as a society which clearly is not stinting on medical expenses. By contrast, if only government expenditures had been considered, the United States would definitely have been classed as a laggard, falling far behind virtually every relevant competitor. For example, in 1974 "public health programs" (as against total expenditures for medical care) absorbed only 2.8 percent of the U.S. GNP at a time when they were taking 7.4 percent of the GNP in Sweden and about 5 percent in other developed countries (USDC 1980: 406, t8/19). If, however, account is taken of private expenditures for medical care, the United States appears in an entirely different light. On that basis the United States was actually spending not a mere 2.8 percent, but rather about 8 percent of its GNP on health care. This was about as much as Sweden was then spending.[†]

---

*Of the total expenditures for health care in the Soviet Union, about three-fourths is accounted for in the state budget. The remainder is accounted for in the budgets of various ministries which have their own medical systems, and in the budgets of trade unions and other social organizations.

[†]In 1970 the figure for Sweden was 7.2 percent and in 1975, 8.4 percent, so 8 percent seems a conservative estimate for 1974 (USDC 1980: 395, t8/2).

In this context we should also note that the USSR is here the laggard. Since virtually all medical care in the Soviet Union is represented in the total calculated by Davis, his figure of 4 percent of GNP spent for medical care in the early 1980s puts the USSR behind both the 10.5 percent for the United States and the European average for the same period. The USSR, by this measure, puts less than half as much effort into total medical care as the leading capitalist nations. It could of course be generating as much benefit as others by this smaller expenditure by using it more efficiently. Alternatively, it may be paying less and getting less.* (We shall examine this issue later.)

What about education, which is another big ticket item? Data on expenditures in the mid-1970s by selected countries, available from the UN and UNESCO, are presented in Table 2. They show

Table 2

GOVERNMENT EXPENDITURE ON EDUCATION AS A
PERCENTAGE OF GROSS NATIONAL PRODUCT, 1979

Country	Expenditures as Percent of GNP
Australia	5.6%
Austria	20.1
Belgium	6.1
Canada	7.7
Czechoslovakia	4.9[a]
Denmark	6.3
Finland	5.7 [1980]
France	3.5
Germany (West)	4.7
Ireland	4.1
Italy	4.6 [1978]
Japan	5.8
New Zealand	5.6
Norway	8.1 [1978]
Poland	3.6 [1971][a]
Sweden	9.1
Switzerland	5.0
United Kingdom	5.7 [1978]
United States	6.4
USSR	7.2[a]
Yugoslavia	5.4

Source: UNESCO, *Statistical Yearbook 1981, 1982.*
[a]Percentage of "net material product."

*For a discussion of public and private spending for medical care and the impact of that spending on disease and health in national populations, see Wilensky (1985).

the United States behind some of the welfare leaders such as Sweden, but well ahead of others such as Germany and France. Around 1979 Germany spent 4.7 percent and France 3.5 percent of their GNP for education, whereas the United States invested 6.4 percent for this purpose. If private expenditures were taken into account, the U.S. figure would be higher, but unfortunately we do not know what comparable adjustments would produce for the other countries.* In any event, the separate examination of the realm of education fails to establish that the United States does not exert itself to maximize individual welfare.

One realm where the United States may show to marked disadvantage in international comparisons of social welfare effort is that of "income maintenance," which is generally defined as including old-age pensions, unemployment insurance, work injury and employer sick pay, exclusive of general health expenditures. Each of these subcategories of income maintenance follows a distinctive pattern influenced by different social forces. The amounts devoted to pensions will obviously be affected by the aging of the population. Since industrial societies have increasingly large aged populations no longer in the workforce, expenditures on pensions can be expected to rise steadily, but without marked fluctuations from year to year. By contrast, the amounts paid out for unemployment insurance, and the sums paid to the needy, can be expected to fluctuate considerably, rising sharply in periods of economic recession and falling in years of prosperity.

Looking first at the investments in old-age, survivors, and disability insurance, the United States was evidently behind most of the welfare leaders in the early 1970s, although doing almost as much as France and England (see Table 3). It fell still further behind by 1977. By then, according to the Senate's Special Committee on Aging (U.S. Senate 1981), the United States was spending 4.3 percent of its GNP for social security and disability pensions as against 10.2 percent in the Netherlands, 9 percent in Germany, 6.2 percent in France. It should be noted that in many European countries the proportion of the population over 65 was up to one-third larger than in the United States. Even with this allowance, however,

---

*According to the Social Security Administration, 85.3 percent of all U.S. education costs in 1975 was paid by government. On that basis the U.S. figure in Table 2 would be raised to about 8 percent, which seems high, however, because the SSA estimated total education expenses, private and public combined, to equal only 6.9 percent of U.S. GNP in 1976 (USDC 1980: 395).

Table 3

EXPENDITURES FOR SELECTED SOCIAL WELFARE PROGRAMS, SELECTED COUNTRIES: 1971 AND 1974

Country	Old-Age, Survivors, and Disability Insurance				Public Aid and Other Social Welfare				Public Health Care Programs			
	Expenditures (millions)		Percent of GNP		Expenditures (millions)		Percent of GNP		Expenditures (millions)		Percent of GNP	
	1971	1974	1971	1974	1971	1974	1971	1974	1971	1974	1971	1974
Belgium [*francs*]^a	$70,583	$123,983	5.0%	5.9%	$14,547	$23,981	1.0%	1.1%	$56,147	$96,270	4.0%	4.6%
Canada [*dollars*]^a	2,205	4,121	2.5	3.1	2,147	2,754	2.5	2.2	4,153	6,150	4.8	4.8
France [*francs*]	38,139	56,803	4.2	4.3	b	43,240	(NA)	3.3	41,062	65,704	4.6	5.1
Germany [*marks*]	58,550	74,482	7.7	7.9	7,621	9,243	1.0	.9	35,377	5,971	4.7	6.0
Japan [*yen*]^a	297,829	723,449	.4	.6	431,228	936,534	.6	.8	2,719,300	3,524,000	3.7	3.1
Netherlands [*florins*]	12,636^c	20,519^c	9.8^c	10.9^c	1,325	2,846	1.0	1.5	5,969	9,919	4.6	5.3
Sweden [*kronor*]	11,045	17,854	6.1	7.2	5,968	8,814	3.3	3.5	11,789	18,386	6.4	7.4
United Kingdom [*pounds*]	2,002	3,320	3.8	4.5	1,079	1,802	2.1	2.4	2,087	3,049	4.0	4.1
United States [*dollars*]^a	35,874	54,870	3.5	4.0	26,415	38,242	2.5	2.8	27,935	38,385	2.8	2.8

Source: USDC (1980: t8/19).

^a Some public expenditures for health care are included under public aid.

^b Public aid expenditures are not separately identified.

^c Includes expenditures for work-connected disability pensions.

a number of European countries were spending larger shares of GNP for old-age pensions—in good part because they permitted earlier retirement and paid more generous benefits than those offered in the United States.

Old-age pensions are, however, only one form of cash transfer designed to maintain the flow of income to persons cut off from earnings. Others are those made for unemployment and work-related illness. When these and related programs are added to old-age pension payments, the total expenditure for income maintenance in the United States for 1976 was estimated by the Social Security Administration to have reached 11.1 percent of the GNP. Of this expenditure, 87 percent was credited to government, but it was acknowledged that the private sector share would have loomed larger if certain excluded benefits had been taken into account.* I have not found a calculation on income maintenance in other countries which considers a range of programs comparable to that used by the Social Security Administration. Martin Rein presented a highly relevant analysis to the Berkeley conference, however, in which he compared pension policies in Europe, and particularly Sweden, with those in the United States. His analysis led him to conclusions markedly congruent with our own. Thus he was struck by the fact that most discussions assume that it is only the state that provides welfare, which leads to the neglect of that part of protection provided by employee pensions and tax-subsidized personal savings. He went on to note that "when we aggregate across sectors, we get a very different insight about the level of social protection in the United States relative to other countries," and "when the institutional details of risk and sector are taken into account, there is virtually no difference in the level of pension expenditures between the United States and Sweden" (1988: 215, 245).

Clearly much remains to be done before we have more meaningful estimates of spending for individual welfare. It will require finding ways to make the definition of different domains more comparable, and to increase the standardization of expenditure categories within those domains. A more complete set of accounts would distinguish between the sources of funding, especially as divided

---

*In weighing the private contributions to income maintenance, only benefits obtained through the place of employment were considered. The various individual and group insurance policy payments, which were excluded, amounted to almost $7 billion as against about $23 billion of benefits which were counted (see Skolnik and Dales 1977: 18-19, t9).

among government agencies, employer organizations, collective or communal organizations, and individual expenditures. It seems likely that when this more complete accounting becomes available, it will show the United States to be much less of a welfare laggard than it is so often represented as being. However, all of these calculations remain, in varying degrees, locked into the framework created by thinking about social welfare programs rather than the total basket of goods and services available to the average individual. When the standard of living as expressed in consumption per capita is the criterion, the United States is unambiguously a world leader, as we shall see below.

V. NORMATIVE ISSUES: EQUALITY, JUSTICE, COMPASSION

For many individuals, all the statistics about effort expressed as a percent of GNP, and the proportion of welfare expenditures going to different categories, will largely fail to respond to their concerns about welfare in contemporary society. They are preoccupied with other matters—issues of equality, compassion, and justice. Such normative concerns are fundamental to the evaluation of any social arrangement. The resultant judgments are, however, the focus of endless debate because values vary greatly, terms are imprecise, and evidence which will be accepted as definitive is so difficult to come by. Nevertheless these issues must be dealt with if we are to deepen our understanding of similarities and differences in Soviet and American welfare policies and practices.

A. EQUALITY

There are some for whom the key characteristic of a good society or community is that it provide as nearly perfect an approximation of equality of treatment and condition as is possible within the limits of human variability. An appropriate model for them might be some of the early years of the Israeli kibbutzim or the communist utopia which is expected to follow in the USSR when the present stage of socialism is finally surpassed. Unable to get everyone into something like a kibbutz, and not ready to wait for utopia, many will still strive to increase equality in the imperfect industrial societies in which we are obliged to live now and in the foreseeable future.

The most direct way to achieve absolute equality in this type of society would be to have an incomes policy such that everyone was paid the same wage or guaranteed income. With one stroke the state could achieve absolute, or near absolute, equality. Moreover, equality could be achieved in this way without need for the usual welfare state apparatus which many assume necessary to achieve equality. Put differently, such an arrangement could be quite consistent with a market economy. It could be left to individuals to buy, with their equal incomes, whatever basket of goods and services they preferred — spending, for example, more for education and less for medical care, or more for housing and less for leisure, as they chose.

Such an incomes policy would obviously be hard to install. Some would feel their idea of equality was undermined if people with equal incomes bought different, hence unequal, baskets of goods and services. In addition, income equality alone would probably not be attractive to those whose preference is to have some collective or the state provide goods and services to people directly. In this conception of the welfare state, things would be arranged so that (quoting Briggs again) "all citizens without distinction of status or class are offered the best standards available in relation to a certain agreed range of social services."

It is not difficult to see how this goal could be attained in the case of medical care. With a national system of health care in place, one would only need to ensure that the service provided at any given clinic was not responsive to the influence of various forms of social stratification. In poor districts, as in rich, doctors and facilities would be distributed so that doctor-to-patient ratios, the qualifications of staff, and the availability of equipment were uniform across all comparable clinics, that referral for special treatment was on grounds of medical condition and not on the basis of personal or social attributes, and so on. To preserve this equality in practice, one would also have to restrict people from buying medical services outside the national health system. In the British case, such restrictions are not seen as appropriate. In the Soviet case, the widespread development of clinics open only to special categories of privileged persons, such as high party members or important scientists, is an officially sponsored departure from the principle of strict equality in providing "the best standard available" to all. Moreover, Soviet citizens can and do buy and sell medical services outside the official network of medical clinics. Although the practice is considered inappropriate and improper, it is not defined as illegal and, in any event, is not prosecuted.

There is something about medical care which makes it possible for the populations of modern industrial societies to accept the principle of absolute equality of treatment, or of treatment determined solely by need, even if the actual practice often departs from the ideal. As with medical care, the principle of equality of access and treatment is also widely accepted with regard to education, at least at the primary school level. Certainly in the United States most will affirm the principle that every child, regardless of background, is entitled to the best education the society can offer and that the child can absorb. Here again the degree of equality actually practiced is much less than might be expected if the principle affirmed were fully implemented, but the potential exists.

A commitment to equality of treatment in medicine and education resolves one issue for the welfare society only immediately to confront it with another. In the search for equality, the initial impulse, strongly influenced by the example of income, is to allocate equal resources to each person. But to do so is to ignore differences in need. People who are critically ill can consume enormous amounts of medical care. For example, average health care costs for those aged 75 or over typically are five times greater than for those aged 14 to 64. Children who are handicapped may require many times the expenditure made for the average child before they have an "equal" chance to learn. We are then confronted by a conundrum: "Is need the enemy of strict equality?"

Different societies have resolved the issue differently, both in general terms and in specific domains such as education for the handicapped. In the case of medicine, it seems agreed among the experts that the Soviet system is oriented to invest its resources most heavily in those individuals who can be returned to productive labor. There is much less interest in medicine for the aged. In the United States the great proportion of medical expenditure devoted to the elderly suggests a quite different orientation. A comparison of Soviet investment in and treatment of handicapped children with the analogous U.S. procedures under the Education for Handicapped Children Act might be revealing.

Beyond medical care and education, in modern societies the degree of commitment to strict equality in the provision of the necessities of life drops off sharply, both on the part of government and of the population. With regard to food, the commitment is only to the principle that hunger should be eliminated and severe malnutrition prevented. In housing, wide variations in the scale and quality of what is consumed seem to be taken for granted, even in nominally very egalitarian societies such as the Soviet Union and Communist China. In housing, as with food, there evidently is a widespread agreement about the right to certain minimum standards, but there is no general commitment to the idea that all should be offered "the same best standard." This is true, even more clearly, with regard to the consumption of leisure, to access to legal services, to the supply of clothing, and to a host of other goods and services.

The widespread acceptance of the idea that, beyond medicine and early education, one need not ensure everyone the same best standard, but may allow differentiation in the quantity and quality of the goods and services available to individuals, is not limited to the capitalist countries. In the Soviet Union it has long been official policy that differentiation must be preserved. Any effort to assure absolute equality in the supply of goods and services is there labelled *uravnilovka*, which roughly translates as "levelling." It is a term of official opprobrium. As Bernice Madison pointed out to the Berkeley conference, Stalin was the fountainhead of the attack on equalization in the awarding of benefits to Soviet workers. He argued instead for favoring those in the most critical industries, and among them the "shock" workers who gave extra effort or otherwise achieved higher productivity. Also favored were those with the longest and steadiest attendance at work. That pattern of differentiation, adjusted to meet changing technologies, and much influenced by differences in personal political power, remains the standard arrangement for Soviet citizens to this day.

Even in the societies which favor the direct provision of services by government agencies, a large part in deciding on the contents of the basket of goods and services each individual consumes has been left to personal choice. This is true not only in the so-called capitalist countries, but applies to a significant degree in the self-defined socialist countries as well. More critical, in the context of this discussion, is the fact that the size and variety of that basket of consumables depends upon the differentiated incomes individuals can command as a result of their wealth, political power, current work, former work, or special condition as part of some minority formed on the basis of race, color, or physical disability.

This introduces us to a different aspect of equality, which might be termed the issue of "equality of burden." It is obviously preferable not to have anyone live in poverty, but if limits on a community's economic means will force *some* members of the community to live at low levels, that burden may be borne equally by all segments of society or disproportionately by only some disadvantaged groups. In the development of the Soviet Union, it was the collective farm population which especially bore the burden of a reduced standard of living to make possible the surplus needed for investment in heavy industry and armaments. The migratory farm worker has been in a comparable disadvantaged position in the United States, although this group, in contrast with the Soviet collective farmer, has been but a small proportion of the population.

Turning to other categories, Ofer and Vinokur found that half of all the households classified as poor in the Soviet Union were made up of retired persons, and one fourth were those headed by women of working age supporting children but not themselves supported by a man. The representation of these groups among the poor is, of course, many times their weight in the population at large. In the United States the elderly do not contribute so disproportionately to the poor. Thus in 1983 they were some 13 percent of the total population and 14 percent of those living in poverty. By contrast, female-headed households were a startling 46 percent of all the poor household units while being only about 12 percent of total U.S. families. Inequalities in carrying the burden of poverty are equally marked when the U.S. population is divided by color and ethnicity. Thus in 1983 the rate of poverty among blacks, at 36 percent, was almost three times that among whites, while among those of Hispanic origin, the rate of poverty was considerably more than double that for whites.

Clearly both the size of incomes and the efforts to limit or ameliorate inequalities will be shaped by many forces—economic, political, and cultural. Whatever the outcome, it will inevitably be judged by current notions about justice.

B. JUSTICE

Justice has many meanings, no less in relation to social welfare than in other realms. Among the words the dictionary associates with justice are "impartiality," "fairness," and "adequate treatment." Where a benefit is available, the exclusion of a person or group which has taken no action to warrant not being included would generally be seen as unjust. In this spirit it might be argued that once a benefit has been recognized and instituted, its extension to all is more just than its restriction to a few. In this context let us consider how extensively different national populations are covered by various welfare schemes, and then turn to a discussion of the fairness issue.

1. Extent of Coverage. It is generally agreed that one major criterion for judging the adequacy of a society's provision of welfare to its population is the extent and depth of the coverage offered by the array of social insurance programs of which individuals can take advantage. Included in a proper assessment would be a review of (a) the range of programs offered, (b) the proportion of the population covered, and (c) the adequacy of the protection against hazards and burdens.

Virtually all the advanced countries provide much the same array of major programs, although there are some outstanding exceptions. Thus the Soviet Union and the other Communist countries are distinctive in not offering unemployment insurance, while the United States is the only one of the twenty leading industrialized nations not to have a program of family allowances. In general, however, all the advanced countries, following broadly similar paths, have found their way to offering basically the same array of programs, ranging from work injury and sickness/maternity benefits through old-age, invalidity, and survivors insurance to unemployment and family allowance programs. Within this common framework there is, however, a sometimes bewildering variety in the details of the programs, the range of individuals covered, and the adequacy of the benefits provided (USDHHS 1983).

Leaving aside for the moment the quality of benefits offered, it seems obvious that those programs which cover the largest proportions of the appropriate populations should be considered the most satisfactory or most just. By this standard some U.S. programs seem highly satisfactory. Thus by 1976 some 98 percent of all wage and salary workers in the United States were covered by a public retirement program, 90 percent by unemployment insurance, and 87 percent by workmen's compensation. Moving away from these nationally mandated programs, however, the proportions covered declined. Accidental death and dismemberment insurance was available to 55 percent of employees, but only some 17 percent could count on long-term disability insurance (USDC 1980: t8/10, t8/12).*

---

*It should be noted that those totally disabled can, if covered by social security, turn to the latter in place of a benefit provided by the employer. Taking this into account makes the proportion covered by long-term disability insurance much greater than 17 percent.

The high level of public retirement coverage in the United States, especially if supplemented by data on privately purchased retirement schemes, would surely make U.S. coverage equal to that of virtually all other countries in the realm of old-age insurance. In this connection it is worth noting that the Soviet Union long lagged behind the United States in extending the protection of a retirement pension to all segments of the population. It was only in 1964 that Soviet law provided that collective farm workers would be guaranteed a pension upon retirement, and what was provided was on a level far below that provided for urban industrial workers. Since close to 40 percent of the Soviet labor force was then employed in agriculture, the proportion of its labor force covered by social security had obviously been, for many decades, much lower than the proportion covered in the United States. Indeed in the late 1950s, according to Madison (1988: 173), when five or six of every ten elderly persons in the USSR were not yet receiving old-age pensions, worker families were paying for their support entirely out of current income. At about the same time the United States, which was paying social security to almost 75 percent of persons over 65, was widely labelled a welfare laggard, but no such labels were applied to the USSR (USDC 1980: 398, t8/6).

Even today there are many groups in the Soviet Union who do not qualify for old-age and disability pensions. Excluded from the old-age pension system are those who work without a labor contract, nonstaff workers in trade and procurement, self-employed craftsmen, free professionals, and, curiously, meat cutters in collective farm markets if their income comes from providing services to private citizens. Most of these categories are covered by social security in the United States. As a result of such exclusions, Madison informs us, at least 13-15 percent of individuals over 65 in the USSR in 1975 were not receiving pensions. In the United States in the same period, 97 percent of married couples over 65 had incomes from at least one pension source, 93 percent were getting money from government, with a quarter of those getting employee pensions in addition, and 89 percent of older unmarried males and females were receiving social security benefits (USDC 1980: 398, t8/7).*

---

*One commentator on this paper suggested that my finding that social security coverage in the United States is greater than in the USSR should be reexamined in the light of the general rule of comparative research that such coverage tends to be greater the higher the economic wealth of a country and the longer a program has been in effect. Yet the Soviet program began in 1917,

In contrast to retirement programs, medical coverage in the United States appears to be quite unsatisfactory when compared with the coverage available in countries such as the United Kingdom, which have national medical schemes encompassing the entire population. In 1976, for example, even with individually purchased medical insurance added to corporate employee benefit plans, only 71 percent of U.S. workers had hospitalization coverage, and only 36 percent were protected by major medical insurance (401, t8/12).

To balance off the less-than-satisfactory coverage of medical programs, a defender of the U.S. performance might suggest we turn to education. There the United States is not only equal to all other countries in providing virtually all children access to primary school education, but at the secondary level it takes the lead. Around 1975 the United States sent 72 percent of those 15 to 19 years of age to school, whereas France and West Germany (social security leaders by ILO standards) provided schooling for only 51 percent of the same age group. The contrast was even greater among the college- and university-age populations: of those 20-24 years of age in 1975, 22 percent were in school in the United States, 10 percent in France, and 11 percent in Germany (303, t6/24).

It would be a formidable task, but one well worth doing, to continue the process initiated above by compiling systematically the data on the extent and depth of coverage provided by different social security and welfare schemes in all advanced countries. Based on the fragmentary data examined here, there is reason to believe that a comprehensive comparative survey would show that the United States does not consistently bring smaller proportions of its population under the coverage of welfare-inducing arrangements than do other advanced countries. This would be even more clearly shown if due allowance were made for individually purchased coverage or access, either as a substitute for or supplement to that provided by public agencies or employers. We would probably find that, in the array of coverage they offer, most countries have distinctive profiles expressing national proclivities, history, and politics, with the United States occupying a rank which on average would be more

---

whereas that in the United States dates from only 1935. As to the effect of wealth, the Soviet doctrinal view is that the nature of capitalism should lead to denying workers social security, whereas in a workers' state, even at lower levels of GNP, the workers' interests will be protected by the state. They would argue that the outcome will be determined not by wealth, but by type of system. The actual outcome does not support their belief.

in accord with its per capita income than its reputation as a welfare laggard.*

2. *A Standard of Fairness.* In the United States, people are likely to think of justice in terms of what is "fair." Thus they will say it is not fair that a woman on welfare should receive as much as a woman who goes out to earn a living. There is a feeling that something is fundamentally wrong if rewards are equal for those who work, pay their taxes, and follow the rules and for those who have made no sacrifice for the benefits they receive. It is likely the resentment against "welfare chiselers," and the assumption that much of the money spent for welfare goes to the "undeserving," that largely accounts for the fact that 60 percent or more of the American public thinks there is too much spending on welfare—four to five times as many as think there is too little spending for this purpose (USDC 1980: 394, t8/1).

At the other end of the scale, the system will be perceived as unjust if it fails to reward properly those who do the right things— who work, produce, earn, pay their taxes, and contribute to social security funds. In this context, one way to make concrete the sense of what is fair is to specify some proper relation between one's condition *before* retirement moves one on to the social security rolls and *after.* For example, Madison found that 96 percent of Soviet refugees felt the minimum pension should provide a level of living "comparable to that of the general population" (1988: 185). Since the minimum pension was only 50 rubles per month, and the majority of her respondents felt 100-150 rubles per month were needed to live according to the "general standard," it is no surprise that some 70 percent of them felt the Soviet social security system failed to provide "social justice."

If we accept the idea widely held by both Soviet and U.S. citizens that it is only "just" that a person who worked all his or her life is entitled to a reasonable standard of living after retirement, we can estimate how much justice is done by calculating how many individuals in retirement enjoy that reasonable standard. Two criteria are often used in evaluating the adequacy of social security benefits for achieving a "reasonable standard." One stresses the proportion of pre-retirement income provided by post-retirement

*Rainwater (1988) notes that nations change a good deal over time in the profile of social security programs they emphasize, which results in "a surprising lack of association . . . between spending measures for 1950 and 1970" for the fourteen advanced countries he examined.

income. The other stresses keeping above a "poverty line" or other minimum base.

Madison's data indicate that Soviet pensions replaced 51 percent of pre-retirement income on average. They also show that the percentages of pre-retirement income replaced varied depending on the size of that income. Thus the pensions of those whose earnings had been low equalled 61 percent of pre-retirement income, while the high earners' pensions were only 46 percent of pre-retirement income.

To obtain her estimates of post-retirement income in the USSR, Madison had to rely on a refugee sample which was highly educated and professional. In the case of the United States, we have detailed breakdowns of earnings replacements for all groups of the population, and must choose among many ways of expressing results. Thus it can make a considerable difference if one concentrates on couples, who have higher earnings replacement rates than single men, or indexes earnings to take account of inflation, or considers incomes before or after taxes.

If we focus on married couples, who are the great majority of retirees, we find that around 1976 their social security payments alone, in the median case, replaced 45 percent of their total pre-retirement earnings. In the lowest quintile of earners, however, the replacement rate was a high 76 percent, whereas among the highest quintile of earners, their social security receipts replaced only 28 percent of pre-retirement total earnings. Thus the social security payments were doing more to cushion the impact of retirement for the poorest segment of the population than for the richest. This pattern, at least in broad outline, is similar to that observed in the USSR, as are the median and range of earnings replacement.

In the United States, however, social security is significantly augmented by pensions from corporate, group insurance, or individually purchased retirement plans, which are virtually unknown in the Soviet Union. Adding such nongovernment pensions pushes the U.S. earnings replacement rate in the 1970s up from 45 to 58 percent for married couples. Since few of the lowest quintile of earners, some 9 percent, had other pensions to supplement social security, their replacement rate did not change much. Among the highest quintile, however, their nongovernment pensions made a considerable difference, raising their replacement rate from 28 to 46 percent. Nevertheless, the lowest quintile were still replacing much more of their pre-retirement earnings than were the highest quintile (USDHHS 1982: t8).* Looking at replacement rates in a broader comparative perspective also shows the United States doing better than might be expected on the basis of its reputation as a welfare laggard. When the criterion is the replacement percentage of the average wage in manufacturing, U.S. social security pensions alone were in 1980 replacing 66 percent of pre-retirement income for couples and 44 percent for single workers. Of twelve industrial countries studied by this standard, the United States ranked fifth in the case of couples and sixth in the case of single workers (Aldrich 1982).

Replacement rates by themselves will not indicate living conditions. Replacing 60 percent of an income which permitted very comfortable living is more desirable than replacing 60 percent of an income which permitted living on the edge of poverty. It is in this respect that the Soviet pension system is least satisfactory.

The Soviet Union has officially defined poverty lines: in 1965 it was drawn at 51.1 rubles per month per person, and between 1970 and 1975 at 66.4 rubles. The minimum wage for workers and employees in the USSR is 70 rubles per month, and Ofer and Vinokur (1988) propose this figure as a more realistic estimate of the poverty line. Madison shows average pensions in the USSR to be consistently below the official poverty line. Thus in 1975 the average pension was only 45.9 rubles. Those receiving pensions from state insurance were mainly just at the poverty line, but the large numbers receiving pensions from other sources—particularly former collective farm members—were far below it. With their low pensions, and in the majority of cases with only modest savings to draw on, half of all pensioners must live with working relatives, according to an official Soviet journal.† It is no surprise that three-quarters of Madison's sample considered that a pension alone would not meet even "modest" needs.

By contrast, retirement incomes in the United States keep the vast majority of retirees well above the poverty line as defined by the

---

*The replacement rates given are those based on "middle-four, price-indexed, estimated total earnings." There is some variation in the replacement reates if different ways of estimating pre-retirement income are used.

†Reported in *Ekonomika i matematicheskiye metody*, 1976, pp. 1196-1200; quoted in Madison 1988. By contrast, no more than 10 to 15 percent of those over 65 years of age in the United States live with relatives. In addition to financial constraints, the shortage of housing in the USSR plays a large role in shaping the Soviet pattern.

U.S. government. This is due in large part to the indexing of social security pensions to take account of inflation, whereas in the Soviet Union they remain fixed for considerable periods of time.* Thus by 1981 the average social security payment to a retired worker in the United States had reached $4,632, whereas the poverty line for a single person over 65 years of age was $4,359.† This cash income, supplemented by savings and a high level of home ownership, makes it possible for all but a small percentage of elderly Americans to maintain their own households rather than live with relatives. Of course many people receive less than the average social security payment, and some have no access to social security at all. Even when savings or work after retirement are taken into account, some people are still left below the poverty line. In 1982 some 14 percent of all persons in the United States 65 and over received incomes below the poverty level (USDC 1985: 456, t760). If the value of noncash benefits were taken into account, the proportion living in poverty would be reduced to some 12 percent (459, t767)—perhaps less than half the comparable figure for the Soviet Union.** Nevertheless, it leaves a considerable number of people in the United States dependent on compassion rather than on entitlement. This leads us to examine how different modern societies deal with the poorest—the destitute with less than the minimum means for subsisting.

C. COMPASSION: CARING FOR THE POOREST

Before the modern welfare state emerged, social welfare was understood to mean mainly those activities, generally private, undertaken to keep people alive and functioning who would simply go under if left to the resources they could command on their own. It meant doing something for those without food or shelter who, by virtue of physical handicap or other misfortune, were in a condition

---

*Madison reports that minimum wages for Soviet workers and employees were increased four times between 1956 and 1978—totalling 160 percent. By contrast, the minimum old-age pension was raised only twice between 1956 and 1981, providing an increase of only 67 percent and creating "a widening gap between the level of living of pensioners and the working population" (1988).

†The social security payment figure is based on average monthly OASDI cash benefits for retired workers of $385.97 for 1981 (USDHHS 1982: 45, tM-13). The poverty line is from USDC (1985: 429).

**Ofer and Vinokur (1988) estimate that 30 percent of the households in the USSR headed by a retired person operate below the poverty line.

of dire poverty and desperate need, or those who, if not aided, would slip into that condition. What they received was not obtained by right—not due to their falling into a social category giving them a legal entitlement to government funds. In brief, what we think of today as "charity"was the major component of all social welfare.

Today, in the advanced countries, social welfare is supported predominantly by *public* funds. As shown in Table 4, the largest part of what is designated by the ILO as social security expenditures— generally about 60-65 percent—is for pensions and related programs (called "social insurance and assimilated schemes" in the table). Old-age pensions alone generally make up 40 percent of the total, while public health schemes, more variable in importance, account for 15-20 percent in the median case.

Pension schemes are generally tied to the individual's work history, so to an important degree they represent a late return on earlier employment. Indeed such payments are often referred to as a "social wage." Medical schemes often have a similar character. On the other hand, some schemes, especially medical and educational, provide national coverage without regard to present or former employment status: the recipients are deemed to have entitlements under law as citizens. Despite the broad coverage frequently available, there are always individuals who fall through the net. Either they have no tie to employment-based schemes, or for other reasons would be destitute beyond what is socially tolerable unless they were given support outside the programs based on work or legal entitlement. Persons whose pensions are not large enough to live on, and children with no one to support them except a mother who must stay at home to care for them, are examples. The aid they receive is included in the ILO social security accounts under "public assistance." In the United States the largest items in this category are food stamps, supplements to social security payments (including assistance for the blind and disabled), and aid to families with dependent children (AFDC)—all of which are based on need rather than on employment history or general entitlement.

Inevitably what is included in the category of public assistance varies from country to country, although the ILO strives to maintain some consistency among different national measures.* Given the common perception of the United States as a place which stresses

---

*However much the ILO may strive to maintain consistency in categorizing specific welfare expenditures as public assistance, that category is generally seen as the least reliable of its indicators, which makes it all the more important to consider other approaches.

Table 4

DISTRIBUTION OF SOCIAL SECURITY BENEFIT EXPENDITURES
AMONG THE DIFFERENT SCHEMES, 1977 OR NEAREST YEAR
(*In percent*)

Country	Social Insurance and Assimilated Schemes	Family Allowances	Public Employees Military Civilian	Public Health	Public Assistance	War Victims
Australia	70.1%	--	6.7%	11.8%	3.7%	7.7%
Austria	63.9	9.5%	20.3	0.4	3.0	2.9
Belgium	65.5	12.1	12.3	3.6	4.6	1.9
Canada	62.3	7.6	1.4	9.8	16.3	2.6
Czechoslovakia	62.6	13.2	--	22.2	2.0	--
Denmark	50.6	4.1	3.8	17.6	23.6	0.3
Finland	46.2	4.4	14.8	20.3	11.7	2.6
France	67.6	11.1	12.1	--	9.2	--
Germany (West)	72.5	5.1	13.2	0.5	4.4	4.3
Ireland	47.5	5.6	11.3	33.0	2.6	--
Italy	69.5	--	9.8	13.7	5.2	1.8
Japan	63.7	1.2	13.8	2.8	12.3	6.2
New Zealand	67.1	--	5.1	25.5	--	2.3
Norway	65.4	4.4	5.3	15.8	7.8	1.3
Poland	58.7	7.7	--	30.6	2.4	0.6
Portugal	67.9	15.3	11.3	3.1	2.4	--
Romania	49.4	18.5	--	28.0	4.1	--
Sweden	50.1	5.1	4.6	24.1	15.8	0.0
Switzerland	73.9	0.3	5.4	12.3	8.1	--
United Kingdom	41.6	2.8	8.4	28.7	17.1	1.4
United States	53.3	--	10.7	6.2	24.0	5.8
USSR	67.4	3.0	--	29.6	--	--
Yugoslavia	84.8	8.1	--	2.3	0.6	4.2

Source: ILO 1981.

Note: "Social insurance and assimilated schemes" includes four main branches of social security: sickness-maternity, employment injury, pensions (old-age, invalidity, and survivors'), and unemployment. Under "public employees, military and civilian" are included the special schemes for such employees. When public employees are covered by a general scheme, these benefits are included under "social insurance and assimilated schemes." The distribution shown is for benefit expenditures only—that is, it does not take account of administrative costs, which are not proportionally the same for all programs.

self-reliance, we would expect it to be a laggard in this type of social security expenditure. Curiously the United States is not a laggard in this respect, but is a world leader. As shown in Table 4, of its total social security expenditures in 1977, the United States devoted 24 percent to public assistance. Of the other countries commonly considered to be welfare state leaders, only Denmark came close to the United States in directing so large a proportion of its welfare expenditures, 23.6 percent, to public assistance. Most of the other countries lagged far behind in this category.

An alternative way of comparing the importance of public assistance programs is to express the expenditure as a percent of GNP. For the Berkeley conference, Rainwater estimated public assistance programs in the United States to equal 1.4 percent of GNP in 1978. Using a similar but evidently broader concept of "public aid and other social welfare," the U.S. Social Security Administration put the figure at 2.8 percent for 1974.* In comparison with eight selected advanced countries, the United States ranked third, surpassed only by Sweden at 3.5 percent and France at 3.3 percent of GNP. Other welfare leaders such as Germany and the Netherlands were far behind (USDC 1980: 406, t18/9).

Given the varying national tendencies to include public assistance expenditures under different headings, one must be cautious in interpreting such comparative data. Thus it might be argued that the United States spends so much on assistance for the poor because it does not offer a broad program of public medical care and does not provide family allowances. Nevertheless, the data do seem to challenge the image of the United States as a welfare laggard. If welfare is understood to mean helping the poorest—those most at risk of suffering destitution—and effort toward that end is measured by the proportion of national income directed to public assistance, then the United States is considerably ahead of most other countries, including virtually all those commonly designated as welfare leaders. Moreover, the calculations of expenditures for public assistance do not take account of spending by charitable organizations, which in the United States are heavily involved in

---

*According to Skolnik and Dales (1977), U.S. expenditures in 1974 for "welfare and other services" equalled 1.4 percent of GNP. This did not, however, include cash transfers made as part of programs for "public assistance and supplemental security income," which when added give a total for public assistance close to 2.8 percent of GNP.

activities which would fit under the rubric of public assistance if the funds were spent by government agencies.*

Apart from the facts about expenditure levels, it would be helpful to have comparisons of what different societies offer by way of support for specific categories of those without means of supporting themselves. We would want to know, for example, how the incomes of those on public assistance compare with those on regular pensions, and how far above the poverty level their public support placed the physically disabled.

The fragmentary evidence available suggests that the pensions paid by the respective social security systems would place a blind or totally disabled person in both the United States and the Soviet Union at least on, and probably somewhat above, the poverty line. In 1975 in the United States, a "permanently and totally disabled" person would, under the supplemental social security program, have received $141 per month, or $1,693 per year. In that year the poverty line was $2,724 for an unrelated individual, but for someone in a two-person household the per capita requirement was $1,763, and in a three-person household, $1,431 (USDC 1980: 403, t18; USDC 1985: 429). Consequently a totally disabled person could pay his share in keeping a household at or above the poverty line. In the Soviet Union in 1975, a worker or employee in the most severe category of disablement would have received 70 rubles per month—an income slightly above the poverty line. A collective farmer, however, would have received only 30 rubles (Madison 1988).

In contrast to the totally disabled person, the situation of an elderly couple with no claim to a pension would be much less satisfactory in the United States and even worse in the Soviet Union. In a typical case in the United States in 1982, an older couple dependent solely on public assistance through the combined federal

*At one time the Social Security Administration did make calculations of total expenditures for social welfare which took account of philanthropic spending. Evidently the last effort to assess the relation of private and public giving for this purpose was made by Skolnik and Dales (1977) for the year 1976. In the category of expenditure for "welfare and other services," which is closest to that for charity, they listed outlays of $27.5 billion, of which $3.4 billion, or some 12 percent, was credited to private contributions. In that same year some $32 billion was given out in the United States as private philanthropy, considerably more than the government spent for welfare-type services. However, the greatest part of the private philanthropy, some 43 percent, went to religious organizations. Contributions to education, health and hospitals, and social welfare combined accounted for 49 percent (USDC 1985: 385, t650).

and state supplemental security income program would have received cash benefits equal only to approximately half of the officially set poverty level income for that year.* Even with supplements in the form of food stamps, they obviously would be struggling to survive, but their situation would still be much better than that of a comparable couple in the USSR. To qualify for public assistance there, persons must meet three criteria. They must be (1) ineligible for a pension, (2) without "any means of existence," and (3) without relatives legally responsible for their support. After all that, and only after 1981, each member of the couple would have received 20 rubles a month—that is, less than one-third the amount required to stay above the poverty line in 1975 (Madison 1988: 183).†

These results serve to illustrate how much that is important is left out when we rely only on averages and medians. Such numbers, often comforting, lead us to overlook the unhappy or desperate situations of groups which are small as a proportion of the total population, but are large enough to demand our attention. Beguiled by averages, we may lose sight of the 14 percent of those over 65 who lived below the poverty line in the United States in 1982. Even this figure is an average which disguises the depressing fact that, by official estimate, 21 percent of single men and 29 percent of single women over 65 in the United States had incomes below the poverty line in 1982 (USDC 1985: 456, t761).** These groups may be only

---

*In 1982 the combined state and federal supplemental social security payment for a needy aged person would typically have been around $120 per month—an annual income of $1,440 for one person and $2,880 for a couple (USDHHS 1982: 51, tM-24). In that year a two-person household with both members over 65 would have been at the poverty line with $5,836 in income (see USDC 1985: 429). The couple without a pension would therefore have had an income just under 50 percent of that required to be at the poverty level.

†Madison notes that before 1980 the grant was only 10 rubles per person, which would have been one-seventh the minimum wage and less than one-sixth the poverty level.

**Somewhat higher rates were reported by Rainwater on the basis of calculations he made using data from the University of Michigan Survey of Consumer Finance. His definition of poverty differs from that of the Bureau of the Census, but he estimated his rates after taking account of various transfers. His calculations for 1979 yielded a rate of poverty for single males 65 and over of 33 percent, and for females, 43 percent. His data indicated some progress was being made because the proportions in these age groups moved out of poverty by transfers was two to three times greater in 1979 than in 1950. Nevertheless, the large numbers remaining in poverty after these transfers are an obvious challenge to the conscience of American society and government.

very small percentages of the total population, but in societies as large as the United States and the USSR, a small percentage of the population can include millions of individuals. That both these societies allow such large numbers of their citizens to live so far below poverty levels which they themselves have defined might be viewed differently if their performance could be compared with that of other countries. Judged on less relative grounds, however, both societies would seem to have no excuse for not mobilizing the resources required to bring everyone up to at least the minimum standard expressed in their national poverty lines. Until they do so, they fail any reasonably strict test of compassion in implementing welfare policy.

VI. OUTCOMES

After all the information about program coverage and expenditures has been gathered and recorded, we still do not know how much social welfare a given system delivers or how many of a society's members are experiencing more well-being. In the United States and other welfare states as well, there is an acute consciousness that throwing money at social problems is no guarantee that they will go away. Indeed chancelleries all over the modern world are haunted by the specter of runaway costs for their national welfare programs. Welfare systems are, therefore, increasingly challenged to prove they are attaining the objectives they were designed to meet.

Tests of the performance of welfare systems can be divided into two broad categories: objective and subjective. In my view the objective performance should be the more decisive—for example, cutting by a half the proportion of persons living below the poverty level, as the United States did between 1959 and 1979. The great majority of social scientists and bureaucrats would most likely incline to the same position. In the world of politics, however, and especially in societies claiming to be participatory democracies, how people feel about the welfare system is likely to prove more important than what objective social indicators suggest it is actually delivering.

A. SUBJECTIVE MEASURES

Madison asked her sample of former Soviet citizens whether the social security system in the USSR served to support or weaken the achievement of certain widely held values such as "elemental humanity" and a "sense of personal worth." Between 60 and 80 percent of her refugee respondents felt the Soviet welfare system acted to *weaken* the attainment of those goals. Her respondents were of course disaffected from the system, but one should not assume their response indicated that they would not, on principle, say anything good about the Soviet system in general and its welfare system in particular. Indeed 80 percent of the refugees interviewed by Gitelman (1988: t3, t4) acknowledged that when they visited the agency in charge of changing job assignments their treatment was "respectful." In other ways as well, the refugees showed themselves to be quite discriminating in their assessment of different features of the Soviet welfare system. It seems reasonable, therefore, to assume that in their summary judgment of the Soviet social security system, these refugees reflected the objective fact that most pensions provided in the USSR make possible a standard of living barely equal to or below the poverty line, and the harsh reality that social assistance for those unable to claim a pension is truly a pittance. Such objective conditions are not likely to yield a subjective evaluation of the pension system as enhancing values such as sense of personal worth or elemental humanity.

If a welfare system were a popular success, it would be singled out by citizens as one of the features of their society for which they are most grateful, or of which they are most proud, or the loss of which they would find most distressing. We know that when Americans are asked what they value most about being Americans, they very frequently mention "freedom." I do not recall any survey of this type in which social security was spontaneously referred to in this way.

It is clear that at least in some respects the social welfare system in the United States does not enjoy a positive image. Only 14 percent of Americans polled in 1977 (and again in 1978) felt that the country was spending too little on welfare programs (USDC 1980: 394, t8/1). "Welfare" is, of course, a "dirty word" in the United States, as Hasenfeld and Zald noted during the Berkeley conference. By contrast, the social security system of old-age pensions enjoys a quite positive image among U.S. citizens. Over many years, surveys of public opinion in the United States have shown 80 percent or more of the population strongly favoring the system of old-age pensions. Indeed Coughlin's (1979) examination of attitudes toward such pensions in other industrial countries led him to the conclusion that "old-age pensions are universally popular." By contrast, unemployment

benefits for those out of work receive a much more limited endorse-
ment, not only in the United States but in Canada and Britain
as well. There is evidently a structure of attitudes toward different
social welfare programs which, as Coughlin notes, is "strikingly
similar across . . . nations."

Similarly the popular judgment of social welfare programs in
both the United States and the USSR manifests a common pattern of
positive and negative sentiments toward different subprograms
within the larger welfare system. In both the Soviet Union and the
United States, individuals going in to get their social security pensions tend to be much more satisfied than those applying for certain
other kinds of benefits. Thus, in the United States, two to three
times as many clients were "very satisfied" after their encounter with
a social security officer than were those who went in to see a welfare
officer (Hasenfeld and Zald 1988, esp. t7). In a similar vein, 82
percent of the former Soviet citizens who had contact with the
pension office reported their cases had been handled either "well"
or "very well," whereas less than half that number, some 34 percent,
responded in the same way with regard to treatment by the housing
authorities (Gitelman 1988: t3).

These findings should sensitize us to the fact that global popular
evaluations of the welfare system may be poor predictors of how
people will judge the particular subprograms which make up the
larger system, and vice versa. They also suggest that the evaluations
of those who have used a service may be quite different from those
who judge that service only at a distance. In addition, these data
point to a notable regularity across societies in how different features
of the welfare system are judged. In both the Soviet Union and the
United States, when programs are based on clear-cut entitlements,
rest on readily ascertained facts, and have benefits calculated by
objective rules, people come away feeling they got what they are
entitled to and were well-treated by the officials. By contrast,
where claims are based on special circumstances, where conditions
cannot be objectively verified, and where claims made greatly exceed
the benefits available, people will much more often come away
frustrated, feeling they did not get their due, that they were not
well-treated, and that something is wrong with the program. A good
example of such a potentially contentious program is one offering
payments for those who are unable to work for health reasons, or
one for those whose resources have so shrunk that they need help
from public assistance funds.

While these insights are valuable, they do not give us the comprehensive comparative popular evaluation of the performance of different national welfare systems which we need. To that end Coughlin (1979) has done yeoman service in drawing together, for eight different countries, the results of public opinion polls testing popular attitudes toward specific social welfare programs. However, very few of these polls provide overall evaluations of the performance of national welfare programs, and the questions were seldom asked the same way in different countries. We should have the answers to comparable questions submitted to comparable audiences evaluating their respective national welfare programs. Included should be evaluations by the people of how successful the programs are in achieving the goals they have been assigned by the governments. Until we have such data we cannot with any assurance say whether, in the subjective view of the populace, the social welfare system of one nation has been more or less effective than those of other nations. While we wait for such comparative surveys of popular evaluations, objective indicators of performance are ready at hand and invite our attention.

B. OBJECTIVE MEASURES

Much of the ambiguity surrounding popular, subjective assessments of the output of welfare programs would seem to be eliminated by using objective measures of performance. A new challenge faces us, however, as soon as we turn to such objective indicators. Suppose, for example, the majority of people in country A live much longer than those in country B. If A has a national health service and B does not, we cannot know if it is that factor or some other which produces such an outcome. Leaving aside the possibility that genetic factors play a role, we would have to consider whether the main explanation lies in the fact that A is wealthier than B, and thus provides a higher standard of living overall. In addition, cultural factors, especially those affecting diet and exercise, would obviously play a role. One might be able to disentangle these and other influences by regression analysis. I do not know of any such efforts, and they certainly are beyond my responsibilities here. Nevertheless, it is of interest to examine what some of the more general objective indices show.

As our first example, let us consider national investment in medical services. An appropriate test of whether this particular effort to improve welfare is effective would be if it produced a population which lives longer and is healthy over a longer portion of that life-time. Data on longevity and morbidity rates for infectious and other communicable diseases would clearly be relevant, as would infant and child mortality rates. Some of these data are incorporated in Table 5, and they suggest that being a welfare laggard has not put the United States at a marked disadvantage as far as health-related outcomes are concerned. For example, deaths from infective and parasitic disease are much less common in the United States than they are in such welfare leaders as France and Italy. While the U.S. infant mortality rate is higher than that of some welfare leaders, it equals that of several others, and is lower than the United Kingdom's despite the latter's universal national health scheme. Moreover, in life expectancy at age 60, for both men and women, the United States is a world leader. In this connection, it is notable that Japan, another notorious welfare laggard, did better than most of the usual welfare leaders.

The Soviet Union's strong point in the medical services area is in the provision of basic facilities. On a per capita basis, it offers its citizens roughly twice as many hospital beds and physicians as are available to the people of the United States. These facilities are, however, widely reputed to be ill-equipped and unsanitary by West-ern standards. Facilities in the rural areas, in which considerable parts of the population are concentrated, are apparently especially poor. These factors surely contribute to the Soviet Union's strikingly high infant mortality rate, which at last report was much more than double that in the United States and three or more times greater than in the Scandinavian countries. Indeed it stopped publishing the rates altogether after 1976 to avoid the embarrassment of having to admit that its already high rate was getting higher year by year. Similar fear of embarrassment may explain why the USSR does not report its rate of deaths from infective and parasitic diseases to the World Health Organization, and for many years has not published life expectancies at older ages.

Turning to education, we can consider several measures of national performance. Providing more people with more years of schooling is one possible indicator of performance, and assessments of how much they have learned in school is another. As shown in Table 6, the United States does considerably better than the welfare leaders in providing places for the eligible age groups in schools at the secondary level, and it is preeminent in the provision of college- and university-level education for its youth. Thus, of women in the 20-24

Table 5

POPULATION AND HEALTH STATISTICS,
SELECTED COUNTRIES: 1980

Country	Infant Mortality Rate per 1,000 Live Births	Life Expectancy at 60		Number of Persons per		Infective and Parasitic Disease Deaths per 100,000 Population
		Male	Female	Hospital Bed	Physician	
Australia	11.1	17.1	21.8	80	559	--
Austria	12.6	16.4	20.4	88	397	6.9
Belgium	11.7	14.8	16.1	108	401	9.0
Canada	10.9[a]	17.2	22.0	112	548	--
Czechoslovakia	16.8	14.6	18.4	81	362	--
Denmark	8.4	17.0	21.4	119	482	4.7
Finland	7.6	15.6	20.7	64	--	9.0
France	9.6	17.1	22.2	82	580	12.8
Germany (West)	12.6	16.3	20.6	85	452	7.6
Hungary	20.6	15.5	19.1	113	434	13.2
Ireland	11.2	15.6	18.7	95	807	10.3[c]
Italy	14.3	16.5	20.3	98	345	10.9[c]
Japan	7.1	18.9	22.6	87	731	9.8
Luxembourg	11.7	15.5	19.7	84	735	6.0[c]
Netherlands	8.2	17.4	22.4	80	541	4.1
New Zealand	11.7	16.1	20.4	97	635	5.5
Norway	8.1	17.7	20.0	66	520	7.1
Poland	20.6	15.2	19.4	131	573	--
Sweden	7.0	17.9	22.1	67	506	--
Switzerland	8.5	16.7	20.4	87	428	6.8
United Kingdom	12.1	16.0	20.6	119	654	4.2
United States	11.7	17.5	22.5	164	524	6.8
USSR	28.8[b]	--	--	80	267	--

Sources: United Nations (1981, 1982, 1983a, 1983b); for infective and parasitic deaths, Eurostat (1980) and WHO (1983).

[a]Data for 1979

[b]Data for 1975-80

[c]Data for 1977

Table 6

STUDENT ENROLLMENT IN SELECTED COUNTRIES EXPRESSED AS
PERCENTAGES OF AGE GROUPS: C. 1980

| | Education Level | | | | | |
| | Primary | | Secondary | | Higher | |
Country	Male	Female	Male	Female	Male	Female
Australia	100%	100%	78%	80%	27.6%	23.9%
Austria	86	87	73	76	26.4	19.4
Belgium	97	98	88	89	26.9	21.8
Canada	100	100	88	90	35.9	35.9
Denmark	97	98	88	85	29.1	28.7
Finland	83	83	85	95	20.6	21.4
France	112	111	81	89	26.7	23.6
Germany (West)		79^a			30.5	22.1
Ireland	91	92	78	83	22.2	15.8
Italy	102	101	75	71	30.6	23.4
Japan		100		93	43.1	23.1
New Zealand	100	100	80	81	29.6	21.1
Norway		99	92	95	26.6	24.2
Poland	98	98	68	73	15.3	19.8
Sweden	97	97	82	90	38.7	34.4
United Kingdom	96	98	81^a	84^a	24.6	14.6
United States		100^a		100^a	53.3	56.5
USSR		106		101		21.2

Sources: UNESCO (1981, 1982).

^{a}Includes student enrollments from other age groups.

Note: The relevant age groups for primary and secondary level education vary among nations. Since some students repeat grades, the percent attending a given level of primary or secondary school may exceed 100 percent of the eligible age group. Enrollment ratios for higher education are based on the number of students in higher education in relation to population of age 20-24.

age group around 1980, the United States enrolled 56.5 percent in higher education institutions, while Sweden managed to enroll only 34 percent, and enrollments in the other welfare leaders were in the 20-25 percent range. Again the Soviet Union's performance put it in the lower range of the distribution.

How much people learn from the years they spend in school is another matter. All the advanced countries provide official statistics indicating virtually universal literacy, which fails to reflect the fact that many of their adult citizens are functionally illiterate. There are frequent reports that this condition is quite widespread in the United States. Moreover, a significant proportion of secondary school graduates in the United States can read only at the sixth- to eighth-grade level. The impact of these students on the national average test scores at the high-school level can be substantial. Thus, at age 14, U.S. children taking a cross-nationally standardized test in science did as well as children of the same age in Sweden, and in general performed as well as children in the other European welfare leaders.* But by the last year of secondary school, the U.S. children lagged substantially behind those in Sweden and the other countries. This did not come about because the U.S. expenditure for education was less. On the contrary, the United States pursued a welfare-oriented policy by keeping most children of high-school age in school. The European countries were more selective or elitist, typically keeping only half as many children in high school. This residual elite inevitably attained higher average test scores than did the less selective group of U.S. high-school seniors.†

We turn next to measures of some of the amenities of daily life. We can probably get general agreement on the principle that amenities have considerable importance in generating social welfare, but there will be much debate about which amenities actually improve the conditions of life. For example, television and the automobile are, for many, seen more as nuisances and pollutants than as potential contributors to personal well-being. Such people are not likely to give much weight to the fact that around 1982 in the United States there were 538 automobiles per 1,000 citizens, whereas in the European Community there were 321, and in the Soviet Union only 32, of which very few were in private hands. The telephone is no doubt more widely accepted as an amenity with potential for enhancing personal welfare. In telephones the United States is far ahead of the welfare leaders. Around 1980 some 790 phones were available to each 1,000 U.S. citizens, compared to 413

---

*This test was administered in nineteen advanced and less developed countries by the International Association for the Evaluation of Educational Achievement. The average score for children in the fifteen advanced countries was 22.3 (of a possible 80 points). The 14-year-olds in the United States averaged 21.6, in Sweden 21.7, in Germany 21.3, and in England only 15.4. Those in Japan and Hungary scored far above the average. For details see the general review of these studies in Inkeles (1977).

†The test for high-school seniors permitted a maximum score of 60. The average score in the developed countries was 20.9, but the U.S. high-school seniors averaged only 13.7 compared to 19.2 for Sweden, 23.1 for Germany, and 15.3 for England (see Inkeles 1977).

for each 1,000 people in the European Community and 84 in the USSR (USDI 1984: 22-23, t2-3).

There is no substitute for the telephone, but the lack of personal automobiles is partly compensated for in the Soviet Union by a much greater elaboration of the means of public transportation. In any event, it can be argued that automobiles and telephones are too high up in the luxury scale to be considered in any serious discussion of popular welfare; we should therefore move down the scale to something as basic as housing. A room of one's own is a very powerful ideal, and by the late 1970s it was an aspiration that had been very nearly fulfilled in most developed countries. The data on housing in Table 7 tell us, among other things, the average number of persons per room in selected countries in the general period 1968-1976. By that formula, most of the advanced countries were close to a standard of one person per room by the early 1970s. In the United States, however, there was an average of *two* rooms per person in 1976, while the Soviet rate, available for urban dwellers in 1965 only, was 1.3 persons per room — a density almost three times that in the United States (UN, *Statistical Yearbooks 1974-81; European Housing Statistics 1978, 80, 81*).

Such averages can of course be markedly influenced by the instances in which a few people occupy many rooms. Considerable control over the effects of such luxury housing is achieved by considering the distribution of *dwellings* rather than *persons*. Approached in this way, it is clear that the favorable person-per-room ratio in the United States was not mainly the effect of having a few rich people occupy an enormous number of rooms. As can be seen in Table 7, in 95.4 percent of the dwellings in the United States there was less than one person per room even by the early 1970s. This compares very favorably with welfare leaders such as Sweden and Germany, with 70.7 and 68.6 percent respectively of dwellings housing less than one person per room. Comparable data for the Soviet Union are not available, but they can be estimated from those of the other Communist countries in Europe, which show at best only one-third of the dwelling units having less than one person per room. This condition is not likely to change much in the near future because housing for people does not command the high priority assigned to housing machinery in the USSR. Thus in 1983 the USSR, with a population 16 percent larger than that in the United States, built 40 percent fewer square meters of housing (USDI 1984: 22, 23, 175).

Table 7

ROOMS PER DWELLING, PERSONS PER HOUSEHOLD AND PER ROOM,
AND DWELLING UNITS WITH 1.5 OR MORE PERSONS PER ROOM,
SELECTED COUNTRIES, LATEST AVAILABLE YEAR: 1968-1976

Country	Year	Average Number[a]			Percent of Dwellings		
		Rooms per Dwelling	Persons per House-hold	Persons per Room	Less than 1.0 Person per Room	1.0 to 1.49 Persons per Room	1.5 or More Persons per Room
Australia	1971	5.0	3.3	0.6	75.3	21.4	3.3
Austria	1972	4.1[a,b]	2.9	.9[c]	29.8[c]	38.3[c]	32.0[c]
Brazil	1972	4.5[a]	NA	1.1	38.3	33.8	27.9
Canada	1971	5.4[a,d]	3.5	.6	78.4	18.7	2.9
Czechoslovakia	1970	3.1[a]	3.3	1.1	32.1	46.0	21.9
Finland	1970	3.1	3.0[e]	1.0	35.7	40.3	24.0
France	1968	3.4	3.1	.9	42.7	37.5	19.8
Germany (West)	1972	4.2	2.7[f]	.7[g]	68.6[g]	27.2[g]	4.2[g]
Hungary	1973	2.8	3.0	1.1	28.5	43.7	27.8
Israel	1971	2.5[a,h]	3.8[c]	1.5	17.8	39.8	42.4
Japan	1970	3.8[b,g]	3.7[g]	1.0	38.4	40.9	20.7
Puerto Rico	1970	4.7	4.2	.9	70.4	17.0	12.6
Sweden	1970	3.8[a,b]	2.6[e]	.7	70.7	26.5	2.9
United Kingdom	1971	4.9[i]	2.9	.6	83.0	13.2	3.8
United States	1976	5.1[a,j]	3.1[j]	.5	95.4	3.7	1.0

Sources: UN, *Compendium of Housing Statistics, 1972-1974* (used with permission); USDC (1980: t3/20).

[a]United Nations estimate. Where the aggregate number of rooms was not available, an approximation of this value was obtained by multiplying each room category by its corresponding dwelling frequency, multiplying the residual category by the lowest number of rooms involved, disregarding the dwellings with an unknown number of rooms, and summing the products. A similar procedure has been used to derive the aggregate number of persons from data on dwellings classified by the number of occupants. The resultant estimates are no doubt low inasmuch as the minimum class limit has been used to calculate the residual category.

[b]Includes rooms used for professional or business purposes.

[c]1971 data.

[d]Refers to housing units.

[e]Refers to occupants of dwellings.

[f]Refers to households in housing units.

[g]1968 data.

[h]Refers to households.

[i]Refers to households in conventional dwellings.

[j]1970 data.

As another aspect of housing, let us consider the convenience of having toilet facilities inside rather than outside one's dwelling. This particular boon to personal well-being is nearly universal in the United States. By the early 1970s some other countries also provided this amenity with great frequency. In Sweden, for example, more than 90 percent of dwellings had inside toilet facilities. Other nominal welfare leaders, however, were much less effective in providing this source of potential comfort, with France managing it for only 52 percent and Austria for only 73 percent of their households (USDI 1980: 155, t3/21). Again the Soviet Union evidently did not provide such information to the UN authorities.*

Such measures of average performance do not, of course, address issues of justice or of compassion for the destitute. Conservative estimates of the homeless in the United States put the figure at some 300,000, and some estimates range as high as two million. Soviet statistical sources are silent on this subject, and we have no idea what their situation might be. But as noted earlier with regard to the poverty line, there seems little reason to excuse any great nation for allowing a considerable number of its people to be without a space they can meaningfully call home.

C. A SUMMARY INDEX

The measures we have been looking at are numerous and diverse. It would obviously be of great advantage to have an index which sumarized all this information in one overall measure succinctly expressing each nation's performance in the provision of goods and services which generate well-being for its citizens.

The most general measure which might be thought to indicate the level of individual welfare in each country would seem to be the GNP per capita—a figure readily available for most countries. Attractive as this measure might be on grounds of availability, there are a number of reasons for challenging its appropriateness and utility as a summary index of individual well-being in a society.

First, we can question the *reliability* of GNP per capita measures. Measures of gross national product capture only those forms of economic activity which involve a financial transaction. Subsistence production for personal consumption and goods and services obtained by barter do not involve any such transactions. As a result,

*At least the Summary of Housing Conditions in United Nations (1985) does not give any data for the USSR.

in some of the poorest countries the official GNP per capita figures are often seriously underestimated, in some cases by as much as one third. Fortunately this problem is rather slight when the comparison is limited to the more highly industrialized countries, where almost all activity is reflected in the monetary system.

A second type of distortion can arise from the arbitrariness of the exchange rates used to convert the GNP of all nations into a single standard currency, such as the dollar. In this case the procedure not only affects the less developed countries, but can also produce a significant distortion for the more developed countries as well.

Challenges to the *validity* of the GNP per capita measure as an index of welfare are perhaps more serious, and adjustments to meet such challenges are not easily made for all, or even most, countries. The average income may be a misleading indicator of individual welfare when it is based on very unequally distributed income. This problem might be dealt with by using the median rather than average income, by limiting cross-country comparisons to certain quintiles of the income distribution considered most representative, or by applying a GINI coefficient or a similar modifier of the GNP per capita figure obtained from official sources.

No matter how far such adjustments are carried, the GNP per capita measure will still be rejected by those who argue it is not a valid index of what they mean by individual welfare. Such a figure gives the monetary value of what was spent per person on average for all activities, but it does not tell how or where the resources available were spent. A society which puts exceptionally large amounts of money into arms is likely to be less concerned with building schools and hospitals, yet both types of construction count equally as GNP expenditures. Putting a man on the moon may be a grand gesture, but it is enormously expensive while contributing little, except some pride, to the day-to-day well-being of most men, women, and children. A preoccupation with investment in heavy industry may make a country militarily strong, but it otherwise adds little to the general daily welfare of individuals. A high rate of savings, especially enforced savings effected through the state's intervention, may contribute to the well-being of the next generation, but it is bought at the expense of consumption by the present generation.

To meet these objections to the use of per capita income as a measure of welfare, we might adopt another model more responsive to the claim that it is not money but the whole range of the basic needs and amenities of daily living which alone can express the level of individual welfare. Admittedly it would not be easy to get precise agreement on what should be included, or to solve the technical problems of constructing a summary measure, but it seems likely that we could get agreement on at least the broad principles which should determine the content of such an index. The technical problems, while formidable, could probably also be solved. Indeed we already have available an approximation of what is required in the frequently used set of "basic needs" indicators.

The elements commonly considered in basic needs indicators include total caloric consumption, grams of protein per day, access to safe water, life expectancy, infant mortality, deaths due to infective and parasitic diseases, literacy, and doctors, nurses, and hospital rooms per 1,000 persons. This particular set might be objected to on the grounds that it is not sensitive enough to distinguish among the more industrialized countries, all of which are at the top of the scale on measures such as literacy and access to safe water. The basic needs index may also be objected to because the elements counted are too few in number, and do not reflect enough of the entire range of supports for individual well-being which should be represented. These objections could, however, be met by expanding the list—say up to as many as one hundred or more different indicators.

An approximation of this expanded list already exists. In a comparison of personal consumption in the United States and the USSR for the year 1976, some 300 items were taken into account, including food products, all types of soft goods and durables, and housing and related household services. Recreation, transportation, and communication were weighed in the calculations, and the input to education and health services was also counted. Moreover, the government's contributions in subsidies and in the form of directly provided services was added to expenditures made by the individual households.*

This detailed comparison of the two societies showed the sum of all personal consumption per capita in the USSR was equal in value to only one-third of all the goods and services consumed by the average individual in the United States.† Extending the analysis, with some

---

*For details concerning the assembly of items included in the personal consumption "basket," and the method of pricing the goods and services, see U.S. Senate (1981: 1-5).

†When this type of comparison is made, there is always a considerable difference in the estimate depending on whether goods and services are priced in the

modifications, to six additional countries showed the individual consumption of goods and services in the Soviet Union to be considerably behind that in the European welfare-leader nations. Indeed, as Table 8 shows, the sum of those items consumed in the USSR was valued at about half or less the basket of goods and services consumed by the average citizen in France and West Germany. In the United States, which was used as the standard for these measurements

Table 8

A COMPARISON OF CONSUMPTION PER CAPITA IN SEVEN
COUNTRIES RELATIVE TO THE UNITED STATES, 1970-1976

Country	Relative Levels 1970	1973	Indexes of Real Consumption Per Capita, 1973-76	Relative Levels, 1976
United States	100.0	100.0	104.4	100.0
France	65.9	67.9	110.8	72.1
West Germany	64.7	63.9	107.9	66.0
United Kingdom	62.5	62.2	96.6	57.6
Japan	49.3	53.5	105.9	54.3
Italy	47.9	47.4	101.9	46.3
Hungary	41.3	42.0	108.9	43.8
USSR				34.4

Source: Originally appeared as Table 7 in U.S. Congress (1981).
Notes: (1) Relative levels in 1970 and 1973 are those given in current prices in *ICP. Phase II*, using the multilateral comparisons carried out in "international prices." (2) Indexes of real consumption per capita for OECD countries were derived from indexes of total private consumption expenditures in 1970 dollars given in OECD, *National Accounts, 1960-1977*, and indexes of population. Because government expenditures on health and education are not taken into account, these indexes probably slightly understate the growth of total consumption in all countries. (3) The index of real consumption per capita for Hungary was calculated from data given in Thad P. Alton and Associates, *Czechoslovakia, Hungary and Poland: Domestic Final Uses of Gross Product, Structure and Growth, Selected Years, 1965-1978*, Research Project on National Income in East Central Europe, Occasional Paper 55, 1979, p. 7. (4) The relative level for the USSR is the geometric mean of the binary comparison carried out in rubles and in dollars. A comparison in "international prices" cannot be made for the USSR with available data.

local currency or in the currency of the country being compared with the local one. Measured in rubles, the basket of goods and services making up Soviet personal consumption per capita was 27.6 percent of the U.S. level. Measured in dollars, Soviet personal consumption was 42.8 percent of the U.S. level. The compromise adopted was to use the geometric mean — 34.4 percent (U.S. Senate 1981: 5).

(U.S. = 100), a typical citizen consumed a basket of goods and services whose value, based on "international prices," was one quarter greater than that enjoyed by French citizens and one third more valuable than that consumed by West Germans, even after allowing for higher levels of "welfare" spending in those countries.* These are averages of course, and as we have already stressed, may disguise major inequities in distribution. It would, however, be quite feasible to perform the same exercise for different income quintiles of the population or to base a comparison on specific socioeconomic categories, such as working class families or retired couples living on pensions.

Although this study was relatively comprehensive, it was limited to the sort of consumption on which one could set a price. Ideally we would like such a monetary index to be supplemented by the evaluation of other inputs to individual welfare and to the generation of personal and familial well-being. In seeking to represent the widest range of the support systems available to individuals, we might follow Mauro Cappelletti's (1981) suggestion, for example, and include ease of access to legal services. Account should also be taken of hours free from work obligations, and the opportunities available for satisfying use of the leisure time thus created. Access to public parks and other recreational facilities, notably omitted from consideration in standard measures of social insurance, might also be included.

This more comprehensive approach would permit us to include what some would characterize as "political system measures," but which can also be seen as contributions to individual well-being. Chief among these are various kinds of personal freedom — freedom to move freely and settle where one wishes, to travel (including travel abroad), to read or see without censorship newspapers, books, plays, and films, and so on. Each country could be given a score for each type of freedom. Indeed, in many cases appropriate ratings and scores already exist and could easily be included (Gastil 1984).

*The data for the additional countries were adapted from the United Nations study of real national product based on purchasing power parities known as *ICP, Phase II*. In that study, consumption was broken down into eight major categories and twenty-five subcategories. These were, with some adaptation, also used in the U.S. Senate study. However, the UN study did not weigh in government expenditures on health and education, as did the U.S. Congress study of Soviet consumption, which might put the U.S. at some advantage in comparison with European countries other than the USSR. The international comparisons discussed in the text are based on "international prices" for all countries except the Soviet Union (see U.S. Congress 1981: 18-22).

The separate scores could then be summed across each domain, such as health, or housing, or income guarantees, and then be summed again across all the realms to yield a total score for the level of welfare provided by each society. Countries could then be compared with reference to their separate realm scores and to their total scores. They could also be arranged according to the distinctive profiles suggested by the pattern of their ratings across realms.

This exercise would show the United States to be much less a welfare laggard than it is generally described as being. On the contrary, it is highly likely that the United States would emerge as a leader in delivering to its citizens the most extensive package of those goods and services which ensure personal welfare and social security and have the potential to advance individual well-being.

REFERENCES

Aldrich, Jonathan. 1982. "The Earnings Replacement Rate of Old-Age Benefits in 12 Countries, 1969-80." *Social Security Bulletin*, November.

Brennan, Geoffrey, and Pincus, Jonathan. 1983. "The Growth of Government: Do the Figures Tell Us What We Want to Know?" In *Why Governments Grow: Measuring Public Sector Size*, ed. Charles L. Taylor. Beverly Hills: Sage Publications.

Campbell, Rita Ricardo. 1977. *Social Security: Promise and Reality*. Stanford, CA: Hoover Institution Press.

Cappelletti, Mauro. 1981. *Access to Justice and the Welfare State*. Florence, Italy: European University Institute.

Coughlin, Richard M. 1979. "Social Policy and Ideology: Public Opinion in Eight Rich Nations." *Comparative Social Research* 2: 3-40.

Davis, Christopher. 1988. "The Organization and Performance of the Contemporary Soviet Health Service." In Lapidus and Swanson, eds.

Davis, Christopher, and Feshbach, M. 1980. "Rising Infant Mortality in the U.S.S.R. in the 1970s." U.S. Bureau of the Census, *International Population Reports*, Series P-95, No. 74, June.

Eurostat [European Community, Statistical Office]. 1980. *Social Indicators for the European Community, 1960-1978*. Luxembourg.

_____. 1983. *Social Protection*. Luxembourg.

Fox, Alan. 1982. "Earnings Replacement Rates and Total Income: Findings from the Retirement History Study," *Social Security Bulletin* 45, 10: 3-22. U.S. Department of Health and Human Services, Social Security Administration, Washington, D.C. October.

Gastil, Raymond. 1984. *Freedom in the World: Political Rights and Civil Liberties, 1983-1984.* New York: Freedom House.

Gitelman, Zvi. 1988. "Unequal Encounters: The Citizen and the Soviet Welfare Bureaucracies." In Lapidus and Swanson, eds.

Hasenfeld, Yeheskel, and Zald, Mayer. 1987. "Client-Organization Encounters in the U.S. Social Welfare Sector." In Lapidus and Swanson, eds.

Inkeles, Alex. 1979. "National Differences in Scholastic Performance." *Comparative Education Review* 23, 3 (October).

ILO [International Labor Office]. 1981. *The Cost of Social Security, Tenth International Inquiry, 1975-1977.* Geneva.

_____. 1985. *The Cost of Social Security, Eleventh International Inquiry, 1978-80.* Geneva.

King, Anthony. 1973. "Ideas, Institutions and the Politics of Governments: A Comparative Analysis," pts. I, II, III. *British Journal of Political Science* 3, 3 (July) and 4, 4 (October).

Kreps, Juanita M. 1971. *Lifetime Allocation of Work and Income: Essays in the Economics of Aging.* Durham, N.C.: Duke University Press.

Lapidus, Gail W., and Swanson, Guy E., eds. 1988. *State and Welfare, USA/USSR.* Berkeley: Institute of International Studies, University of California.

Lapman, Robert J. 1984. *Social Welfare Spending: Accounting for Changes from 1950 to 1978.* Orlando: Harcourt, Brace, Jovanovich, Academic Press.

Madison, Bernice. 1988. "The Soviet Pension System and Social Security for the Aged." In Lapidus and Swanson, eds.

Moon, Marilyn, ed. 1984. *Economic Transfers in the United States.* Chicago: University of Chicago Press.

Morgan, James, et al. 1966. *Productive Americans.* Ann Arbor, Mich.: Institute of Social Research, University of Michigan.

Ofer, Gur, and Vinokur, Aaron. 1988. "The Distributive Effects of the Social Consumption Fund in the Soviet Union." In Lapidus and Swanson, eds.

Page, Benjamin I. 1983. *Who Gets What from Government.* Berkeley: University of California Press.

Peters, B. Guy, and Heisler, Martin O. 1983. "Thinking About Public Sector Growth." In *Why Governments Grow*, ed. Charles L. Taylor. Beverly Hills: Sage Publications.

Rainwater, Lee. 1988. "The Growth of Social Protection in the United States: 1929-1979." In Lapidus and Swanson, eds.

Rein, Martin. 1988. "A Comparative Study of Pension Policies in the United States and Europe." In Lapidus and Swanson, eds.

Simanis, Joseph G., and Coleman, John R. 1980. "Health Care Expenditures in Nine Industrialized Countries, 1960-76." *Social Security Bulletin.* U.S. Department of Health and Health Services, Social Security Administration. January.

Skolnik, Alfred M., and Dales, Sophie R. 1977. "Social Welfare Expenditures, Fiscal Year 1976." *Social Security Bulletin.* Washington, D.C.: U.S. Department of Health and Human Services, Social Security Administration. January.

Titmuss, Richard M. 1971. *The Gift Relationship: From Human Blood to Social Policy.* New York: Random House.

UNESCO. 1981. *Statistical Yearbook, 1981.* Paris: United Nations Educational, Scientific and Cultural Organization.

_____. 1982. *Statistical Yearbook, 1982.* Paris: United Nations Educational, Scientific and Cultural Organization.

United Nations. 1981. *Statistical Yearbook, 1979/80.* New York: United Nations.

_____. 1982. *Demographic Yearbook, 1980.* New York: United Nations.

_____. 1983a. *Demographic Yearbook, 1981.* New York; United Nations.

_____. 1983b. *Statistical Yearbook, 1981.* New York: United Nations.

_____. 1985. *Statistical Yearbook, 1982.* New York: United Nations.

U.S. Congress. 1981. *Consumption in the USSR: An International Comparison.* Washington, D.C.: U.S. Government Printing Office.

USDC [U.S. Department of Commerce]. 1985. Bureau of the Census. *Statistical Abstract of the U.S. 1985.* Washington, D.C.

_____. 1980. Bureau of the Census. *Social Indicators III: Selected Data on Social Conditions in the United States.* Washington, D.C. December.

USDHHS [U.S. Department of Health and Human Services]. 1982. Social Security Administration. *Social Security Bulletin* 45, 10. Washington, D.C. October.

_____, Social Security Administration. *Social Security Programs Throughout the World, 1983.* Research Report No. 59. Washington, D.C.: SSA Publications No. 13-11805.

USDI [U.S. Directorate of Intelligence]. 1984. *Handbook of Economic Statistics, 1984.* Washington, D.C. September.

U.S. Senate. 1981. Special Committee on Aging. *Social Security in Europe: The Impact of an Aging Population.* Washington, D.C.: U.S. Government Printing Office.

Wedderburn, Dorothy. 1965. "Facts and Theories of the Welfare State." In *The Socialist Register, 1965,* eds. Ralph Miliband and John Saville. New York: Monthly Review Press.

Wilensky, Harold. 1975. *The Welfare State and Equality.* Berkeley: University of California Press.

_____. 1976. *The 'New Corporatism,' Centralization, and the Welfare State.* Beverly Hills: Sage Publications.

_____. 1980. Foreword to Richard Coughlin, *Ideology, Public Opinion, and Welfare Policy.* Berkeley: Institute of International Studies, University of California.

_____. 1983. "Political Legitimacy and Consensus." In *Evaluating the Welfare State*, eds. S. Spiro and E. Yuchtman-Yaar. N.Y.: Academic Press.

Wilensky, Harold, et al. 1985. *Comparative Social Policy*. Berkeley: Institute of International Studies, University of California.

Wilensky, Harold L., and Lebeaux, Charles N. 1958. *Industrial Society and Social Welfare*. New York: Russell Sage Foundation.

WHO [World Health Organization]. 1983. *World Health Statistics*. Geneva.

Zapf, Wolfgang. 1980. "The Welfare State and Welfare Production." Working Paper No. 25. Sonderforschungsbereich 3 Frankfurt/Mannheim; published in German as "Wohlfahrtsstaat and Wohlfahrtsproduktion." In *Politische Parteien*, eds. L. Albertin and W. Link. Dusseldorf: Droste, 1981: 379-400.

INDEX

Alcohol: campaign against, 137; consumption of, 98, 109, 112
Aliev, Gaidar, 343
All-Union Central Committee of Trade Unions (AUCCTU), 165, 167, 193
Almond, Gabriel, 347
Amenities: automobiles, 446; public transportation, 447; telephones, 446-7
American Medical Association (AMA), 147
Andropov, Yuri, 195, 199
Armstrong, John, 323
Ashby, Eric, 64
Austria: percentage of elderly in, 225; welfare spending in, 213, 219, 289, 293
Avis, George, 53
Azarova, E.G., 200

Bauer, Raymond, 328
Belgium: pensions in, 215, 220; welfare spending in, 289, 290, 293
Bendick, M., 365
Blat (connections), 46, 47n, 336-7, 340, 344; in Romania, 346
Braniff International Airlines, 231
Brennan, Geoffrey, 403
Bribery, 8-9, 46-7, 338, 340-1, 345-6
Bureaucracies. *See* Bureaucratic encounters
Bureaucratic encounters:
——in United States: characteristics of clients in, 358, 365, 370-3; citizens' evaluations of, 10, 327-8, 353-4, 362-3, 366, 371-3, 377; citizens' input into, 354, 356; and culture, 355, 357, 359-60, 367; diversity of, 353, 355; frequency of, 321, 358; and higher education, 72-3, 75, 76; and housing, 375; and job placement, 344; and mental health, 360, 367-74; and minorities, 375; organi-

zational factors, 354-5, 357-61, 376; and pensions, 360-6, 441; and policymaking, 348; and public assistance, 355-6, 359-60, 363-7, 441; rights of citizens in, 354, 357, 358, 360-1, 364-5, 373-7, 441
——in USSR: citizens' evaluations of, 326-8, 331-7, 347; citizens' input into, 337; characteristics of clients in, xi, 330, 337; and culture, 321, 325-6, 346-8; data on, 328-30; and family health, 103; frequency of, 321-2, 347-8; and government control, 321; and higher education, 332, 335, 340-1, 343; and housing, 332-3, 335-6, 339-40, 441; and Jews, 330, 340-2, 344; and job placement *(raspredelenie)*, 335, 343-4; and military, 345; and nationalities, 330-2, 338-44; and organizational factors, 10, 322-3, 326, 331, 347; orientation of, 322, 336; and patronage *(protektsiia)*, 345; and pensions, 195, 197-9, 204, 206, 332-3, 335-6, 340, 345, 347, 441; and policy 322, 336-7, 347-8; political influence on, 325; political significance of, 321-2; and resource allocation, x, 325; rights of citizens in, 196-9, 323-6, 347, 390, 441; role of CPSU in, 342, 345

Canada: health insurance in, 155-7; perceptions of welfare in, 441
Cantu, M.G., 365
Cappelletti, Mauro, 453
Carnegie Commission, 62
Carter administration, 147, 237
Central All-Union Social Security Fund for Collective Farmers, 173, 193
Chernobyl, 107
Clark, Burton R., 356

459

INSTITUTE OF INTERNATIONAL STUDIES
UNIVERSITY OF CALIFORNIA, BERKELEY

215 Moses Hall   Berkeley, California 94720

CARL G. ROSBERG, *Director*

Monographs published by the Institute include:

RESEARCH SERIES

1. *The Chinese Anarchist Movement.* R.A. Scalapino and G.T. Yu. ($1.00)
7. *Birth Rates in Latin America.* O. Andrew Collver. ($2.50)
16. *The International Imperatives of Technology.* Eugene B. Skolnikoff. ($2.95)
19. *Entry of New Competitors in Yugoslav Market Socialism.* S.R. Sacks. ($2.50)
20. *Political Integration in French-Speaking Africa.* Abdul A. Jalloh. ($3.50)
21. *The Desert & the Sown: Nomads in Wider Society.* Ed. C. Nelson. ($5.50)
22. *U.S.-Japanese Competition in International Markets.* J.E. Roemer. ($3.95)
24. *Urban Inequality and Housing Policy in Tanzania.* Richard E. Stren. ($2.95)
25. *The Obsolescence of Regional Integration Theory.* Ernst B. Haas. ($6.95)
27. *The SOCSIM Microsimulation Program.* E. A. Hammel et al. ($4.50)
28. *Authoritarian Politics in Communist Europe.* Ed. Andrew C. Janos. ($8.95)
31. *Politics of Oil Pricing in the Middle East, 1970-75.* R.C. Weisberg. ($4.95)
32. *Agricultural Policy and Performance in Zambia.* Doris J. Dodge. ($4.95)
34. *Housing the Urban Poor in Africa.* Richard E. Stren. ($5.95)
35. *The Russian New Right: Right-Wing Ideologies in USSR.* A. Yanov. ($5.95)
37. *The Leninist Response to National Dependency.* Kenneth Jowitt. ($4.95)
38. *Socialism in Sub-Saharan Africa.* Eds. C. Rosberg & T. Callaghy. ($12.95)
39. *Tanzania's Ujamaa Villages: Rural Development Strategy.* D. McHenry. ($5.95)
40. *Who Gains from Deep Ocean Mining?* I.G. Bulkley. ($3.50)
43. *The Apartheid Regime.* Eds. R. Price & C. Rosberg ($12.50)
44. *Yugoslav Economic System in the 1970s.* Laura D. Tyson. ($5.95)
45. *Conflict in Chad.* Virginia Thompson & Richard Adloff. ($7.50)
46. *Conflict and Coexistence in Belgium.* Ed. Arend Lijphart. ($10.50)
47. *Changing Realities in Southern Africa.* Ed. Michael Clough. ($12.50)
48. *Nigerian Women Mobilized, 1900-1965.* Nina E. Mba. ($12.95)
49. *Institutions of Rural Development.* Eds. D. Leonard & D. Marshall. ($11.50)
50. *Politics of Women & Work in USSR & U.S.* Joel C. Moses. ($9.50)
51. *Zionism and Territory.* Baruch Kimmerling. ($12.50)
52. *Soviet Subsidization of Trade with East Europe.* M. Marrese/J. Vanous. ($14.50)
53. *Voluntary Efforts in Decentralized Management.* L. Ralston et al. ($10.00)
54. *Corporate State Ideologies.* Carl Landauer. ($5.95)
55. *Effects of Economic Reform in Yugoslavia.* John P. Burkett. ($9.50)
56. *The Drama of the Soviet 1960s.* Alexander Yanov. ($9.50)
57. *Revolutions & Rebellions in Afghanistan.* Eds. Shahrani/Canfield. ($14.95)
58. *Women Farmers of Malawi.* D. Hirschmann & M. Vaughan. ($8.95)
59. *Chilean Agriculture under Military Rule.* Lovell S. Jarvis. ($11.50)
60. *Influencing Political Behavior in Netherlands and Austria.* J. Houska. ($11.50)